Access® 2000 Programming Weekend Crash Course

Access® 2000 Programming Weekend Crash Course

Cary Prague
Jennifer Reardon
Lawrence S. Kasevich
P. V. Phan
Diana Reid

IDG BOOKS
WORLDWIDE

IDG Books Worldwide, Inc.
An International Data Group Company
Foster City, CA • Chicago, IL • Indianapolis, IN • New York, NY

Access® 2000 Programming Weekend Crash Course
Published by
IDG Books Worldwide, Inc.
An International Data Group Company
919 E. Hillsdale Blvd., Suite 400
Foster City, CA 94404
www.idgbooks.com (IDG Books Worldwide
Web site)

Library of Congress Card Number: 00-102379
ISBN: 0-7645-4688-0
Printed in the United States of America
10 9 8 7 6 5 4 3 2
10/RQ/QV/QQ/FC
Distributed in the United States by IDG Books Worldwide, Inc.
Distributed by CDG Books Canada Inc. for Canada; by Transworld Publishers Limited in the United Kingdom; by IDG Norge Books for Norway; by IDG Sweden Books for Sweden; by IDG Books Australia Publishing Corporation Pty. Ltd. for Australia and New Zealand; by TransQuest Publishers Pte Ltd. for Singapore, Malaysia, Thailand, Indonesia, and Hong Kong; by Gotop Information Inc. for Taiwan; by ICG Muse, Inc. for Japan; by Intersoft for South Africa; by Eyrolles for France; by International Thomson Publishing for Germany, Austria, and Switzerland; by Distribuidora Cuspide for Argentina; by LR International for Brazil; by Galileo Libros for Chile; by Ediciones ZETA S.C.R. Ltda. for Peru; by WS Computer Publishing Corporation, Inc., for the Philippines; by Contemporanea de Ediciones for Venezuela; by Express Computer Distributors for the Caribbean and West Indies; by Micronesia Media Distributor, Inc. for Micronesia; by Chips Computadoras S.A. de C.V. for Mexico; by Editorial Norma de Panama S.A. for Panama; by American Bookshops for Finland.

For general information on IDG Books Worldwide's books in the U.S., please call our Consumer Customer Service department at 800-762-2974. For reseller information, including discounts and premium sales, please call our Reseller Customer Service department at 800-434-3422.

For information on where to purchase IDG Books Worldwide's books outside the U.S., please contact our International Sales department at 317-596-5530 or fax 317-572-4002.

For consumer information on foreign language translations, please contact our Customer Service department at 800-434-3422, fax 317-572-4002, or e-mail rights @idgbooks.com.

For information on licensing foreign or domestic rights, please phone +1-650-653-7098.

For sales inquiries and special prices for bulk quantities, please contact our Order Services department at 800-434-3422 or write to the address above.

For information on using IDG Books Worldwide's books in the classroom or for ordering examination copies, please contact our Educational Sales department at 800-434-2086 or fax 317-572-4005.

For press review copies, author interviews, or other publicity information, please contact our Public Relations department at 650-653-7000 or fax 650-653-7500.

For authorization to photocopy items for corporate, personal, or educational use, please contact Copyright Clearance Center, 222 Rosewood Drive, Danvers, MA 01923, or fax 978-750-4470.

ABOUT IDG BOOKS WORLDWIDE

Welcome to the world of IDG Books Worldwide.

IDG Books Worldwide, Inc., is a subsidiary of International Data Group, the world's largest publisher of computer-related information and the leading global provider of information services on information technology. IDG was founded more than 30 years ago by Patrick J. McGovern and now employs more than 9,000 people worldwide. IDG publishes more than 290 computer publications in over 75 countries. More than 90 million people read one or more IDG publications each month.

Launched in 1990, IDG Books Worldwide is today the #1 publisher of best-selling computer books in the United States. We are proud to have received eight awards from the Computer Press Association in recognition of editorial excellence and three from Computer Currents' First Annual Readers' Choice Awards. Our best-selling ...For Dummies® series has more than 50 million copies in print with translations in 31 languages. IDG Books Worldwide, through a joint venture with IDG's Hi-Tech Beijing, became the first U.S. publisher to publish a computer book in the People's Republic of China. In record time, IDG Books Worldwide has become the first choice for millions of readers around the world who want to learn how to better manage their businesses.

Our mission is simple: Every one of our books is designed to bring extra value and skill-building instructions to the reader. Our books are written by experts who understand and care about our readers. The knowledge base of our editorial staff comes from years of experience in publishing, education, and journalism — experience we use to produce books to carry us into the new millennium. In short, we care about books, so we attract the best people. We devote special attention to details such as audience, interior design, use of icons, and illustrations. And because we use an efficient process of authoring, editing, and desktop publishing our books electronically, we can spend more time ensuring superior content and less time on the technicalities of making books.

You can count on our commitment to deliver high-quality books at competitive prices on topics you want to read about. At IDG Books Worldwide, we continue in the IDG tradition of delivering quality for more than 30 years. You'll find no better book on a subject than one from IDG Books Worldwide.

John Kilcullen
Chairman and CEO
IDG Books Worldwide, Inc.

*Eighth Annual
Computer Press
Awards ≥1992*

*Ninth Annual
Computer Press
Awards ≥1993*

*Tenth Annual
Computer Press
Awards ≥1994*

*Eleventh Annual
Computer Press
Awards ≥1995*

IDG is the world's leading IT media, research and exposition company. Founded in 1964, IDG had 1997 revenues of $2.05 billion and has more than 9,000 employees worldwide. IDG offers the widest range of media options that reach IT buyers in 75 countries representing 95% of worldwide IT spending. IDG's diverse product and services portfolio spans six key areas including print publishing, online publishing, expositions and conferences, market research, education and training, and global marketing services. More than 90 million people read one or more of IDG's 290 magazines and newspapers, including IDG's leading global brands — Computerworld, PC World, Network World, Macworld and the Channel World family of publications. IDG Books Worldwide is one of the fastest-growing computer book publishers in the world, with more than 700 titles in 36 languages. The "...For Dummies®" series alone has more than 50 million copies in print. IDG offers online users the largest network of technology-specific Web sites around the world through IDG.net (http://www.idg.net), which comprises more than 225 targeted Web sites in 55 countries worldwide. International Data Corporation (IDC) is the world's largest provider of information technology data, analysis and consulting, with research centers in over 41 countries and more than 400 research analysts worldwide. IDG World Expo is a leading producer of more than 168 globally branded conferences and expositions in 35 countries including E3 (Electronic Entertainment Expo), Macworld Expo, ComNet, Windows World Expo, ICE (Internet Commerce Expo), Agenda, DEMO, and Spotlight. IDG's training subsidiary, ExecuTrain, is the world's largest computer training company, with more than 230 locations worldwide and 785 training courses. IDG Marketing Services helps industry-leading IT companies build international brand recognition by developing global integrated marketing programs via IDG's print, online and exposition products worldwide. Further information about the company can be found at www.idg.com.   1/26/00

Credits

Acquisitions Editor
Greg Croy

Project Editor
Matthew E. Lusher

Technical Editor
Allen Wyatt

Copy Editors
S.B. Kleinman
Chrisa Hotchkiss

Media Development Specialist
Jason Luster

Permissions Editor
Lenora Chin Sell

Media Development Manager
Stephen Noetzel

Project Coordinators
Danette Nurse
Marcos Vergara

Graphics and Production Specialists
Robert Bilhmayer
Jude Levinson
Michael Lewis
Ramses Ramirez
Dina F Quan
Victor Pérez-Varela

Book Designer
Evan Deerfield

Design Specialist
Kippy Thomsen

Illustrators
Mary Jo Richards
Shelley Norris

Proofreading and Indexing
York Production Services

About the Authors

Cary Prague is an internationally known best-selling author and lecturer in the database industry. He is the president of Database Creations, Inc. the world's largest Microsoft Access add-on company. This direct-mail company creates and markets add-on software, books, and video training for personal computer databases. Cary also manages a very successful consulting company which is a Microsoft Certified Solution Provider, specializing in Microsoft Access application development. He is one of the best-selling authors in the computer database management market, having written over 40 books (which have sold nearly one million copies) on software including Microsoft Access, Borland's dBASE IV, Paradox, R:Base, and Framework. Cary's books include eight different editions of the *Microsoft Access Bible*. Other books have included *Access 97 Secrets*, *dBASE for Windows Handbook*, *dBASE IV Programming* (winner of the Computer Press Association's Book of the Year award for Best Software Specific Book), and *Everyman's Database Primer Featuring dBASE IV*.

Cary is certified in Access as a Microsoft Certified Professional and has passed the MOUS test in end-user subjects in Access and Word. He is a frequent speaker at seminars and conferences around the country. Cary holds a Master of Computer Science degree from Rensselaer Polytechnic Institute, and an M.B.A and Bachelor of Accounting degree from the University of Connecticut. He is also a Certified Data Processor.

Jennifer Reardon is considered a leading developer of custom database applications. She has over 10 years' experience developing client/server and PC-based applications. She has accumulated much of her application development experience working as lead developer for Database Creations. She has worked with Cary Prague to develop applications for many Fortune 500 companies. Ms. Reardon owns her own consulting firm, Advanced Software Concepts, which provides custom applications to both the public and private sectors. She has contributed several chapters for books on dBase and Microsoft Access, including the *Microsoft Access 2000 Bible*, *Microsoft Access 97 Bible*, and *Access 97 Secrets*, published by IDG Books. Jennifer holds a Bachelor of Science degree from the University of Massachusetts.

Lawrence S. Kasevich is presently vice president of development for Database Creations, Inc. He oversees the consulting division and manages the project efforts for numerous clients and new product development. Before joining Database Creations, Mr. Kasevich was an independent consultant assisting companies with their information and project management needs. He is currently a member of the adjunct faculty at Rennselear Polytechnic Institute where he has been teaching information systems courses since 1989. His previous books include *Mastering Framework III*, Windcrest Books., 1989, *Controlling Your Resources*, TAB Books, Inc., 1986, *Framework II*, TAB Books, Inc., 1986, *Using Framework — A Pictorial Guide*, TAB Books, Inc., 1985. He earned a Bachelor of Science degree in Engineering from the University of Connecticut in 1974. In 1986, he received a Master of Management degree from the Hartford Graduate Center.

P. V. Phan currently serves as director of information & technical services/developer for Database Creations, Inc. In this capacity he heads the support team for in-house support as well as customer technical support to end users and developers. He is also a member of the development and consulting team for the full line of Database Creations, Inc. products as well as numerous consulting projects for many Fortune 500 companies. He has been programming and developing and conducting training with Access for over five years and has had over 12 years of computer experience.

Diana Reid is responsible for managing the daily operations of Database Creations, Inc. She is responsible for the company's e-commerce site and all Web-related activities, including design and programming of the company's Web site and client Web sites. She is a contributing editor for several books on Microsoft Access and has been a technical editor for many of the Access Bible books. She also is a speaker at Microsoft sponsored developer conferences, speaking on Frontpage, HTML and many other Web technologies. Ms. Reid received a Bachelor of Science degree in Finance from Central Connecticut State University in 1991.

This book is dedicated to my wife Karen in honor of our twentieth wedding anniversary and for putting up with me for nearly 25 years. I love you with all my strength and devotion. I look forward to spending the rest of my life with you and our greatest accomplishments — David, Jeffery, and Alexander. — Cary Prague

To Cary Prague — Thanks for including me on this great opportunity and thanks for being so perpetually generous and so appreciative of everything I do. Thanks to my husband, Jeff, for doing such a good job pretending I was not around while writing this book — even when I complained so loudly. — Jennifer Reardon

This book is dedicated to the memory of my father, Stanley Kasevich, who will be remembered for his devotion, caring, and ambition. To my mother for her strength with life's challenges. To Alissa, may your dreams come true. To Cheryl and Tom, with best wishes as they start their lives together. To my sister, Sandy, for all her help. To Ashley, and especially to Debbie for her caring and love.
— Lawrence S. Kasevich

This is dedicated to my father, Vinh Phan, for all of his sacrifice, dedication and love to his children. — P.V. Phan

To my husband Matt, my biggest supporter, who has had to learn to cook during the writing of this book. To my stepdaughter Elizabeth for leaving me all those cute little notes while I disappeared over the weekends. To my parents, Bob and Joan Smith, who taught me to achieve to be the best. And finally to Cary Prague, my mentor and good friend, who has taught me how to be successful and still have fun.
— Diana Reid

Preface

Microsoft Access is an outstanding environment for application development on any level. It is one of easiest database managers to use, and one of the most powerful. People with all levels of skill and experience have found that Microsoft Access can help them create applications to meet nearly any need. New users can quickly master simple tables, queries, forms, and reports. Even macros can be easily learned and used. However, when modules and VBA code are needed, many users run into a virtual brick wall and cannot proceed.

This book will teach you how to program in Microsoft Access and VBA whether you have never programmed before or you are an experienced information system professional who wants to add another language to your box of tools. Organized according to the Weekend Crash Course approach, this book consists of 30 short chapters. Each chapter will teach you a different part of Access VBA development. Starting with programming basics, the first few chapters will teach you system design, an understanding of logical constructs, an introduction to the VBA editor environment and testing and debugging. After the initial chapters, you will learn hard-core VBA and ADO programming with a variety of topics including client/server, working with data, and even programming external data imports and exports.

Using one cohesive example of a common check writer, register, and reconciliation form along with a banking interface, you will learn visual programming using Microsoft Access. Each chapter features easy-to-follow text and lots of screen pictures to keep you on track. The check writer example is completely written in ADO for Microsoft Access 2000. You will also see an .ADP version linked to an MSDE (SQL Server 7.0) back end database.

Structure of the Book

Each part of this book is organized into four or six sessions. Each session is designed to be completed in about half an hour and contains review questions as well as questions and answers at the end of each part.

Part I will teach you the basics of programming. You will how to make the transition from macros to modules and then learn about the Visual Basic Editor and how to debug programs with the built-in tools like syntax checking, auto quick info and auto list members. You will learn the basics of system design and learn the concentric circle method of development that Microsoft follows. You will learn how to trigger code from various types of events and how to declare the various types of variables.

Part II will move you beyond the basics. You will first learn the logical constructs that every programmer uses, including decision-making and looping. You will learn the difference between functions and procedures and write your first program in Visual Basic, the language of Microsoft Access. A good starting point is calendars and you will learn how to add date and time processing to your applications. ADO and DAO are next as you learn how to access and manipulate data in tables. You will learn how to not only retrieve data from tables, but how to add, update, and delete data.

Part III will teach you how to create switchboards and menus and how to handle keypress events programatically. You will learn about unbound forms which are used in client-server systems. The rest of Part III will teach you how to work with the various controls on a form or report through programs. You will first learn how to program combo and list boxes and how to work with option groups through programming. Next, you will learn how to manipulate subforms through code and how to use tabbed controls in ways you never thought possible.

Part IV starts with a session on advanced message boxes and error handling. Next you will learn how to import and export data programatically from other databases, spreadsheets, and text type files including delimited and fixed-width file types. You will learn the secrets of improving processing speed and keeping your programs compiled. Finally in this session you will learn how to create animated splash screens, about boxes and other forms that appear when a program starts. Part IV ends with a session on adding help systems to Microsoft Access programs.

Part V begins to cover how to handle more advanced types of requirements. It starts with dialog boxes for printing and then covers finding data using dialog boxes for searching any field in a table. The next session covers topics after your development is complete like packaging your application using the Office Developers edition and Access runtime and Setup utilities. You will also learn how to create wizards for getting started or shepherding the user through complex tasks.

The final part of the book, Part VI covers a group of advanced programming topics. It begins with building Add-in libraries and using references. You will see how to programatically check file attachments and an interface to link to files. You will learn how to program Access security and create true client-server applications using .ADPs and the Microsoft Database Engine (MSDE) or SQL Server 7.0. Finally, you will learn how to build the new Data Access Pages to move live Access data to the Web with Web-based forms.

Layout and Features

No one should try to simply power through this material without a break. We've arranged things so the sessions in this book each last about half an hour, and they're grouped into parts of two or three hours. After each session, and at the end of each part, you'll find some questions to check your knowledge and give you a little practice at exercising your new-found skills. Take a break, grab a snack, refill that coffee mug, and plunge into the next one!

30 Min. To Go

Along the way, you'll find some features to help you keep track of how far along you are, and point out interesting bits of info you shouldn't miss. First, as you're going through each session, check for this in the margin:

This icon and others like it let you know how much progress you've made through each session as you go. There are also several icons to point out special tidbits of info for you:

This is a flag to clue you in to an important piece of info you should file away in your head for later.

This gives you helpful advice on the best ways to do things, or a neat little technique that can make your work easier.

Don't do this! 'Nuff said.

SYNTAX ▶ Watch for places where we've flagged a passage where essential syntax is modeled for you. The bar to the left shows you the extent of the passage. Usually, it'll be something like this:

To check something and make a decision based on it, you use the `If...Then` statement. The `If...Then` statement works like this:

```
If this is true Then do this
```

Here's an example:

```
If Check1.Value = 1 Then Form1.Text1.FontBold = True
```

The part after the `If` is a condition; if the condition is true, the computer will do whatever comes after `Then`.

Conventions Used in this Book

Aside from the icons you've just seen, such as *Tip*, there are only three conventions in this book:

- To indicate a menu choice, we use the ⇨ symbol, as in:

  Choose File ⇨ Save Project to save your work.

- To indicate programming code within the body text, we use a special font, like this:

  Notice that line at the end: `Form2.Hide`. When the user clicks the OK button, you want Form2 to disappear. The `Hide` command does just that.

- To indicate a programming example that's not in the body text, we use this typeface:

  ```
  Private Sub Command2_Click()
  Form2.Hide
  End Sub
  ```

Acknowledgments

We wish to thank the following people who greatly contributed to the success of our book. First and foremost to the staff of Database Creations Inc and Database Creations Consulting LLC for supporting our band of writers as we completed the book. To Julie Frattaroli, Kim Cote, Sarah Andrews, Karen Prague, Debbie Schindler, Jerry Boutot, Jr., and Tom Schindler. Your work keeping the lights on and the customers happy is most appreciated.

One of our motivations was the desire to create a book that could be used to teach Access programming. We needed a test bed and found it at at a high school in South Windsor, Connecticut. When we approached the Board of Education with an idea, we thought we had no chance of actually convincing them to let our developers teach a course that didn't even exist. To our amazement, they agreed.

To Allan Mothersele, a true educator who lives more hours than not at South Windsor High School. He lets us practice our ideas on the students as we muddle through our Access database and programming course. His love for children, robots, things mechanical, and the entrepreneurial spirit truly lives within his teachings. A special thanks to Salvatore Randazzo, the principal at South Windsor High School, for cutting through the bureaucracy and bringing concept to reality in just a few months. We never would have imagined it possible and we are glad almost everyone said YES!

To our agents Matt Wagner and Bill Gladstone and our financial guru Maureen at Waterside Productions. They are the best agents and people in the business! Thanks for making our trips through contract-land easy and profitable.

To our friends at IDG books. First to our acquisitions editor for this book, Greg Croy. Our favorite pilgrim, he always has a calming hand and a great suggestion. He also has the cleanest desk I have ever seen. He relentlessly pursued us until we agreed to write this book. We fondly remember the unique dinner we had at Buca di Beppo in Indianapolis. We are still full six months later. We appreciate Greg's politically correct suggestions when we are ready to shoot our editors. To Matt Lusher, our project editor at IDG Books, whom we never wanted to shoot. You are organized, communicate well, and always get back to us quickly. We thank you for being a great editor. We also wish to thank the copy editors, S.B. Kleinman and Chrisa Hotchkiss, who read, changed, complained, whined, insisted, ranted, raved, and wrote us voluminous explanations about English grammar, gerunds, and apocryphal references to the late Admiral Grace Hopper (who, on a nice summer day in 1979 in Sturbridge Massachusetts, personally told me the story of how debugging got its name).

Thanks to our other friends at IDG Books including John Kilcullen, Walter Bruce, Richard Swadley, Joe Wikert, and Mary Bednarek. A special thanks to my friend Andy Cummings (who should immediately be promoted to senior executive). Thanks for your help, advice, conversations, and helping out the cause. You will be an executive some day. You have a unique ability to get the job done.

To Jeff Bezos at Amazon.com for selling lots of our books and giving us a way to watch how good our books perform.

Finally, to all of our families, loved ones, and friends whom we ignore for months at a time when we write our books.

Contents at a Glance

Contents

☑ **Friday**

☐ Saturday

☐ Sunday

Part I — Friday Evening

PART

I

Friday Evening

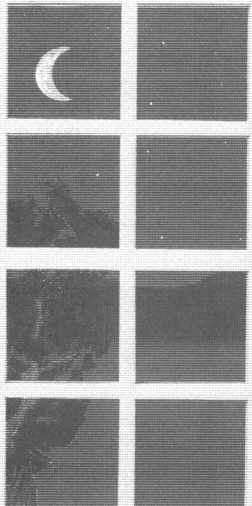

Introduction to Microsoft Access and Programming

Session Checklist

✔ What is programming?

✔ Why Use the Visual Basic language?

✔ Programming in the year 2000 and beyond

✔ Database programming

✔ Using the Check Writer example database

✔ Basic Access program structure: modules, functions and subprocedures

30 Min. To Go

Microsoft Access is an outstanding environment for both database users and professional developers. In this session, you will learn the difference between using Microsoft Access tables, queries, forms, and reports and programming with the Visual Basic language. You will learn how professional developers use Microsoft Access to create applications and get an introduction to the Check Writer application example used throughout this book.

In order to get the most from this book, it is assumed that you are already familiar with most of the Microsoft Access objects including tables, queries, forms, and reports. You should also know the basic concepts of building tables and creating relationships. If you have never created a Microsoft Access form, then this book will not help you very much. All of the examples start from forms that have been created and explain how to add functions and procedures using Access' internal Visual Basic language.

If you have already created simple or complex macros, then you already understand the basics of events and programming. This book does not teach macros, as professional developers only use macros on rare occasions. These may include creating certain types of menus, avoiding .MDA referencing problems, and other specific situations. It does explain how to convert your macros to modules and thoroughly explains event-driven programming, which is used in Microsoft Access applications.

What is Programming?

Programming is the name given to the process of creating instructions to accomplish a task. This is just one of the many phases of development. Microsoft Access contains a set of tools, one of which is called a language. Just as you build words, sentences, and thoughts when you speak or write using human language, you use the programming language to create the program. The language consists of a series of commands that tells the computer how to accomplish the task at hand. Computer programming languages have rules and grammar just like spoken languages.

Computer grammar is called *syntax*.

Programming can be defined in many ways but usually words like *logic*, *structure*, *commands*, *sequence*, and *order* are part of the definition. Professional programmers today prefer the term *developer*. A developer is a person who creates computer applications. It doesn't matter if traditional programming is used. Creating a form using Microsoft Access can be considered development. When an error message or process is added to the form with a macro or language element, it is considered programming. Programming is only one element of development. Analysis, design, testing, and debugging are other key elements of application development.

Microsoft Access contains a variety of tools that allow you to build applications without using the built-in language. These include queries, forms, and reports. Microsoft Access is known as a database management package because it gives you the ability to create tables that hold the data you use. If you have created macros using Microsoft Access, then you already have programmed, whether you knew it or not.

Visual Basic is the language that is used internally with Microsoft Access. It is also called VBA or Visual Basic for Applications, Visual Basic – Applications Edition, and the Visual Basic language. It used to be called Access Basic in the first versions of Microsoft Access. Whatever you prefer to call it, the Visual Basic language is an integral part of Microsoft Access. For the purposes of this book, the Microsoft Access programming language will be referred to simply as VBA.

Why Use the Visual Basic Language?

While Microsoft Access allows you to create process-oriented programs using macros, it is the language that gives you unlimited flexibility. Many Microsoft Access programmers started with macros and eventually realized they couldn't do everything they wanted. Eventually, you will find that only programming using the Visual Basic language will meet all of your needs.

There are many things that macros cannot do. Macros cannot

- Create error trapping routines and run a process based on the error
- Use repetitive looping, or incrementing of variables
- Perform complex decision making
- Replace runtime parameters to change form display

 Don't confuse the Visual Basic language within Microsoft Access with the product Microsoft sells called Visual Basic. Though Visual Basic (the product) and Microsoft Access share the common Visual Basic language, the products themselves are very different.

Programming in the Year 2000 and Beyond

If you are fairly new to Microsoft Access and have been a programmer for several decades, you may be wondering, Why program at all? You may have already discovered the incredible power of tables, queries, forms, and reports. You may have created fairly complex forms including combo box, option groups, OLE Objects and the like, which provide more power than many programs you used just 10 years ago. You also may be very comfortable using macros.

If you have already been programming in languages like COBOL or dBASE, you may be looking for the window that lets you type in commands so you can start programming. While there is such a screen in Microsoft Access, you don't use the Visual Basic Editor window as you might have to write a program in the 1980s. In the early days of personal computers, you started with a blank screen and an editor similar to a simple word processor. You would write line after line of computer language code to do such mundane things as:

Draw a rectangle	@12,15 To 25,40
Display a text label	@13,17 SAY "Customer Name:"
Allow the user to enter data	@13,31 GET CUSTNAME

You always had to worry about where the cursor was and where it was going. Today's visual tools, such as the form design window, make it easy to build forms without ever entering a line of computer code. In fact, using Microsoft Access you can build fairly sophisticated applications without ever writing a single line of VBA code. Creating a simple form in dBASE II could easily take a day to program. In Microsoft Access, you can create the same form with a wizard in a couple of minutes or from the form design screen in half an hour.

Microsoft Access uses an event-driven visual programming environment. This means that, generally, you create a form to display something and then in the design view of the form you use the events of the form, the form's controls, mouse movements, or keyboard keypresses to add programmed instructions that go beyond just simple form display and data editing. It is a visual environment because you see the user interface at all times. Additionally, as you will learn in the next session, you can view the results of your work nearly instantaneously and with only a few mouse clicks. If you are used to the mainframe world, you know the pain of compiling and linking.

An event is just that — an event, such as a form being opened, a user placing the cursor in a field on a form, a data value being changed, your mouse moving to a specific control, or more than 50 other distinct occurrences that you can write VBA code with. You can also write VBA code for many other things that happen to forms and reports, printing reports, trapping for potential errors, and even to check the passage of time and perform some task after a certain number of seconds. Each of these events serves as a trigger for code to be run (or *executed*, as it is also called in programming vernacular). Figure 1-1 shows some of the events that are behind a form, and a VBA window where a simple program has been created to check the value of text box entry and display an error message if it is null.

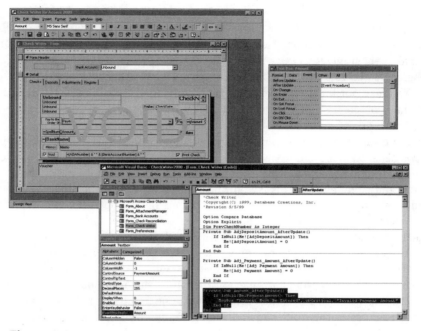

Figure 1-1
Sample events behind a form and the VBA window showing a simple program.

You will learn about many different events in the next session.

**20 Min.
To Go**

Database Programming is Incredibly Flexible

There are many popular computer software products today that include or are built primarily around programming languages. Some of these are C++, Java, Visual FoxPro, Delphi, Visual Basic, Microsoft Access, and Microsoft Excel. There are many, many more products with smaller followings from many small companies, but Microsoft Access is one of the most flexible because it is built around a database management system. Database management systems include the ability to build tables and relationships and the ability to store data.

Microsoft Access is a multi-dimensional product because it also includes an easy-to-use but powerful set of form and report tools. Its VBA language capability allows the automation or addition of extensions to your simple forms and reports and makes them incredibly powerful.

Microsoft Access uses a database management system known as Jet to manage data. You may not know this because the Jet engine is built into Microsoft Access. Each time you create a new database, design a table, or write a query, you are using the Jet database engine.

If you create professional Microsoft Access applications, you should always create two separate .MDB database files. One database file contains just your tables while the other contains links to those tables along with your queries, forms, reports, and module code. This is known as *file/server computing*. You may have heard it referred to as *client/server computing* but the Jet database engine is not a true client/server database engine but rather a file/server database engine.

Real client server database engines such as SQL Server or Oracle actually do all their processing on the database server hardware and minimize data sent across the network. While Microsoft Access uses Jet as a database manager, all processing is done on each client workstation every time after the entire data table is sent across the network. The optimum solution for large database applications is to use Microsoft Access as the front-end and use SQL Server or Oracle as the back end.

While SQL Server and Oracle are also very powerful database managers, they do not include a set of integrated tools and have no specific programming language. In fact, SQL Server uses VBA to handle its own internal event model known as *triggers* and *stored procedures*. Triggers are events that respond to a change in a data value that triggers (or starts) a block of code known as a stored procedure because it is also stored in the data table.

Microsoft Access 2000 contains a new client-server database model called *projects* and uses the file extension .ADP. This built-in client/server model uses the personal desktop version of SQL Server known as the Microsoft Database Engine (MSDE). You can create applications that work with MSDE instead of Jet and then instantly use the more powerful SQL Server when you are ready.

Using the Check Writer Example Database

Included in the back of this book is a CD containing the example files used in the sessions in this book. There are also many free software samples and demo versions of business systems and third-party tools from leading Microsoft Access add-on vendors.

The example used in this book is a fairly simple application that is very representative of the types of applications you can develop with Microsoft Access. The example is a working check writer, which is an electronic version of the checkbook you probably use all the time. The example is written in Microsoft Access and programmed with the latest version of Access 2000, VBA, and the internal data access language ADO.

There are two files you will need to use:

CheckWriter2000.mdb   The program file including Queries, Forms, Reports, and Modules

CheckWriter2000Data.mdb   The data file containing just the tables used in the example

If you have never worked with linked databases, this is a great time to start.

Professional Microsoft Access application developers always keep the program and data in two separate database files. This way, if the programs or design objects (forms, reports, etc.) need some changes, the developer can replace the customer's program file without disturbing the data files.

The sessions in this book use various parts of this example to show how to build any professional application. The application was constructed specifically to show many of the things you have to do to be successful in application development. This includes both VBA programming as well as data design and forms and report creation.

Using the Check Writer main menu

When you first open the Check Writer application, the main menu is displayed as shown in Figure 1-2. The main menu consists of a few simple buttons and some graphics. When you click a button, the function runs.

The functions include the following:

Check Writer/Register   A tabbed dialog where you can add, edit, delete, or display checks, deposits, adjustments, and a visual check register.

Bank Accounts   A data entry form to enter bank account information for your accounts.

Check Reconciliation   A complete electronic check reconciliation screen to help you balance your checkbook.

| Setup | A simple form to enter your company name and address |
| Exit | A function that closes Check Writer application and exits Microsoft Access. |

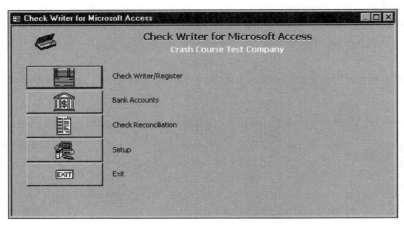

Figure 1-2
The Check Writer example main menu

Using the Check Writer tabbed data entry form

The main Check Writer/Register application consists of four tabs. Each tab contains a separate subform that displays one or more records. The tabs filter the data to only show checks, deposits, or adjustments in the first three tabs while the fourth tab shows a check register containing all types of transactions. Figure 1-3 shows the first tab, displaying the check form itself. The check form lets you enter the check number, enter the check date, select or enter a new payee, and enter the amount of the check.

As you will learn throughout the book, there are many great examples of programming behind this form. A function behind the amount field is used to automatically convert the amount to words. A pair of spin buttons in the upper right corner of the check let you automatically increase or decrease the check number. When a new payee is added, a program makes sure you wanted to add the new value and adds a record to the separate payee database.

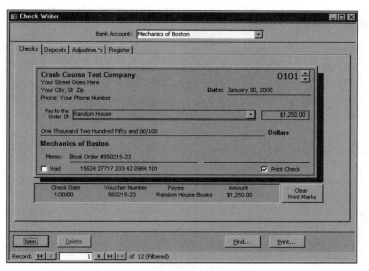

Figure 1-3
The Check Writer/Register example tabbed data entry form

At the bottom of the form there are several check boxes. One voids the check and displays a large VOID stamp across it while the other prints the check. You can fill in the stub below the check using a button to retrieve values from the check and format them into a single string.

The area in the footer of the form also contains buttons that will display great examples of a search-and-print dialog as well as New and Delete buttons that use professional error-trapped subprocedures for handling new and delete tasks.

Understanding the Check Writer data model

The data model used in the Check Writer example is shown in Figure 1-4. Most of the transaction data is stored in the Check Writer table. This table is used to store checks, deposits, and adjustments.

While all of the data fields necessary to enter check, deposit, and adjustment data are contained in this table, there are also some fields used for reconciliation (balancing your checkbook), printing, and voiding. The TransType field is used to identify the type of transaction and to filter the records for each tab in the Check Writer form.

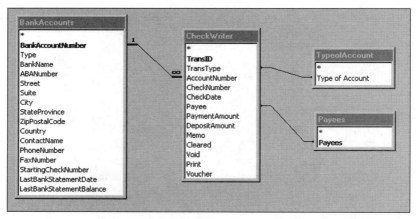

Figure 1-4
The Check Writer example data model

The BankAccounts table contains all necessary information for adding bank accounts and relating this information to the Check Writer table. The primary key field for the Bank Accounts table is BankAccountNumber, while the primary key in the Check Writer table is an AutoNumber field named TransID. The foreign key field to the bank accounts table is the AccountNumber field in the Check Writer table. The reason an AutoNumber field is used is that other more distinctive keys don't make sense in a check writer. While checks usually have sequential numbers, deposits and adjustments do not. Therefore, there is no foreign key combination that will work. BankAccountNumber, Date, and TransType cannot work because you can have multiple checks, deposits, or adjustments on the same day.

There are two additional tables used for lookups in the example. The TypeofAccount table contains a list of transaction types including check, deposit, and adjustments such as Error Correction, Interest, Wire Transfer, ATM, etc. The Payees table contains a list of unique payees used by the checks. Each time you enter a new payee into the Check Writer form payee line, you have the option to add any new payees into the table.

Using the Check Register

The Check Register is found in the last tab of the Check Writer form as shown in Figure 1-5. There is not a lot of code behind this form, but the subform is a great example of a continuous form with a complex calculation to display the continuous balance.

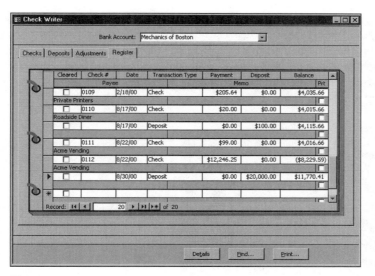

Figure 1-5
The Check Register form

The Check Register subform is made up of multiple lines. You will learn how to use multiple line subforms that include a surrounding OLE object and an editable data source. You will also learn how to change the record source of the subform programmatically (using code) when the form is initially opened and also change a controls calculated control source programmatically.

Viewing the Print Checks dialog

The Print Checks dialog shown in Figure 1-6 is displayed by pressing the Print button at the bottom of the Check Writer form. This example is used in several chapters to show interaction between VBA and dialog boxes. Based on the choices the user selects in the dialog box, different blocks of VBA code are run to select different reports, change query dynasets (the results of a query) that are passed to different reports, and even determine fields that are printed or hidden on reports.

Managing the Check Reconciliation process

The Check Reconciliation screen is shown in Figure 1-7. This screen contains a set of tools allowing the user to visually reconcile a checkbook by first entering the bank balance to view the difference between the check book balance and bank balance, and then clicking on the Cleared button and watching the difference shrink. Using the combo box on the form, the user uses VBA code to switch between bank accounts. The EDIT button in the continuous subform also allows the user to display the selected transaction by opening the Check Writer form, changing the tab, and finding the record programmatically. This provides a good lesson for navigation within multiple forms.

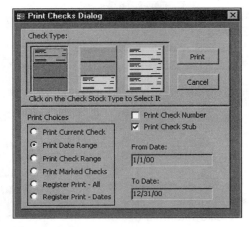

Figure 1-6
The Print Checks dialog box

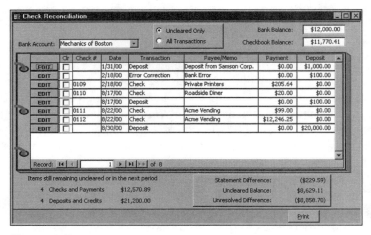

Figure 1-7
The Check Reconciliation dialog box

A Typical VBA Screen

10 Min. To Go

In the next chapter you will learn how to create VBA programs and begin to understand the process of working with VBA programs. Figure 1-8 shows the Visual Basic editor window that in Microsoft Access 2000 is a separate program in a separate window.

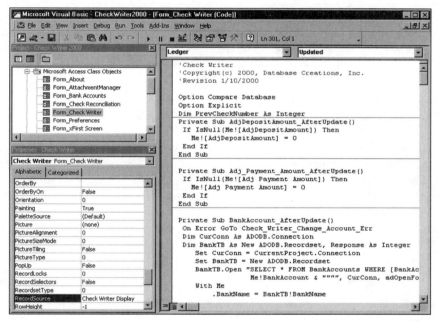

Figure 1-8
Editing VBA code

This means that you will see both Microsoft Access and the Visual Basic Editor in your task bar at the bottom of your Windows screen. While this is a huge difference internally to Access, it simply means that you can view both windows simultaneously and the editor does not use memory that could otherwise be used by Access. This results in more memory being available to Access, which can increase programmer productivity and be less taxing on machines running Access programs, as Windows itself is more stable.

The more clean and free memory you give Microsoft Access, the faster your programs will run and the more stable they will be. You should reboot your machine at least once a day, and if you have been moving between design screens and running your Access forms programs a lot, you should close Access once in a while (every hour perhaps) and restart it. Each time you move from a design screen to a datasheet or forms view, Access leaves behind a little dirt known as a memory leak. Eventually, your system will report "out of memory," or Access will report errors where there are none. Closing Access and restarting it or rebooting your system will clean up the internal memory. These problems are well known to professional Access developers.

Modules, Subprocedures, and Functions

There are a few more terms you should understand before moving on to the next chapter. When programmers think of programming in Microsoft Access, they think of VBA modules. You already know that there is a Module tab in the database container. The Modules tab in the database container displays the module libraries created by you. You can have up to 1024 module libraries in a database. Each module library can contain many procedures, just as a bookcase can contain many books.

There are two types of procedures: functions and subprocedures. Functions and subprocedures are the building blocks of modules. Each one contains VBA statements.

You will often see the term *procedure* used interchangeably with the Microsoft Access term *subprocedure* and sometimes *function*.

Procedures hold the VBA program statements that make up modules. Just as a library has both hard-cover and soft-cover books, a module library has two different types of modules. Both work exactly the same, allow passed parameters to be used to affect the way they process VBA statements, can contain error checking, and can use any VBA statement. The only difference is in the way they are called (started) and whether they return a value when processing is completed. Functions return a value when processing is complete, while subprocedures do not.

Later in this book, when you learn how to run VBA procedures, you will see in greater detail how these are run.

Done!

The module tab is not the only place where VBA modules are found. VBA modules can also be placed behind any form or report. These are known as *class modules* when they "live" behind a form or report. They behave exactly as functions or subprocedures in a module library do. They just are stored in a different place.

Generally, if a function or subprocedure is used only by a form or report, you store it behind the object. If it is to be used by more than one form or report, you should store it in a module.

REVIEW

In this chapter, you learned the definition of programming and how Microsoft Access objects interact with the VBA programming environment. You learned about database programming and the types of procedures used in Microsoft Access modules. You also learned about the Check Writer example used in this book and the two types of procedures that are found in an Access module library.

- Programming is the name given to the process of creating instructions to accomplish a task.
- Visual Basic for Applications (VBA) is the language used within Microsoft Access modules.
- Microsoft Access uses an event-driven visual programming environment.
- Microsoft Access uses a file server based database management system known as Jet to manage data. You can also create applications that work with the Microsoft Database Engine (MSDE) instead of Jet, and then instantly use the more powerful SQL Server when you are ready.
- The example used in this book is a working check writer, which is an electronic version of the checkbook you probably use all the time.
- Each module library can contain many procedures. Functions and subprocedures are the building blocks of modules.
- While module libraries contain only VBA procedures, form and report objects can also contain procedures embedded within the form or report object.

In the next chapter, you will be introduced to the VBA window and learn how to display, create and edit VBA programs.

Quiz Yourself

1. Define the term programming. (See "What is Programming?")

2. Name three reasons to use VBA instead of macros. (See "Why Use the Visual Basic Language?")

3. What are the two internal database management systems that Microsoft Access contains? (See "Database Programming is Incredibly Flexible.")

4. What is the difference between file/server and client/server database management systems? (See "Database Programming is Incredibly Flexible.")

5. What are the main functions of the Check Writer example? (See "Using the Check Writer Example Database.")

6. Name the two types of procedures. (See "Modules, Subprocedures, and Functions.")

From Macros to Modules

Session Checklist

✔ The benefits of using VBA vs. macros

✔ Converting macros to VBA

✔ Using the Command Button Wizard to create VBA code

✔ Using the Visual Basic Editor

**30 Min.
To Go**

Many tasks can be carried out through the application's user interface along with some simple macros. However, there are some tasks that macros cannot perform. VBA modules provide the most power and control of your application development environment.

When to Use Macros

Macros provide a quick and easy way to perform simple actions. The macro window provides a drop-down list of commands available and prompts you for the appropriate arguments for each command. You don't have to memorize complicated commands and arguments. In Access, some actions actually run faster in a macro than in a VBA module. Here are some of the situations where macros are a sensible solution:

- Opening and closing forms
- Running reports
- Deleting all of the records in a table or updating all of the values in a field

The Open Bank Accounts macro uses the OpenForm command to open the Bank Accounts form. Figure 2-1 shows the Open Bank Accounts macro in the Macro window.

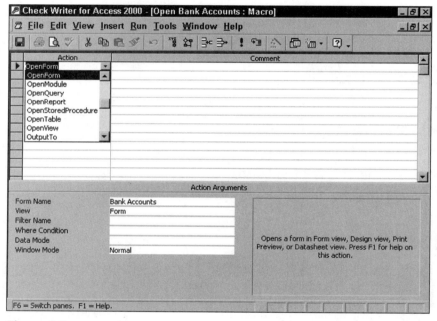

Figure 2-1
Using the macro window to create a simple macro.

Macros are most commonly used with command buttons. You can attach a macro to a command button on a switchboard, for example, for a quick and simple method of navigating to the various forms in your application.

Figure 2-2 shows the Bank Accounts command button for the Check Writer switchboard. The Open Bank Accounts macro is associated with the command button's OnClick event. When the user clicks the Bank Accounts command button, the Open Bank Accounts macro runs to open the Bank Accounts form.

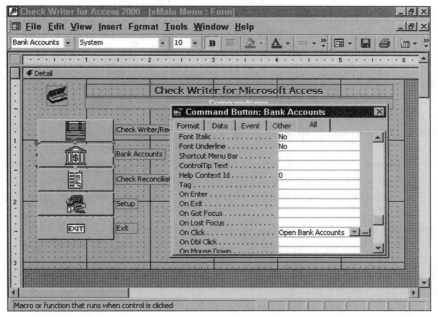

Figure 2-2
Running a macro from a command button

When to Use VBA

While macros provide a simple way to perform many actions in an application, more sophisticated applications use VBA as the tool of choice. Even though creating a VBA procedure is more complex than creating a macro, you will see that VBA provides a more robust set of commands and more control for handling any user and application errors that might occur in your application. VBA is the best solution for the following situations:

- Creating your own functions
- Handling errors and displaying message boxes
- Integrating with other applications using OLE and DDE (e.g., Microsoft Word or Microsoft Excel)
- Calling Windows functions (i.e., File Open and File Save dialogs)
- Stepping through a group of records in a table

- Manipulating the application's objects
- Passing variables to a procedure or function
- Displaying a progress meter

In a nutshell, VBA makes your application more professional by providing better error handling and lots more horsepower.

**20 Min.
To Go**

Converting macros to VBA code

Now that you see the advantages of using VBA procedures over macros, you will want to replace many of the macros in your existing applications with VBA code. Even for an application of modest size, analyzing and rewriting each macro as equivalent VBA code can be a daunting task.

Fortunately, Access provides a quick and easy solution for converting macros to VBA code automatically. You can save a macro library either as a macro object, or as a module. When you save a macro library as a module, Access automatically creates a module object for you in the Database window. This module contains a separate VBA procedure for each macro in the original macro library.

To save a macro library as a module, select the macro in the macro objects tab of the Database window. Then choose File⇨Save As. The Save As dialog displays, as shown in Figure 2-3.

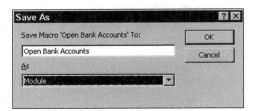

Figure 2-3
Saving a macro as a module.

In the Save As dialog, enter a name for the new module and select Module for the As option. Then select the OK button. The Convert Macro dialog box displays, as shown in Figure 2-4.

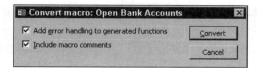

Figure 2-4
Specifying the macro to module conversion options.

Select the options to include error handling and comments. Then select the Convert button.

During the conversion process, each new procedure displays in the Visual Basic Editor. When the process is finished, the Visual Basic Editor closes and the Conversion Finished message box displays. Select the OK button to close the message box. The new module displays in the Modules object window of the Database window. When Access names the new module, it adds the prefix "Converted Macro –" to the name you specified in the Save As dialog. Figure 2-5 shows the converted code for the Open Bank Accounts macro.

When the macro is converted to a module, the original macro library remains in the macro objects window.

When you open the new module in Design view, the Visual Basic Editor displays the VBA code for the new procedures. You can examine the VBA code to see how it compares to the macro actions in the macro library. In fact, this is an excellent way to learn how to write VBA code.

As you can see in Figure 2-5, Access created a function called Open_Bank_ Accounts. At the top of the function, Access inserted four comment lines. The comment lines here are simply used to display the name of the function. You can add additional comment lines here as appropriate.

It is a good idea to add comment lines to the top of each function and procedure. You should include details about the purpose of the function or procedure and any special notes that may be necessary to understanding the code.

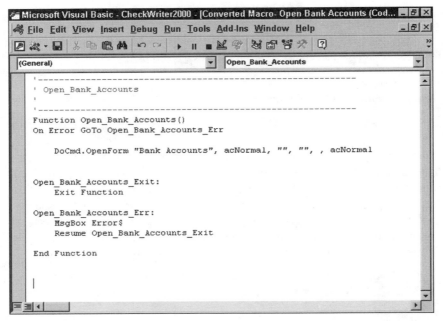

Figure 2-5
The code for the converted macro

When you specify in the conversion dialog that you want to include error process-ing, Access automatically creates the OnError statement. The OnError statement is the first statement in a function or procedure. The OnError statement tells Access where to find the error processing code section if an error occurs when the code runs. The error processing section includes a statement to display an appropriate error message and the command to exit the procedure or function.

Error processing is covered in more detail in Chapter 16.

The statement beginning with DoCmd.OpenForm is the code equivalent to the OpenForm action in the macro. The DoCmd methods run Access actions from Visual Basic. Access actions include tasks like opening and closing forms and reports, and setting the value of controls. The arguments for the macro's actions are converted to the parameters for the DoCmd method.

For macros that are used in a form, you can convert these while in the form's Design view by choosing Tools→Macro→Convert Form's Macros to Visual Basic. In addition to creating the VBA code, Access will replace the macro name in the form with a reference to the new procedure.

Using the Command Button Wizard

Another easy way to learn how to write a VBA procedure is to use the Command Button Wizard. The screens in this Wizard prompt you for the information Access needs to create the command button and its attached procedure. Figure 2-6 shows the Actions screen of the Command Button Wizard.

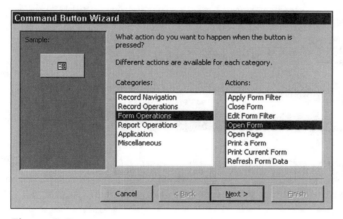

Figure 2-6
The Command Button Wizard

When the Command Button Wizard is finished, you can view the procedure that it created for the command button. You can use this procedure as is, or you can use it as a starting point and modify it as necessary.

To view the command button's procedure, follow these steps:

1. Display the form in Design view.

2. Display the Property window for the command button.

3. Click on the Builder button (...) for the OnClick event property.
   The command button's procedure displays in the Visual Basic Editor.

Part I–Friday Evening Session 2

Figure 2-7 shows the procedure for the Bank Accounts command button in the Visual Basic Editor.

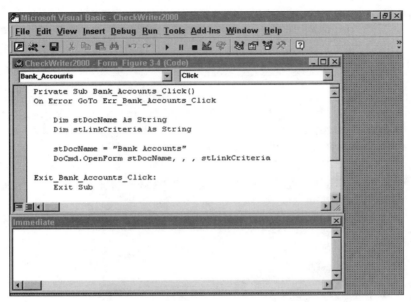

Figure 2-7
The Bank Accounts command button's On Click procedure.

Event procedures are covered in more detail in Chapter 4.

10 Min.
To Go

Cross-Ref

Understanding the Visual Basic Editor

The Visual Basic Editor is the design tool provided with Access for creating and editing the VBA code in your application.

Components of the Visual Basic Editor

The Visual Basic Editor has four basic areas:

- Menu bar (command bar)
- Toolbar

- Code window
- Immediate window

The menu bar helps you create new modules and procedures quickly. The toolbar contains buttons for the actions you use most often while working with VBA code.

The code window is the most important area of the Visual Basic Editor. This is where you actually write the VBA code.

 You can resize, minimize, maximize, and move the code window. You can also split the window into two areas so that you can edit two procedures simultaneously. To split the window choose Window→Split.

The Immediate window allows you to "test drive" a line of code while your procedure is still open. This is handy when you are unsure of the result of some expression.

To display the Immediate window, choose View→Immediate window. To test an expression, type **?** and the expression to test, and then press Enter. Figure 2-8 shows testing the result of subtracting 30 days from the current date.

Figure 2-8
Testing code in the Immediate window.

You can also run a procedure in the Immediate window. This is useful for checking to see if the procedure works as expected. To test a procedure, type **?** and the name of the procedure to test. If the procedure requires arguments, be sure to specify them as well. Figure 2-9 shows testing the SpellNum procedure.

Figure 2-9
Using the Immediate window to test a procedure.

Writing code in the code window

While you are learning VBA syntax, working in the code window can seem awkward compared to everything else you may have developed in your Access application. The Visual Basic Editor, however, has some built-in features to help you on your way to becoming a VBA expert.

As you type each line of code in your procedure, on-screen help, called Auto List Members and Auto Quick Info, displays to guide you through the vast array of commands and options available for your procedure.

Auto List Members automatically displays when you type the beginning of a command. For example, when you enter DoCmd., a list of possible commands displays, as shown in Figure 2-10. You can either select one of the commands in the list, or continue typing the command if you already know the one you want to use.

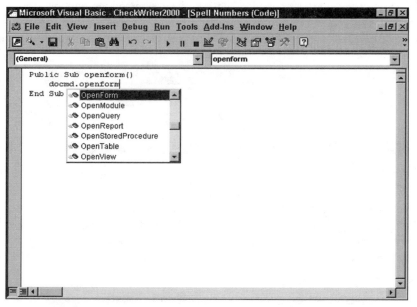

Figure 2-10
Auto List Members help in the code window.

Auto Quick Info help displays the options for the command you entered. The next parameter to enter displays in bold. As you specify each parameter and enter the

comma separator, the next parameter to enter displays in bold. Figure 2-11 shows
the Auto Quick Info help for all of the parameters of the Openform command.

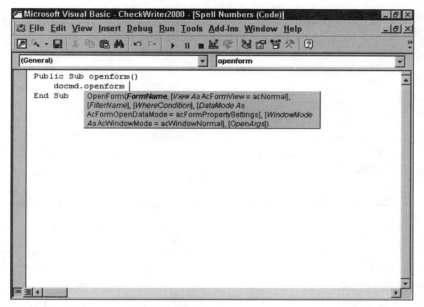

Figure 2-11
Auto Quick Info help for the OpenForm command.

Compiling procedures

After you create a procedure, you should compile it by choosing Debug→Compile.
This action checks your code for errors and converts your VBA code to a format that
your computer can understand. If the compile process fails, a message box displays
to advise you of the type of error that was encountered and the offending line of
code is highlighted in the code window.

**Access compiles all currently uncompiled procedures, not just the
one you are currently viewing.**

If you receive a compile error, you should immediately modify the code to rectify the problem. Then try to compile the procedure again.

When your application is compiled, the Debug→Compile menu choice is disabled. Before implementing an application at the customer's site, you should make sure that your application is compiled. More information on distributing applications is available in Chapter 23.

Done!

Saving a procedure

While you are creating a procedure, you should save it often to avoid the loss of important code should there be any sudden hardware failure. To save the procedure, choose File⇨Save.

REVIEW

In this chapter, you learned how to use some of the built-in tools to create VBA procedures automatically and how to use the Visual Basic Editor. The following topics were covered:

- You can save a macro library as a module to automatically convert the macro actions to VBA code.
- The Command Button Wizard automatically creates the VBA procedure to run a command button's OnClick event.
- You can use the Immediate window to test your code.
- The Visual Basic Editor provides the Compile action for checking your code for errors.

You should be familiar now with some of the tools for creating VBA code. But before you jump into writing your first program, you need to put some thought into the overall design for the program. The next chapter discusses how to come up with a good design for your system.

QUIZ YOURSELF

1. Name the situations where macros are a better solution than VBA code. (See "When to Use Macros.")

2. Name the Access feature that automatically converts a macro to a module. (See "Converting macros to VBA code.")

3. Name the VBA statement that handles an error when a program runs. (See "Converting macros to VBA code.")

4. Name the feature that allows you to quickly test a line of code. (See "Components of the Visual Basic Editor.")

5. How can you tell if your code is compiled? (See "Compiling procedures.")

3

System and Process Design, Testing, and Debugging

Session Checklist

✔ Designing your system

✔ Planning for programming

✔ Testing your programs

✔ Syntax checking and compiling

✔ Debugging, breakpoints, and the immediate window

**30 Min.
To Go**

Before you begin any programming activities, you should have a firm understanding of the tasks you need to accomplish. System design is one of the first steps to building any computer application and may encompass hardware, networks, and software. With Microsoft Access, the first two are usually all taken care of. As long as the computer system and network can run Microsoft Access, any program you create using Microsoft Access will usually run without any problems.

Since you have already created applications with tables, forms, reports, and possibly macros, you already have designed systems. This session will review some basic design concepts and concentrate on taking a working set of forms and table designs and planning for the next step — programming. This session will also introduce the concepts of testing and debugging VBA programs.

Designing your System

When you begin writing an application, you start with the most general of design goals and then get more and more specific. When the authors of this book decided to use a comprehensive example, they brainstormed for a representative application. We decided to use our award-winning Check Writer application, which we have used for previous versions of Microsoft Access, and to rewrite it using the new ADO data access method used in Microsoft Access 2000.

Building an application is like building a house. You start by deciding you want a house. Next, you get more specific. The house will be colonial, two stories tall, and about 2,500 square feet. Then you decide how many rooms each floor will have and the dimensions and layout of each floor. Now its time to draw up some blueprints and order the materials. Only then can you start the building process.

As you build the house, you are constantly checking to make sure everything is square. Just as professional carpenters use a variety of tools including levels, chalk lines, and squares, you will use a variety of VBA tools to insure quality in your application such as the syntax checker, compiler, built-in debugger, immediate window, and breakpoints.

With Microsoft Access, it is much the same. The difference is you can build the system at a much lower cost as there are no materials, just labor. However, just because a computer system can be less expensive to build then a house, doesn't mean the up-front design time should be any less. Though you can always take down a wall in a house after it is built, you would probably want to build it right the first time. It would be nice if each time you made a door opening too small, the house would tell you. The good news is that the built-in tools in Microsoft Access constantly give you this kind of feedback as you program your application.

You may not need a set of detailed blueprints to begin your system design with Microsoft Access but you should create a set of specifications with increasing details. Your specifications should first address the general problem, and then a set of details, and then a specification with even more details. Microsoft Access' own visual forms designer and user-friendly table design environment makes it a wonderful system development environment. You can create prototypes as quickly as you can brainstorm features, and make changes as you go.

Because of this, you do not need to spend as much time designing your systems up front as with other less visual languages. However, the more time you spend discussing and defining your system before you start, the easier it will be to complete it successfully.

When building a computer system, there are several distinct phases. These include:

- General Design (Also Known as System Design)
- Detail Design
- Programming and Documentation
- Testing
- Debugging

General design

The overall system design is defined from a business point of view as opposed to a technical or computer outlook. A general design will ordinarily take just a few pages and lay out the most important aspects of the system. Major functions will be mentioned by name only. Later all the details can be filled in. The output of the system (reports) should also be discussed because you generally can't create data designs or forms without knowing what information will ultimately be needed from the system.

When we first built this application, we decided that we wanted to build an application that would closely resemble something everyone used all the time. We decided on a checkbook. After we decided the overall application, we moved to the next level. We first wrote a small group of bullets.

Design is a Never-Ending Process, Not Just a Phase

Designing anything is a fluid process. It never ends. You keep reviewing and working and reviewing. You start with an idea, refine it, discuss it further, add some new ideas, and continue changing it until you are satisfied with the result. This can occur during any of the phases of design. Sometimes, when testing a completed form, you may realize you left out a very basic set of data items that may require you to create a new lookup table, rearrange the form, or even redesign portions of the entire application. Don't be discouraged if this happens. It is a normal part of development and even the most experienced developers go through this process. In fact, sometimes it is better to prototype your first idea without even discussing it!

We will design a checkbook that works like a manual checkbook. It will have the following functions:

- A form to enter and edit bank account information
- Separate forms to enter and edit checks, deposits, and adjustments
- A check register listing all checks, deposits, and adjustments with a running balance
- A system to reconcile cleared checks
- A main menu to navigate among these functions

Detail design

Once you have a general conceptual model of the system and a rough idea of what you want to build, you can get specific. For the purposes of this book, we assume that someone on your design team has the necessary business knowledge to produce detailed specifications of the system regardless of the program being used. Detail design should include sketches of the forms and reports you think you will need. From the form and report designs, you can lay out the raw data elements you may need and then begin to create tables and relationships and normalize the data design. You can do this on paper or use Microsoft Access as a prototyping tool.

One good place to start is with customers and their existing systems. In virtually every consulting job we have ever had, the customer is either automating a manual system that already exists on paper or index-type cards, or creating a new system. In new systems, we were usually shown another company's system that was to be cloned. It is very unusual for a system to be developed with no basic template to start with.

The very first thing our team did was to each get our checkbooks out and copy a check and the check register. We looked at five different examples that were all similar with a few minor differences. Bank names were in different places, one of the checks had a place for the payee's address, the memo area was a little different. Most of us had checks in small pocket-size checkbooks, while one of our team members had a multi-part check with the check itself on top and areas for the stub in the middle and on the bottom.

We decided that businesses would probably want the multi-part check forms. Once we had established this basic template, it was easy to come up with many of the print options, such as a choice of three kinds of check stock and the option to print check numbers if the paper didn't have pre-printed numbers.

We decided to start with the most fundamental of needs — the check. We looked at the check and designed a simple table consisting of just five fields:

- Check Number
- Check Date
- Payee
- Check Amount
- Memo

We then designed a simple form and moved the fields into position as shown in Figure 3-1. As you can see, with just this simple table and form, the application is already beginning to look like a check and could theoretically be used for data entry and reporting.

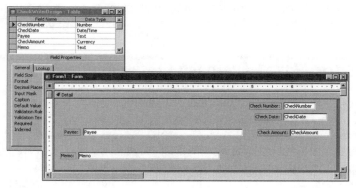

Figure 3-1
Simple check writer table and form design

Once we had seen the basic form, we discussed adding some basic text, such as labels, for the bank account information — bank account number, bank name, bank address, and routing numbers. This then led to a discussion about customers who had more than one bank account. We decided to add a bank account table and enable the check writer table and form to handle more than one bank account.

This meant that we not only had to design and create the Bank Account table and form, but also add some additional fields to the Check Writer table. We added the Bank Account Number field to the Check Writer table and related the two tables so each Check Writer record would record the bank account number and could then be used for more than one bank account.

We then added a combo box to the Check Writer form to display all of the bank accounts and knew that we would have to add some VBA code to change or filter bank accounts. At the same time, we discussed the fact that while we had a form for checks, we needed other forms for balance adjustments.

Eventually, we realized that multiple forms would be hard to navigate through and packaged all of the forms into the tabbed dialog you see in the example.

This process took several weeks of work and many prototypes. This is a normal part of programming: design, programming, testing, refinement, and more design. It never really stops. You can continue to add more and more functionality. Our check register was developed using several different prototypes and, in fact, we started over several times before finding a design we really liked.

Eventually, you will have a form that is as complete as it can be without macro or VBA programming. While a form can be used for simple data entry or display, it usually needs some sort of processing to complete your design. Error checking, calculations, moving data between tables, filling combo box row sources, filtering data, or building menus are just a few of the reasons you must write program code.

The "Concentric Circle" Approach to Development

Microsoft has always followed a philosophy of development that includes the design, programming, and testing of a core set of features followed by increasing functionality in phases. Microsoft develops a blueprint that includes small sets of features. First, the most fundamental features are developed. Then, this feature set can be distributed to customers for comments and testing. While one small team of developers is working on testing and debugging one of the feature sets, another team is working on programming the next feature set while still another team is working on design refinement of the next set of features. This continues until Microsoft is ready to release the product. When it is ready, features that have not passed the testing criteria are simply removed.

The product could be released at many different times with different feature sets. Based on market dynamics and customer feedback, the product will either be released or development will continue. Think of a set of concentric circles that keep getting bigger and bigger. At any time, the product could be released — but the longer development continues, the more features are added.

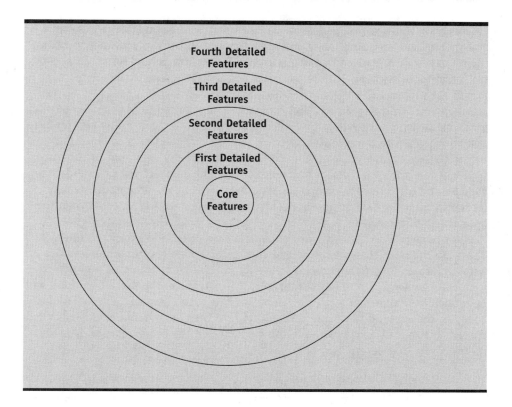

Fourth Detailed
Features

Third Detailed
Features

Second Detailed
Features

First Detailed
Features

Core
Features

**20 Min.
To Go**

Planning for Programming

After you have designed your basic data entry objects on paper or used Microsoft
Access to prototype your table, form, and report designs, you can turn your attention to adding process code. Having data entry forms without any programs behind
them gives you very little flexibility. Adding VBA code or macros behind Access
forms give you unlimited flexibility to handle errors, create calculations and for-
mulas, add navigation (getting from one form to another), handle data inter-
change between tables, find records, and create flexible dialog boxes for printing.
You may also want to have a splash screen, user-definable setup options, an about
box, programmable security, and a menu system or switchboard. The best way to
learn how to write the specific lines of code to accomplish a task is to find some
code that does what you want and modify it to fit your tables and forms.

This book will give you plenty of examples. But before you start writing code you should have an idea of what you want to write and where you want to write it. In Chapter Two, you learned about events. Events live behind forms, form controls, and form processes (before and after you insert, update, or delete records), and in other places as well.

When you begin to plan any VBA coding you might need, it is generally a good idea to start with data validation as it is entered at both a control-by-control basis and possibly before the record is saved. When you put validation code behind Before Update events, you can stop the data from actually being put in the control. You can display a message and require different input. If you put validation code behind After Update events, the data has already been accepted. You may be transferring the data to another control or storing it in a table other than the bound field of the control.

A lot of code is written to process numeric data or to follow business rules. These are the rules that the business dictates. For example, after a line item is entered into an invoice application, the subtotal will be recalculated and then the item will be checked to see if it is taxable. If it is taxable, the taxable subtotal will be recalculated and than a calculation of Tax Rate × the Taxable Subtotal will be added to the subtotal to calculate Total Owed. In the Check Writer example, voided checks must not be added to the running balance on the check register. It is the business rule that determines what has to be designed and then programmed to do this.

Once you have built a few applications, you will also be building your toolbox of routines. The more you build, use, discover, craft, or create, the easier it gets.

One way to jumpstart your development efforts is to purchase some of the low-cost libraries of preprogrammed utilities, interfaces, and source code repositories. Some of the best are the Total Access SourceBook, a library of VBA code from FMS Corporation www.fmsinc.com **and the EZ Access Developer Tools, a library of interface designs and VBA code from Database Creations,** www.databasecreations.com. **See the CD in the back of this book for demos of these and many other products.**

As you go through your design process and define things you can't do with just forms, you will turn them into business and process designs and eventually VBA designs. There are hundreds and even thousands of different types of VBA statements, constants, variables, and constructs. Don't worry about trying to learn every one. Learn the ones you need for the type of programming you are doing. Pay special attention to the statements you use a lot and learn new ones as you need to.

While only experience can teach you how to create algorithms (specific designs in a language), this book will show you many algorithms for a wide variety of situations.

Testing and Debugging your Applications

Testing is the first step in a process that lets you insure that your application is working as designed. Each time you move from form or report design or the Visual Basic Editor to running those same forms, reports, and VBA code, you are testing your application. Each time you write a line of code and move to another line, you (or Access) is testing your code. Each time you change a property in a form or report and move your cursor to another property, you and Access are testing your form or report.

Testing is the time to see if your application runs the way you designed it, or even runs at all. When you run an application and it doesn't work, you have found a bug.

Fixing problems is known as debugging. This term dates back to the earliest electron tube computers. Legend has it that a moth shorted out a hardware circuit. Removing the moth was known as "debugging the system" a phrase attributed to the late Admiral Grace Hopper, an early pioneer in computing.

You may have already learned a lot about testing and debugging. When you run a report and no data appears, you have probably learned to check the report's Record Source property and to view the data in the query or table to see if the data source is the problem. If you run a form and you see #Name or #Error in individual controls, you have learned to check the Control Source of the Control. Perhaps you have an incorrect reference to a table field or spelled something wrong. Maybe you had too many parentheses or have used a control name in a formula that uses the control name. Each time you had this problem, you probably asked someone with more experience than you what the problem was or perhaps you looked it up in a manual or researched the syntax of the formula.

When you run forms and reports, Access may report an error if it finds something seriously wrong. When you create VBA code, there are a wide variety of tools built in to the editor to help you.

Syntax checking — the first step

When you type a line of code in VBA, each character is being evaluated against the known but limited set of valid VBA commands. In the last chapter, you learned about the Access 2000 Auto List Members and Auto Quick Info tools that help you enter code correctly. When you have completed entering each line of code, another built-in tool known as the syntax checker is used to make sure the line of code contains valid entries

Syntax is the name given to computer grammar. Figure 3-2 shows a statement typed incorrectly and the error message that is displayed as you try to leave the line. You may also notice the lines are different colors. Black indicates a valid line of code. Green is used for comments and red is used when a line has been flagged by the syntax checker and not yet corrected.

Unlike some other languages, VBA will let you leave a line of code that has an error and fix it later. Sometimes, you need to add or change another line of code in order to fix a subsequent line.

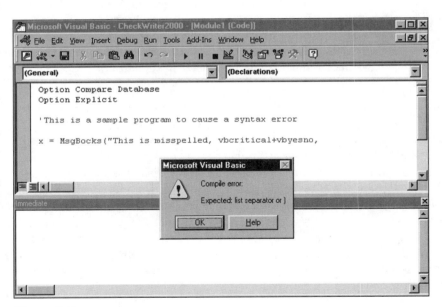

Figure 3-2
The Microsoft Access 2000 Syntax Checker

Compiling procedures

After you create a subprocedure or function and want to make sure all of your syntax is correct, you should compile your procedures by choosing Debug⇨Compile *projectname* from the VBA menu as shown in Figure 3-3. This action checks your code for errors and also converts the programs to a form your computer can understand. If the compile operation is not successful, an error window appears. This level of checking is more stringent than the single-line syntax checker. Variables are checked for proper references and type. Each statement is checked for all proper parameters. All text strings are checked for proper delimiters such as 'text string.'

While your database is named with a standard Windows name such as Check Writer for Access 2000, there is a separate project name that Microsoft Access uses internally. You will see this when you compile your database. When the database file is first created, the project name and the Windows file name will be the same. The project name is not changed when you change the Windows file name. You can change the project name by selecting Tools⇨*projectname* Properties where *projectname* is the current internal project name.

When you compile your application, Access checks each and every uncompiled procedure and then converts it to a form that can be run. If Access finds any errors, it stops and reports the error. It stops at the first error it finds. You must correct the error and then run the compile operation again.

Compiling your database does more that just make sure that you have no syntax errors. It also checks to ensure that object references are appropriate. The compiler can only check for language problems by first recognizing the VBA statement and then checking to see that you specify the right number of options and in the right order.

After you compile your program you should also compact your database. Each time you make a change to your program it stores both the changes and the original version. When you compile your program, it may double in size as the compiled and uncompiled versions of your code are stored. When you compact the database, it will reduce the size of the database by as much as 80% as it eliminates all previous versions internally.

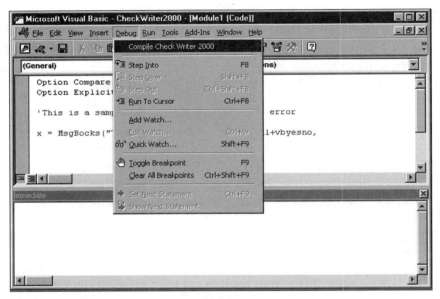

Figure 3-3
Compiling the VBA Code in Your Database

Handling runtime errors

You might create a line of code that refers to a specific form. The form is expected to have been opened already by a previous line of code in a different procedure. If that form is not already open when the program runs, an error will occur. You cannot determine that this might happen during the compile step because the compiler evaluates each procedure separately and does not try to compare the logic between procedures or modules. There is no way to know if the code might have already been run to open the form since that code could be run from a variety of events. However, when the program runs, you will get an error message.

When you get an error message, you can likely respond to it. However, some errors are harder to understand than others and some require you to instantly recognize the problem. For example, Figure 3-5 shows a simple program that declares and creates a text string variable and a numeric variable and then tries to assign the numeric variable the value of the text string. You probably already know that you can't put letters in a numeric field.

The error message in Figure 3-4 reports a Run-time error '13:' which happens to be a Type mismatch. Unless you know the problem, how does this message help you? Without a great deal of experience, how do you then fix this type of problem? In fact, how do you determine what the problem is?

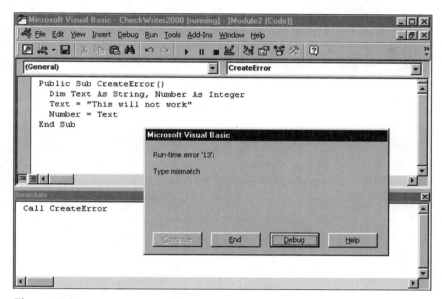

Figure 3-4
A Runtime Error Message

In the error dialog in Figure 3-4, you can see a button labeled Debug. The Debug button will stop the program where it is running and place you on the offending statement. The program is in a state of limbo. All of the values of temporary variables are intact and you can view them to help you solve the error. The End button will stop the program and you will not be able to use any tools to check the problem.

Figure 3-5 shows this statement. It is highlighted by a yellow background indicating it is the offending statement. There are several tools you can then use to find your problem.

If you place your cursor over any variable in the highlighted area you can see the current value. If you examine Figure 3-5, you can see the arrow in the left margin indicating the highlighted line is the currently running line of code. You can also see the rectangle containing the text Text = "This will not work," the current value of the variable named Text. You can see that the value of Number is currently 0.

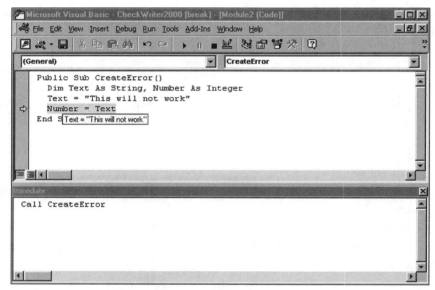

Figure 3-5
Displaying the Value from a Running Variable

While you can place your cursor on the running variable and determine the values, you may want to see the value of other variables as well. Sometimes, depending on how the program is structured, you can do this, but usually you are limited to the latest values created.

Variables are user-defined values stored in memory and are covered in detail in Chapter 6.

10 Min. To Go

Using the Immediate, Locals, and Watches Window

There are several more tools that can help you debug a program. These include the Immediate, Locals, and Watches windows. You can display any of them as part of the Visual Basic editor window by selecting View⇨Immediate Window, View⇨Locals Window, or View⇨Watch Window. Any may be necessary depending on the severity of your problems and the mysteriousness of the error.

The Immediate Window is an area where you can run procedures, check the value of variables, check an expression, or run a single line of VBA code. You can run a VBA subprocedure by using the syntax Call *procedurename* where *procedurename* is a subprocedure. You can also run a function by placing a ?

in front of the call and adding a variable for the return value such as ? x = *functionname*. You can check the value of any variable running in your program by placing a ? in front of the variable name.

You can see the values of the running variables as displayed in Figure 3-6. Here in the immediate window you see that ? Number was entered and produced the value 0. Then on a separate line ? Text was entered and the text "This will not work" is displayed as this is the value of the variable named Text.

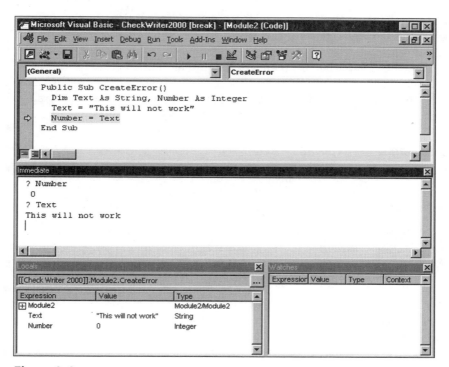

Figure 3-6
Using the Immediate, Locals, and Watches Window

The Locals window can be used to display all of the active memory items in your running program. These include forms, modules, and variables. In Figure 3-6, you can see the Locals window in the bottom left-hand corner of the figure. Since only a simple module is running, you only see the reference to that object. If you were also running a form, you would see a reference to the form object along with a tree diagram that could be exploded to show each control on the form and the value of each control for the current record. This is important when you are debugging a module behind a form or report.

Generally, you start with just the module debugger and then if necessary move into the Immediate window. If you need to view more variables, you might display the Locals window. There is also an advanced window known as the Watches window. While this is outside the scope of this book, the Watches window lets you set up specific values to watch for and then stop the program when a value is reached. For example, if you are expecting an incremental value to reach 500 by 1 and it never does, you might set a Watch variable to see if it hits 100 rather than to randomly check the program when it runs. If the watchpoint (as it is called) hits 100, the program is stopped and the line of code highlighted that the program was on when the value reached 100. This is the same as a run-time error without the actual error.

When the program stops, there are some other tools you can use to step through the program one line at a time. You can also move to previously executed lines to check your program logic. Besides the Watch window, you can stop your program at a specific point by using a breakpoint.

Creating a breakpoint

There is one last code-debugging tool that professional developers use: breakpoints. Whereas the watch window watches for a specific value, breakpoints simply watch for a specific line to be executed and stop the program at that statement.

Professional developers often refer to running a program as *executing* it. You execute a program to start it. Either term is appropriate.

A breakpoint is often used to stop a running program before it causes an error. This way all the variables and conditions of the objects can be checked before the error occurs.

To set a breakpoint, display your program in design view and press the F9 function key or select the Toggle Breakpoint menu item from the Debug menu. Figure 3-7 shows a breakpoint on the line that sets the value of the variable Text in the simple program you have seen in this chapter. After you set the breakpoint, you can close the module and the breakpoint will be remembered until the database file is closed. When you run the program and that module is executed, the program will stop on that line and display the program at the breakpoint.

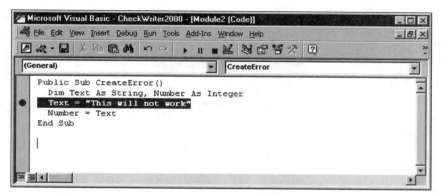

Figure 3-7
Setting a breakpoint

Once the program has run and stopped, you can use options on the Debug menu to control the execution. The Debug menu is shown in Figure 3-8 with the line stopped where the breakpoint is set. Notice the solid red circle and the yellow arrow in the margin. The red circle indicates the breakpoint and the arrow the current line.

You can set as many breakpoints as you want but more than one may be confusing unless you are trying to determine if a block of code is being run at all.

The Debug menu is broken into five areas. The first area lets you compile the application. You generally don't do this while the program is running.

The next area lets you use four different methods to continue running your program one or more statements at a time.

Step Into	Run the next one line of code
Step Over	Run the next line of code and all the code in any called procedures
Step Out	Run the entire current procedure and then stop with the next line in the original called procedure
Run to Cursor	You can move your cursor to later line and run all the statements between the current line and the line where the cursor is.

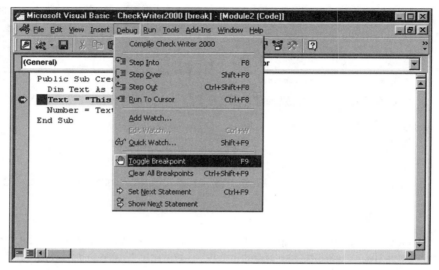

Figure 3-8
Using the Debug Menu

The next group lets you add or edit a watchpoint in the watch window. You can also run a quick watch just to see the value of a variable, much like entering ? somevariablename in the Immediate Window.

The next group lets you toggle a breakpoint on or off or clear all breakpoints. When you close a database file, all breakpoints are automatically cleared.

The final menu choices are perhaps the most powerful. Set Next Statement lets you move the cursor to any line of code and then run the program starting with that line. If you are trying to correct an error and keep getting it wrong, being able to go backwards is very important. Show Next Statement simply highlights without running the next statement that will run.

There are also several options on the Run menu that will help you debug a program.

Continue	Continues running the program without stopping until the next error, breakpoint, or to the program's conclusion.
Break	Stops the program where it is running. You can also use Ctrl-Break to stop a running program and cause a manual break. If you accidentally create an endless loop, this will stop the program.
Reset	Stops the error process and lets you restart the program from any desired line of code.

When you are debugging a running program and finally get a line of code corrected, make sure you press the Save icon or your changes will not be saved when you close the procedure.

Done!

By using the wide variety of debugging tools, you will be able to diagnose your coding problems and quickly solve them. You can also use the Visual Basic help system to help you understand the problem being reported, but generally errors will be yours to solve.

REVIEW

In this chapter, you learned about various design phases and how to properly think about your program design. You learned how to use the various debugging tools to trap for errors and fix them.

- Design is an ongoing process that contains many iterative phases.
- Development includes conceptual or general design, detail design, programming, testing, and debugging.
- You can use Microsoft Access itself to prototype your systems during design phases instead of using paper and pencil.
- Debugging is the name given to the process of finding problems with your systems and correcting them.
- Syntax is the name given to computer grammar. Access program statements follow types of rules of grammar similar to spoken language.
- Compiling checks all of your program statements for correct syntax and translates your code into a form that Access can run quickly and efficiently.
- When a run-time error is displayed, you can use the Debug button to display the problem line.
- The Immediate, Locals, and Watches windows help you display your program variables.
- The Debug menu contains many options to help you run your program one line at a time to find and correct your errors.

In the next chapter you will learn about Events and which form and report events are used to call procedures from.

Quiz Yourself

1. Define the term "general design." (See "Designing Your System.")

2. What is the "concentric circle" approach to development? (See "Detail design.")

3. Define the term syntax. (See "Syntax checking — the first step.")

4. What are the two main reasons to compile your programs? (See "Compiling procedures.")

5. When you get a runtime error, how do you display the offending line of code? (See "Handling runtime errors.")

6. What are some of the ways to watch your variables as your program runs? (See "Using the Immediate, Locals, and Watches Window.")

7. How can you stop your program anywhere you want and run it one line at a time? (See "Creating a breakpoint.")

Events — A Place to Run Your Code

Session Checklist

✔ Understanding events

✔ Responding to events

✔ Creating an event procedure

✔ Using an event procedure to validate data

✔ Understanding event sequences

**30 Min.
To Go**

Forms and reports are the objects that are most apparent to your application's users. The text boxes, labels, and command buttons in the forms and reports provide the visual components that allow the users to interact with the application. While developing forms and reports constitutes a significant amount of the entire application development effort, a considerable amount of thought and planning, and a little code, are required to tie all of these forms and reports together seamlessly.

Understanding Events

An event is a process that occurs whenever a user performs some action in a form or report. Microsoft Access is referred to as an event-driven environment because it can respond to actions like clicking a command button, opening a form or report, or updating data in a field. In an event-driven environment, the user has more control over the flow of the application. The user can update the fields on a form in any order, for example, or click any one in a set of buttons. Events provide a way to respond to actions that occur in an application. An event can occur when the user performs some action, like clicking a button. An event can also occur in response to an action that the user did not perform directly, like the timer event that occurs when a form opens.

Every control you place on a form has a set of event properties. You can check the event properties that are available for a form, report, or control by displaying the property sheet. Figure 4-1 shows the Events page of the property sheet for the Bank Accounts command button.

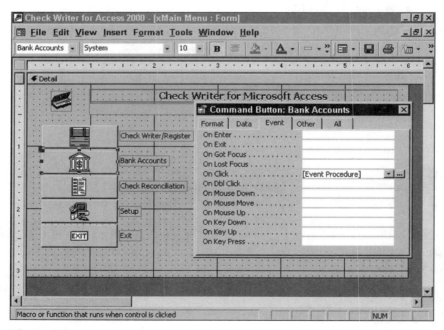

Figure 4-1
The event properties for the Bank Accounts command button.

Responding to Events

Event properties provide a way to respond to any of the actions a user might perform with a form, report, or control. You respond to an event by associating a macro or event procedure with a specific event property. The macro or event procedure contains the instructions that Access should perform whenever the associated event happens.

The Bank Accounts command button has an event procedure associated with its OnClick event property. The OnClick event occurs whenever the user selects the command button by clicking it with the mouse or by moving to the command button and pressing Enter. Whenever the Bank Accounts command button's OnClick event occurs, the event procedure runs automatically.

You learned how to associate a macro with a command button in Chapter 3.

An event procedure is a VBA program that you create and associate with an event. Figure 4-2 shows the OnClick event procedure for the Bank Accounts command button. The Bank_Accounts_Click procedure opens the Bank Accounts form.

Creating an Event Procedure

You can associate an event procedure with an individual control, or with an entire form or report. To create an event procedure, follow these steps:

1. Open the form or report in design view.
2. Select the control in the design window and display the property sheet.

To display the property sheet for the form or report, select the square at the top left of the design window.

3. Click the event property in the property sheet for the event that you want to respond to. For a command button, for example, select the OnClick event property.

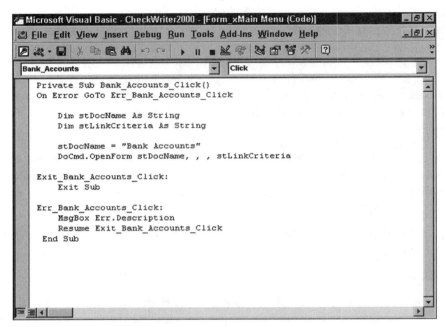

Figure 4-2
The event procedure for the OnClick event of the Bank Accounts command button.

4. Click the Build button next to the event property. The Choose Builder dialog displays.

5. Select Code Builder in the Choose Builder dialog. The Visual Basic Editor opens and automatically displays the first and last lines of the new event procedure.

There are two other methods for creating an event procedure: Choose Build Event from the shortcut menu (see Figure 4-3), or select Event Procedure from the event property's combo box.

When an event property has an associated event procedure, the text "[Event Procedure]" displays next to the event property.

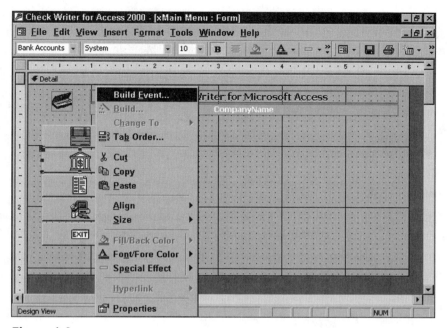

Figure 4-3
Using the shortcut menu to create an event procedure.

When you create a new event procedure, Access automatically inserts the first and last statements for the procedure. This built-in feature acts as a template to help you create procedures quickly and easily.

The first statement in a procedure contains a lot of information about its type and behavior. The `Private` keyword indicates that only this form or report can execute this procedure. The `Sub` keyword describes the type of event procedure. The third element of the procedure statement is the procedure's name.

The `Public` keyword makes the procedure available to any form or report in the application.

Chapter 1 discusses the difference between `Sub` and `Function` procedures.

Access automatically assigns an appropriate name to an event procedure to correspond with the associated event property. The name is the associated object's name followed by an underscore and the associated object's event. For example, the name for the Bank Accounts command button's OnClick procedure is `Bank_Accounts_Click`.

When assigning a name for an event, Access converts a space in the control's name to an underscore.

Never change the name of an event procedure. The name maintains the connection between the control, the control's event, and the event procedure code. Likewise, never change the name of a control that has associated event procedures.

The last statement in the procedure is `End Sub`. This statement indicates the end of the procedure.

Running a Function for an Event

20 Min. To Go

Event procedures are the recommended method of running VBA code for an event. However, you can also associate a function with an event. Figure 4-4 shows the function associated with the `BankAccountNumber` text box in the Bank Accounts Unbound form.

In the Bank Accounts Unbound form, whenever the `BankAccountNumber` text box is updated, the `uf_SetEditedFlag` function runs. The `uf_SetEditedFlag` function is shown in Figure 4-5.

The `uf_SetEditedFlag` function changes the value of the `FlagEdited` field in the form to True. Notice that the `uf_SetEditedFlag` function is declared as `Public`. This indicates that it can be executed by any event in any form. This function is stored in the Unbound Form Utilities module. By storing the function in a module, you can use it for multiple unbound forms in your application.

More on Modules in Session 7.

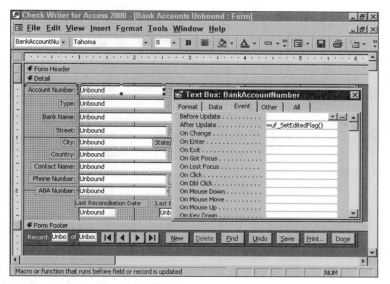

Figure 4-4
Associating a function with an event.

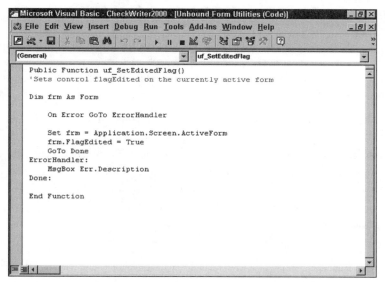

Figure 4-5
A public function can be called by events in any form.

To associate a function with an event, follow these steps:

1. Click the event property in the property sheet for the event that you want to respond to.
2. Enter an equals sign (=), followed by the function name and a pair of parentheses.

Entering the function name directly into the event property saves development time by eliminating the need for a separate event procedure for every control and event that needs to run it. Alternately, you can call the function from an event procedure like this:

```
Private Sub BankAccountNumber_AfterUpdate()
    Dim x As Integer
    x = uf_SetEditedFlag()

End Sub
```

To call the procedure using the event procedure method, you would have to create an event procedure and write the same code for each field in the unbound form.

Using an Event Procedure to Validate Data

In most cases, you can use the Validation Rule property for a field to verify acceptable field values. By using an event procedure, though, you have much more power and flexibility available for data entry validation. You should use an event procedure when you need to validate data using any of these scenarios:

- You need to verify that multiple fields have been completed. For example, the user must enter a name and a Social Security number.
- You want to display a different error message for certain types of incorrect values. You might want to display one message if the value is below a certain amount, and a different message if the value exceeds another amount.
- When you want to allow a potentially invalid entry and simply display a warning message.
- To validate the data against fields on other forms.

Figure 4-6 shows an event procedure for validating the CheckDate in the Check Writer form.

```
Microsoft Visual Basic - CheckWriter2000 - [Form_Figure 4-6 (Code)]
File  Edit  View  Insert  Debug  Run  Tools  Add-Ins  Window  Help

CheckDate                              BeforeUpdate

Private Sub CheckDate_BeforeUpdate(Cancel As Integer)
On Error GoTo CheckDate_BeforeUpdate_Err
    Dim CutoffDate As Date

    CutoffDate = Date - 30
    If Me!CheckDate < CutoffDate Then
        MsgBox "The check date must be within the past 30 days.", vbCriti
        Cancel = True
    Else
        If Me!CheckDate > Date Then
            MsgBox "You cannot enter a future check date.", vbCritical, "
            Cancel = True
        End If
    End If
    Exit Sub

CheckDate_BeforeUpdate_Err:
    MsgBox "Error is " & Err.Description & " entering Check Date in Check
    Exit Sub

End Sub
```

Figure 4-6
Displaying separate error messages for types of incorrect values.

The CheckDate's BeforeUpdate event compares the date entered to two possible scenarios. If the CheckDate falls into either scenario, a message appears and the user must enter a different CheckDate in order to continue.

In the first scenario, the event checks to see if the CheckDate is within the past 30 days. In order to test this condition, the procedure performs the following steps:

1. The CutoffDate variable is calculated as the current date minus 30 days.

 The Date keyword refers to the current date.

2. The CheckDate is compared to the CutoffDate. If the CheckDate is before the CutoffDate, the message box displays.

3. If the CheckDate is before the cutoff date, the Cancel variable is set to True. Setting Cancel to True causes Access to stop processing the update.

Notice that the BeforeUpdate **event receives the** Cancel **variable as a parameter. When an event procedure includes** Cancel **as a parameter, this indicates that you can cancel the event in process.**

The Else portion of the CheckDate_BeforeUpdate procedure tests the second scenario. This scenario checks to see if the CheckDate is a future date. If the CheckDate is greater than the current date, then a different error message displays and the event is cancelled.

Understanding the Order of Events

10 Min. To Go

You have learned that forms, reports, and controls have many associated event properties. You have also learned that the user's actions can trigger these events. It is extremely important to note, however, that a single action can trigger multiple events. These events are processed in a prescribed sequence. Understanding this sequence is fundamental to creating effective event procedures.

When the user clicks on a field, for example, the Enter event occurs followed by the GotFocus event. If you create event procedures for both of these events, you must be aware of which event occurs first.

Events for updating data in controls

When the user updates data in a control and then moves to another control, the order of events is the following:

BeforeUpdate ⇨ AfterUpdate ⇨ Exit ⇨ LostFocus

If the BeforeUpdate event is cancelled, either through its Validation Rule or through its event procedure, then none of the other events are triggered.

If, after updating the data in a control, the user moves to another record, the form's BeforeUpdate and AfterUpdate events also occur.

Events for deleting records

The order of events for deleting a record are:

Delete ⇨ BeforeDelConfirm ⇨ AfterDelConfirm

When a user attempts to delete a record, Access automatically displays a confirmation message. If the user cancels the deletion, none of the events occurs.

Events for opening a form

When a form opens, the following events occur:

Open ⇨ Load ⇨ Resize ⇨ Activate ⇨ Current

The Current event also runs whenever the user moves to another record or to a new record.

Events for creating a new record

When the user creates a new record, these events occur:

Current ⇨ BeforeInsert ⇨ AfterInsert

Events for closing a form

These events occur when a form closes:

Unload ⇨ Deactivate ⇨ Close

Done!

Working in an event-driven environment is confusing at first. But once you become familiar with events and how they are processed, you will find many opportunities to use them to your advantage as you strive to make your application run as smoothly and efficiently as possible.

REVIEW

In this chapter, you learned how events allow the user to control the flow of the application. The event-driven environment used by Access allows you to create event procedures that perform specific instructions in response to the user's actions.

- Forms, reports, and controls have many associated event properties.
- An event property can contain a macro, a function, or an event procedure.
- Event properties occur in a prescribed order.
- You can use an event procedure to accept or reject an update to a control or form.

In the next chapter you will learn about logical constructs. These are the decision-makers that help you write efficient event procedure code.

Quiz Yourself

1. How do you determine what events are available for a control on a form or report? (See "Understanding Events.")

2. What event is triggered when the user selects a command button? (See "Responding to Events.")

3. Name the three components of the first line of a procedure. (See "Creating an Event Procedure.")

4. When should you use an event procedure instead of the Validation Rule property when validating data entered by a user? (See "Using an Event Procedure to Validate Data.")

5. When data in a control is updated, which event occurs first: `Exit` or `AfterUpdate`? (See "Understanding the Order of Events.")

PART

I

Friday Evening

1. Define the term *database management system*.
2. Is the Visual Basic window a separate window or part of Microsoft Access 2000?
3. What are the two types of procedures and what is the difference between them?
4. What are VBA, Jet, and MSDE?
5. True or false: You should use a macro to handle application errors.
6. For which of the following situations are macros a sensible solution?
    a. Creating functions
    b. Calling Windows common dialogs
    c. Integrating with Word or Excel
    d. Opening a form from a command button

7. When you begin typing a command in the code window, the built-in feature _____ automatically displays a list of commands.
8. You know your application is compiled when
    a. the "Compile Complete" message box displays.
    b. the Debug⇨Compile menu choice is disabled.
    c. the code in the code window changes to green
    d. the computer speaker beeps

9. What are the five major steps of development?

10. Why is compiling important and what should you do after you compile your program?

11. What are the names of the three windows that help you debug a program?

12. What is the difference between a watchpoint and a breakpoint?

13. The _____ lists the events that are available for a form.

14. True or false: An event procedure is a special type of macro.

15. The first statement of the event procedure for the Bank Accounts command button's `OnClick` event procedure is:

    a. `Private Sub Bank_Accounts_Click()`

    b. `On Error GoTo Bank_Accounts_Err`

    c. `Function Bank_Accounts_Click()`

    d. `Dim strName as String`

16. You must use an event procedure to validate data in which of the following scenarios?

    a. The check amount must be greater than zero.

    b. You must enter check date.

    c. The check amount must be less than $500 and the check amount must be greater than zero.

    d. The check date cannot be in the future.

17. What statement allows you to declare a variable?

18. Why should you use the `Option Explicit` statement at the beginning of every procedure?

19. What are the keywords used to make a variable known to your entire program or just to a specific procedure?

20. Which of the following are valid Visual Basic variable types?

    a. `Integer`

    b. `Text`

    c. `Number`

    d. `Long`

☑ Friday

☑ **Saturday**

☐ Sunday

P A R T

II

Saturday Morning

Declaring and Understanding Variables and Using Naming Conventions

Session Checklist

✔ Types of variables

✔ Declaring variables

✔ Public and private variables

✔ Naming conventions

**30 Min.
To Go**

When you create programs in any computer language, you must create temporary storage areas known as variables. They are called variables just as x in the algebraic expression $x = 5 + 9$ is called the variable. The value within the variable changes or varies based on the expression.

Variables can be used to store numbers, text strings, control names, or data values. Variables can be used to store the value of a control or the name of a form. There are variables at every object level in Microsoft Access. You can store the value of any object including control names of forms or reports, table field names, the names of tables, queries, forms, or reports. You can use a variable for the name of a database or even a Windows file name. Anytime you need a temporary storage area, you can create a variable and assign a value to it.

Creating and using variables is a two-step process. First you give the variable a name and assign it a type (data type, object type, etc.). Then you assign it a value.

In this chapter, you will learn how to declare variables and assign values to them. You will learn how to make variable values available to one module or your entire program. You will also learn about some of the standard naming conventions for objects and variables used by professional developers and some alternative object-naming guidelines.

Using Variables

One of the most powerful concepts in programming is the variable. A variable is a temporary storage location for some value and is given a name. You can use a variable to store the result of a calculation, or you can create a variable to make the value of a control available to another procedure.

To refer to the result of an expression, you create a name to store the result. The named result is the variable. To assign an expression's result to a variable, you use the = operator. Following are some examples of calculations that create variables:

```
counter = 1
counter = counter + 1
today = Date()
```

Naming variables

Every programming language has its own rules for naming variables. In VBA, a variable name must meet the following conditions:

- Must begin with an alphabetical character
- Must not contain an embedded period or type-declaration character
- Must have a unique name — one not used elsewhere in the procedure or in modules that use the variables
- Must be no longer than 255 characters.
- Must not contain spaces. Field names can contain spaces but it is not recommended
- Although you can make up almost any name for a variable, most programmers adopt a standard convention for naming variables. Some common practices include:
  - Using uppercase and lowercase characters when you are representing multiple words, as in TotalCost.

■ No spaces. Do not create a field named `Total Cost`.

■ Using all lowercase characters, as in counter. While this contradicts the first bullet, it is also a practice of some programmers.

■ Preceding the name with the data type of the value. A variable that stores an integer type number might be called `intCounter`. This type of naming convention is used by some professional programmers so religiously, it makes code harder to read.

When you need to see or use the contents of a variable, you simply use its name. When you specify the variable's name, the computer program goes into memory, finds the variable, and gets its contents for you. This procedure means, of course, that you need to be able to remember the name of the variable.

Declaring variables

Declaring a variable before assigning anything to it sets up a location in the computer's memory for storing a value for the variable ahead of time.

VBA, like many other programming languages, allows you to create variables on the fly. In the `Counter = 1` example, the `Counter` variable was not declared before the value 1 was assigned to it. Because you assigned an integer to the variable named `Counter`, the variable is implicitly (automatically) declared as an integer data type.

The amount of storage allocated for the variable depends on the type of data that you plan to store in the variable. More space is allocated for a variable that will hold a currency amount (such as $1,000,000) than for a variable that never will hold a value greater than, say, 255.

Even though VBA does not require that you declare your variables before using them, it does provide various declaration commands. Getting into the habit of declaring your variables is good practice. Declaring a variable assures that you can assign only a certain type of value to it — always a number or always characters, for example. You can attain real performance gains in VBA by predeclaring (known as explicitly naming) variables. For purposes of maintenance, most programmers like to declare their variables at the top of the procedure.

Although VBA does not require initial declaration of variables, you should avoid using undeclared (implicitly named) variables. If you do not declare a variable, the code may expect one type of value in the variable when another is actually there.

If, in your procedure, you set the variable TodayIs to "Monday" and later change the value for TodayIs to a number (such as TodayIs = 2), the program generates an error when it runs because the first value set was a string.

Using the Option Explicit statement

At the top of your VBA module (either the module behind a form or report or a standard module object) in the Declarations section, you should always enter the text **Option Explicit** as shown in Figure 5-1. This tells VBA that you want the compiler to report an error for any variable that is not explicitly declared.

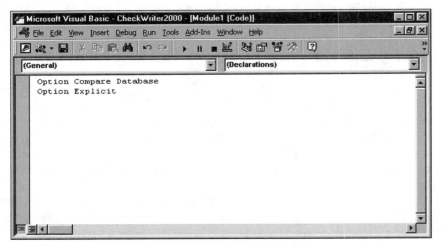

Figure 5-1
Using the Option Explicit statement with the Declarations section of your Module

Why would you want to do this? Since Access and VBA can automatically assign a data type the first time you assign a value, why bother to make sure you define every variable? Besides potential errors if you assign a different data type value, the answer is speed. Access will run a VBA program much faster if Option Explicit is used once at the top of each module and all your variables are declared.

You can go to the Declarations section of a module while you are creating an event procedure in a form by selecting declarations from the Procedure combo box. Another way to move to the Declarations section is to select (general) in the Object combo box. Figure 5-1 shows the Module window combo boxes.

Using the Dim statement

SYNTAX ▶ To declare a variable, you most often use the Dim statement. When you use the Dim statement, you must supply the variable name that you assign to the variable. The format for the Dim statement is:

```
Dim variablename [As type]
```

Figure 5-2 shows the Dim statement for a simple procedure named VariableTest. As you can see in the figure, the displayed Message Box is shown below the Visual Basic window. The vbInformation + vbOKOnly displays the informational icon and the single OK button.

This program declares two variables, assigns values to them, and uses them in a message box. The message box is shown running below the Visual Basic window in Figure 5-2. The message box is shown concatenating (joining together) string text, string variables, and numeric variables. You can also see the Immediate Window is open, where the Call statement is used to run the program in order to display the message box.

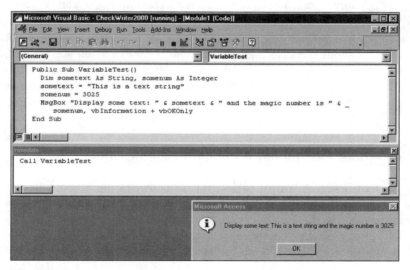

Figure 5-2
A Simple Dim statement for a simple program

The Dim statement declares two different variables, each with a different data type. The first part of the declare statement, Dim sometext As String, declares a variable named sometext and assigns a String data type to the variable. Notice the comma following the declaration and that a second variable named somenum is declared and assigned the numeric Integer data type.

You could have used two separate statements like the following:

```
Dim sometext As String
Dim somenum As Integer
```

Sometimes it is easier to declare multiple variables on one line but it makes it easier to read if the variables are declined on their own line.

Notice that the variable name follows the Dim statement. In addition to naming the variable, you can use the optional As clause to specify a data type for the variable. The data type is the kind of information that will be stored in the variable: String, Integer, Currency, and so on.

If you don't have the As clause, the default data type is known as Variant. A Variant data type can hold any type of data but requires Access to figure out what type of data is put into it. Using Variant data types or not declaring your variables can slow down your application and should be avoided.

When creating variables, you can use uppercase, lowercase, or mixed-case characters to specify the variable or call it later. Visual Basic variables are not case-sensitive. This fact means that you can use the TodayIs **variable later without having to worry about the case that you used for the name when you created it;** TODAYIS, todayis, **and** tOdAyIs **all refer to the same variable. Visual Basic automatically changes any explicitly declared variables to the case that was used in the declaration statement or the last entered reference(**Dim **statement).**

20 Min.
To Go

Making variables available to the entire application

When you use the Dim statement to declare a variable in a procedure, you can refer to that variable only within that procedure. Other procedures, even if they are stored in the same module, do not know anything about the variable. This is known as a *private* variable because it was declared in a procedure and is only known in the procedure where it was declared and used.

Variables can also be declared in the Declarations section of a module. Then all the procedures in the module can access the variable. Procedures outside the module in which you declared the variable, however, cannot read or use the variable.

To declare a variable for use by procedures in different modules, you use the Public statement.

The Public statement

To make a variable available to all modules in the application, use the `Public` keyword when you declare the variable. Figure 5-3 illustrates using the `Public` keyword to declare a variable. Notice that the statement is in the declarations section of the module. Public variables must be declared in the Declarations section of the module.

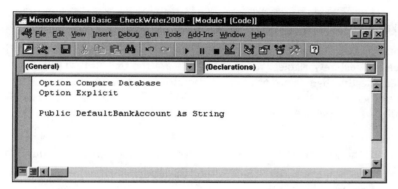

Figure 5-3
Declaring a public variable.

Although you can declare a public variable in any module, it seems logical to declare public variables only within the module that will use them the most. The exceptions to this rule are true global variables that you want to make available to all procedures across modules and that are not specifically related to a single module. You should declare global variables in a single standard module so you can find them easily.

Global variables are declared by entering **Global variablename** in the Declarations section of a module. It is then known to the entire application. You can set the value anywhere. However, if for any reason Access crashes, the value in a global variable is lost.

You cannot declare a variable public within a procedure. It must be declared in the Declarations section of a module. If you attempt to declare a variable public, you receive an error message.

In a standard, report, or form module, you can refer to a public variable from a different form or report module. To access the value of a public variable from another module, you must qualify the variable reference, using the name of the form or report object. `CheckWriter.somevariable`, **for example, accesses a form named Check Writer and obtains the value of the variable** `somevariable`**.**

The Private statement

The declarations section in Figure 5-2, earlier in this chapter, shows the use of the `Dim` statement declare variables. You could substitute the text `Private` instead of `Dim`. Technically, there is no difference between `Private` and `Dim`, but using `Private` at the module (Declarations) level to declare variables that are available to all procedures is a good idea. Declaring private variables does the following things:

- Contrasts with `Dim`, which must be used at the procedure level, distinguishing where the variable is declared and its scope (Module versus Procedure)

- Contrasts with `Public`, the other method of declaring variables in modules, making understanding your code easier

When you declare a variable, you use the `As` clause to assign a data type to the variable. Data types for variables are similar to data types in a database table definition.

Working With Data Types

The main reason to declare any variable is to save internal resources, which in turn makes programs run more quickly and efficiently. If you rely on using an undeclared variant for a variable when you could use an integer, for example, you waste 14 bytes of memory for every variable you use.

When you declare a variable, you also can specify the data type for the variable. All variables have a data type. The type of variable determines what kind of information can be stored in the variable.

A *string variable* — a variable with a data type of string — can hold any values ranging from A–Z, a–z, and 0–1, as well as formatting characters (#, -, !, and so on). Once created, a string variable can be used in many ways: to compare its contents with another string, to pull parts of information out of the string, and so on. If you have a variable defined as a string, however, you cannot use it to do mathematical calculations. Conversely, you cannot assign a number to a variable declared as a string.

Table 5-1 describes the 11 data types that Visual Basic supports.

Table 5-1
Data Types Used in Visual Basic

Type	Range	Storage
Boolean	True or false	2 bytes
Byte	0 to 255	1 byte binary data
Currency	–922,337,203,685,477,5808 to 922,337,203,685,477,5807	8-byte number with fixed decimal point
Decimal	+/-79,228,162,514,264,337,593,543, 950,335 with no decimal point; +/-7.9228162514264337593543950335 with 28 places to the right of the decimal; smallest non-zero number is +/0.0000000000000000000000000001.	14 bytes
Date	01 Jan 100 to 31 Dec 9999	8-byte date/time value
Double	–1.79769313486231E308 to –4.94065645841247E–324	8-byte floating-point number
Integer	–32,768 to 32,767	2-byte integer
Long	–2,147,483,648 to 2,147,483,647	4-byte integer
Object	Any object reference	4 bytes
Single	negative values: –3.402823E38 to –1.401298E – 45 positive values: 1.401298E –45 to 3.402823E38	4-byte floating-point number
String	0 to approximately 2,000,000,000 (variable-length)	10 bytes plus length of string
String (fixed-length)	1 to approximately 65,400	Length of string
Variant (with numbers)	Any numeric value up to the range of Double	16 bytes

Continued

Table 5-1 *Continued*

Type	Range	Storage
Variant (with characters)	0 to approximately 2,000,000,000	22 bytes plus length of string
User-defined (using Type)	Same as Range of its data type	Number required by elements

Most of the time, you use the string, date, integer, and currency or double data types. If a variable always contains whole numbers between −32,768 and 32,768, you can save bytes of memory and gain speed in arithmetic operations if you declare the variable an integer type.

When you want to assign the value of an Access field to a variable, you need to make sure that the type of the variable can hold the data type of the field. Table 5-2 shows the corresponding Visual Basic data types for Access field types.

Table 5-2
Comparative Data Types in Access and Visual Basic

Access Field Data Type	Visual Basic Data Type
AutoNumber (Long Integer)	Long
AutoNumber (Replication ID)	—
Currency	Currency
Computed	—
Date/Time	Date
Memo	String
Number (Byte)	Byte
Number (Integer)	Integer
Number (Long Integer)	Long
Number (Single)	Single
Number (Double)	Double

Access Field Data Type	Visual Basic Data Type
Number (Replication ID)	—
OLE object	Array of bytes
Text	String
Yes/No	Boolean

If a variable may have to hold a value of Null, it must be declared as variant. Variant **is the only data type that can accept Null values.**

Now that you understand variables and their data types, you're ready to learn how to use them in writing procedures.

Using Standard Naming Conventions

As you can imagine, you can use quite a few variables in a program. This can make it difficult to remember what all of your variables are used for. The same is true of objects in your Access databases, such as tables, forms, and reports. As the number of objects and variables increases, so does the inherent complexity of the programs that use those objects and variables.

Part of the solution to this problem is to use descriptive names for both objects and variables. This is only part of the solution, however. The other part involves using some sort of standard naming convention so you can immediately understand the type of data referred to by a variable or object name.

For professional developers, adhering to a standard makes it easier to maintain other developer's programs. In development projects with multiple programmers, naming conventions can make it easier to understand what each object or variable is used for, the data type of a variable or other critical information needed to properly code and debug a program efficiently

However, for a casual or power user or even the novice developer, adhering to naming conventions can be a less than productive experience. Where naming conventions are supposed to make programs easier to read and maintain because they instantly tell the VBA developer, they can do the exact opposite.

In this portion of the chapter, you will learn about the standard naming conventions that most professional developers use and see some alternatives to using them.

Figure 5-4 shows two Microsoft Access database containers. The database container on top uses no special naming conventions. The database container on the bottom uses one of the standard naming conventions for objects. Which do you think is easier to read?

Figure 5-4
Object naming conventions

There are several competing naming conventions used for Microsoft Access. One is the *Leszynski Naming Conventions* (LNC) developed by Stan Leszynski (www.kwery.com) and the other is the *Reddick Naming Conventions* developed by Greg Reddick. The tables in the remaining portion of this chapter provide an overview of these standards. If you wish to obtain the entire detailed naming conventions, you can go to this website.

Both of these naming conventions suggest using prefixes for several different types of Microsoft Access items – objects (tables, queries, forms, reports, data access pages, macros, modules), table fields, form and report controls, ADO and DAO recordset objects, and variables.

Microsoft Access database object naming conventions

These naming conventions suggest using leading tags also known as prefixes. This means that the naming convention precedes the standard business name such as strCustomerName. The standard Microsoft Access object names are shown in Table 5-3.

Table 5-3
Object Naming Conventions

Prefix	Object	Example
Tbl	Table	tblBankAccounts
Qry	Query	qryCheckWriterDisplay
Frm	Form	frmCheckWriter
Rpt	Report	rptCheckRegister
Mcr	Macro	mcrAutoexec
Bas	Module	basFileUtilties
Fsub	Subform	fsubCheckRegisterDetails
Rsub	Subreport	rsubCheckPrintContinuous

**10 Min.
To Go**

Microsoft Access table field naming conventions

Another portion of the naming conventions covers fields in tables. Figure 5-5 shows the Check Writer table modified to use these prefixes. Table 5-4 shows these table-field naming conventions.

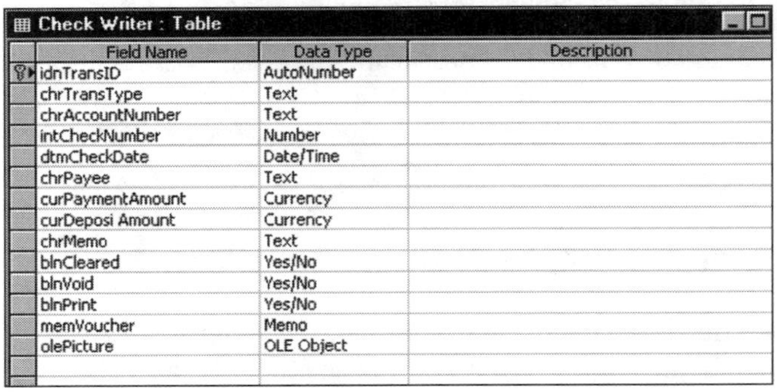

Check Writer : Table		
Field Name	**Data Type**	**Description**
idnTransID	AutoNumber	
chrTransType	Text	
chrAccountNumber	Text	
intCheckNumber	Number	
dtmCheckDate	Date/Time	
chrPayee	Text	
curPaymentAmount	Currency	
curDeposi Amount	Currency	
chrMemo	Text	
blnCleared	Yes/No	
blnVoid	Yes/No	
blnPrint	Yes/No	
memVoucher	Memo	
olePicture	OLE Object	

Figure 5-5
Table field naming conventions

Table 5-4
Table Field Naming Conventions

Prefix	Object
idn	Autonumber (Random)
idr	Autonumber (Replication ID)
ids	Autonumber (Sequential)
bin	Number (Binary)
byt	Number (Byte)
cur	Currency
dtm	Date/Time
dbl	Number (dbl)
hlk	Hyperlink
int	Number (Integer)

Prefix	Object
lngz	Number (Long)
mem	Memo
ole	OLE Object
sng	Number (Single)
chr	Text (Character)
bln	Yes/No (Boolean)

Microsoft Access form/report control naming conventions

Another area covered by naming conventions are control names on forms on reports. These are used whenever you are naming a control on a form or report. Table 5-5 shows these conventions.

Table 5-5
Form/Report Control Naming Conventions

Prefix	Object
frb	Bound Object frame
cht	Chart (Graph)
chk	Check Box
cbo	Combo Box
cmd	Command Button
ocx	ActiveX Custom Control
det	Detail (section)
gft[*n*]	Footer (group section)
fft	Form footer section
fhd	Form header section
ghd[*n*]	Header (group section)

Continued

Table 5-5 *Continued*

Prefix	Object
hlk	Hyperlink
img	Image
lbl	Label
lin	Line
lst	List Box
opt	Option Button
grp	Option Group
pge	Page (tab)
brk	Page break
pft	Page Footer (section)
phd	Page Header (section)
shp	Rectangle
rft	Report Footer (section)
rhd	Report Header (section)
sec	Section
sub	Subform/Subreport
tab	Tab Control
txt	Text Box
tgl	Toggle Button
fru	Unbound Object Frame

Microsoft Access VBA variable naming conventions

The final major area covered by the standard Access naming conventions are VBA data variables. Table 5-6 shows these conventions.

Table 5-6
VBA Data Variable Naming Conventions

Prefix	Object
Bln	Boolean
Byt	Byte
Ccc	Conditional Compilation Constant (#xxx)
Cur	Currency
Dtm	Date
Dbl	Double
Err	Error
Int	Integer
Lng	Long
Obj	Object
Sng	Single
Str	String
Typ	User-Defined Type
Var	Variant

There are many more tags that are defined by the standard naming conventions. In fact, there are close to one thousand different tags. Professional developers use these standards to varying degrees. Some ignore them for anything but data variables while others ignore them completely. Others try their best to follow them.

Are naming conventions really necessary in Access?

The human mind is a wonderful thing. It can provide wondrous creative solutions to problems. It can turn manual nightmares into automated algorithmic processes. But give the human mind something just a little foreign and processing slows to a crawl as the brain's disruptive subroutine circuitry is invoked with a nearly endless loop. Having to filter out the characters that precede the business names makes it much more difficult to read and understand the purpose of the application.

The same could be true for variable and field naming in tables. Figure 5-6 shows two table definitions for the same objects. The table definition on the top shows the standard prefixed naming conventions where each different data type uses a different prefix. The table definition on the bottom shows only the business names.

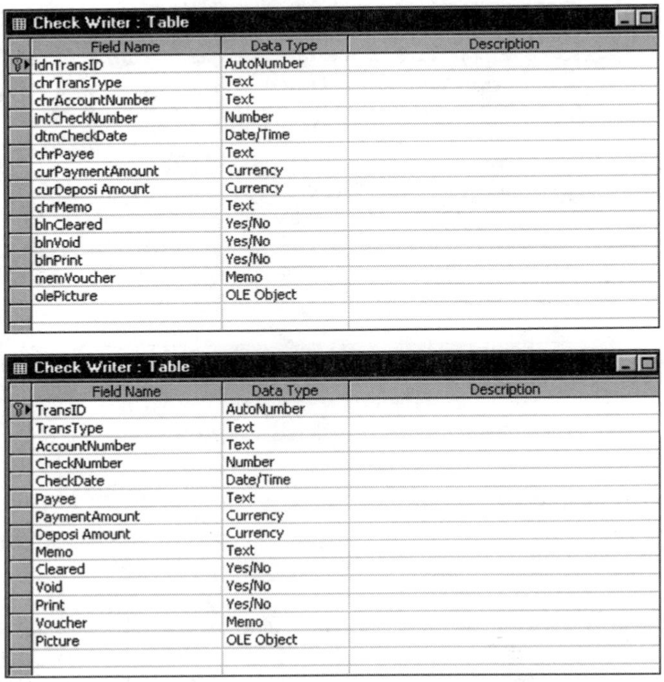

Check Writer : Table

Field Name	Data Type	Description
idnTransID	AutoNumber	
chrTransType	Text	
chrAccountNumber	Text	
intCheckNumber	Number	
dtmCheckDate	Date/Time	
chrPayee	Text	
curPaymentAmount	Currency	
curDeposi Amount	Currency	
chrMemo	Text	
blnCleared	Yes/No	
blnVoid	Yes/No	
blnPrint	Yes/No	
memVoucher	Memo	
olePicture	OLE Object	

Check Writer : Table

Field Name	Data Type	Description
TransID	AutoNumber	
TransType	Text	
AccountNumber	Text	
CheckNumber	Number	
CheckDate	Date/Time	
Payee	Text	
PaymentAmount	Currency	
Deposi Amount	Currency	
Memo	Text	
Cleared	Yes/No	
Void	Yes/No	
Print	Yes/No	
Voucher	Memo	
Picture	OLE Object	

Figure 5-6
A comparison of two table-naming conventions

Again, the database container on the bottom is far easier to read. Imagine if written English words required naming conventions. Perhaps all predicates could be prefixed with pre, verbs with vrb, nouns with nou, adverbs with adv, adjectives with adj, and so on. The sentence below:

```
The Quick Brown Fox Jumps Over The Big Computer
```

would become:

```
preThe adjQuick adjBrown nouFox vrbJumps advOver preThe adjBig
nouComputer
```

Though it can be read, it makes it much harder to understand the words as you first must filter out the prefixes. Only in rare instances would a word be questionable as to its meaning or content. Our experience is far more important than our need to explicitly understand sentence structure or grammar.

How does a professional developer know that ZIP codes, phone numbers, and Social Security numbers are almost always defined as text strings? Fields like Salary, Total Expense, or Amount Paid are obviously currency or numeric data types, while Date of Birth or the Last Sale Date is probably always stored as a date data type. This simply takes experience and common sense. This same experience or training lets us all know how to read a sentence with the correct understanding of words, intonation, or grammar.

The bottom line is that sometimes less is more. You have to program in a style that suits you and your environment. While naming conventions can be good, consistency is always better. If you are investing in a set of naming conventions, check a few simple things:

1. Do they make sense? Do they seem like common sense dictated them rather than some committee whose sole purpose was to get something on paper through compromises, endless debate, and finally exhaustion and frustration?

2. Are they endorsed by an international board such as ISO or even Microsoft? Notice the main Microsoft Access sample file named Northwinds.mdb does not use any naming conventions.

Done!

REVIEW

In this chapter, you learned about variables and how to define them. You learned the difference between public and private variables and how to use both of them. Finally, you learned about the standard naming conventions that professional developers use.

- Variables are temporary storage because the value within the variable changes or varies based on the expression.

- Variables can be used to store numbers, strings, control names, or data values. Variables can also be used to store the value of a control or the name of a form.

- Every programming language has its own rules for naming variables.

- You should always use `Option Explicit` at the beginning of a module to tell VBA that you want the compiler to report an error for any variable that is not explicitly declared.
- You define a variable with the `Dim` statement and the As clause to specify the data type for the variable.
- There are `Public` and `Private` variable types.
- Professional developers usually use some type of standard naming convention.

In the next chapter you will learn about logical constructs including conditional processing, choices, looping, and repetition.

QUIZ YOURSELF

1. Define the term variable. (See "Using Variables.")
2. What are the most important rules for naming variables? (See "Naming variables.")
3. Why is the Option Explicit statement important to have in every module? (See "Using the Option Explicit statement.")
4. Why would you use the Public variable definition instead of Dim? (See "Making variables available to the entire application.")
5. What are some of the variable data types? (See "Working with Data Types.")
6. Should you use naming conventions? (See "Are naming conventions really necessary in Access?")

Logical Constructs — Loops, Decisions, Choices, and Quick Exits

Session Checklist

✔ Understanding logical constructs

✔ Handling single conditions (If – Then – Else – End If)

✔ Handling multiple conditions (Select Case – Case – End Select)

✔ Creating repetitive loops (Do ... Loop)

✔ Creating loops that count (For ... Next)

✔ Constructs that remember (With... End With)

**30 Min.
To Go**

Logical constructs are a certain class of VBA statements that control the way a program runs. Generally, programs run one statement after another in the order they appear. Logical constructs are used to make the program run in the order that makes sense for the business purpose. Logical constructs include:

* Conditional processing (single condition decision making)

    If... Then... Else ... End If

* Conditional processing (multiple condition decision making)

    Select Case... Case ... End Select

- Repetitive looping

  ```
  Do ... Loop
  For ... Next
  ```

Using logical constructs, you make the program respond to values in your variables to run or skip one or more statements or run a group of statements repeatedly. In this chapter, you will learn the three types of logical constructs and how to create counters and variables that react within these constructs.

Each of these logical constructs requires specific syntax to operate correctly. Generally, there is an opening statement, statements in the middle, and a closing statement, also known as an end statement. Sometimes the syntax makes sense, like starting a conditional statement with If and ending with End If. Select Case starts a multiple condition decision- making construct, while End Select completes it.

Repetitive looping is a little different. A Do statement ends with a Loop, and a For statement ends with Next. This chapter explains all of these differences.

Conditional Processing

One of the real powers of a programming language is the capability to have a program make a decision based on some condition. Often, a program in VBA performs different tasks based on some value. If the condition is True, the code performs one action. If the condition is False, the code performs a different action.

Procedures are evaluated to see if they are true or false. For example, suppose you code the following:

```
If CheckAmount > 200 Then
    Call largedollarprocedure
Else
    Call smalldollarprocedure
Endif
```

The first part of the expression checks to see if the value of the variable CheckAmount is greater than 200. If it is the expression evaluates to True and the code after the Then is run until the line before the Else clause. If the expression is not evaluated to True, the lines of code within the Else clause are run. In this example, a False condition (actually not True) would occur if the value of CheckAmount is less than or equal to (<=) 200.

This procedure is similar to walking down a path and coming to a fork in the path; you can go to the left or to the right. If a sign at the fork points left for home and right for work, you can decide which way to go. If you need to go to work, you go to the right; if you need to go home, you go to the left. Conditional processing of code works the same way. A program looks at the value of some variable and decides which set of code should be processed.

When writing code, you need to be able to control which actions execute. You may want to write some statements that execute only if a certain condition is True.

An application's capability to look at a value and, based on that value, decide which code to run is known as *conditional processing*.

The If. . .Then. . .Else. . .End If statement

The If. . .Then and If. . .Then. . .Else constructs allow you to check a condition and, based on the evaluation, perform a single action. It is a binary evaluation. With an If-Then-Else statement, there are only two choices — one or the other. You can have one or more statements after both the Then and the Else clause. In fact, you can have no statements after one or both conditions, but it would be easier to eliminate the clause. For example. You do not have to include an Else statement with an If Then construct..

SYNTAX ▶ Following is the general syntax of the If-Then-Else statement:

```
If test_expression Then
    code statements here (test expression = true)
Else
    code statements here (test expression = not true)
End If
```

The If-Then-Else construct does not have to have an Else statement. You can have just an If Then condition that, if met, runs the statements to the End If and skips any processing within the construct if the condition is not met.

Figure 6-1 shows a conceptual diagram of an If-Then-Else condition:

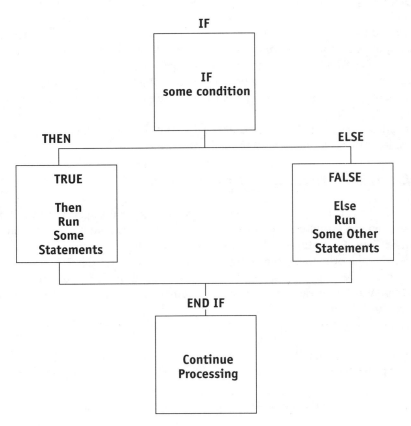

Figure 6-1
A conceptual diagram of an If-Then-Else statement

The condition must evaluate to True or Not True. The reason it says True and Not True is that just because something is true doesn't mean the opposite is necessarily false. The condition can evaluate to unknown if one of the values is null or blank. You must make sure when you use an If-Then-Else statement that the condition you use has a binary selection (one or the other)

If the condition is True, the program moves to the next statement in the procedure and runs each statement between the Then and any Else statement, or if there is no Else statement, to the End If. If the condition is Not True (or False), the program skips to the statement(s) following the `Else` statement and then continues to the `End If` statement. Once the `End If` statement is reached, processing continues normally to the next logical construct.

Figure 6-2 shows the `OnClick` event subprocedure code from the Print button on the `yBank Print Dialog` form. The procedure is used to handle user selections to determine where a report will print and which records or which report will print. Notice the `If-Then-Else` statement.

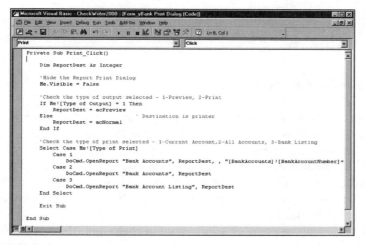

Figure 6-2
A simple If-Then-Else condition

The `If` statement checks the value of the `Type of Output` control on the `yBank` Print Dialog form. If the condition `Me![Type of Output] = 1` is true, the value of `ReportDest` is set to `acPreview`. If the value of `Me![Type of Output]` is anything other than 1, the `Else` condition is met and the value of `ReportDest` is set to `acNormal` (the default printer).

Remember, the `Else` statement is optional. You can use `Else` to test for a second condition when the `If` statement evaluates to False. When the `If` statement is True, the program executes the statements between the `If` statement and the `Else` statement. When the If statement evaluates to False, the program skips to the `Else` statement, if it is present. Then, if the `Else` statement is True, the program executes the following statement. If the `Else` statement is False, the program skips to the statement following the `End If` statement.

You can also use the Not **operator to check for conditions that are expected to be false, as in the following example. Generally, the most common condition is first. These are easier for some people to read.**

```
If Not Check Type = 'Deposit' Then
    Process Checks
Else
    Process Deposit
End If

This is also equivalent to:

If Check Type <> 'Deposit' Then ....
```

Nesting If-Then-Else statements

You can also put an If-Then-Else statement within another If-Then-Else statement. This is known as *nesting*. For example, the following code shows an example of a nested If-Then-Else statement.

20 Min. To Go

The first If statement checks the value of the variable ClassType to see if it is equal to "Elementary School". If the condition is true, the next statement is run. This is another If statement that checks to see if the value of Grade is between 1 and 3 and if this is true, runs the grade 1–3 process. If the value of ClassType is "Elementary School" and the value of Grade is not between 1–3, the statements after the Else are run.

Listing 6-1
A Nested If–Then–Else Statement

```
If ClassType = "Elementary School" Then
    If Grade Between 1 and 3 Then
        'Process something for grades 1-3
      Else
        'Process something for other elementary grades
    End If
  Else
    'Process Middle and High School
End If
```

If the value of the variable ClassType is not "Elementary School", processing moves to the corresponding Else statement and the process for middle and high school is run. While these are just comments, you would substitute the real statements in place of or after the comments.

It is a good idea when creating nested constructs to begin by typing the constructs themselves along with any End statements, and then enter some comments about what each If or Else statement will do. This is known as *pseudocoding*. You can then enter the code to be run after the comments and leave the comments in place.

You can nest any logical construct within another logical construct.

Suppose you had to test for five different conditions. You could write a set of If-Then-Else statements like this:

```
If Salary Between 0 and 20000 Then
  'Do Some Processing (0-20000)
End If
If Salary Between 20001 and 40000 Then
  'Do Some Processing (20001-40000)
End If
If Salary Between 40001 and 60000 Then
  'Do Some Processing (40001-60000)
End If
If Salary Between 60001 and 80000 Then
  'Do Some Processing (60001-80000)
End If
If Salary Not Between 0 and 8000
  'Do Some Other Processing (Not Between 0-80000)
End If
```

However, this would be very inefficient, as each condition would be tested for even if only one condition or the first condition is met. A better but more complex set of code is shown here:

```
If Salary Between 0 and 20000 Then
  'Do Some Processing (0-20000)
Else
  If Salary Between 20001 and 40000 Then
    'Do Some Processing (20001-40000)
  Else
```

```
    If Salary Between 40001 and 60000 Then
      'Do Some Processing (40001-60000)
    Else
      If Salary Between 60001 and 80000 Then
        'Do Some Processing (60001-80000)
      Else
        'Do Some Other Processing (Not Between 0-80000)
      End If
    End If
  End If
End If
```

However, this would be complex to write and maintain. Even though processing would stop once a condition was satisfied, the nested If statements can get very complicated.

When you have many conditions to test, a better approach is to use the Select Case construct.

The Select Case. . .End Select construct

In addition to the If. . .Then statements, VBA offers a command for checking more than one condition. You can use the Select Case construct to check for multiple conditions. Figure 6-3 shows a conceptual diagram of a Select Case statement.

SYNTAX ▶ The Case statement contains the opening Select Case statement, an unlimited number of Case *test_expression* clauses, a potential Case Else clause, and finally, an End SelectSelect statement. The following is the general syntax of the Case statement:

```
Select Case test_expression
    Case expression value1
        code statements here (test expression = value1)
    Case expression value2
        code statements here (test expression = value2) ...
    Case Else
        code statements (test expression = none of the values)
End Select
```

Notice that the syntax is similar to that of the If. . .Then statement. Instead of a condition in the Select Case statement, however, VBA uses a test expression. Then each Case statement inside the Select Case statement tests its value against the test expression's value. When a `Case` statement matches the test value, the program executes the next line or lines of code until it reaches another `Case` statement or the `End Select` statement. Visual Basic executes the code for only one matching `Case` statement.

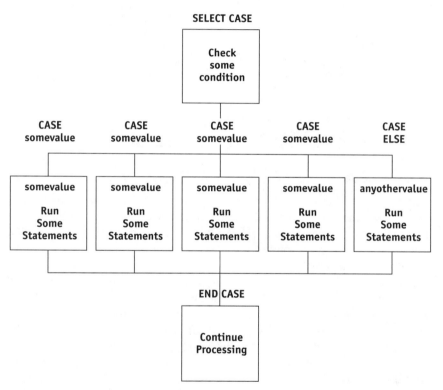

Figure 6-3
A conceptual diagram of a Select Case statement

Figure 6-4 again shows the `OnClick` event subprocedure code from the Print button on the yBank Print Dialog form. The procedure is used to handle user selections to determine where a report will print and which records or which report will print. Notice the `Select Case` statement.

If more than one `Case` statement matches the value of the test expression, only the code for the first match executes. If other matching `Case` statements appear after the first match, VBA ignores them.

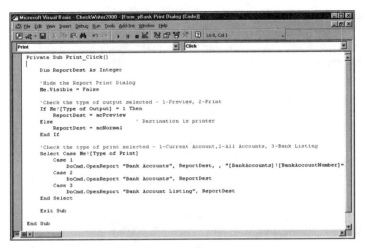

Figure 6-4
A simple Select Case statement

In Figure 6-4, the Select Case statement looks at the value of the control Type of Print and then checks each Case condition. If the value of Type of Print is 1 (Current Bank Account), the Case 1 statement evaluates to True, and the Bank Account report prints but limits the value to the current record through the report's filter parameter.

An If-Then-Else construct can theoretically run every If condition in a group of statements. It must test each branch until one is satisfied. A Select Case statement will stop testing and running conditions once the first condition is true.

If Type of Print is not 1, Visual Basic goes to the next Case statement to see whether Type of Print matches the next test value, which is 2. If this is true, the Bank Accounts report is run for all records. There is no Case Else clause, so theoretically, if the value of Type of Print was not 1, 2, or 3, no statements within the Select Case construct would be run. Each Case statement is evaluated until a match occurs or the program reaches the End Select statement.

The Case Else statement is optional. The Case Else clause is always the last Case statement of Select Case. You use this statement to perform some action when none of the Case values matches the test value of the Select Case statement.

Repetitive Looping

**10 Min.
To Go**

Another very powerful process that VBA offers is *repetitive looping* — the capability to process some group of code over and over. The statement or group of statements is processed continually while or until some condition is met.

Visual Basic offers two types of repetitive-looping constructs:

Do...Loop   generally used to process data

For...Next   used when you know the exact number of repetitions

The Do...Loop statement

The Do...Loop statement is used to repeat a group of statements while a condition is true or until a condition is true. This statement is one of the most common commands that can perform repetitive processes.

SYNTAX ▶ The following is the format of the Do. . .Loop statement:

```
DO [While | Until condition]
    code statements [for condition = TRUE]
    [If some additional condition Then Exit DO]
    code statements [for condition = TRUE]
LOOP [While | Until condition]
```

Notice that the Do. . .Loop statement has several optional clauses. The While clause tells the program to execute the code inside the Do. . .Loop as long as the test condition is True. When the condition evaluates to False, the program skips to the next statement following the Loop statement.

The Until clause works in just the opposite way; the instructions in the construct execute as long as the condition is False. Where you place the While or Until clause determines whether the code inside Do. . .Loop executes.

The Do While may never run any statements if the condition is not initially true, while the Do Until will always run the loop at least once.

The Exit Do statement is used to terminate Do. . .Loop immediately. The program then skips to the next statement following the Loop statement. Figure 6-5 shows a conceptual diagram of the Do Loop. As long as the condition of the Do Loop is True and any condition to run the Exit Do remains False, the loop will execute over and over again.

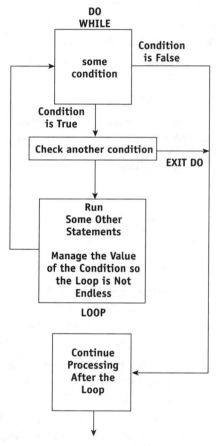

Figure 6-5
A conceptual diagram of a Do ... Loop statement

Generally, inside the loop you will process records in a table, recordset or dynaset. Figure 6-6 shows the Clear Marks OnClick event from the Check Writer form. This code is used to change the value of the Print field to False in the Check Writer table for all records.

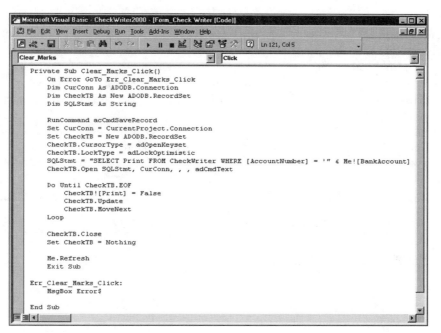

Figure 6-6
A simple Do Until loop

The first part of Figure 6-6 uses some ADO statements to set up and open a recordset of all records in the Check Writer table for the specific bank account open in the Check Writer form. The Do loop in the middle of the figure runs through all of the records.

While you haven't learned ADO yet or how to create or process a recordset, the code in Figure 6-6 will be described so you can follow it. The important part is the loop construct syntax and not the ADO in this example.

The Do statement is typical of a loop that processes recordset data. Generally, you want to start at the top of the recordset defined in the SQL statement and process all of the records. In this example, CheckTB is the name of the recordset, and the Do Until CheckTB.EOF statement will run the loop until the CheckTB recordset has reached the end of file.

The next line CheckTB![Print] = False sets the value of the current record to False. The line CheckTB.Update actually updates the value of Print in the Check Writer table. Without the Update method, the change would not be saved.

When you create a loop, you must set up code to manage coming out of the loop. There are two ways to do this. You can use an `Exit Do` statement or change the condition at the top of the loop that the `Do` clause is repetitively checking.

The final statement inside the loop `CheckTB.Movenext` moves the record pointer of the recordset to the next record. When the last record has been processed, the value of the .EOF (end of file) marker is set to True. This causes the loop to terminate, as the `Do Until CheckTB.EOF` condition is satisfied. The statements after the `Loop` statement are then executed, which close the open recordset.

The `While` and `Until` clauses provide powerful flexibility for processing `Do.. .Loop` in your code. Table 6-1 describes the various alternatives for using the `While` and `Until` clauses and how they affect the processing of code.

Table 6-1
Repetitive Looping, Using Do. . .Loop with the While and Until Clauses

Pseudocode	Purpose of Do. . .Loop

Do	Code starts here
	If condition Then
	Exit Do
	End If

Loop	The code always runs at least once. The code has some conditional statement (If. . .Then) that, if True, runs the Exit Do statement. The Exit Do statement allows the user to get out of Do. . .Loop. If that statement were missing, the code inside the loop would run forever.
Do	While condition code starts here for the condition on the Do While line being TRUE
Loop	The code inside the Do While loop runs only if the condition is True. The code runs down to the Loop statement and then goes back to the top to see whether the condition is still True. If the condition is initially False, Do. . .Loop is skipped; if the condition becomes False, the loop is exited when the code loops back to the Do While line. Exit Do is not needed for this purpose.

Pseudocode	Purpose of Do. . .Loop
Do	Until *condition* *code starts here for* *the condition on the* *Do Until line being* *FALSE*
Loop	This code works the opposite way from Do While. If the condition is False (not True), the code begins and loops until the condition is True; then it leaves the loop. Regardless if the condition is true, the loop and its code are run at least once even if the Until condition is True.
Do	*Code starts here for* *the condition on the* *Do While line being* *TRUE*
Loop While *condition*	This code always runs at least once. First, the code is executed and reaches the Loop While line. If the condition is True, the code loops back up to process the code again; if not, the code loop ends.
Do	*Code starts here for* *the condition on the* *Do Until line being* *FALSE*
Loop Until *condition*	This code works similarly to the preceding code. The code always runs at least once. When the code reaches the Loop Until line, it checks to see whether the condition is True. If the condition is True, the code drops out of the loop. If the condition is False, the code loops back up to redo the code.

The For. . .Next statement

The For. . .Next construct is another method for the Do. . .Loop construct. You can use For. . .Next when you want to repeat a statement for a specific number of times. In the previous example in Figure 6-6, rather than process the recordset until .EOF, you could have counted the number of records in the recordset and then processed that many records. This code might look like Figure 6-7.

Figure 6-7
A simple For Next loop

Notice the differences between the Do Loop and this For Next code. First, several variables are defined. NumRecs holds the total number of records, and RecNum holds the number of the record being processed. The variable NumRecs is set to the recordset variable for the number of records (CheckTb.RecordCount).

The loop is executed by running through the recordset from record number 1 to record number *n*, where *n* is the number of records counted by the RecordCount method.

This example uses a default Step clause of 1. You actually do not need the Step clause if you are using the default value. The Step clause followed by an increment lets you process the loop in a nonsingle step amount. For example, if the start number was 1, the end number was 100, and you wanted to increment the counter by 10 each time, you would use step 10. Although the loop would be executed only 10 times, the value of the counter would be 1, 11, 21, and so on, instead of 1, 2, 3, and so on.

SYNTAX ▶ Following is the general syntax of the For. . .Next statement:

```
For counter = start number To end number [Step increment]
    Some code goes here
    [If somecondition is True Then Exit For]
```

```
    Other code can continue here after the Exit for
Next [counter]
```

At the start of the For. . .Next loop, the program initializes the value of the counter variable RecNum to 1; then it moves on and executes each statement. Whenever the program encounters the Next statement, it automatically increments the counter variable by 1 and returns to the For statement. The program compares the value of RecNum with the value in NumRecs. If the test is True, the code executes again; otherwise, the program exits the loop.

You can execute the same basic code with a Do While or Do Until loop by managing the counter yourself just as you manage the recordsets. Below are equivalent loops using both a For Next and a Do While loop:

Do While Loop

```
Dim Counter As Integer

Do While Counter <= 20
    Some process goes here
    Counter = Counter + 1
Loop
```

For Next Loop

```
Dim Counter As Integer

For counter = 1 To 20
    Some process goes here
Next Counter
```

Constructs That Remember: With . . . End With

You should understand one additional construct, as it simplifies large amounts of coding and can process form data much faster. Hopefully, you are familiar with form and control referencing. To reference a specific property on a form, you might code something like this:

```
Forms!CheckWriter!CheckAmount.Visible = True
```

If you have a number of different properties to set or methods to run, you would have to reference the form over and over again. For example:

```
Forms!CheckWriter!CheckAmount.Visible = True
Forms!CheckWriter!CheckAmount = 0
Forms!CheckWriter!Void.Visible = False
Forms!CheckWriter!Memo = ""
```

This is an incredibly inefficient way to reference controls. Each time you run a statement that references a form, Access has to find that form in the list of all forms in your database. Believe it or not, it starts at the top alphabetically and looks at each one until it finds the one you are referencing. If you are looking for the forms that begin with the letter A versus forms that begin with the letter Z, you can actually see the difference on a slower machine when you have a lot of forms.

There is a better way: define a form type variable and then use the variable to reference the controls. For example:

```
Dim frmControl As Form
Set frmControl = Forms!CheckWriter
frmControl!CheckAmount.Visible = True
frmControl!CheckAmount = 0
frmControl!Void.Visible = False
frmControl!Memo = ""
```

This way, the form variable is set and referenced only once. Each time you refer to `frmControl` (or any name you use), Access knows where to find the form in the list. In effect, you are creating an index, and you will see a big performance gain throughout your programs.

The best way, however, is to use the `With...End With` construct:

```
With Forms!CheckWriter
  !CheckAmount.Visible = True
  !CheckAmount = 0
  !Void.Visible = False
  !Memo = ""
End With
```

As you can see, you specify the form variable in the `With` statement and just precede each control with the ! symbol. Everything within the `With....End With` construct references the value of the `With` clause.

Done!

REVIEW

In this session, you learned about logical constructs that are used to make a program run in the order that makes sense for the business purpose. Logical constructs include conditional processing and repetitive looping.

- Logical constructs refer to a certain class of VBA statements that control the way a program runs.
- An application's capability to look at a value and, based on that value, decide which code to run is known as conditional processing.
- If-Then-Else statements are used to process binary conditions.
- Select Case statements are used to process multiple conditions.
- Do While or Do Until loops let you perform repetitive processing.
- For Next loops allow processing with counter variables.
- Any logical construct can be nested within another construct.
- The With construct can speed up processing when referencing form variables.

In the next session, you will learn how to find and change records using VBA code.

QUIZ YOURSELF

1. Define the term logical construct. (See the beginning of the session.)
2. Name two types of conditional processing. (See "Conditional Processing.")
3. Can you run one If statement within another? (See "Nesting If-Then-Else statements.")
4. When would you use an If-Then over a Select Case? (See "The Select Case...End Select statement.")
5. What are the two types of repetitive loops? (See "Repetitive Looping.")
6. What's the difference between a Do While and a Do Until? (See "The Do...Loop statement.")
7. What type of looping construct includes an automatic counter variable? (See "The For...Next statement.")
8. How do you speed up processing when using referenced form variables? (See "Constructs That Remember: With...End With.")

Procedures, Modules, and Class Modules

Session Checklist

✔ Understanding procedures

✔ Working with modules

✔ Using class modules

✔ Creating and running procedures

30 Min. To Go

You have seen in previous chapters how event procedures expand the capabilities of your Access application. Event procedures are just one of several available types of procedures. While event procedures run automatically in response to some action in a form or report, subprocedures and function procedures provide another way to process actions in your application.

Understanding Subprocedures

A **subprocedure** is a series of programming statements that carries out some action. Subprocedures begin with the Public Sub keywords and end with the

End Sub statement. They can receive arguments, but they cannot return a value. The following is an example of a subprocedure:

```
Public Sub IsWeekday(DateToCheck As Date)
 If Weekday(DateToCheck) = vbSaturday Or _
Weekday(DateToCheck) = vbSunday Then
     MsgBox DateToCheck & " is not a weekday.", vbInformation
 Else
     MsgBox DateToCheck & " is a weekday.", vbInformation
 End If
Exit Sub
End Sub
```

Event procedures are also declared with the Sub...End Sub **statements. They are a special type of subprocedure because they are associated with a form or report's event properties.**

The IsWeekday subprocedure receives the DateToCheck argument. An *argument* is simply a value that the procedure needs in order to process the procedure statements. The IsWeekday subprocedure displays a message indicating whether DateToCheck is a weekday or not.

If the procedure does not have any arguments, leave the parentheses empty. For example, this procedure declaration statement

Public IsWeekday()

does not have any arguments.

Understanding Function Procedures

Function procedures are similar to subprocedures. *Function procedures* are composed of a series of statements that perform some action, and they, too, can receive arguments. Unlike subprocedures, however, they can return a value.

Function procedures begin with the keywords Public Function and end with the End Function statement. If the function receives arguments, the argument declarations are enclosed by parentheses following the Function keyword. The beginning statement ends with the declaration of the function's return value. The following is an example of a function procedure:

```
Public Function CalcTax(PurchaseAmt As Currency, TaxRate As Double) As Currency
```

```
        CalcTax = Round(PurchaseAmt * TaxRate, 2)
    Exit Function
    End Function
```

The `CalcTax` function receives two arguments: one for the amount of the purchase, and one for the current tax rate. The keywords `As Currency` at the end of the function declaration statement indicate that the function will return a currency value. The `CalcTax` function calculates the tax amount for the amount purchased based on the supplied tax rate. The function returns the calculated tax amount to the procedure that called it by assigning the result of the calculation to the function name (`CalcTax`).

Access provides numerous built-in procedures for common operations like working with date/time data, string manipulation, and conversion between data types. Some examples include:

- `Round()` rounds a number to the specified number of decimal places.
- `IsWeekday()` returns the position in the week for the specified date.
- `Now()` returns the current date and time.
- `Left()` returns the specified number of characters in a string starting from the first letter.

Consult Microsoft Visual Basic Help for a complete list of all of the available built-in procedures.

20 Min. To Go

Understanding Modules

Before you can create a subprocedure or function procedure, you need to understand modules. A *module* is an Access object that stores a collection of procedures. There are four types of Access modules: form modules, report modules, standard modules, and class modules.

Form and report modules

All of the event procedures for a form or report are stored in a *form module* or *report module*. When you create the first event procedure for a form or report, Access automatically creates the form or report's module.

To view a form or report's module, open the form or report in Design view. Then select View Code from the menu. The module displays in the Visual Basic Editor. Figure 7-1 shows the module for the xMain Menu form.

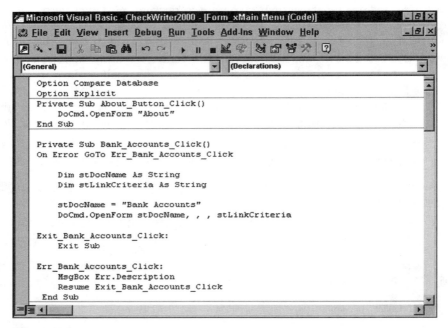

Figure 7-1
Viewing the module for a form

Form and report modules provide a way to keep all of the code that pertains only to an individual form together in one place. While form and report modules usually contain only event procedures, you can also add sub- and function procedures as well.

Standard modules

Standard modules are a place where you can store procedures that you want to use in any form and report in your application. Standard modules are stored in the Modules tab of the Access database window.

To view the procedures in a module, select one of the modules listed on the Modules page, then click the Design button. The module displays in the Visual Basic Editor. Figure 7-2 shows the Utility Functions module.

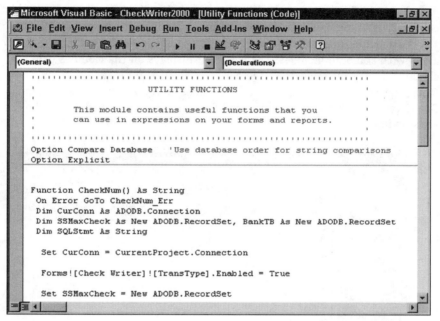

Figure 7-2
Viewing a standard module in the Visual Basic Editor

The *Utility Functions module* contains some common procedures that you can use throughout the Check Writer application. These procedures include:

- CheckNum( ) generates the next check number for the Check Writer form.
- IsLoaded( ) determines whether the specified form is currently open.
- NullToZero( ) converts the specified value to 0 if it is Null.

  While the CheckNum function is associated with the Check Writer form, the IsLoaded and NullToZero functions could be used in any form, report, or query in any application.

Keep generic procedures together in one module. This way, you can easily import the module into other applications as needed.

Class modules

Class modules allow you to create new custom objects for your application. For most applications, the built-in user-interface objects provide the framework for just about anything you need to build. Once you start developing more sophisticated applications, however, you may want to build your own objects.

Class modules are stored on the Modules tab of the Access database window along with standard modules. The icon that displays on the Modules page for class modules is different than the one that displays for standard modules. Figure 7-3 shows a Modules page that includes both standard and class modules. The WelcomeMsg module is a class module, while the other modules in the list are standard modules.

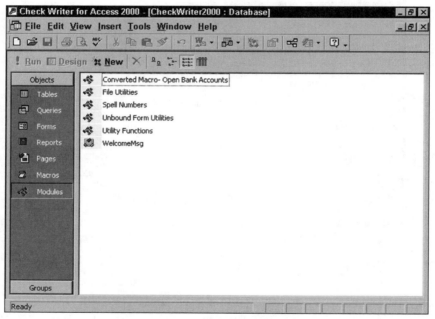

Figure 7-3
The Modules tab displays different icons for standard and class modules.

To view the procedures in a class module, select one of the modules listed on the Modules page, then click the Design button. The module displays in the Visual Basic Editor. Figure 7-4 shows the WelcomeMsg class module.

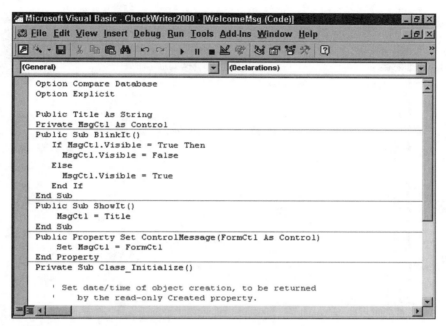

Figure 7-4
Viewing a class module in the Visual Basic Editor

You use the WelcomeMsg class module to create a custom text object. You can use this object in any form where you might want to display a flashing message. For example, you might use the objects in this class module to display a welcome message on your application's splash screen or main switchboard. You can use this class module in any application because it does not include references to any specific form or report in the application.

To see how the WelcomeMsg class module works, open the form called Figure 7-4 in the Check Writer database.

Creating a New Module

To create a new standard module, follow these steps:

1. Click the Modules object button in the Database window.

2. Click the New toolbar button.

The Visual Basic Editor opens and creates a new module named Module1. Figure 7-5 shows the new module Module1.

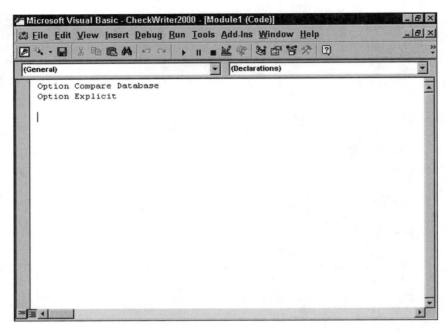

Figure 7-5
A new module in the Visual Basic Editor

When you create a new module, the Code window automatically displays these two statements: `Option Compare Database` and `Option Explicit`. These two statements are optional, but it's good practice to include them. The `Option Compare Database` statement tells Access what the sort order should be when comparing data for strings. The `Option Explicit` statement forces you to declare all variables used in the procedures in this module.

There are two advantages to including the `Option Explicit` **statement in your modules: it speeds up execution of the module code, and it makes the code easier for others to read later on.**

Each module is composed of a declarations section and a separate section for each procedure. The two combo boxes at the top of the Code window help you locate a section in the module. Figure 7-6 shows the available sections in the Utility Functions module.

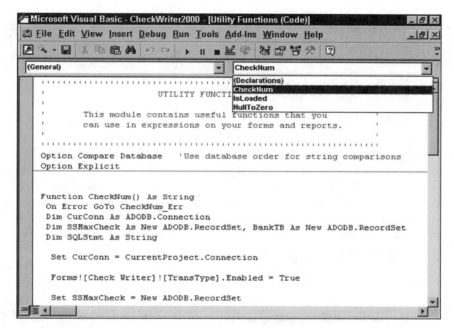

Figure 7-6
Using the combo boxes to locate a section in a module

When you create a new module, the declarations section is created automatically. The two Option statements are always placed at the beginning of the declarations section. The declarations section can also include any variables that you want to be available to all procedures in the current module, or to any module in the application.

Creating a New Procedure

After completing the declarations section of the new module, you are ready to create a procedure. Follow these steps to create a procedure called ShowMessage:

10 Min. To Go

1. Select Insert Procedure from the Visual Basic Editor menu. The Add Procedure dialog box displays, as shown in Figure 7-7.

2. Enter **ShowMessage** for the new procedure's name. Select the Sub option for the Type and the Public option for the Scope.

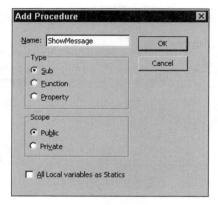

Figure 7-7
Creating a new procedure.

3. Click the OK button. The new procedure displays in the Code window.
The new procedure should look like the one in Figure 7-8.

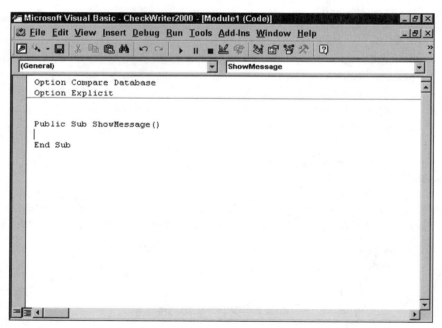

Figure 7-8
A new procedure in the Code window

You enter the statements for the procedure between the Sub and End Sub statements. Enter the following statements for the ShowMessage procedure:

```
Dim MsgTxt As String
MsgTxt = "Running the ShowMessage procedure."
Beep
MsgBox MsgTxt, vbInformation, "ShowMessage Procedure"
```

The completed procedure should look like Figure 7-9.

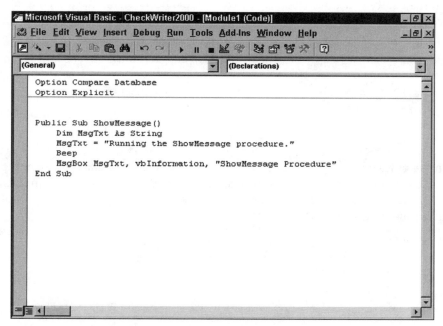

Figure 7-9
The ShowMessage procedure

To see how the ShowMessage procedure works, you can run it from the Visual Basic Editor. To run the ShowMessage procedure, open the Immediate window. Then type **ShowMessage** and press Enter. When ShowMessage runs, it beeps and then displays the message.

You should always compile your procedures before running them.

Using a Procedure in a Form

Once you have created a procedure, you can use it in any form, report, or query. To use the procedure in a form or report, you simply enter the procedure name as a statement or part of a statement in one of the event procedures. When entering the procedure name, also be sure to include the procedure's arguments inside the parentheses.

The OnOpen event for the Check Writer form calls the IsLoaded function stored in the Utility Functions module. The code listing below shows the a section of the code for the Check Writer form's OnOpen event.

```
If IsLoaded("Check Reconciliation") Then
  Me![BankAccount] = [forms]![Check Reconciliation]![BankAccount]
Else
Me![BankAccount] = DLookup("[DefaultBankAccountNumber]",_
"[Preferences]")
End If
```

When the OnOpen event procedure calls the IsLoaded function, it passes the name of the form to check, Check Reconciliation, as an argument. When the IsLoaded function runs, it checks to see if the Check Reconciliation form is open. If the form is open, the function returns True; otherwise, it returns False. The code for the IsLoaded function is shown below.

```
Function IsLoaded(MyFormName)
' Accepts: a form name
' Purpose: determines if a form is loaded

IsLoaded = (SysCmd(acSysCmdGetObjectState, acForm, MyFormName)_
<> 0)
End Function
```

The IsLoaded function receives the parameter MyFormName. MyFormName is used to specify the name of the object you want to check — the Check Reconciliation form, in this case. The IsLoaded function calls the built-in function SysCmd to check the status of the object specified in MyFormName.

Using a Procedure in a Query

Done!

You can use function procedures in a query because they return a value. You can include function procedures in queries to convert data or to calculate expressions. You can include either a built-in function like Left, Date, or Now, or you can include one of your own functions. To use a function in a query, you simply pass the column name as the argument for the function. Figure 7-10 shows a query that calls the NullToZero function.

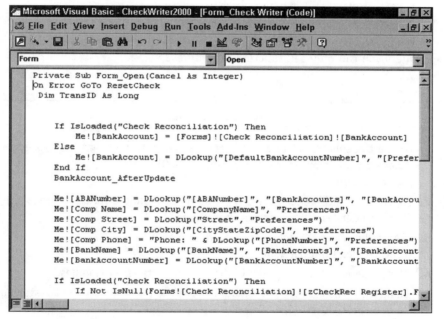

Figure 7-10
Calling a function from a query

REVIEW

This chapter discussed working with procedures and modules. The following topics were covered:

- The two types of procedures are subprocedures and function procedures.
- Function procedures return a value. Both subprocedures and function procedures can receive arguments.
- Procedures are stored in modules.
- Class modules are used for creating custom object definitions. All other procedures are stored in standard modules.
- You can call function and subprocedures from forms and reports. In a query, you can only call function procedures.

QUIZ YOURSELF

1. Name the component of a subprocedure that tells you that the procedure needs a value from another program. (See "Understanding Subprocedures.")
2. What is the difference between a subprocedure and a function procedure? (See "Understanding Function Procedures.")
3. Name the Access object used to store procedures. (See "Understanding Modules.")
4. Name the four types of modules. (See "Understanding Modules.")
5. Name two reasons why you should include the Option Explicit statement in your procedures. (See "Creating a New Module.")

Programming Calendars

Session Checklist

✔ Understanding pop-up calendars

✔ Using a pop-up time clock

✔ Opening a pop-up calendar from a form

✔ Updating a date/time field from the pop-up calendar

✔ Calculating the difference between two dates

✔ Using the Access Calendar Control

**30 Min.
To Go**

One of the most intimidating data entry tasks is entering date information. A blank text box for a date field provides no hint as to what users should type. Should they type month, day, then year, or is it year, month, then day? Should they type a slash or a dash to separate each date part? This is a classic example of where professional user-interface techniques come into play. Providing a graphical calendar control takes the guesswork out of entering and manipulating date information in your application.

Using Pop-Up Calendars for Date Information

A *pop-up calendar* is useful for several different purposes. You can use it to view a calendar just like you would reference a desk or wall calendar. Or, you can use it as a date selector for a field on a form.

Three pop-up calendars are included with the Check Writer: a monthly calendar, a three-month calendar, and a calendar calculator. These are self-contained forms that can be opened individually or called by another form to fill a value in a control.

Each of the calendars included on the CD-ROM contains buttons to move ahead or behind a month or year at a time. You can also select time information by clicking the button with a picture of a clock on it to display a clock where you can easily choose a time to go along with the date in the pop-up calendar.

Pop-up calendars are used frequently to fill a form control with a date. While Microsoft Access provides an ActiveX calendar control, you can use the pop-up calendars included on the CD instead of the ActiveX calendar control when you want the flexibility to modify the appearance and the functionality of the calendar. The calendars provided have the following features:

- A stand-alone form that can be opened to view just a monthly calendar
- A pop-up form that returns the selected date (and optionally time) to the calling form
- A monthly calendar subform that provides an easy means to create a form with more than one calendar
- Sizable calendars
- Calendars that can be changed in appearance (fonts, colors, control locations, sizes, etc.)
- Display pictures on each day
- The ability to set the starting day of the week
- Developer control of the calendar interface components

- Self-contained calendars with no global variables, modules, or external references
- Code written completely in VBA

An example of each of the pop-up calendars is shown in Figures 8-1 to 8-3.

Figure 8-1
The monthly pop-up calendar

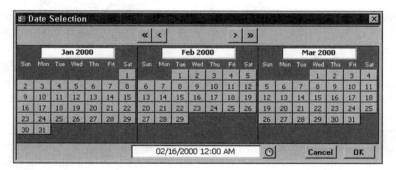

Figure 8-2
The three-month pop-up calendar

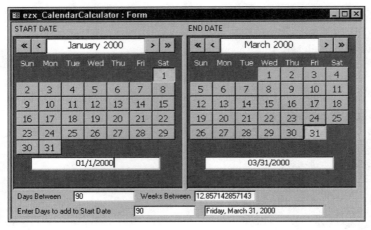

Figure 8-3
The pop-up calendar calculator

Selecting a date from a pop-up calendar

When a form contains a date field, you can provide a pop-up calendar so that the user can simply point and click with the mouse to select the appropriate date. The pop-up calendar displays a graphical representation of a calendar month just like an everyday calendar. Figure 8-4 shows the monthly pop-up calendar for the Check Writer form's CheckDate field.

When the pop-up calendar opens for the Check Writer form, it initially displays the calendar for the month and year shown in the Check Date field — in this case, January, 2000. The current value of the Check Date field, January 30, 2000, displays at the bottom of the pop-up calendar.

To select a different date for the selected month and year, press the button for the day of the month you want. The date you select displays in the field on the bottom of the pop-up calendar. Click the OK button to update the date field on the Check Writer form.

You can move to a different month by clicking one of the single arrow (< or >) buttons on the top of the calendar. You can change the year by clicking one of the double arrow (<< or >>) buttons on the top of the calendar.

- << Move back one year
- >> Move forward one year
- < Move back one month
- > Move forward one month

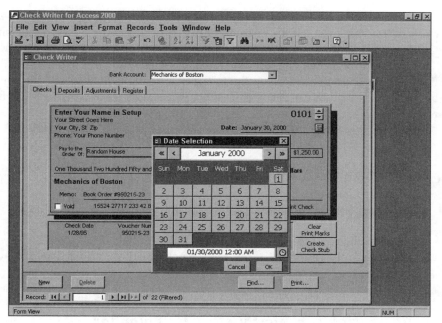

Figure 8-4
A pop-up calendar provides a flexible way to choose a date.

Selecting a time from a pop-up time clock

For date/time combination fields, you can also select a time for the date. You can add a time to a selected date by clicking the clock button located next to the date field at the bottom of the calendar. The clock button pops up a time clock that you can use to choose a time. Figure 8-5 shows the time clock pop-up form.

Figure 8-5
A pop-up time clock provides a way to enter time information.

Just like the pop-up calendar is a useful tool to select a date, this pop-up time clock makes it easy to select a time. You can choose the current time by pressing the Current Time button or click the number buttons to choose the time you want.

The time clock includes an Hour section and a Minute section. To enter a time, first click the appropriate hour button in the Hour section. Then choose the minute by clicking the minute buttons in the Minute section. Then click the AM or PM button located in the Minute section of the time clock.

For example, follow these steps to enter 9:32 AM:

1. Press the Hour 9 button
2. Press the Minute 3 button
3. Press the Minute 2 button
4. Press the AM button

**20 Min.
To Go**

When you click OK, the time clock closes and the time you selected displays on the calling form. If you press Cancel, the time clock closes, but no time displays on the calling form.

Implementing the Monthly Pop-Up Calendar

The Monthly pop-up calendar interface consists of two form objects: ezx_PopUpCalendar and ezx_TimeClock. You can import these objects into your own application as is. They are completely application-independent and ready to use in any application where you want to provide a graphical date interface.

Renaming these objects is not recommended because they include Visual Basic code that depends on the objects named the way they are currently.

The pop-up calendar object names include the prefix "ezx_". These objects were imported from the EZ Access Developer Suite available from Database Creations, Inc. These pop-up calendars are just a sample of the interfaces included in the EZ Access Developer Suite, a collection of predesigned forms, reports, and interfaces that are ready to go with no additional programming. Just link these objects to your application and save hours of programming time. Contact Database Creations, Inc., at (860) 644-5891, or at their Web site www.databasecreations.com.

Using the monthly pop-up calendar by itself

To use the monthly pop-up calendar by itself, include the `ezx_PopupCalendar` in your application and open it either directly or through a button on a form.

Calling the monthly pop-up calendar to fill a control

To display the monthly pop-up calendar for updating a control on a form, you use the `OnClick` event for a command button. The following is the `OnClick` event procedure for the Check Writer form's Calendar command button:

Listing 8-1
Opening the monthly pop-up calendar from a form

```
Private Sub Calendar_Click()
DoCmd.OpenForm "ezx_PopupCalendar", acNormal, , , , acDialog, _
Me.Name & ".[CheckDate]"
Me!CheckDate.SetFocus
End Sub
```

The `Calendar_Click` procedure opens the pop-up calendar as a modal dialog box, which means the form has focus until it is closed. It also passes an opening argument to the form. This argument is the name of the calling form (`Me.Name`), followed by the name of the control on the form that will receive the date/time value. The name of the form and the name of the control must be separated with a period ".".

The monthly pop-up calendar has some unique features:

- It knows when it has been opened as a subform and then hides the Cancel, OK, and Time buttons.
- It knows if it has been called from a form and is to return a value.
- It can be resized automatically when it is opened.
- The user can resize it.
- The first day of the week can be changed.
- It initially displays the current month and displays the current day in red.

Figure 8-6 shows the design view of the ezx_PopupCalendar form. The controls on the form are straightforward with the exception of the day buttons. This is actually an option group made up of 42 buttons.

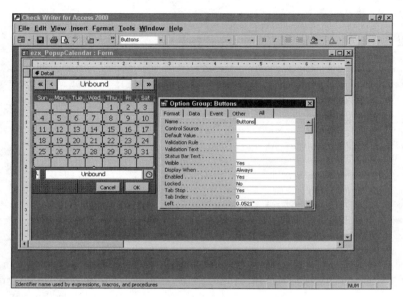

Figure 8-6
Using an option group for the pop-up calendar's days of the month

The Caption property for each button in the Buttons option group changes as each month changes. When the pop-up calendar opens, it runs the DisplayMonth procedure to determine how to set up the days of the month. Figure 8-7 shows the DisplayMonth procedure.

The DisplayMonth procedure determines how many days there are in the displayed month (28, 29, 30, or 31) and what weekday the month starts on (e.g., Sunday through Saturday). The rest of the code in the procedure numbers the buttons to match the days in the month (e.g., 1 through 31 for January) starting the numbering so that day 1 falls on the correct weekday (e.g., Saturday for January, 2000). If the calendar is showing the current calendar month, it also displays the button for the current day in red.

Clicking a day button triggers the OnClick event of the option group Buttons. The code for the OnClick event is shown in Figure 8-8.

```
Microsoft Visual Basic - CheckWriter2000 - [Form_ezx_PopupCalendar (Code)]
File  Edit  View  Insert  Debug  Run  Tools  Add-Ins  Window  Help

(General)                                    DisplayMonth

Public Sub DisplayMonth()
    FirstWeekdayOfMonth = WeekDay(DateSerial(Year(dispMonth), Month(dispMonth), 1))
    NumDaysInMonth = Day(DateSerial(Year(dispMonth), Month(dispMonth) + 1, 0))
    FirstBut = FirstWeekdayOfMonth - FirstDay + 1  'calculate first button of month
    If FirstBut <= 0 Then FirstBut = FirstBut + 7

    For dispButton = 1 To FirstBut - 1
        Me.Controls("D" & dispButton).Visible = False
    Next dispButton

    For dispButton = FirstBut To FirstBut + NumDaysInMonth - 1
        With Me.Controls("D" & dispButton)
            .Visible = True
            .caption = dispButton - FirstBut + 1
            If DateSerial(Year(dispMonth), Month(dispMonth), dispButton - FirstBut + 1) _
               = Date Then
                .ForeColor = 255
            Else
                .ForeColor = 0
            End If
        End With
    Next dispButton

    For dispButton = FirstBut + NumDaysInMonth To 42
        Me.Controls("D" & dispButton).Visible = False
    Next dispButton

    Me.Buttons = 0
End Sub
```

Figure 8-7
Determining the correct days to display in the pop-up calendar

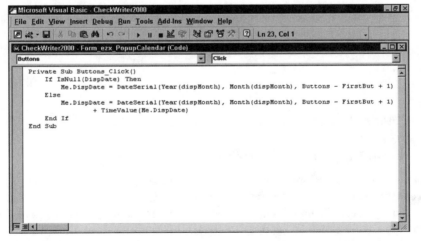

```
Microsoft Visual Basic - CheckWriter2000
File  Edit  View  Insert  Debug  Run  Tools  Add-Ins  Window  Help
                                                    Ln 23, Col 1

CheckWriter2000 - Form_ezx_PopupCalendar (Code)
Buttons                                      Click

Private Sub Buttons_Click()
    If IsNull(DispDate) Then
        Me.DispDate = DateSerial(Year(dispMonth), Month(dispMonth), Buttons - FirstBut + 1)
    Else
        Me.DispDate = DateSerial(Year(dispMonth), Month(dispMonth), Buttons - FirstBut + 1) _
            + TimeValue(Me.DispDate)
    End If
End Sub
```

Figure 8-8
Displaying the selected date in the pop-up calendar

The `Buttons_Click` procedure calculates the date to display using three components: the year of the displayed month, the displayed month, and the day number for the button number of the selected option group button. The day number is calculated by subtracting the number of the button for the first day of the displayed month from the number of the selected button. The three date components are formatted into a date value using the `DateSerial` function. The `DateSerial` function is a built-in Access function that formats the year, month, and day parameters into an acceptable date format.

Clicking the OK button runs the `OK_Click` event. The `OK_Click` event processes the selected date and closes the pop-up calendar form. Figure 8-9 shows the code for the `OK_Click` event.

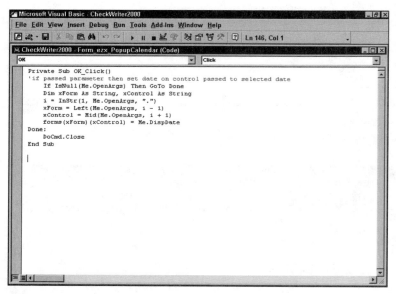

Figure 8-9

Passing the selected date in the pop-up calendar to the calling form

Since the pop-up calendar can be opened as a stand-alone form, the `OK_Click` procedure first checks to see if its `Openargs` property contains any data. If the `Openargs` property is empty, the form was opened in stand-alone mode and the procedure simply closes the pop-up calendar. If it contains data, then it was opened from another form. The procedure then formats the `Openargs` data into the statement that updates the calling form's date field with the selected date from the pop-up calendar. After the date field is updated, the OK_Click procedure closes the pop-up calendar.

Implementing the Three-Month Calendar

To use the three-month pop-up calendar in your application, include the ezx_Calendar3Month as well as the ezx_CalendarSub forms in your application. To use the ezx_Calendar3Month form by itself, open the ezx_Calendar3Month either directly or through a button on a form.

Using the three-month pop-up calendar to fill a control on a form is the same as using the monthly pop-up calendar. You need to add a button on your form with an OnClick event and the following code:

```
DoCmd.OpenForm "ezx_Calendar3Month", acNormal, , , , acDialog, _
Me.Name & ".[NameOfControl]"
```

**10 Min.
To Go**

The OK_Click procedure in the three-month pop-up calendar passes the selected date to the calling form the same way the monthly pop-up calendar passes it.

Working with the Calendar Calculator

A third type of pop-up calendar is the calendar calculator. It provides a means of determining the number of days and weeks between two dates, as well as the ability to add or subtract a certain number of days from a selected date.

To use the calendar calculator, you need to include the ezx_CalendarCalculator and the ezx_PopupCalendar forms in your application. Then simply provide a means of opening the ezx_CalendarCalculator form in your application.

The calendar calculator uses the ezx_PopupCalendar form as a subform for the two calendars that display and is designed to be opened by itself. It does not receive any arguments when opened and does not return any arguments when closed.

The calendar calculator includes three calculated date fields: Days Between, Weeks Between, and a third field that displays the result of adding a specified number of days to the selected date. The calculated dates display each time you select a new date from either of the two calendars.

There is actually no VBA code behind the Calendar Calculator form — all calculations are performed using the ControlSource properties of the fields.

Determining the number of days/weeks between dates

The DaysBetween and WeeksBetween fields on the Calendar Calculator form calculate the number of days or weeks between two dates. The fields display when you select a date from each of the two calendars. Select the start date from the calendar on the left labeled *Start Date*, and the end date from the calendar on the right labeled *End Date*. To calculate the difference between another set of dates, simply select the new start and end date, and the Days Between and Weeks Between fields display the new results. Figure 8-10 shows the ControlSource for the DaysBetween field.

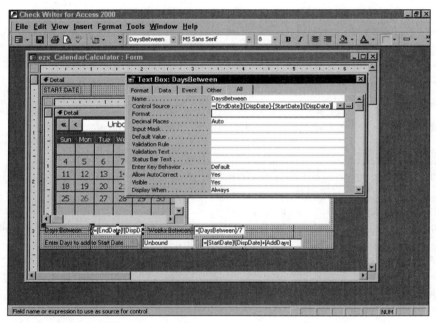

Figure 8-10
Calculating the number of days between two dates

The ControlSource property for the DaysBetween field simply subtracts the date selected in the EndDate subform from the date selected in the StartDate subform.

The ControlSource property for the WeeksBetween field uses the value in the DaysBetween field and divides that by 7. Figure 8-11 shows the ControlSource for the WeeksBetween field.

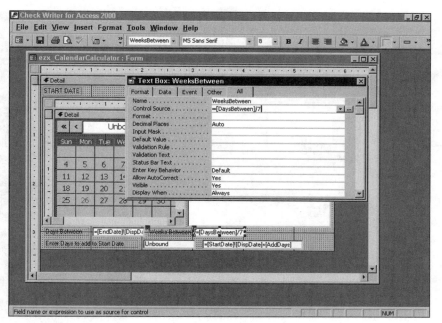

Figure 8-11
Calculating the number of weeks between two dates

Calculating the days from the start date

The calendar calculator determines an end date by adding the specified number of days in the AddDays field to the selected date in the StartDate subform. This is a useful feature if you want to determine when an invoice, project, or payment is due. To add a certain number of days to a given date, first choose a date using the calendar labeled *Start Date*. Then enter a number in the field labeled *Enter days to add to start date*. The result displays in the field to the right of the *Enter days to add to start date* field.

To subtract a certain number of days from the selected start date, type a negative number in the *Enter days to add to start date* field.

Figure 8-12 shows the ControlSource property for calculating the days from the start date.

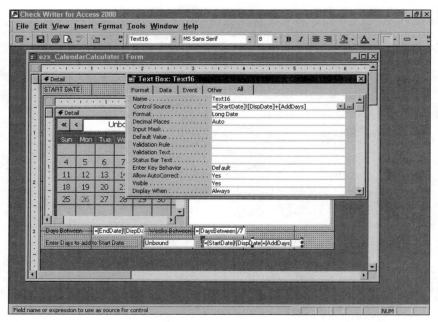

Figure 8-12
Calculating an end date by adding days to the start date

Using the ActiveX Calendar Control

Access provides a built-in ActiveX Calendar Control that you can plug into any form. As shown in Figure 8-13, the Calendar Control displays a monthly calendar. As you click on each day of the month, the day number appears sunken. You can modify the appearance of the control using the control's properties box.

Figure 8-14 shows the Calendar Properties dialog box, which allows you to change how the control displays all of the date components on the calendar. On the General tab, you can change the control to display the month in short format (Jan, Feb, Mar, etc.) or long format (January, February, etc.). You can also format the days of the week (Monday, Tuesday, Wednesday) to short, medium, or long. The check boxes on the right side of the Properties dialog box allow you to turn the display of the various components on and off. The Font and Color tab allow you to change the font and color of each component that displays in the control. The events provided with the control allow you to retrieve the date the user has selected in the control.

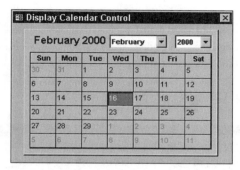

Figure 8-13
The Access ActiveX Calendar Control displays a monthly calendar

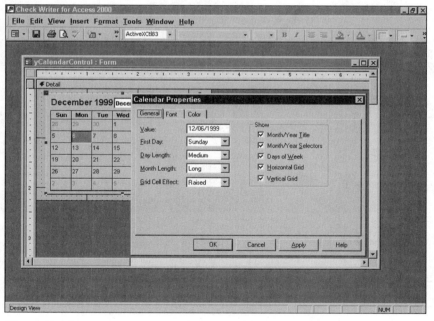

Figure 8-14
Configuring the appearance of the ActiveX Calendar control

While the Access Calendar control is easy to add to any form, it provides limited programmable features. Additionally, the Calendar control is not installed automatically when you install Access. When you distribute your application to users, you must also distribute and register the files required to run the Calendar control.

Done!

Another popular ActiveX calendar control is the Monthly Daytimer Calendar control available in a collection of controls called Solutions::PIM Professional, available from DBI Technologies, Inc. Figure 8-15 shows an example of the Monthly Daytimer Calendar. This control provides some neat capabilities like dragging and dropping, displaying a picture for each day, and showing individual day colors. You can contact DBI Technologies, Inc., at (204) 957-5770 or www.dbi-tech.com.

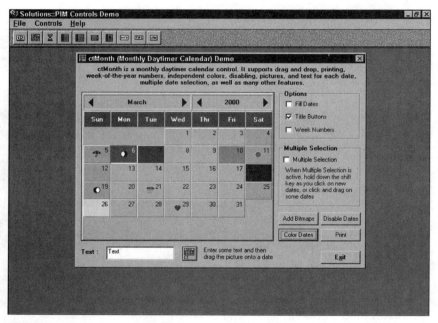

Figure 8-15
The Monthly Daytimer Calendar from DBI Technologies, Inc.

REVIEW

This chapter provided tips and techniques for implementing graphical date selection into your application. Using these techniques along with the prebuilt calendar forms included on the CD, you will be able to provide a great-looking, easy-to-use application. The following topics were covered:

- Pop-up calendars can be used alone as an easy reference tool.
- A form can call a pop-up calendar and retrieve the date selected by the user.

- The calendar calculator provides a useful tool for performing date math on two dates.
- The Access Calendar control provides a quick and easy way to display a calendar.

QUIZ YOURSELF

1. What type of control and which event procedure do you use to open a pop-up calendar from a form? (See "Calling the monthly pop-up calendar to fill a control.")

2. What built-in Access function is used to display the selected date on the pop-up calendar? (See "Calling the monthly pop-up calendar to fill a control.")

3. Which pop-up calendar event updates the calling form's date field? (See "Calling the monthly pop-up calendar to fill a control.")

4. Identify a drawback of using an ActiveX calendar control. (See "Using the ActiveX Calendar Control.")

Working with Data Programmatically

Session Checklist

✔ Viewing SQL Statements

✔ Creating SELECT, UPDATE, and DELETE SQL statements

✔ Using SQL statements in procedures

✔ Using DAO and ADO to retrieve data

✔ Understanding the limitations of ADO

**30 Min.
To Go**

By now, you are familiar with using fields on forms and reports to display and update data in a table. At some point, however, you will eventually need to work with data in a table that is not available in the form's record source. The Visual Basic language provides a rich set of powerful commands that allow you to retrieve and update data programmatically. This chapter provides an overview of SQL, DAO, and ADO. These are the Visual Basic tool sets you use to manipulate data in local and remote databases.

What is SQL?

SQL is a programming language used to retrieve and manipulate data in databases. Like the Visual Basic language, it has a unique set of commands and syntax that you must follow. The three most common commands that you will use are SELECT, UPDATE, and DELETE.

You are familiar with building queries using the Access Query Designer. When you use the Query Designer, you create the query graphically by pointing and dragging tables and fields to the Design view workspace. What may not be apparent to you, however, is that as you select each table and field, Access is building a structured query language (SQL) statement simultaneously.

To view the SQL statement that Access creates, select View ⇨ SQL View from the Query menu. Figure 9-1 shows the SQL statement for the Check Writer Display query.

Figure 9-1
Viewing the SQL view of an Access query

The Check Writer Display query retrieves fields from the Check Writer table. The query includes a filter to limit the result to include only the records where the Bank Account Number matches the BankAccount field in the Check Writer form.

The SELECT statement

The SELECT command is the one you will use most often. The syntax for the SELECT statement includes the keywords SELECT, FROM, WHERE, and ORDER BY. This powerful statement performs the following functions:

- Retrieves specific fields or all fields
- Can retrieve the fields from one or more tables
- Includes all of the rows from the table or uses a filter expression to limit the rows to include
- Sorts the rows by a specific field or fields

The SELECT keyword

The SELECT keyword must be the first word in the statement and precedes the list of field names that you want to include in the query. A comma separates each field name in the list. Optionally, each field name can be preceded by the table name where it is found, followed by a period.

If you are retrieving fields from multiple tables, you should always include the table name prefix. In fact, if a field name appears in multiple tables and you do not include the table name, you will get an error when you run the query.

The SELECT statement for the Check Writer Display query includes 13 fields. The first field name in the list is [CheckWriter].[TransID]. The brackets around the table and field names are optional if the name does not include any spaces. For example, the same item could have been coded as CheckWriter.TransID.

If you want to retrieve all of the fields from the table, you can use an asterisk (*) in place of the field name list. The Check Writer Display query could have been coded like this:

```
SELECT * FROM CheckWriter
```

The FROM keyword

You use the FROM keyword, as you may have guessed, to list the table names for the fields listed for the SELECT clause. This keyword is required and always follows the SELECT clause.

If the query includes fields from more than one table, you must include a join type expression in the FROM clause. The join type expression tells Access how the tables relate to one another. There are three join type keywords:

- INNER JOIN. Combines the records from two tables where the values in the joined fields in both tables match
- LEFT JOIN. Includes all of the records from the table in the left side of the clause even if no records from the table on the right side match
- RIGHT JOIN. Includes all of the records from the table in the right side of the clause even if no records from the table on the right side match

The FROM clause syntax using a join type expression is:

```
FROM <left side table name> <join type> <right side table name> ON
<left side join field> = <right side join field>
```

The following is an example of a query using a RIGHT JOIN clause:

```
SELECT CheckWriter.*, BankAccounts.BankName
FROM BankAccounts RIGHT JOIN CheckWriter ON
BankAccounts.BankAccountNumber = CheckWriter.AccountNumber;
```

In this example, the query retrieves all of the fields from the Check Writer table and just the BankName field from the BankAccounts table. The RIGHT JOIN clause tells Access to match the BankAccountNumber field in the BankAccounts table with the AccountNumber field in the Check Writer table. Because the join type is RIGHT JOIN, all of the Check Writer rows will be retrieved, even if the AccountNumber field does not match any of the values in the BankAccountNumber field in the BankAccounts table.

The WHERE keyword

The WHERE keyword is optional. If you include it, it always follows the FROM clause. You can use this as a filter to limit the rows that the query retrieves.

The WHERE clause always begins with the WHERE keyword followed by some condition that must be met. The condition is an expression that evaluates to either True or False. It includes a field name from one of the tables included in the FROM clause followed by a test expression. An example of a query using a WHERE clause might look something like this:

```
WHERE ((CheckWriter.TransType = 'Check') AND (CheckWriter.Payee =
'Random House'))
```

In this example, the test expression involves comparing the values in the field name TransType to the value 'Check'. In this case, the WHERE clause includes two test expressions joined by the AND operator. The second test expression compares the values in the field Payee with the value 'Random House'. The AND operator tells Access that both of these expressions must evaluate to True for the record to be included in the result.

The ORDER BY keywords

The ORDER BY keywords are also optional. When used, they always appear at the end of the SQL statement. You can use this to sort the query results.

The ORDER BY clause always begins with the ORDER BY keywords followed by the field names by which to sort. The following is an example of an ORDER BY clause:

```
ORDER BY CheckWriter.CheckDate;
```

In this example, the query results will be sorted by CheckDate in ascending order. To sort the results in descending order, use the DESC keyword. For example:

```
ORDER BY CheckWriter.CheckDate DESC;
```

The semicolon at the end of the SQL statement tells Access that there are no more keywords to process. If you omit it, however, Access will insert it for you.

**20 Min.
To Go**

The DELETE statement

Another SQL command that you will use quite often is the DELETE command. The syntax for the DELETE command includes the keywords DELETE, FROM, and WHERE. You use the DELETE command to remove records from one or more of the tables listed in the FROM clause that satisfy the WHERE clause. The following is an example of a delete query:

```
DELETE CheckWriter.* FROM CheckWriter;
```

In this example, all of the rows would be deleted from the Check Writer table.

The UPDATE statement

You can use the UPDATE statement to change the data in a field for many records simultaneously. The syntax for the UPDATE statement is a little different from the SELECT and DELETE statements. The keywords for this statement are UPDATE, SET, and WHERE. Figure 9-2 shows an example of a DELETE statement.

The SQL statement in this example changes the value in the Void field to True if any rows in the Check Writer table have a zero in the CheckNumber field.

The DELETE and UPDATE statements do not return any records.

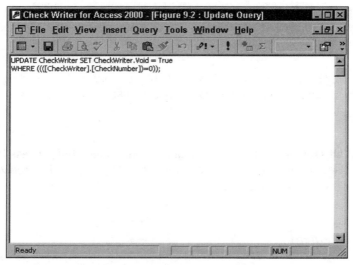

Figure 9-2
An UPDATE statement changes many rows simultaneously

Using SQL statements in procedures

You can use SQL statements in procedures. For example, you can use a SQL statement to set the RecordSource property for a subform. Listing 9-1 shows the code for the AfterUpdate event of the Recon Display option group in the Check Reconciliation form.

Listing 9-1
Using a SQL statement in a procedure

```
Private Sub Recon_Display_AfterUpdate()
    Select Case Me![Recon Display].value
        Case 1    'Uncleared Only
            Me![zCheckRec Register].Form.RecordSource = "SELECT *
"FROM [CheckWriter] WHERE " & _
                "Not [Cleared] AND [AccountNumber] =
Forms![Check Reconciliation]![BankAccount] And Not [Void]"
        Case 2    'All Transactions
            Me![zCheckRec Register].Form.RecordSource = "SELECT *
```

```
FROM [CheckWriter] WHERE " & _
                "[AccountNumber] = Forms![Check
Reconciliation]![BankAccount] And Not [Void]"
    End Select
End Sub
```

The `Recon_Display_AfterUpdate` procedure checks the value of the Recon Display option group. The procedure sets the `RecordSource` property for the zCheckRec Register subform based on the selected Recon Display option. If the Uncleared Only option is selected, the SQL statement filters the `RecordSource` to include only the records that have Cleared values set to False and where the AccountNumber matches the BankAccount field in the Check Reconciliation form. If the All Transactions option is selected, the SQL statement filters the `RecordSource` only on the AccountNumber field.

Instead of attempting to write your SQL statement from scratch in a procedure, you can use the Query Design window to create and test the query. Then switch to SQL view for the query, copy the SQL statement to the clipboard, then paste it into your procedure.

Creating Procedures to Validate Data

In Access, it is simple to display or update the data for a field in a form. You simply drag one of the fields from the field list to the Design view of the form. When the form runs, it displays the current value for the field. If the user changes the value, Access automatically stores the new value in the field.

In many cases, however, you want to validate the data the user entered against other values that are already stored in the form's table. For example, if the user is creating a new account in the Bank Accounts form, you should check to make sure that the new account number does not already exist in the Bank Accounts table. If the account number is a duplicate, you should display an error message to the user and cancel the update.

To validate the new account data, you must check all of the records in the table to see if the new account already exists. There is no built-in function that you can enter into the `ValidationRule` property that can span multiple records in a table automatically. You must write your own procedure.

Note

Since the BankAccountNumber field in the BankAccounts table is the primary key, Access will not allow a duplicate entry for this field. You could omit the validation procedure and let Access accept or reject the new account. However, this could be annoying to the user entering the data because Access would not perform the check until the user has completed all of the information for the new record and attempted to save it.

You use a field's BeforeUpdate event to validate potential new data. Figure 9-3 shows the BeforeUpdate event for the BankAccountNumber field. This event combines the use of a SQL statement along with some special VBA commands called DAO commands.

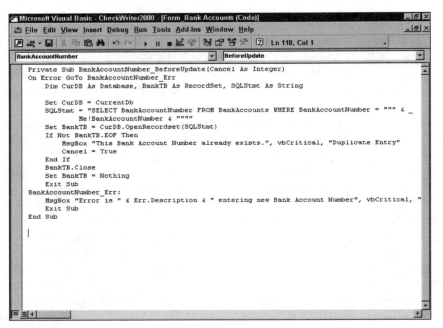

Figure 9-3
Using a procedure to validate data

Understanding DAO

The `BankAccountNumber_BeforeUpdate` procedure checks to make sure the new data entered into the BankAccountNumber fields does not already exist in the BankAccounts table. This procedure uses a SQL statement along with some VBA code. The VBA code consists of a special set of commands called *Data Access Objects*, or DAO. DAO commands are used to retrieve and manipulate data in tables and queries within a procedure.

The DAO command set was designed specifically to work with the Microsoft Jet database engine, usually referred to as Jet. *Jet* is the data-access manager that resides between your application and the source of the data. The data source can be an Access database, or even an ODBC data source like Paradox or DBASE. When your application retrieves or updates data in a table, Jet is the system that actually moves the data between the tables and your application.

Declaring DAO variables

The first step in creating a DAO procedure is to declare DAO object variables. The `Dim` statement in this example declares DAO object variables for the database and the recordset. A *recordset* is a special object variable that you use to refer to the records in a table. In this example, the variable `CurDB` refers to the name of the database, and `BankTB` refers to the recordset.

Assigning values to DAO objects

The second step is to assign values to the object variables that were declared in the `Dim` statement. To assign the object variables, you use the `Set` statement. In this example, the `Set` statement

```
Set CurDB = CurrentDb
```

assigns the currently active database to the `CurDB` object variable. The assignment to the `BankTB` recordset variable is a little more complicated.

Assigning values to object variables requires special handling. You cannot simply assign some value like you can with an integer or string variable — `LastName = "Smith"`**, for example. The** `Set` **statement tells Access that you are assigning a value to an object variable.**

Part II—Saturday Morning
Session 9

To assign a value to a recordset object variable, you use the `OpenRecordset` method. Object variables are like controls on a form or report. They have a limited set of methods and properties that are available to perform on the data that they represent. `OpenRecordset` is one of the methods available when you are working with a database object. When you want to use one of the object variable's methods, you must preface the method with the name of the object on which it is to be used.

All objects in Access are members of a hierarchical tree. The currently active database is at the top of the tree. The recordset object is a descendent of the currently active database. To assign a new descendent object of some object in the tree, you use one of the parent object's methods. Methods are special functions that can be used only with specific objects. You can determine which methods are available for an object using Auto List Members. Auto List Members is an option available in the Visual Basic Editor Code window. If this option is enabled when you type an object name followed by a period, Auto List Members automatically displays a list of available methods and properties for that object.

Opening a recordset

The `Set` statement for the `BankTB` recordset:

```
Set BankTB = CurDB.OpenRecordset(SQLStmt)
```

uses the `OpenRecordset` method on the `CurDB` object. The `OpenRecordset` method has one required argument — the data source. The data source can be a table name, a query name, or a SQL statement. In this example the data source is a variable that stores a SQL statement. The SQL statement:

```
SQLStmt = "SELECT BankAccountNumber FROM BankAccounts WHERE
BankAccountNumber = """ & Me!BankAccountNumber & """"
```

retrieves the BankAccountNumber field from the BankAccounts table where the BankAccountNumber field matches the value that was entered in the BankAccountNumber field in the Bank Accounts form.

Working with recordsets

Once the recordset is open, you can begin working with the data that it contains. In this example, the statements between the If and End If statements perform the validation:

```
If Not BankTB.EOF Then
    MsgBox "This Bank Account Number already exists.", & _
    vbCritical, "Duplicate Entry"
    Cancel = True
End If
```

When you open a recordset and it contains no data, the property end of file (EOF) status is True.

The validation code tests the BankTB recordset to see if it is *not* at the end of the file. If the recordset does contain data (the recordset status is *not* at end of file), then the SQL statement did find a match on the new account number data — an undesirable result. Then an error message displays to notify the user of the duplicate entry and the update is cancelled.

If the recordset status was EOF, then the SQL statement did not find a match and the procedure does nothing. The update will not be cancelled.

Closing object variables

The two statements:

```
BankTB.Close
Set BankTB = Nothing
```

after the End If statement are basic housekeeping statements that you should always use when working with objects. The Close method tells Access that you are finished working with the object. If you needed to work with the object later on in the procedure, you would then have to code another Set statement to reopen the object. Assigning Nothing to an object variable releases all the system and memory resources associated with the object.

The Data Access Objects interface has evolved to become more and more powerful with each new version of Access. Starting with Access 2000, a new data access interface, which you can use as an alternative to DAO, is now available called ADO.

Understanding ADO

10 Min. To Go

You have seen how easy it is to work with Access databases whether they reside on your local desktop or on a remote server. As a powerful client/server development tool, Access makes it just as easy to connect to non-Access databases, like Oracle and SQL Server, as well.

With Access 2000, the DAO data access interface has been refined into a new command set called *ActiveX Data Objects*, or ADO. ADO is a simpler, more powerful command set designed specifically to work with non-Access databases.

You can perform the same tasks using DAO as you can with ADO — Access currently supports both. However, Microsoft plans to incorporate any further enhancements to data access technology only into ADO.

While you can achieve the same result using DAO or ADO, the ADO interface is more efficient. Some of the advantages of ADO over DAO include the following:

- Has a simpler command set
- Executes faster
- Uses less memory
- Consumes less disk space
- Includes new features specifically designed for client/server and Web-based applications

Figure 9-4 shows the `BankAccountNumber_BeforeUpdate` procedure rewritten using the ADO data access interface.

Declaring ADO variables

The first step in creating an ADO procedure is to declare ADO object variables. The `Dim` statement in this example declares ADO object variables for the connection and the recordset. A connection, similar to the database object in DAO, opens a communication line into the database. In this example, the variable `CurConn` refers to the name of the connection, and `BankTB` refers to the recordset.

```
Microsoft Visual Basic - CheckWriter2000 - [Form_Bank Accounts (Code)]
File  Edit  View  Insert  Debug  Run  Tools  Add-Ins  Window  Help
                                                          Ln 32, Col 9

BankAccountNumber                          BeforeUpdate

   Private Sub BankAccountNumber_BeforeUpdate(Cancel As Integer)
   On Error GoTo Errout
   Dim CurConn As New ADODB.Connection
   Dim BankTB As New ADODB.RecordSet, Response As Integer

        CurConn.Open CurrentProject.Connection
        BankTB.Open "SELECT * FROM BankAccounts WHERE [BankAccountNumber] = """ & _
                 Me!BankAccountNumber & """", CurConn, adOpenForwardOnly
        If Not BankTB.EOF Then
          Response = MsgBox("Duplicate Bank Account Number!" & Chr$(10) & Chr$(13) & _
                   "Do You Want to Cancel the Entry?", 20, "Duplicate Bank Account Number")
          If Response = vbNo Then
            Cancel = True
            BankTB.Close
            Set BankTB = Nothing
            Exit Sub
          Else
            Cancel = True
            Me.Undo
            BankTB.Close
            Set BankTB = Nothing
            Exit Sub
          End If
        End If
        BankTB.Close
        Set BankTB = Nothing
        CurConn.Close
        Set CurConn = Nothing
   Exit Sub
```

Figure 9-4
Using ADO to validate data

DAO and ADO share some objects. To distinguish between a DAO and an ADO object variable, you must preface the variable declaration with the appropriate class type. For ADO objects, the class type is ADODB. **For DAO objects, the class type is** DAO. **You don't have to specify the DAO class type because it is the default type.**

Assigning values to ADO objects

With ADO, the Set statement is optional. If you use the New keyword when you declare an ADO object variable, you do not need to code the Set statement.

Opening connections and recordsets

To open a connection or recordset, you use the Open method preceded by the name of the object to open. When you use the Open method on a connection object, you also specify the name of the connection string for the database you want to open. In this example, the connection string is ActiveProject.Connection — the currently active database connection. The Open method for the recordset in this example has three arguments: the source (a SQL statement here), the name of an open connection object (`CurConn`), and the cursor type (`adOpenForwardOnly`). Four recordset cursor types are available:

- `adOpenForwardOnly`. A read-only recordset with the ability to scroll through the records in the recordset only in a forward movement.

- `adOpenKeyset`. An updateable recordset where additions and deletions to the data source by others are not available to the recordset. However, updates made to the data source are automatically applied to the recordset.

- `adOpenDynamic`. An updateable recordset where additions, deletions, and updates to the data are automatically applied to the recordset. This type is not available for Jet databases.

- `adOpenStatic`. A read-only recordset where additions, deletions, and updates to the data are not visible to the recordset.

The `adOpenForwardOnly` **cursor type is the most efficient option when you are opening a recordset to simply find a record.**

Opening a connection for a non-Jet database

When developing in a client/server environment, you will need to establish connections to many different database systems like Oracle or SQL Server. When you open a connection for these external databases, you must use a connection string that is appropriate for the data source. The connection string is different for each database provider. The following is an example of a connection string for a SQL Server database:

```
CurConn.Open "DSN=pubs;uid=sa;pwd=;database=pubs"
```

This connection string opens the pubs database (the example database supplied with SQL Server). Each of the four parameters in this connection string is separated by a semicolon. The `DSN` parameter refers to the data source name of the database. The `pubs` data source name contains the drive letter and directory of the location of the database. Most external databases require a user ID and password to gain access. The `uid` and `pwd` parameters contain these values. The database parameter refers to the actual name of the database in SQL Server.

Chapter 29 has more information on working with client/server databases.

Closing ADO object variables

Just as in DAO, when you have finished using ADO object variables, you should close them and set them to Nothing.

When to use ADO and DAO

While much of the information that you may have read about working with Access 2000 data probably emphasizes using ADO exclusively, you should proceed with caution. In some situations, DAO still outperforms ADO and, in some cases, DAO is the only solution that works.

The ADO object model was designed to be a generic interface to multiple database providers. It offers many key features for building client/server and Web-based applications that are not available in DAO. When you are working with server-type databases like Oracle and SQL Server, ADO is the most strategic solution. For Jet databases, on the other hand, the ADO object model falls short in several situations.

Using ADO with a Jet database *can* result in five to ten times slower performance than using DAO. When you query a database using ADO, it must retrieve information about the database before it can communicate with it. ADO treats all databases as external databases. So, even though you are building an Access application against an Access database, ADO still has to retrieve this information. Since DAO was optimized for accessing Jet databases, it already has most of the information it needs about the database.

ADO does not currently fully support managing database security for Jet databases. When creating new users and groups programmatically, ADO does not return the personal identifier (PID) for the new user or group. This is a serious flaw. If you lose your System.mdw file (the file that stores users and groups by PID), you will not be able to recreate it.

Chapter 28 discusses database security.

Done!

Until ADO evolves into a more mature data access interface, you may want to stick with DAO when working only with Jet databases. A sensible alternative might be to mix ADO and DAO in your procedures wherever one has the advantage over the other.

REVIEW

This chapter provided information on how to use procedures to retrieve information from a database. You learned how to create SQL statements and how to use them with the DAO and ADO object models. The following topics were covered:

- Access queries are actually stored as SQL statements, and you can view them by selecting View ⇨ SQL View from the Query Design window menu.
- The SELECT statement retrieves a set of records from one or more tables and, optionally, can filter and sort the set of records.
- If the SELECT statement uses more than one table, you must include a join type in the FROM clause.
- The DELETE statement removes one or more records from a table.
- The UPDATE statement changes the values for one or more fields in a table.
- You can use a SQL statement in a BeforeUpdate event to validate data.
- In procedures like the BeforeUpdate event procedure, you use DAO or ADO to send a SQL statement to a database and to access the recordset it returns.
- ADO is a more refined version of the DAO command set.
- When working with Jet databases, DAO outperforms ADO.

QUIZ YOURSELF

1. How can you view the SQL statement for an Access query? (See "What Is SQL?")
2. Name four keywords used in a SELECT statement. (See "The SELECT statement.")
3. Name two SQL statements that do not return any records. (See "The UPDATE statement.")
4. Which object model was specifically designed to work with Jet databases? (See "Understanding DAO.")
5. Which object model was designed to work with external databases? (See "Understanding ADO.")

Adding, Updating, and Deleting Records Using DAO and ADO

Session Checklist

✔ Using a `NotInList` event procedure to add a new record

✔ Saving changes to a recordset

✔ Locking records for update

✔ Handling update errors

✔ Minimizing update conflicts

✔ Navigating throughout a recordset

✔ Deleting a record

**30 Min.
To Go**

I n the preceding session, you learned how you can retrieve data from a table in a procedure using DAO or ADO code. This session expands on that topic to show you how you can also add, change, and delete data in a table. Manipulating data using a procedure may seem intimidating at first. However, the power that these command sets give you to develop a full-featured multi-user application makes it well worth the investment of effort to become familiar with them.

Adding a Record to a Table

You can create a Visual Basic procedure to add a record to a table programmatically. To use ADO and DAO to add a new record to a table, you use the AddNew method. Figure 10-1 shows the ADO procedure for adding a new payee to the Payees table.

```
Microsoft Visual Basic - CheckWriter2000 - [Form_Check Writer (Code)]
File  Edit  View  Insert  Debug  Run  Tools  Add-Ins  Window  Help

                                              Ln 319, Col 1

Payee                                    NotInList

Private Sub Payee_NotInList(NewData As String, Response As Integer)
On Error GoTo Payee_NotInList_Err
    Dim CurConn As ADODB.Connection
    Dim PayeeTB As New ADODB.RecordSet
    Dim Answer As Integer

    Answer = MsgBox("This Payee is not on file. Add it to the Payees list?", _
        vbQuestion + vbYesNo, "New Payee")
    If Answer = vbNo Then
        Response = acDataErrContinue
    Else
        Response = acDataErrAdded
        Set CurConn = CurrentProject.Connection
        PayeeTB.CursorType = adOpenKeyset
        PayeeTB.LockType = adLockOptimistic
        PayeeTB.Open "Payees", CurConn, , , adCmdTable
        With PayeeTB
            'Add new payee to Payees table
            .AddNew
            !Payees = NewData
            .Update
        End With
        PayeeTB.Close
        Set PayeeTB = Nothing
        CurConn.Close
        Set CurConn = Nothing
    End If
    Exit Sub
Payee_NotInList_Err:
```

Figure 10-1
Adding a new record to a table using ADO

When the user enters a payee name in the Check Writer form that does not appear in the combo box list of payees, the Payee_NotInList procedure runs. The message box prompts the user to confirm whether to add the new payee to the Payees combo box list. If the user selects Yes, the ADO code to add the new payee to the Payees table runs.

Adding a new record to a table using DAO is very similar. Listing 10-1 shows the Payee_NotInList procedure coded using DAO.

Listing 10-1
Using DAO to add a new record to a table

```
On Error GoTo Payee_NotInList_Err
    Dim CurDB as database
    Dim PayeeTB As Recordset
    Dim Answer As Integer

    Answer = MsgBox("This Payee is not on file. Add it to the
Payees list?", _
            vbQuestion + vbYesNo, "New Payee")
    If Answer = vbNo Then
        Response = acDataErrContinue
    Else
        Response = acDataErrAdded
        Set CurDB = Currentdb
        Set PayeeTB = CurDB.OpenRecordset("Payees")
        With PayeeTB
            'Add new payee to Payees table
            .AddNew
            !Payees = NewData
            .Update
        End With
        PayeeTB.Close
        Set PayeeTB = Nothing
    End If
    Exit Sub
    Payee_NotInList_Err:
        MsgBox "Error is " & Err.Description & _
        " adding new Payee to Payees list in Check Writer.", _
        vbCritical, "System Error"
Exit Sub
End Sub
```

Using the AddNew method

As you can see from these two examples, you use the AddNew method the same
way for both ADO and DAO. The AddNew method creates a buffer for a new record.
You assign values to fields from the recordset by coding a separate statement for

each field assignment. The field assignment statements are always coded between the AddNew statement and the Update statement. As each field assignment statement runs, the new field information is copied into the buffer.

Completing the new record

The Update method, when used with the AddNew method, moves the information from the buffer to the end of the recordset. The Update method is used the same way for both ADO and DAO. With ADO, however, you can omit the Update method. When you move to a new record in ADO or close the recordset, the changes are saved automatically. It is a good idea, though, to include the Update statement so that others who may read the code later on understand that the update section of the code is complete.

With DAO, if you forget to include the Update **statement, the changes will be lost if you move to another record in the recordset or close the recordset. No warning message or runtime error will occur.**

To cancel any pending updates in ADO, you use the CancelUpdate method. Once an Update method has executed, however, you cannot issue the CancelUpdate method. You cannot undo any changes once they have been saved.

Making a recordset updateable

To add, change, or delete records in a recordset, the recordset must be updateable. You can make a recordset updateable by setting specific properties for the recordset before opening it using the Open method. The CursorType property, in conjunction with the LockType property, determine whether changes can be made to the recordset. The adOpenKeyset cursor type is the only updateable cursor type available for Jet databases.

Session 9 discusses all of the available cursor types.

Table 10-1 describes the lock types available for recordsets. The lock type determines which type of lock to place on the record to prevent other users from modifying the record you are about to update.

Table 10-1
Recordset Lock Types

ADO Lock Type	Description
adLockReadOnly	Read only. No changes allowed.
adLockPessimistic	Lock the record immediately upon editing.
adLockOptimistic	Attempt to lock the record when the record is saved.
adLockBatchOptimistic	Use for updating records in batch mode.

The adLockReadOnly lock type is used with the adOpenForwardOnly and adOpenStatic cursor types when you are simply querying data. For updateable recordsets, you will use the adLockPessimistic and adLockOptimistic lock types most of the time.

If you specify an invalid CursorType/LockType combination for a Jet database, Jet automatically opens the recordset using a valid LockType for the specified CursorType. Valid CursorType/LockType combinations for Jet databases include: adOpenForwardOnly/ adLockReadOnly, adOpenKeyset/adLockOptimistic, **and** adOpenStatic/adLockReadOnly**.**

Using the adLockPessimistic lock type is called *pessimistic locking*. With pessimistic locking, the record is locked as soon as an edit occurs. The record stays locked until the record is saved. This is the disadvantage of using pessimistic locking. Other users cannot edit the record until the record is saved. If your procedure must execute many statements before the update is complete, the record could be unavailable to others for a long time.

Remember, with DAO, using the Update **method saves the record. With ADO, using the** Update **method, moving to another record, or closing the recordset saves the changes.**

Optimistic locking, using the adLockOptimistic lock type, does not lock the record until the record is saved. This approach minimizes the amount of time that the record is unavailable to other users.

Part II–Saturday Morning
Session 10

**20 Min.
To Go**

With both optimistic and pessimistic locking, an error will occur if a lock cannot be obtained on a record. In most multi-user applications, multiple users will likely attempt to change the same record at the same time. Your procedures must be able to at least attempt to resolve editing conflicts rather than just drop to a default error message.

Handling lock errors

You can include a special error-handling section in your procedure to handle the errors that can occur when updating a recordset. With Jet databases, the three most common error codes that can occur are listed in Table 10-2.

Table 10-2
Common Locking Error Messages

Code	Message	Description
3218	Could not update. Currently locked.	The record is already locked by another user.
3197	The database engine stopped because you and another user attempted to change the same data at the same time.	Another user has already started editing the record.
3260	Couldn't update. Currently locked by \<user> on machine \<machine name>.	The record is already locked by another user.

Listing 10-2 shows an example of an ADO error-handling routine for managing locking errors.

Listing 10-2
Handling locking errors

```
Proc_Sql_Err:
Dim Response As Integer, LockCount As Integer,  RndCtr As Integer
Dim I As Integer

Const MULTIUSER_EDIT As Integer = 3197
Const RECORD_LOCKED As Integer = 3218

Select Case CurConn.Errors(0).SQLState
```

```
Case MULTIUSER_EDIT    'someone else already changed the data

    Response = MsgBox("This record was changed by another" _
            & "user. Save anyway?", vbYesNo + vbQuestion
    If Response = vbYes Then
        Resume
    Else
        Resume Proc_Exit
    End If

Case RECORD_LOCKED
    ' The record is locked.
    LockCount = LockCount + 1
    ' If more than 2 retries, then ask the user what to do
    If LockCount > 2 Then
        Response = MsgBox("Could not complete update due to " _
                & Err.Description & " Retry?", vbYesNo + _
                vbQuestion)
        If Response = vbYes Then
            LockCount = 1
        Else
            Resume Proc_Exit
        End If
    End If

    ' Yield to Windows.
    DoEvents
    ' Delay a short random interval, making it longer each
    ' time the lock fails.
    RndCtr = LockCount ^ 2 * Int(Rnd * 3000 + 1000)
    For I = 1 To RndCtr
    Next I
    Resume                 ' Try the edit again.
Case Else                  ' Some other kind of error
    MsgBox "Error " & CurConn.Errors(0).SQLState & ": " _
            & Err.Description, vbOKOnly, "ERROR"
    Resume Proc_Exit

End Select
```

The `Proc_Sql_Err` error-handling routine evaluates the type of error that occurred and attempts to resolve it. The `SQLState` property of the active connection's current error returns the error number for the error. The `Case` statement in the routine compares the SQL error to two different SQL error conditions.

Instead of using error numbers in your code like 3218, 3197, and 3260, you can use constants to make them easier to understand.

If the error was due to a multi-user error (`MULTIUSER_EDIT`), then another user already changed the data before this update could be completed. The message box prompts the user to decide how to resolve this. If the user selects Yes to retry, the code returns to the `Update` statement and executes it again. If the user selects No, the code jumps to the exit routine for the procedure canceling the update.

If the error was due to a failed lock problem (`RECORD_LOCKED`), then another user has locked the current record. The statements in this branch of the routine attempt to automatically retry the update after waiting a short time. The `DoEvents` and the `For...Next` loop tick off some time, thereby making the procedure "wait" before returning to retry the `Update` statement. The error routine keeps track of how many times the retry process has occurred. If a third attempt occurs, the message box prompts the user to decide if further retry attempts should be made.

Error-handling programs are covered in more detail in Session 16.

Locking multiple records

When you lock a record for a Jet-based recordset, more than one record may actually be locked. In previous versions of the Jet database engine, issuing a lock on a recordset locked a section of records in a table called a page. A *page* consists of approximately 4K of data. If the size of the current record in a table is less than 4K, contiguous records are also locked until the total size of the locked records reaches the page size.

Beginning with version 4.0 of the Jet database engine, the ability to lock individual records in a table became available. Locking an individual record is called *record-level locking*. Record-level locking is an optional feature in Access 2000.

To turn on record-level locking, select the option *Open databases using record-level locking* in the Tools ⇨ Options window under the Advanced tab. Figure 10-2 shows the Options window.

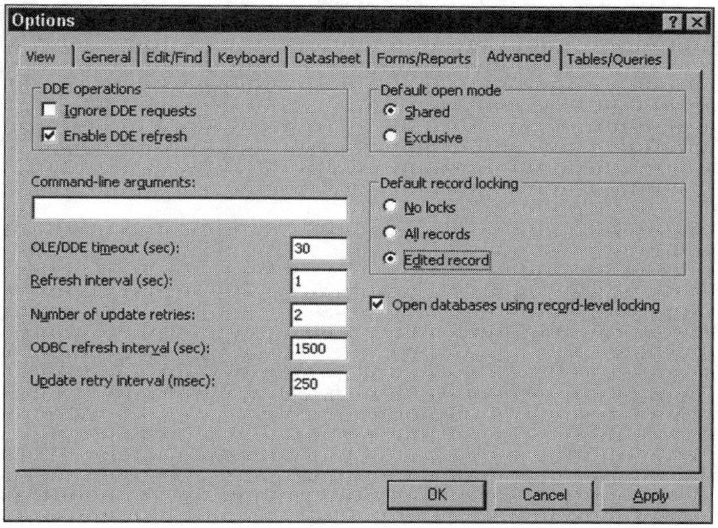

Figure 10-2
Setting the record-level locking feature

To use *page-level locking* (locking an entire page of records), you can clear the *Open databases using record-level locking* option.

Using page-level locking generally provides better performance. However, in an application where many simultaneous updates occur, you can imagine how often locking conflicts can occur. The likelihood of two users attempting to update records within 4K of each other at the same time is probably very high. If you have included a good error routine for conflict resolution, your users probably won't get any update rejection messages. However, the system will slow down as it makes each retry attempt.

Updating a Record

Changing a record in a table is very similar to adding a new record. To update a field in a table using ADO, you simply assign a new value to the field you want to update.

Figure 10-3 shows the ADO procedure for changing the `DefaultBankAccountNumber` field in the Preferences table.

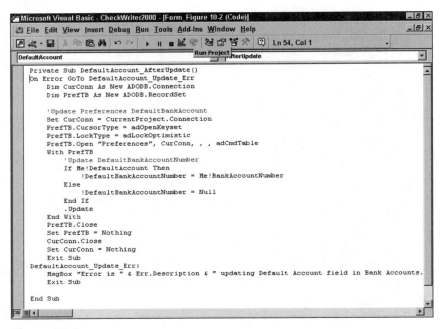

Figure 10-3
Updating a record using ADO.

The Bank Accounts form is bound to the BankAccounts table. The DefaultBank AccountNumber check box in the Bank Accounts form is an unbound field because it refers to the DefaultBankAccountNumber field in the Preferences table. You must use a procedure to update a field in a table that is not bound to the form.

When the user selects the Default Account check box in the Bank Accounts form, the `DefaultAccount_AfterUpdate` procedure runs. This procedure changes the value in the DefaultBankAccountNumber field in the Preferences table. If the Default Account check box is selected, the procedure changes the Preferences table's DefaultBankAccountNumber to the BankAccountNumber value in the Bank Accounts form. If the Default Account check box is cleared, the procedure erases the value in the DefaultBankAccountNumber.

When the `Update` method runs, the change to the Preferences table is saved.

Updating a record using DAO is a little different. Listing 10-3 shows the `DefaultAccount_AfterUpdate` procedure coded using DAO.

Listing 10-3

Using DAO to update a record.

```
Public Sub DefaultAccount_AfterUpdate()
On Error GoTo DefaultAccount_Update_Err
    Dim CurDB As database
    Dim PrefTB As RecordSet

    'Update Preferences DefaultBankAccount
    Set CurDB = CurrentDb
    Set PrefTB = CurDB.OpenRecordset("Preferences")
    With PrefTB
        'Update DefaultBankAccountNumber
        .Edit
        If Me!DefaultAccount Then
            !DefaultBankAccountNumber = Me!BankAccountNumber
        Else
            !DefaultBankAccountNumber = Null
        End If
        .Update
    End With
    PrefTB.Close
    Set PrefTB = Nothing
    Exit Sub

DefaultAccount_Update_Err:
    MsgBox "Error is " & Err.Description & " updating Default " & _
        "Account field in Bank Accounts.", vbCritical, "System Error"
Exit Sub

End Sub
```

Using the Edit method

Before you can update any of the fields in a DAO recordset, you must use the Edit method. This is one of the biggest differences between DAO and ADO. With ADO, the recordset automatically opens in edit mode.

10 Min.
To Go

The Edit method copies the current record in the recordset to a buffer. When you assign a value to a recordset field, the changes are stored in the buffer. When the Update method executes, the changes in the buffer are copied to the recordset's table. The Edit method can be used only on updateable recordsets.

Creating updateable DAO recordsets

The type parameter of the OpenRecordset method determines whether a DAO recordset can be updated. Setting the type parameter is similar to using the CursorType and LockType properties for ADO recordsets. Table 10-3 compares the DAO recordset types to the ADO CursorType and LockType combinations.

Table 10-3
Comparing DAO and ADO Open Arguments

DAO Type	ADO CursorType	ADO LockType
dbOpenDynaset	adOpenKeyset	adLockOptimistic
dbOpenSnapshot	adOpenStatic	adLockReadOnly
dbOpenForwardOnly	adOpenForwardOnly	adLockReadOnly

Note

These types are the ones that you can use for Jet-linked tables. Other types are available for other database providers. If you do not specify a type when you open a DAO recordset, the recordset type defaults to dbOpenDynaset.

To set the type of locking to use for a DAO recordset, you use the LockEdits parameter of the Open method. The three LockEdits settings that you will use most often for Jet databases are:

dbReadOnly	Prevents other users from making changes to the table while the recordset is open.
dbPessimistic	Uses pessimistic record locking. A record is locked in the recordset as soon as the Edit method executes.
dbOptimistic	Uses optimistic record locking. The record is not locked until the Update method executes.

If you do not specify a LockEdits parameter, the recordset opens using pessimistic record locking (dbPessimistic).

Moving between recordset records

Before you edit a record in a recordset, you need to make sure that the recordset contains records and that you are on the correct record. In `DefaultAccount_AfterUpdate` (Listing 10-3), the Preferences table used in the recordset happens to always contain only one record. Many recordsets that you will use, however, will contain any number of records.

If a recordset contains no records, the beginning of file (BOF) and end of file (EOF) properties are True. When you open a recordset that contains one or more records, the first record in the recordset automatically becomes the current record, and the BOF and EOF properties are both false.

Listing 10-4 shows some of the methods you can use to move around in a recordset.

Listing 10-4
Navigating through a recordset

```
Public Sub Moving_Methods()
    Dim CurDB as database
    Dim PayeeTB As Recordset

    Set CurDB = CurrentDb
    Set PayeeTB = CurDB.OpenRecordset("Payees")
      If Not PayeeTB.EOF Then
        With PayeeTB
            .MoveFirst
            MsgBox "Payee is " & !Payees, vbInformation
            .MoveNext
            If Not .EOF Then
                MsgBox "Payee is " & !Payees, vbInformation
            End If
            .MovePrevious
            MsgBox "Payee is " & !Payees, vbInformation
            .MoveLast
            MsgBox "Payee is " & !Payees, vbInformation
        End With
      End If
      PayeeTB.Close
      Set PayeeTB = Nothing
    Exit Sub
End Sub
```

The Moving_Methods procedure uses the MoveFirst, MoveNext, MovePrevious, and MoveLast methods to move around in a recordset that contains multiple records. This example is a DAO procedure, but the methods work the same way for both DAO and ADO. Notice that after the MoveNext statement, the code checks the status of the EOF property. When the EOF property is true, an error will occur if you try to access data from the recordset or attempt to move forward in the recordset.

Before moving to another record in the recordset, always be sure to issue the Update **command if the current record has any pending changes.**

Deleting a Record

You can use ADO and DAO to delete a record in a table. Both ADO and DAO use the Delete method to delete a record. Listing 10-5 shows the ADO procedure for deleting a bank account.

Listing 10-5
Using ADO to delete a record

```
Public Sub Delete_Click()
 On Error GoTo Delete_Err
 Dim CurConn As New ADODB.Connection
 Dim BankTB As New ADODB.RecordSet, Response As Integer

 Response = MsgBox("Are you sure you want to delete this Bank" & _
Account?", vbQuestion + vbYesNo)
 If Response = vbYes Then
    CurConn.Open CurrentProject.Connection
    BankTB.Open "SELECT * FROM BankAccounts WHERE " & _
BankAccountNumber = """" & _ Me!BankAccountNumber _
              & """", CurConn, , , adCmdText
    If Not BankTB.EOF Then
       With BankTB
          .Delete
       End With
    End If
    BankTB.Close
    Set BankTB = Nothing
```

```
   CurConn.Close
     Set CurConn = Nothing
  End If
  Exit Sub

Delete_Err:
     MsgBox ("Error is " & Err.Description)
  Exit Sub
End Sub
```

When you are writing SQL statements, you must use two sets of double quotation marks to represent a single set of double quotation marks. For example, "...WHERE [LastName] = """ & CustName & """"

Listing 10-6 shows the same delete bank account procedure using DAO.

Listing 10-6
Using DAO to delete a record

```
Public Sub Delete_Click()
On Error GoTo Delete_Err
 Dim CurDB as Database
 Dim BankTB As RecordSet, Response As Integer
 Dim SQLStmt as String

 Response = MsgBox("Are you sure you want to delete this Bank" & _
    Account?", vbQuestion + vbYesNo)
 If Response = vbYes Then
    Set CurDB = CurrentDb
    SQLStmt = "SELECT * FROM BankAccounts WHERE " & _
            BankAccountNumber = """ & Me!BankAccountNumber _
            & """"
    Set BankTB = CurDB.OpenRecordset(SQLStmt)
    If Not BankTB.EOF Then
       With BankTB
          .Delete
       End With
    End If
    BankTB.Close
```

Continued

isting 10-6 *Continued*

```
    Set BankTB = Nothing
  End If
  Exit Sub

Delete_Err:
    MsgBox ("Error is " & Err.Description)
  Exit Sub
End Sub
```

When you use the Delete method, you do not precede it with the Edit method or follow it with the Update method. Once the Delete method executes, the record is permanently deleted from the recordset.

Done!

When you delete a record, the record remains the current record in the record-set. However, if you try to retrieve any data from the record, an error will occur. Once you move to another record, you cannot move back to the deleted record.

REVIEW

The DAO and ADO command sets provide powerful capabilities for building Access applications. While these concepts may represent some of the more challenging topics presented in this book, you will use them in just about every application you develop. This session included the following topics:

- The AddNew method adds a new record to a recordset.
- The Update method saves pending changes to a recordset.
- With DAO, you must issue the Update method before moving to another record to avoid losing any pending changes.
- With ADO, the Update method is optional but highly recommended.
- The Open method includes parameters for opening an updateable recordset.
- With pessimistic record locking, the record is locked as soon as you edit it.
- With optimistic record locking, the record is not locked until you update it.
- Page-level locking can lock multiple records, while record-level locking locks an individual record.
- You can use error-handling routines to resolve locking conflicts.
- The Delete method deletes a record from a recordset.

QUIZ YOURSELF

1. What method is used to save the changes to a recordset? (See "Completing the new record.")

2. When editing a record, what is the major difference between using ADO and DAO? (See "Updating a Record.")

3. Name the two ADO properties that determine if a recordset is updateable. (See "Making a recordset updateable.")

4. Which locking scheme locks the record as soon as you edit it? (See "Making a recordset updateable.")

5. What is the default DAO recordset type? (See "Creating updateable DAO recordsets.")

6. Name four methods for moving through the records in a recordset. (See "Moving between recordset records.")

7. How is the Delete method different from the methods used to add or edit a record? (See "Deleting a Record.")

PART

II

Saturday Morning

1. Define the term *logical construct*.
2. What are some of the classes of logical constructs?
3. What is a nested statement?
4. What is the difference between `Do While` and `Do Until`?
5. True or false: The procedure declaration `Public IsWeekday()` does not have any arguments.
6. What kind of procedures return a value?
7. Which of the following is true: Using the `Option Explicit` statement in a module
   a. slows down code execution.
   b. automatically declares the procedure's variables.
   c. runs the procedure's error processing statements when an application error occurs.
   d. speeds up code execution.
8. A subprocedure cannot be called from which of the following objects?
   a. Form
   b. Report
   c. Query
   d. Module

9. Which function is a built-in Access function that formats the year, month, and day parameters into an acceptable date format?

10. Which event is typically used to run the code for a command button?

   a. OnOpen

   b. OnClick

   c. OnActivate

   d. OnLostfocus

11. True or false: There is a built-in Calendar Control within Microsoft Access.

12. Which one of the following is the command for opening a form?

   a. DoCmd.OpenForm

   b. Call Form

   c. DoCmd.RunForm

   d. Run Form

13. Which of the following is not performed by the SELECT command?

   a. Retrieve specific fields or all fields.

   b. Retrieve the fields from one or more tables.

   c. Change the values in a group of rows in a table.

   d. Sort the rows by a specific field or fields.

14. True or false: The Update statement returns a group of records.

15. In DAO and ADO, a _____ is a special object variable that you use to refer to the records in a table.

16. Which of the following is not an attribute of ADO?

   a. It's optimized for working with Jet databases.

   b. It executes faster.

   c. It uses less memory.

   d. It includes new features specifically designed for client/server and Web-based applications.

17. True or false: When making changes to a DAO recordset, the Update statement is unnecessary.

18. Locking a record as soon as an edit occurs is called _____.

19. Which one of the following ADO lock types does not allow changes to the recordset?

    a. adLockReadOnly

    b. adLockOptimistic

    c. adLockPessimistic

    d. adLockBatchOptimistic

20. If you do not specify a type for a DAO recordset, which default type is automatically applied?

    a. dbOpenReadOnly

    b. dbOpenStatic

    c. dbOpenDynaset

    d. dbOpenForwardOnly

P A R T

III

Saturday Afternoon

Navigating an Application Using Switchboards, Custom Menus, and Keyboard Events

Session Checklist

✔ Creating an application switchboard

✔ Adding functionality to the switchboard

✔ Adding custom menus to your application

✔ Using keyboard events

**30 Min.
To Go**

Every application should provide an easy way for users to navigate to other components of the application. One way this can be done is to create a user interface that provides access to other forms or functions within the application. These types of interfaces are normally called switchboards. A *switchboard* is actually a type of menu system. One type of switchboard is a form-based switchboard, which consists of a set of buttons that allow users to access other forms and functions in the application.

Another method for navigating an application is through the use of a customized menu system. Similar to the Microsoft Access menu, you can create your own custom menu bar to provide access to components of your application.

Creating a switchboard is fairly easy. You can create your own custom switchboard or use the Access Switchboard Manager to quickly create a professional-looking application interface.

In this session, you will learn how to create a basic application switchboard and add navigation links to the switchboard. You will also learn how to create your own menu system. In addition, you will see how you can add keyboard events to help users navigate through the switchboard or menu system without using a mouse.

Creating a Switchboard with Switchboard Manager

Switchboard Manager is an add-in included with Access 2000 that guides you through the process of building an application switchboard. It is useful if you want to quickly create a basic switchboard that you don't intend to modify extensively.

The form named Switchboard in the Check Writer application is an example of a simple switchboard created with the Switchboard Manager. You can create your own switchboard by following these steps.

1. Start Switchboard Manager by selecting Tools ⇨ Database Utilities ⇨ Switchboard Manager from the Access menu. The Switchboard Manager dialog is displayed as shown in Figure 11-1. You can create a single switchboard or multiple switchboards for your application and add any number of buttons to each form to control navigation through your application.

 Before opening the Switchboard Manager, Access will search your database for a valid switchboard. If no switchboard is found, a message box will be displayed providing you with the option to have Access create one for you.

2. Press the New button to create a new switchboard. You can edit an existing switchboard by selecting the switchboard from the Switchboard Pages area and pressing the Edit button.

Adding Items to the Switchboard

Once you've created a switchboard, you will want to add items to it so users can easily access various parts of your application. Each item you add will be displayed on the switchboard as a button with text that identifies its purpose. Selecting a button will perform a specific action, such as opening a form or executing a macro. Follow these steps to add items to a switchboard.

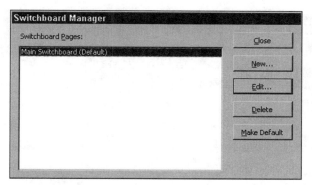

Figure 11-1
Switchboard Manager

1. Press the Edit button to add new items to the switchboard. The Edit Switchboard Item dialog is displayed as shown in Figure 11-2. This dialog allows you to select the text to appear on each button as well as the command to be performed when the button is pressed.

2. Enter the text to appear on the switchboard in the Text box. The text you enter should be descriptive of the function that will be performed when the user selects this item from the switchboard.

3. Enter the command to be performed in the Command box. Eight commands are available, including the ability to open forms, run macros or modules, and close the application.

4. Some commands require additional selections. Depending on the command selected, a third box may be displayed under the Command box. Select an item from this box, if necessary. For example, as shown in Figure 11-2, a new item named Write Checks is being added to the main switchboard. This item uses the "Open Form in Add Mode" command to open a form in Add mode. When this command is selected, the Form box is displayed under the Command box. This box contains a list of forms found in the current database. Select the form you want to open from the list provided.

5. Press OK when you are finished to have the new item added to the switchboard. Repeat these steps to add additional items to the switchboard.

6. You can test your switchboard by opening the switchboard form from the Forms tab in the database container.

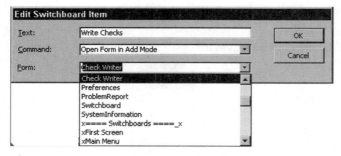

Figure 11-2
Adding buttons

Once you create a switchboard, Microsoft Access automatically creates a Switchboard Items table that describes what the buttons on the form do. If you want to make a switchboard automatically open when you open the database, select the switchboard name in the Switchboard Manager dialog box, and then click Make Default.

An example of a finished switchboard is shown in Figure 11-3.

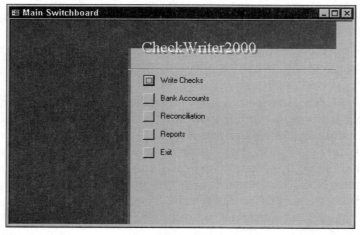

Figure 11-3
A sample switchboard

When you create a switchboard with the Switchboard Manager, Access adds quite a bit of code to the switchboard, referencing items in the Switchboard Items table as well as objects on the form. If you make design changes to the Switchboard, such as deleting or renaming objects on the form, the switchboard may no longer function properly.

If you expect to customize your switchboard by changing the interface, or adding, deleting or renaming objects on the form, it's better to create your own switchboard from scratch. Then, set it as the startup form, which is the first form displayed when a database is opened.

Creating a Custom Application Switchboard

An *application switchboard* is typically a form that allows a user to navigate to other components of the application. You can even create a main switchboard that will bring the user to additional switchboards, such as a data entry switchboard, a reports switchboard, or a utility switchboard. A switchboard can contain several different types of objects, including labels, text boxes, tabs, list boxes, buttons, or ActiveX controls. Controls you add to a switchboard can perform several types of functions, including the following:

- Opening a form
- Printing a report
- Running a query
- Running a macro, function, or subroutine

Figure 11-4 shows the application switchboard for the Check Writer application, named xMain Menu. This form is displayed automatically when the user starts the application. It consists of six buttons that, when pressed, open other forms contained within the application. One of the buttons is also used to close the application. Other fields on the form are used to display a product logo, application title, and company name.

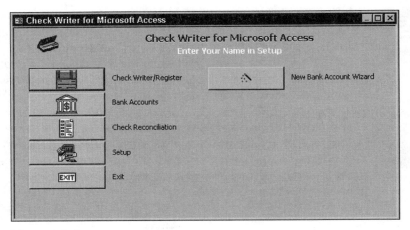

Figure 11-4
The Check Writer application switchboard

Creating a simple custom switchboard is easy.

1. Create a new form and work in the design view of the form.

2. Set the form so it doesn't show any scroll bars or record selectors.

3. Create the title and subtitle by adding text and label fields to the form. You can manually enter titles and other information to be displayed on the form or you can set the record source to point to a table or query that contains the information you want to use. For example, with the xMain Menu switchboard, the record source is set to the Preferences table. This allows you to display the company name entered in the Preferences table in the Company Name field on the switchboard form.

4. Add a company logo or other graphics, as desired, by inserting a graphic or unbound object frame onto the form. In the Check Writer switchboard, the graphic located in the upper left corner of the form also serves as a link to display the About box. You accomplish this by adding the code shown below DoCmd.OpenForm "About" to the graphic's OnClick event.

   ```
   DoCmd.Openform "About"
   ```

5. Next, you add command buttons for each major function of the application to which you want to give users access. Set these up in some organized manner so it's easy for users to locate and navigate items on the form.

Each command button should contain code to execute a specific function. For example, the New Bank Account Wizard performs the following when its button is pressed:

```
Private Sub Account_Wizard_Click()
    DoCmd.OpenForm "AddAccountWizard"
End Sub
```

This opens the AddAccountWizard form when the button is pressed. This is an example of a simple button. Other buttons may contain more advanced functions such as error checking and lookup functions. The OnClick event of the Checkwriter/ Register button contains more advanced functions. See listing 11-1.

Listing 11-1
The OnClick event for the Check Writer/Register button

```
Private Sub Check_Writer_Click()
On Error GoTo Check_Writer_Click_Err
    Dim BA As String
    Dim curconn As ADODB.Connection
    Dim BankTB As New ADODB.RecordSet, CheckTB As New ADODB.RecordSet
    Dim Response As Integer

    If IsNull(DLookup("[DefaultBankAccountNumber]", "Preferences")) Or _
        DLookup("[DefaultBankAccountNumber]", "Preferences") = "" Then
        Response = MsgBox("You Must Enter a Default Bank Account" & vbCrLf & "in
        the User Choices Form", 16, _"Missing Default Bank Account")
        Exit Sub
    Else
        BA = DLookup("[DefaultBankAccountNumber]", "Preferences")
        Set curconn = CurrentProject.Connection
        Set BankTB = New ADODB.RecordSet
        BankTB.Open "SELECT [BankAccountNumber] FROM [BankAccounts] WHERE _
            [BankAccountNumber] = '" & BA & "'", curconn, adOpenForwardOnly
        If BankTB.EOF Then
        Response = MsgBox("You Must Select a Valid Default Bank Account" & _
        vbCrLf & "           in the User Choices Form", 16, _"Invalid Default Bank
        Account")
            BankTB.Close
            Set BankTB = Nothing
            Exit Sub
        End If
        BankTB.Close
        Set BankTB = Nothing
```

Continued

Listing 11-1 *Continued*

```
    End If
    DoCmd.OpenForm "Check Writer"
Check_Writer_Click_Err:
MsgBox "Error is " & Err.Description & " in Check Register button in Main
Menu.", vbCritical, "System Error"

Exit Sub
```

Adding intelligence to switchboard buttons

While you can program buttons to simply open a form or perform a function, you can also create buttons with more intelligence behind them. This includes adding error handling, opening recordsets, or performing other actions before a form is opened. You can learn more about using error handling in Session 16.

Let's look at Listing 11-1 again. The code uses error trapping to provide the user with a specified error message if a problem occurs running any portion of the code. It's always a good idea to add error trapping and error checking to your application. This helps users identify a problem when it occurs, and it helps you — as the application developer — to troubleshoot and resolve the error.

Besides adding some error trapping, the code checks the DefaultBankAccountNumber field in the Preferences table to make sure a default account number has been entered. If the field is Null, a message is displayed alerting the user to enter a default bank account. This is performed in the following portion of code:

```
If IsNull(DLookup("[DefaultBankAccountNumber]", "Preferences")) Or
DLookup("[DefaultBankAccountNumber]", "Preferences") = "" Then
    MsgBox "You Must Enter a Default Bank Account" & vbCrLf & _
    "        in the User Choices Form", vbCritical, _
    "Missing Default Bank Account"
Exit Sub
```

If a default bank account number is found, the number is stored as a string using the code:

```
BA = DLookup("[DefaultBankAccountNumber]", "Preferences").
```

A recordset is created using ADO, and a SQL SELECT statement is run to check that the number in the Preferences table matches a number in the Bank Accounts table. The following code accomplishes this task:

```
        Set curconn = CurrentProject.Connection
        Set BankTB = New ADODB.RecordSet
        BankTB.Open "SELECT [BankAccountNumber] FROM [BankAccounts] WHERE
[BankAccountNumber] = '" & BA & "'", curconn, adOpenForwardOnly
```

If the number is not found, a message is displayed to the user. If the number does match, the Check Register form is opened.

**20 Min.
To Go**

Multilevel switchboards

You can design a switchboard to have a single level or multiple levels. When a switchboard has more than one level, this means that selecting a button or control on the switchboard will bring up another set of controls. This is similar to having a drop-down menu display another submenu. The design of a switchboard with multiple levels can get very involved from both a programmer's standpoint and also from a user-interface standpoint. Working with multilevel switchboards is beyond the scope of this book, since they use more advanced programming techniques than we're going to get into, but let's examine a multilevel switchboard so you can see what they look like.

Figure 11-5 is an example of a multilevel switchboard. This is a sample switchboard found in the EZ Application Builder demo found on the CD that accompanies this book. You can view the form named eza_SwitchboardDeluxe in the EZ Application Builder demo to test the functionality of this form.

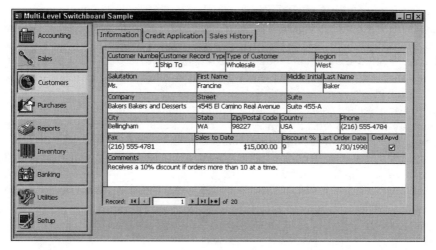

Figure 11-5
A multilevel switchboard

The switchboard consists of two sets of tab controls. The first tab control is located on the left side of the form and contains a column of buttons that are used to navigate through the switchboard. Each time the user selects a button in the tab control area on the left side of the form, the main area of the form changes.

The main area of the form contains the second tab control. Notice there are three tabs located at the top of the form. Each of these tabs contains a subform that is displayed when a tab is selected.

You set navigation links to the main functions in your application, such as to Accounting or Sales functions, in the left tab control area. Then, display the forms available within each function in the main tab control area. For example, as shown in Figure 11-5, selecting the Customers function from the left tab control displays subforms that contain a customer's general Information, Credit Application, or Sales History in the main tab control area. You can even add a third level by placing a tab control within each of the subforms in the main tab control area to open other forms or even other switchboards.

Since creating a multilevel switchboard can be complex, you may want a head start. The EZ Application Builder by Database Creations, Inc., is a product that lets you select from one of several predefined, fully functioning application switchboards. You can then customize them to work with your application's components.

Building a Custom Menu

Another way to add navigation to your application is to build a customized menu bar. You can add commands to the menu that are appropriate for your application. You can even use a custom menu bar with a switchboard to provide users with an alternate method for selecting items normally displayed on a switchboard.

Figure 11-6 shows the Check Writer switchboard with a custom drop-down menu bar attached. Notice that this menu bar replaces the default menu bar normally displayed with a form. Each of the five choices on the menu bar (File, Forms, Reports, Utilities, and Help) has a drop-down menu attached. You can view this form by opening the form named xSwitchboard with Menu Bar from the Check Writer sample application included with this book.

Adding a custom menu to a form is fairly easy. There are two ways to create custom menus in Access 2000:

- Use the Access 2000 CommandBar object
- Use macros

Using macros was the only way to create menus in Access 2.0 and Access 95.

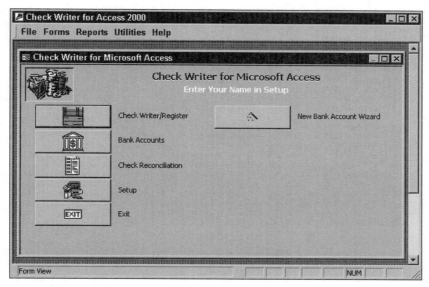

Figure 11-6
A switchboard with a custom menu bar

 If you have menus previously created in Access 97, you do not need to convert them to Access 2000. Access 97 menus can be used as is in Access 2000.

Creating custom menu bars

You can create the custom menu bar shown in Figure 11-6 by first creating the top-level menu consisting of five elements: File, Forms, Reports, Utilities, and Help.

1. You create the top-level menu by selecting View, Toolbars, Customize, etc. from the Access menu. The Customize dialog box is then displayed, as shown in Figure 11-7.

   This dialog box contains three tabs:

   - **Toolbars:** Displays all of the toolbars, including built-in toolbars and custom toolbars. You can use this tab to create new toolbars or edit existing bars.

Figure 11-7
The Customize menu bar dialog box

- **Commands:** Lists commands sorted by category that you can add to your menu and toolbars.

- **Options:** Provides various options for personalizing menu bars and toolbars.

2. To create a new menu bar, select New from the Toolbars tab of the Customize dialog box. A dialog box appears asking you to provide a name for the custom menubar. In this example, the custom menu bar is named CheckWriter.

   Once created, a small, gray rectangle appears in the center of the screen. This represents the new menu bar you have created. The name of the new menu bar also appears at the bottom of the Customize menu list.

3. Before you begin adding functions or commands to this bar, you first need to decide which type of menu bar you want to create. To do this, select the menu bar you created from the Toolbars tab of the Customize dialog box and click the Properties button. The Properties dialog box is displayed, as shown in Figure 11-8.

   Three types of bars are available for you to choose:

   - **Menu Bar:** Used for drop-down menus of commands containing text and optionally, pictures

   - **Toolbar:** Used for button bars only of pictures

   - **Popup:** Used either for drop-down menu lists or shortcut menus; can contain pictures and text

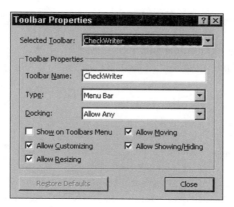

Figure 11-8
The Toolbar Properties dialog box

4. For this example, you want to create a menu, so choose the Menu Bar option. Several other options are available when you select this option. Select the options you want to apply to your menu. If you do not want the user to have the option of customizing your menu or other options, you may want to clear some of these options. Click on the Close button when finished.

Adding a submenu to a custom menu bar

Most menu commands are placed on submenus. It is very rare for a top-level menu to do anything but display a submenu. The submenu contains the actual menu item that, when clicked, runs the desired action, such as opening a form or printing a report.

To create a submenu:

1. Display the Customize dialog box shown in Figure 11-7. You can do this by right-clicking the top-level menu bar you created and selecting Customize from the shortcut menu.

2. Click the Commands tab and select the New Menu choice from the bottom of the Categories list box.

3. Select the New Menu item in the Commands area, and then drag and drop it from the Customize dialog box to your new menu bar. The text *New Menu* appears on the menu bar.

4. Click it again, and a rectangle appears around the name. This is the submenu. Figure 11-9 shows the custom menu bar with the new submenu. You can change the name of the new submenu by right-clicking it and entering a name in the Name area.

Figure 11-9
The Main Menu Bar with a submenu

Repeat this process for each submenu you want to add to your menu bar. Once you have finished adding submenus, you can add commands to the submenus.

 After you add submenus to a menu bar, you cannot change it to a toolbar or pop-up menu.

Adding commands to a submenu

You can add commands to a custom menu bar by dragging pre-existing commands to the menu bar or by adding any of your tables, queries, forms, reports, or macros to the menu bar. You can also add your own ActiveX controls to a menu bar. If you add your own items, you may need to add functionality behind them. Using a pre-existing command completes all the necessary actions and options for you. However, unless you are planning to use an action found on one of the Access 2000 menus, you should create your own menus by first creating a new command bar and making it a menu bar, as discussed in the previous section.

 With the Customize dialog box open, you can add commands from other menus by simply clicking the menu on the menu bar or toolbar, or click the shortcut menu that contains the command you want to copy or move. Use the Ctrl key when selecting a command to copy the command.

 If you move or copy a command to a built-in menu (for example, the Edit menu), the command appears on that menu in all views that have that menu.

After you have defined the blank submenus on the menu bar, you can drag controls to them. For example, you might want to display the About dialog box in your Help submenu. To do this, follow these steps:

1. Select Commands from the View, Toolbars, Customize dialog box.

2. Select All Forms from the Categories list.

3. Select About from the Commands list and drag it over the Help submenu. Notice that a gray box appears below the Help submenu text. Drop the item in this area to have it displayed under the Help submenu.

 If you simply drop the item on the menu bar, it will appear as a command on the main menu bar. You must place the item in the gray box beneath a submenu if you want the item to be accessible from the submenu.

When the user selects About from the Help menu, Access opens the About form. Access automatically opens the form because any time you add an existing object to a submenu, Access assumes the object should be opened and adds the appropriate open action to the command. If you want to perform some other action, you will need to change the On Action property in the Properties dialog for the selected item. This is covered in further detail below.

Setting properties for menu items and commands

Each command or item you add to a submenu has its own shortcut menu that allows you to further customize the item. You can display the shortcut menu by right-clicking the item you want to modify. Several options are available such as the ability to delete the command, add graphics to the command, add a hyperlink, or edit properties for the command. These options provide you with the flexibility to control how your menu items behave.

Once you have added an item to your menu, follow these steps to display the properties dialog and add a graphic to the menu item.

1. Make sure the Customize dialog is displayed. If it is not, right click on the menu bar and select Customize... from the shortcut menu. You can only make changes to menu bar items if this dialog is displayed.

2. Right-click the item you want to modify to display the shortcut menu.

3. To add a graphic to appear next to the item, select the Change Button Image option, as shown in Figure 11-10.

4. Select a graphic from the ones displayed.

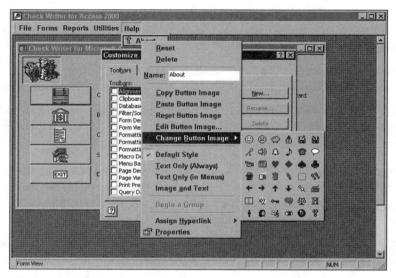

Figure 11-10
Adding a graphic to a submenu item

You can create your own image and add it to a command by copying the image to the clipboard and selecting the Paste Button Image option from the shortcut menu.

If you select the Begin a Group check box, Access places a horizontal separator line before the menu item.

You can further customize each item by changing its properties. The Properties form for a command or menu item is displayed when you click the Properties button on the shortcut menu for a menu item, as shown in Figure 11-10. The Properties dialog box is displayed in Figure 11-11.

Changing the caption changes the text displayed on the menu. In Figure 11-11, notice that an ampersand (&) is added in front of the word *About*. This defines the hot key for this command and allows the user to press the letter *A* after selecting the Help menu to display the About form.

To define a hot key for the menu item, add an ampersand in front of the hot-key letter you want to use.

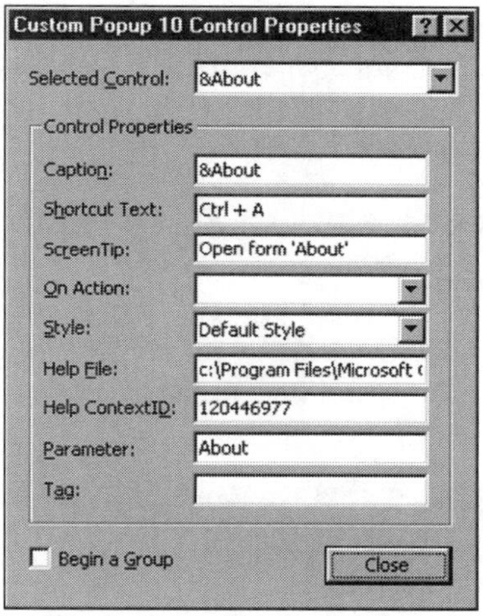

Tip

Figure 11-11
Customizing properties for a control

If you set up an AutoKeys macro list, you can specify the action behind the shortcut text. Notice the Ctrl + A in the Shortcut Text box. In an autoexec macro, this key combination would be set to open the About form. AutoKeys are explained in more detail later in this session.

If you assign a set of actions to a key combination that is already being used by Access (for example, Ctrl + C is the key combination for Copy), the actions you assign this key combination replace the Access key assignment.

Note

You can also define ToolTip text for the control by entering text in the ToolTip area.

The most important option in the Properties dialog box is normally the On Action option. This allows you to specify a VBA function or macro that should run when the menu item is selected. If you selected a predefined menu item, this may already be completed for you.

The other options let you choose the Help File name and entry point if you click Help while selecting the menu. The Parameter entry is used to specify optional parameters when calling a VBA function.

Attaching the menu bar to a form

**10 Min.
To Go**

After you have completed your custom menu bar, you can attach the menu bar to a form. To do this:

1. Open the form in Design view.

2. Display the Property sheet for the form by selecting the Properties icon from the tool bar or by selecting View, Properties.

3. As shown in Figure 11-12, you select the Menu Bar property and choose a menu bar from the list. When you display the form in Form view, notice that the only menu bar that displays is the custom menu bar.

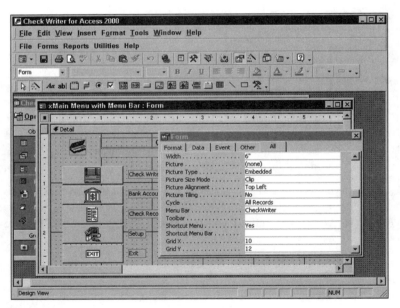

Figure 11-12
Choosing a menu bar to display with a form

You can specify a menu bar to be displayed with a form using VBA code behind the form. The code shown below displays the CheckWriter menu bar each time the Preferences form is opened.

Forms!Preferences.MenuBar = "CheckWriter"

To display the built-in menu bar for a form or the application global menu bar, you set the MenuBar **property to a zero-length string (" "):**

Forms!Preferences.MenuBar = ""

You can use the StartupMenuBar property to specify a custom menu bar to use as the global menu bar for your application. The StartupMenuBar property is a string expression that identifies the name of a custom menu bar in the current database.

The easiest way to set this property is by using the Menu Bar option in the Startup dialog box, as shown in Figure 11-13. You display this dialog box by selecting the Startup option from the Tools menu.

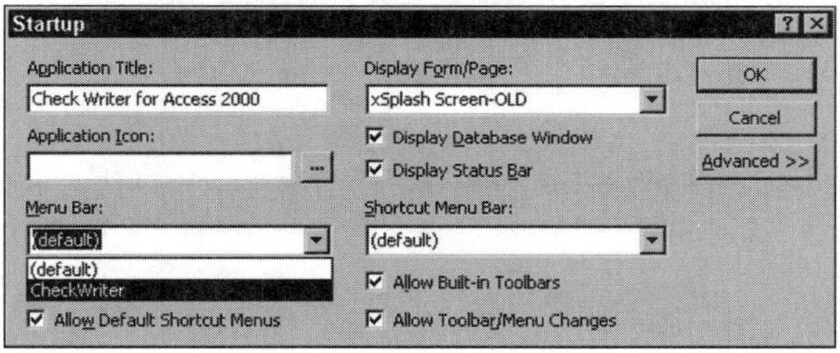

Figure 11-13
Setting a custom menu bar as the global menu bar

You can also set the StartupMenuBar property, as well as other startup properties, by using code. If you use your own custom properties, you need to be sure the property you want to set exists for the Database object before you set it. If it does not exist, you will need to add it.

There are two ways you can set startup properties using code:

- Create a macro named AutoExec and use the RunCode action to execute a VBA procedure that sets the properties. An AutoExec macro is automatically executed after a database is loaded.

- Add code to the Open event of a splash screen or other startup form in your database to set the startup properties. This method is the preferable method over using a macro since most database applications use some type of startup form. However, it is much easier to just use the Startup Option if the property you want to set is displayed here.

Using Keyboard Events

Since forms are a core part of most applications, it is important to understand the different form and control events that are available to you. This will help you to learn which events control certain tasks, allowing you to control the behavior of your forms.

Microsoft Access traps for about 30 form events, each of which has a specific purpose. Some of these events include keyboard events, which are the focus of this section. Trapping for these types of events are often used to control what action occurs when a user presses a specific key combination. These are helpful when you are building applications where the user is not solely relying on using a mouse, for example, in a point of sale application.

You can use three types of key events within your application:

KeyDown	Occurs when the user presses a key or key combination
KeyUp	Occurs when the user releases a key or key combination
KeyPress	Occurs when the user presses and releases a key or key combination

These key events apply only to forms and controls on forms, not controls on reports.

Keyboard characters for key events are passed as ASCII. You can determine the ASCII equivalent for each key by viewing the Character Set listing in Microsoft Access VBA Help.

Using KeyUp and KeyDown events

You use the KeyDown and KeyUp events to set actions when a key or key combination is pressed or released. These events use the following syntax. Notice two arguments are used with this event: KeyCode and Shift.

```
Sub controlname_KeyDown(KeyCode As Integer, ByVal Shift As Integer)
```

As an example, the xMain Menu form in the Check Writer sample application contains the following KeyDown event code:

```
Private Sub Form_KeyDown(KeyCode As Integer, Shift As Integer)
If KeyCode = vbKeyF6 Then   'F6 Key
  MsgBox "This is an example of a KeyDown event"
End If
KeyCode = 0
End Sub
```

When the user presses the F6 key, designated by the KeyCode vbKeyF6, a message box is displayed. The KeyCode is then set to 0. There is a separate KeyCode constant for each key on the keyboard. A list of these keys is found in Microsoft Access VBA Help.

The previous code will display the message box if the user presses F6, Ctrl + F6, Shift + F6, or Alt + F6. Suppose you want the message box to display only if the user presses the Ctrl + F6 key combination. In this case, you would need to revise the KeyDown event to the following:

```
Private Sub Form_KeyDown(KeyCode As Integer, Shift As Integer)
If KeyCode = vbKeyF6 And Shift=acCtrlMask Then   'Ctrl F6 Key
  MsgBox "This is an example of a KeyDown event"
End If
KeyCode = 0
End Sub
```

The Shift argument checks for the state of the Ctrl, Shift, and Alt keys at the time of the event. By including a check for this, you can determine the key combination used and the action to take. The following constants are used for each of these special keys:

acCtrlMask	Constant for the Ctrl key
acShiftMask	Constant for the Shift key
acAltMask	Constant for the Alt key

Part III—Saturday Afternoon
Session 11

Each Shift argument is assigned a separate value. For example, the value for Ctrl is 2, while the value for Ctrl + Alt is 6. You can view the Access Help for a list of values for each special key type used in the Shift argument.

You can use the arguments for the KeyDown, KeyPress, **and** KeyUp **events, in conjunction with the arguments for the** MouseDown, MouseUp, **and** MouseMove **events to make your application work smoothly for both keyboard and mouse users.**

In some cases, you may want to control what does not happen when the user presses a specific key or key combination. For example, in Microsoft Access, whenever the F11 key is pressed, the database container is displayed. You can stop your users from being able to access the database container by adding the following code behind a form's KeyDown event.

```
Private Sub Form_KeyDown(KeyCode As Integer, Shift As Integer)
If KeyCode = F11 Then  'F11 Key
KeyCode = 0
End If

End Sub
```

This automatically sets the KeyCode to 0 when the F11 key is pressed, so the F11 key event, in essence, becomes disabled.

Using the KeyPress event

The KeyPress event occurs when the user presses and releases a key or key combination that corresponds to an ANSI code while a form or control has the focus. The event can involve only printable characters, such as the Ctrl key combined with a character from the standard alphabet or a special character, and the Enter or Backspace key. The syntax of this event is the following:

```
Private Sub Form_KeyPress(KeyAscii As Integer)
```

Unlike the KeyUp and KeyDown events, the KeyPress event does not indicate the physical state of the keyboard. Instead, it indicates the ANSI characters that correspond to the key or key combination that is pressed. Because it handles only ANSI keys, you can use the Chr and Asc functions to convert the KeyAscii argument between an ASCII character and the equivalent ANSI character. For example:

```
fkey=Chr(KeyAscii)
KeyAscii=Asc(fkey)
```

If you want to use a keyboard event for a nonprinting character, such as the function keys or navigation keys, you should use the KeyDown or KeyUp **event.**

KeyPress **interprets the uppercase and lowercase of each character as separate key codes and, therefore, as two separate characters.**

If you hold down a key, the KeyPress **event occurs repeatedly.**

Understanding the KeyPreview property

You can use the KeyPreview property to create a keyboard-handling procedure for a form. This allows you to specify whether form-level keyboard events are invoked before a control's keyboard events. The KeyPreview property is set to False (No) by default. With this setting, only the active control will receive keyboard events. If the KeyPreview property is set to True (Yes), as shown in Figure 11-14, the form will receive the keyboard event first, and then the active control will receive the keyboard event.

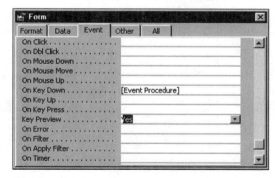

Figure 11-14
Setting the KeyPreview property

Part III—Saturday Afternoon
Session 11

Using AutoKeys

You can assign an action to a specific key or key combination using an AutoKeys macro group. When the user presses the key or key combination, Access performs the action. AutoKeys are useful if you want to perform an action behind shortcut keys you have used in custom menu bars or toolbars. Selecting the shortcut key on the bar will automatically perform a specific action.

 If you assign an action to a key combination that Access is already using, the action you assign to the key combination will replace the Access key assignment.

You can create an AutoKeys macro by performing the following steps:

1. Create a new macro.
2. In the Macro Name column, type the key or key combination to which you want to assign an action or set of actions.
3. Add the action(s) you want the key or key combination to carry out.
4. Save the macro group with the name *AutoKeys*.

The new key assignments are in effect as soon as you save the macro group and will be available each time you open the database. You can select one of several types of key assignments for the Macro Name field. Table 11-1 lists the types of key assignments you can use.

Table 11-1
Key Assignments for Macros

Key Code	Key Assignment
^B or ^3	Ctrl + any letter or number key
{F3}	Any function key
^{F3}	Ctrl + any function key
+{F3}	Shift + any function key
{INSERT}	Ins
+{INSERT}	Ctrl + Ins
{DELETE} OR {DEL}	Del

Key Code	Key Assignment
^{DELETE} OR {DEL}	Ctrl + Del
+{DELETE} OR {DEL}	Shift + Del

Figure 11-15 shows the properties for a submenu item located on a custom menu bar. Notice that a shortcut has been set up for this item. When the user presses Ctrl + A, you want the About form to open.

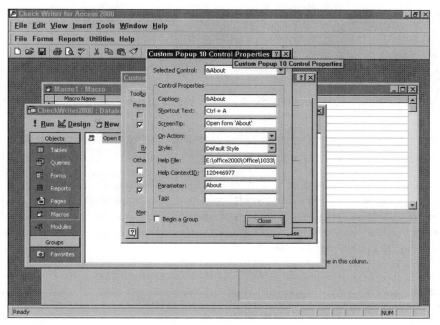

Figure 11-15
A shortcut key for a submenu item

Done!

If you haven't set up an AutoKeys macro with this key combination defined, nothing will happen when the user presses the key combination. To make it work, add the following macro name and action to the AutoKeys macro as shown in Figure 11-16.

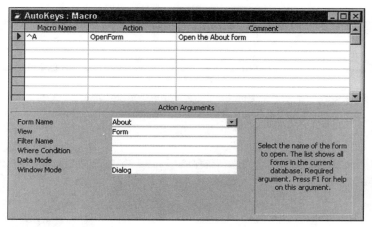

Figure 11-16

Adding a macro name to the AutoKeys macro group

REVIEW

In this session, you learned it is important to provide users with a means for navigating through an application. You learned two ways to accomplish this — creating switchboards and creating custom menu bars. You also learned how to use keyboard events behind various forms in an application to control various actions, including the overall behavior of the form.

QUIZ YOURSELF

1. What are two ways to provide navigation for your application?
   (See "Creating a Switchboard with Switchboard Manager," "Creating a Custom Application Switchboard," and "Building a Custom Menu.")

2. What types of functions can be performed from switchboards?
   (See "Creating a Custom Application Switchboard" and "Adding intelligence to switchboard buttons.")

3. How can you create a custom menu bar? (See "Building a Custom Menu.")

4. How do you create and enable a shortcut key on a menu or submenu?
   (See "Setting properties for menu items and commands.")

5. How can you make a custom menu bar the global menu bar?
    (See "Attaching the menu bar to a form.")

6. What are the three types of keyboard events?
    (See "Using Keyboard Events.")

7. Why are AutoKeys macro groups used? (See "Using AutoKeys.")

Using Unbound Forms — True Client/Server Programming

Session Checklist

✔ Unbound forms

✔ Record locking and functionality of unbound forms

✔ ADO programming for unbound forms

✔ How to create a simple unbound form

**30 Min.
To Go**

This session will cover the use and programming associated with unbound forms. These types of forms require a significant amount of programming and provide a good foundation for learning how to connect to data sources programmatically as well as work with the properties and methods of an Access form.

What Are Unbound Forms?

Access makes it easy to create a form and bind it to a record source. Let's repeat that last sentence: Access makes it easy to create a form and bind it to a record source. Many Access features work behind the scenes to simplify form design and form use not only for the developer, but for the end user as well. With little training, a user can create a form bound to a table or query and have a completely functional form with the ability to add, edit, or delete records, including navigation between records. Access provides wizards with which the users can build the forms. It doesn't get much easier. But these are all bound forms. A *bound form* is a form tied directly to a record source providing a constant connection and open view of the underlying data. Bound forms are simple to build but not always the best approach when the application is running.

An *unbound form* is a form that does not have a constant connection and open view of the underlying data. It can behave like a bound form, but instead of a constant connection, it retrieves one record at a time programmatically. In other words, VBA code needs to be behind the form that controls the retrieval and saving of data. The code has to do a lot more besides that, which will be covered later in this session.

Why Use Unbound Forms?

There are several reasons to use unbound forms:

- You can use them to solve record-locking conflicts.
- They request the minimal amount of data, thereby improving performance.
- You can include a means to cancel the changes to a record in case the user changes his or her mind.
- You can include a means for the user to confirm saving a record.
- You can programmatically perform a record validation before the record is saved.
- All record changes are under the control of code rather than Access or the property setting of a bound form.
- They are required for transaction processing.
- They are necessary for client/server architecture.

With all these great reasons, why wouldn't you want to use unbound forms? First, a lot of code is required to duplicate the functionality of a bound form. You need to handle not only data retrieval and saving, but also navigation, error checking, data validation, etc. It is also difficult to provide continuous forms or a datasheet view, which a bound form can easily do.

Considerations for Using Unbound Forms

When you use unbound forms, you need to handle functions that are automatic with Access bound forms. This includes such things as record locking, and the functions that connect the form to a data source, handle reading and writing the data, searching for data, etc.

Record locking

Using an unbound form can limit the time a record is locked. For a bound form, the record is locked from the time the user first makes a change in the first fields to the time the record is saved. This could take a few seconds to several minutes. For unbound forms, the record is locked only for the split second it takes to update it. When a record is saved by the unbound form, a check should be made to see if the record was changed since it was first retrieved. This is necessary when the record was not locked when it was loaded onto the form.

 It may make sense to first design the form based on the bound record source so that controls relating to the fields can easily be added to the form. Then, after the form layout is designed, remove the record source and add the necessary code to make the form work.

Functionality

When using an unbound form, you need to create code to handle the following functions since you can't rely on Access to do this anymore:

- Connecting to the record source
- Selecting/finding a record or records from a record source
- Loading up the controls on the form with data
- Retrieving the record(s)
- Editing a record
- Saving a record
- Adding a new record
- Deleting a record
- Moving among multiple records to include going to the first record, last record, next record, and previous record
- Undoing changes made to the record before it is saved

These functions are the basic ones; in this session, you will use ADO to learn about them.

It is always good programming practice to make your code as modular and flexible as possible. Therefore, the code we'll create for the previous functions will be as generic as possible so you can use it over again. To do that, we'll put the general functions into a module rather than the class module associated with the form. This will allow the general functions to be shared by other unbound forms and not be repeated in each form. Code specific to a form should be located with the form. This also minimizes the code behind the form, which will make it faster to load.

Although you can create a generic form to use for different record sources, this task is beyond the scope of this session. To keep things simple, this session covers recordsets with only one key field.

Programming for Unbound Forms

You can find the code for this section in the module "Unbound Form Utilities" and the form "Bank Accounts Unbound" in the sample application.

The Unbound Form Functions

The module "Unbound Form Functions" contains several of the functions required to make an unbound form work. These include:

uf_NewRecord	Adds a new record
uf_SaveRecord	Saves the current data on the form to a new or existing record
uf_FindRecord	Finds a set of records meeting a criterion
uf_DisplayRecord	Retrieves and displays a selected record
uf_DeleteRecord	Deletes a record
uf_ClearForm	Clears all fields on the form contained in the record source
uf_SetEditedFlag	Is called by a field on the form when it is updated

Most of these functions will require a form parameter to be passed, which is the form that called the function and contains the data.

The Unbound Form references

To use the aforementioned functions, the unbound form must contain the following text- box controls loaded with the appropriate values to tell the functions which data to connect to and what the key field is. These controls will be subsequently referred to as the form's "X" controls.

```
xProvider              xRecordset
xDataSource            xKey
```

In Session 9 and 10 you learned about ActiveX Data Objects (ADO). These objects are used here to connect to the data sources. To simplify the code for this session, these functions are limited to a single key field. The key field(s) could be retrieved from an ActiveX Data Objects Extensions (ADOX) table definition, but we don't want to use ADOX here to provide for maximum flexibility since we may connect to a non-Jet database. The only reference needed is for the object ADODB, which is the standard object for the ActiveX Data Objects library.

In addition, the unbound form must contain the following check-box controls:

flagEdited	The default value of False, used to determine if user has changed any data.
flagFind	The default value of True, used to allow instant find when the form is opened. Used with the Find function to determine if search criteria was entered.

The controls on the form that are to relate to fields in the record source must be named with the same name as the fields. To handle default values on the form, we cannot use the default value property since the unbound controls will automatically display that value. Instead, we will put any default values in the control's Tag property, which is a property Access doesn't use.

We will also use the form's Filter property to store the criteria for the recordset. This can be set to determine the initial recordset or just left blank. If left blank initially, the form will open in a find mode.

Each function will be discussed in detail because they are an important part of understanding unbound forms and record handling with ADO. Some of the code will also be discussed in detail as necessary, but the discussion will not be repeated for the same code in other functions.

Adding a new record

To add a new record to the recordset as specified by the form's "X" controls, you must establish a connection to the recordset. The New Record function does this after it first checks to see if any data has been changed or entered on the form. (See Listing 12-1.) The form's control flagEdited is used for this.

The flag works similarly to the Access form's property `Dirty`. Whenever a value in a field on the form has changed, the flag is set to True. This is done by adding the function call `uf_SetEditedFlag()` to the `AfterUpdate` event property for all the controls on the form that are part of the recordset.

If data has been entered or changed, the New Record function will display a message asking the user whether he or she wants the record saved. If so, the `uf_SaveRecord` function is called first before a new record is added.

Adding a new record is a three-step process:

1. Clear the fields on the form, set them to their default value, and set focus to the first field.
2. Allow the user to enter the data.
3. Save the record.

Step 1 is accomplished by the remaining section of the New Record function. Control is then passed to the user. When the user presses a Save button, the record is saved using the `uf_SaveRecord` function.

Note that the `uf_NewRecord` function iterates through the controls on the form that are enabled and also has a corresponding field in the recordset. This prevents controls that don't contain data on the form from being cleared.

Listing 12-1
The New Record Function

```
Public Function uf_NewRecord(frm As Form)
'Adds a new record

Dim strConnection As String
Dim cnn As New ADODB.Connection
Dim rst As New ADODB.RecordSet
Dim fld As ADODB.Field
Dim ctl As Control
Dim vartemp As Variant

    On Error GoTo ErrorHandler

    'reset find flag if set
    frm.FlagFind = False

    'Check to see if data has been changed
    If frm.FlagEdited Then
```

```
        If MsgBox("Do you want to save your changes", _
            vbYesNo) = vbYes Then
            uf_SaveRecord frm
        Else
            frm.FlagEdited = False
        End If
End If


'Open connection
cnn.Open frm.Controls("xProvider") & _
    frm.Controls("xDataSource")

'Open recordset with no records
rst.Open "Select * From " & frm.Controls("xRecordset") & _
    " Where True;", cnn, adOpenStatic

'Iterate through controls on form that match fields in
'recordset
For Each ctl In frm

    'if error the field is not on the form
    On Error Resume Next
    Err = 0
    vartemp = rst.Fields(ctl.Name).Name
    If Err = 0 Then
        On Error GoTo ErrorHandler
        'if control enables then set default value from tag
        '   and set focus if tab index 0
        If ctl.Enabled Then
            If IsNull(ctl.Tag) Then
                ctl.Value = Null
            Else
                ctl.Value = ctl.Tag
            End If
            If ctl.TabIndex = 0 Then ctl.SetFocus
        End If
    End If
Next
```

Continued

Listing 12-1 *Continued*

```
GoTo Done

ErrorHandler:
    MsgBox Err.Description
Done:

End Function
```

After the user has pressed a Save button, the form's `On Click` event for that button should call the function `uf_SaveRecord`, passing it the name of the form containing the data. Listing 12-2 shows the code for this function.

The function first checks to see if the form has been edited. If not, the function simply exits. Otherwise, it opens a connection to the recordset without any records retrieved, simply to find out the type of field the key field is so a criteria string can be created. The criteria string is used to search the recordset for a record with the same key field. This is necessary so the function can determine whether to update an existing record or create a new record.

If it is a new record, the function will use the `AddNew` method and iterate through the controls on the form that match the fields in the recordset and create a record with the new data. If a record exists with the same key field, then the fields are copied to the recordset and the record is updated. The fields are also checked to see if the field is an Auto Increment type and whether it is enabled. If it is, the field value is not updated.

For simplicity, the example here does not deal with checking the existing record to see if another user has changed the record since it was last retrieved. This code should be added for a multi-user system.

After the record has been successfully saved, the user is informed and `flagEdited` is reset.

Listing 12-2
The Save Record Function

```
Public Function uf_SaveRecord(frm As Form)
'Saves the record on the form

Dim strConnection As String
Dim cnn As New ADODB.Connection
Dim rst As New ADODB.RecordSet
```

```
Dim fld As ADODB.Field
Dim ctl As Control
Dim vartemp As Variant
Dim strCriteria As String

    'On Error GoTo ErrorHandler

    'Check to see if data has been changed
    If Not frm.FlagEdited Then
        MsgBox "Nothing to save"
        GoTo Done
    End If

    'Open connection
    cnn.Open frm.Controls("xProvider") & frm.Controls("xDataSource")

    'Open recordset to determine type of key field and setup Criteria
    rst.Open "Select * From " & frm.Controls("xRecordset") & " Where False;", _
        cnn, adOpenStatic
    Select Case rst(frm.Controls("xKey").Value).Type
        Case adChar, adVarWChar, adLongVarWChar
            strCriteria = frm.Controls("xKey") & " = " & Chr(34) & _
                frm.Controls(frm.Controls("xKey")).Value & Chr(34)
        Case adDate
            strCriteria = frm.Controls("xKey") & " = " & "#" & _
                frm.Controls(frm.Controls("xKey")).Value & "#"
        Case Else    'assume numeric
            strCriteria = frm.Controls("xKey") & " = " & _
                str(frm.Controls(frm.Controls("xKey")).Value)
    End Select
    rst.Close

    'Determine if this is a new record or a changed record
    rst.Open "Select * From " & frm.Controls("xRecordset") & " WHERE " & _
        strCriteria, cnn, adOpenKeyset, adLockOptimistic
    If rst.RecordCount = 0 Or rst.RecordCount = -1 Then

        'Create new record
        rst.AddNew
        'Iterate through controls on form that match fields in recordset
        For Each ctl In frm
            'if error the field is not on the form
            On Error Resume Next
            Err = 0
            vartemp = rst.Fields(ctl.Name).Name
            If Err = 0 Then
                On Error GoTo ErrorHandler
                'if control enabled then
                '    if it is not an auto increment field
                '        if data is not null or an empty string
                If ctl.Enabled Then
```

Continued

Listing 12-2 *Continued*

```
                           If Not rst.Fields(ctl.Name).Properties("IsAutoIncrement") Then
                                If Not IsNull(ctl.Value) And Not ctl.Value = "" Then
                                    vartemp = ctl.Value
                                    rst(ctl.Name).Value = vartemp
                                End If
                           End If
                       End If
                   End If
               Next
               'Update the recordset
               rst.Update
               rst.Close
           Else
               'Change record
               'Need to add code to determine if record was changed since last retrieved
               'Iterate through controls on form that match fields in recordset
               For Each ctl In frm
                   'if error the field is not on the form
                   On Error Resume Next
                   Err = 0
                   vartemp = rst.Fields(ctl.Name).Name
                   If Err = 0 Then
                       On Error GoTo ErrorHandler
                       'if control enabled then
                       '    if it is not an auto increment field
                       '        if data is not null or an empty string
                       If ctl.Enabled Then
                           If Not rst.Fields(ctl.Name).Properties("IsAutoIncrement") Then
                                If Not IsNull(ctl.Value) And Not ctl.Value = "" Then
                                    vartemp = ctl.Value
                                    rst(ctl.Name).Value = vartemp
                                End If
                           End If
                       End If
                   End If
               Next
               'Update the recordset
               rst.Update
               rst.Close

           End If
           'reset edited flag on form
           frm.FlagEdited = False
           MsgBox "Record Saved"
       GoTo Done

       ErrorHandler:
           MsgBox Err.Description
       Done:

       End Function
```

Finding records

You find records with the function uf_FindRecord. This function is based on the ability to enter criteria on the form in any field control. The function works in two passes as determined by the control flagFind on the form. If this flag is True, then the form contains the criteria to do the find. If it is False, then the form is cleared so the user can enter the criteria. A message is displayed telling the user to enter the criteria and to press the Find button again to retrieve the records.

You can set the default value of this flag to True so that when the form is opened, the user can start entering criteria right away. After the function is done, the resulting criteria is stored in the Form's filter property for later use. The function checks to see if the current record has been saved before clearing the form out for the criteria.

Listing 12-3 provides the code for this function. There is an option set by a constant named AllowAllRecords, which, when set, will retrieve all records from the recordset if no criteria is specified. If set to False, the user will be warned that no criteria was entered and not retrieve any records.

The heart of this function's operations is creating a criteria string. It provides a very flexible mechanism for the user to find a record. Any combination of fields on the form can be used, and the function will create a criteria using AND logic between all the fields selected. For example, in our sample application, you can enter a state, and all records for that state will be retrieved. If a user knows an account or a bank, he or she can enter those as well. The trick to making the criteria string is to find the fields on the form that the user has filled in and then look up the type of field in the recordset to determine how to format the criteria string.

For text fields, you must enclose the search value in quotes; for dates, you must enclose the search value with a pound (#) sign. For numbers, no delimiter is needed. To create the criteria string, the recordset is opened without retrieving any records. This is done with the Where clause equal to False. The code then cycles through all the controls on the form that match the field names. If the control value is not a zero-length string or is not null, then the field name and the field value are added to the criteria string.

When all the controls have been checked, the recordset is opened with the criteria. If the record count is not zero, the criteria string is stored in the forms Filter property and the first record is displayed on the form.

Listing 12-3
The Find Record Function

```
Public Function uf_FindRecord(frm As Form) As Integer

Dim strConnection As String
Dim cnn As New ADODB.Connection
Dim rst As New ADODB.RecordSet
Dim fld As ADODB.Field
Dim ctl As Control
Dim strCriteria As String
Dim vartemp As Variant

Const AllowAllRecords = True 'Set to true to display all records when no
criteria is entered

    On Error GoTo ErrorHandler

    If Not frm.FlagFind Then
        'Check to see if data has been changed
        If frm.FlagEdited Then
            If MsgBox("Do you want to save your changes", vbYesNo) = vbYes Then
                uf_SaveRecord frm
            Else
                frm.FlagEdited = False
            End If
        End If
        uf_ClearForm frm
        frm.FlagFind = True
        frm.FlagEdited = False
        MsgBox ("Enter your criteria on the form and then press the Find" & _
        " button again.")
        GoTo Done
        Else
        If Not frm.FlagEdited Then
            If Not AllowAllRecords Then
                MsgBox ("You have not entered any criteria")
                frm.FlagFind = False
                GoTo Done
            End If
        End If

        'Create a find criteria string
        'Open connection
        cnn.Open frm.Controls("xProvider") & frm.Controls("xDataSource")

        'Open recordset with no records
        rst.Open "Select * From " & frm.Controls("xRecordset") & " Where _
            False;", cnn, adOpenStatic
```

```
'Iterate through controls on form that match fields in recordset
strCriteria = ""
For Each ctl In frm
  'if error the field is not on the form
  On Error Resume Next
  Err = 0
  vartemp = rst.Fields(ctl.Name).Name
  If Err = 0 Then
    On Error GoTo ErrorHandler
    If ctl.Enabled Then
      If Not IsNull(ctl.Value) And Not ctl.Value = "" Then
        If Len(strCriteria) > 0 Then strCriteria = strCriteria & " AND "
        Select Case rst(ctl.Name).Type
          Case adChar, adVarWChar, adLongVarWChar
            strCriteria = strCriteria & ctl.Name & " = " & Chr(34) & _
                ctl.Value & Chr(34)
          Case adDate
            strCriteria = strCriteria & ctl.Name & " = " & "#" & _
                ctl.Value & "#"
          Case Else    'assume numeric
            strCriteria = strCriteria & ctl.Name & " = " & _
                str(ctl.Value)
        End Select
      End If
    End If
  End If
Next
rst.Close

'Open recordset with criteria
If Len(strCriteria) > 0 Then strCriteria = " WHERE " & strCriteria
rst.Open "Select * From " & frm.Controls("xRecordset") & strCriteria & _
    " ORDER by " & frm.Controls("xKey"), cnn, adOpenStatic, _
    adLockBatchOptimistic
If rst.RecordCount = 0 Then
  MsgBox ("No records found")
  uf_FindRecord = 0
Else
  uf_FindRecord = rst.RecordCount
  frm.Filter = Mid(strCriteria, 8)    'store the criteria for later
  frm.FlagFind = False
  frm.FlagEdited = False
  'Display first record
  uf_DisplayRecord frm, 1
End If

End If

GoTo Done
```

Listing 12-3 *Continued*

```
ErrorHandler:
   MsgBox Err.Description
Done:

End Function
```

The actual retrieval of the data and populating of the form is done with the uf_DisplayRecord function shown in Listing 12-4. Since only one record is retrieved at a time, the DisplayRecord function gets only one record based on the record source, the filter property of the form, and the record number passed as an argument to the function. The function returns the current number of recordsets based on those parameters, which is useful when you want to fill in a control on a form such as the total number of records.

Before processing, this function checks to see if the user has changed any data on the form. If data has been entered and changed and not saved, as determined by the flagEdited control, then the user is prompted to save the record.

The connection to the data is opened using the "X" controls and the Filter property of the form, if it exists. The function then moves to the specified record based on the argument intRecord. As in previous functions, the code iterates through the controls on the form that match a field in the recordset and populates the control.

Listing 12-4
The Display Record Function

```
Public Function uf_DisplayRecord(frm As Form, intRecord As Integer) As Integer
'Displays the record determined by intRecord
'Returns the number of records in the recordset

Dim strConnection As String
Dim cnn As New ADODB.Connection
Dim rst As New ADODB.RecordSet
Dim fld As ADODB.Field
Dim ctl As Control
Dim vartemp As Variant

    'On Error GoTo ErrorHandler

    'Check to see if data has been changed
    If frm.FlagEdited Then
        If MsgBox("Do you want to save your changes", vbYesNo) = vbYes Then
```

```
            uf_SaveRecord frm
        Else
            frm.FlagEdited = False
        End If
    End If

    'Open connection
    cnn.Open frm.Controls("xProvider") & frm.Controls("xDataSource")

    'Open recordset
    If Len(frm.Filter) = 0 Then
    rst.Open "Select * From " & frm.Controls("xRecordset") & _
    " Order by " &  frm.Controls("xKey"), cnn, adOpenStatic
    Else
    rst.Open "Select * From " & frm.Controls("xRecordset") & _
    " WHERE " & frm.Filter & " Order by " & _
    frm.Controls("xKey"), cnn, adOpenStatic
    End If

    'move to selected record
    rst.Move intRecord - 1

    'Iterate through controls on form that match fields in recordset
    For Each ctl In frm

        'if error the field is not on the form
        On Error Resume Next
        Err = 0
        vartemp = rst.Fields(ctl.Name).Name
        If Err = 0 Then
            On Error GoTo ErrorHandler
            'if control enables then set default value from tag
            '    and set focus if tab index 0
            If ctl.Enabled Then
                ctl.Value = rst.Fields(ctl.Name).Value
                If ctl.TabIndex = 0 Then ctl.SetFocus
            End If
        End If
    Next

    uf_DisplayRecord = rst.RecordCount

    GoTo Done

ErrorHandler:
    MsgBox Err.Description
Done:

End Function
```

Deleting records

The uf_DeleteRecord function shown in Listing 12-5 has a similar flow as the previous functions. It first prompts the user to confirm the deletion, then opens the recordset and moves to the record based on the argument intRecord. It then uses the Delete and UpdateBatch methods to carry out the delete action.

It is up to the VBA code in the calling form to determine what to do next. In our sample application, the calling form will display the first record of the current recordset after the deletion is completed.

Listing 12-5
The Delete Record Function

```
Public Function uf_DeleteRecord(frm As Form, intRecord As Integer)
'Deletes the record determined by intRecord

Dim strConnection As String
Dim cnn As New ADODB.Connection
Dim rst As New ADODB.RecordSet
Dim fld As ADODB.Field
Dim ctl As Control
Dim vartemp As Variant

    On Error GoTo ErrorHandler

    If MsgBox("Do you really want to delete this record", vbYesNo) = vbNo Then
GoTo Done
    End If

    'Open connection
    cnn.Open frm.Controls("xProvider") & frm.Controls("xDataSource")

    'Open recordset
    If Len(frm.Filter) = 0 Then
        rst.Open "Select * From " & frm.Controls("xRecordset") & " Order by " _
            & frm.Controls("xKey"), cnn, adOpenStatic, adLockBatchOptimistic, _
            adCmdText

    Else
        rst.Open "Select * From " & frm.Controls("xRecordset") & " Where " & _
            frm.Filter & " Order by " & frm.Controls("xKey"), cnn, _
            adOpenStatic, adLockBatchOptimistic, adCmdText
    End If

    'move to selected record
    rst.Move intRecord - 1
```

```
      rst.Delete adAffectCurrent
      rst.UpdateBatch
      GoTo Done

ErrorHandler:
   MsgBox Err.Description
Done:

End Function
```

**10 Min.
To Go**

How to Create a Simple Unbound Form

In this section, we will use the sample Check Writer application and a form to work with the Bank Accounts table. The form name is called "Bank Accounts Unbound" and can be found in the sample application on the enclosed CD.

Figure 12-1 shows the form in Normal view.

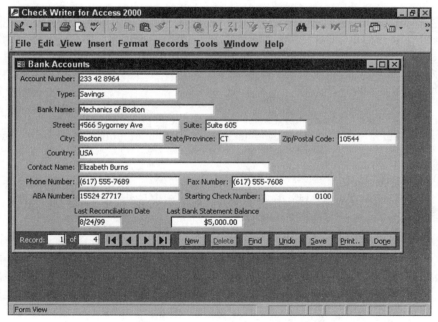

Figure 12-1
An unbound form in Normal view

Part III–Saturday Afternoon
Session 12

This form contains almost all the features you need to add, edit, delete, and find records. The form footer contains a series of buttons to provide these functions and more. The Undo button allows the user to redisplay a record after changes have been made but before the Save button is pressed. The Print button opens another form in our application, which is a dialog box providing choices about what to print. Finally, the Done button closes the form and if the record wasn't saved, prompts the user to save it.

When dealing with an unbound form, the changes to the record are not saved until the Save button is pressed.

The record navigation buttons that are found in a bound Access form are recreated here. We cannot use the Access record navigation buttons because the form is not bound to a record source. There are also controls to show the user the current record number as well as the total number of records.

Because of the unique functions we created to handle unbound forms as described in the previous section, this form needs to have some special controls that are invisible to the user. These are shown on the form with white print on a dark background in the upper right portion of the form (see Figure 12-2). The Visible property of these controls is set to False so they cannot be seen when the user is using the form.

On the top right of the form are four controls referred to previously as the "X" controls. They are named and must be set to the appropriate values to work. The values below are used in our sample application and are put in the control source property:

xProvider ="Provider=Microsoft.Jet.OLEDB.4.0;"

xDataSource ="Data Source=d:/ccb/CheckWriterData2000.mdb"

xRecordset ="BankAccounts"

xKey ="BankAccountNumber"

Also, the unbound form contains the following check-box controls, also hidden, located on the bottom right portion of the screen.

flagEdited with default value of False

flagFind with default value of True

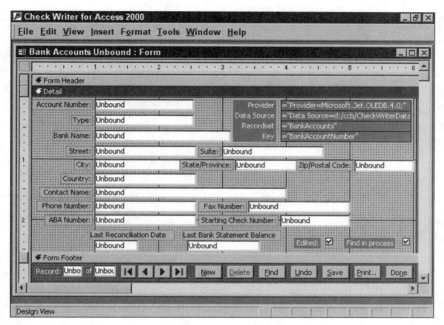

Figure 12-2
An unbound form in Design view

The form's remaining controls have no `Control Source` property set, and the form has no `Record Source` property set. You can optionally include a filter for the form with the `Filter` property. This is used by the `Form Load` event subroutine if initially set. The fields that you will be using from the recordset need a control on the form with the same name as the recordset field name. Default values for the fields, if needed, are set in the `Tag` property, not the default property. Also, the controls for the fields need to have an entry for the `After Update` event property. This is a call to the function `uf_SetEditedFlag()` to set the `flagEdited` control when the field value has changed.

This form has a minimum amount of code. Most of the code is in the module "Unbound Form Utilities." The code behind the form falls into two categories: form subroutines (see Listing 12-6) and button subroutines (see Listing 12-7). When the form loads, a subroutine checks to see if a filter property of the form exists and, if so, displays the first record based on the "X" controls and the filter. If there is no filter, then the form will open in a find mode, waiting for the user to enter criteria to retrieve records. When the form closes, the `flagEdited` control is checked to see if data has changed on the form and if the data has changed, the function will prompt the user to save it.

Listing 12-6
Form Subroutines

```
Private Sub Form_Load()
    If Len(Me.Filter) > 0 Then
        Me.tbxRecordCount = uf_DisplayRecord(Me, 1)
        If Me.tbxRecordCount > 0 Then Me.tbxRecordNumber = 1
        Me.FlagFind = False
    End If
End Sub

Private Sub Form_Unload(Cancel As Integer)
Dim Answer As Integer
    If Me.FlagEdited Then
        Answer = MsgBox("Do you want to save your changes?", vbYesNoCancel)
        If Answer = vbCancel Then Cancel = True
        If Answer = vbYes Then uf_SaveRecord Me
    End If
End Sub
```

Each button has a subroutine. These subroutines use calls to the general functions as described in the previous sections. Also referenced frequently are the controls tbxRecordNumber and tbxRecordCount, which are text-box controls containing information about the current record number and the total number of records. These are referenced by almost all of the subroutines to keep track of the location in the current recordset.

Listing 12-7
Button Subroutines

```
Private Sub btnDelete_Click()
    If Not IsNull(Me.tbxRecordNumber) Then
        uf_DeleteRecord Me, Me.tbxRecordNumber
        Me.tbxRecordCount = uf_DisplayRecord(Me, 1)
        Me.tbxRecordNumber = 1
    End If
End Sub

Private Sub btnDone_Click()
    On Error Resume Next
    DoCmd.Close acForm, Me.Name
End Sub

Private Sub btnFind_Click()
```

```
    Me.tbxRecordCount = uf_FindRecord(Me)
    If Me.tbxRecordCount > 0 Then Me.tbxRecordNumber = 1
End Sub

Private Sub btnFirst_Click()
    Me.tbxRecordCount = uf_DisplayRecord(Me, 1)
    Me.tbxRecordNumber = 1
End Sub

Private Sub btnNew_Click()
    Me.tbxRecordCount = Null
    Me.tbxRecordNumber = Null
    uf_NewRecord Me
End Sub

Private Sub btnPrevious_Click()
    If Me.tbxRecordNumber > 1 Then
        Me.tbxRecordCount = uf_DisplayRecord(Me, Me.tbxRecordNumber - 1)
        Me.tbxRecordNumber = Me.tbxRecordNumber - 1
    End If
End Sub

Private Sub btnNext_Click()
    If Me.tbxRecordNumber < Me.tbxRecordCount Then
        Me.tbxRecordCount = uf_DisplayRecord(Me, Me.tbxRecordNumber + 1)
        Me.tbxRecordNumber = Me.tbxRecordNumber + 1
    End If
End Sub

Private Sub btnLast_Click()
    Me.tbxRecordNumber = uf_DisplayRecord(Me, Me.tbxRecordCount)
End Sub

Private Sub btnSave_Click()
    uf_SaveRecord Me
End Sub

Private Sub btnUndo_Click()
    If Me.FlagEdited And Me.tbxRecordNumber > 0 Then
        uf_DisplayRecord Me, Me.tbxRecordNumber
        Me.FlagEdited = False
    End If
End Sub

Private Sub btnPrint_Click()
    DoCmd.OpenForm "yBank Print Dialog"
End Sub
```

Done!

REVIEW

A lot of good reasons exist to use unbound forms, but some very strong reasons also exist not to use them.

- Unbound forms can improve performance significantly, but they also require a lot of development time.
- When using unbound forms, you need to duplicate in code the functionality that Access provides with bound forms.

ADO provides the necessary functionality to program unbound forms.

QUIZ YOURSELF

1. What is the difference between a bound and unbound form? (See "What are Unbound Forms?")

2. When should you use unbound forms instead of bound forms? (See "Why Use Unbound Forms?")

3. What are the precautions for record locking for unbound forms? (See "Record locking.")

4. Why would you use ADODB rather than ADOX as the data object for unbound forms? (See "The Unbound Form references.")

5. What functions need to be programmatically added to an unbound form to achieve the same functionality as an Access bound form? (See "Programming for Unbound Forms.")

Programming Check Box, Option Group, Combo, and List Box Controls

Session Checklist

✔ Handling true/false selections with a check box

✔ Programming option control groups

✔ Working with combo and list boxes

✔ Handling items not in a combo/list box listing

✔ Selecting and handling multiple choices in list boxes

**30 Min.
To Go**

Learning to program check box, option group, combo box, and list box controls will give you a powerful and flexible arsenal of interfaces. With a little ingenuity, creativity, and programming knowledge, you can make the forms that use these controls more robust and dynamic. Used alone or in conjunction with other controls, you will be able to collect data, control how your forms look, and limit or expand options and choices.

Handling True/False Selections with a Check Box

You most certainly have already used check box, option button, or toggle button controls for instances when you are recording Boolean data types. For simple yes/no or true/false information, these controls are ideal. When coupled with some code, they can become even more useful controls. This example focuses on the check box control. You could easily apply the same technique to an option button or a toggle button.

Figure 13-1 and Figure 13-2 show the Checks form from the Check Writer database. The figures show two instances of the same form. There is a Void check box on the bottom left of both forms. The form in Figure 13-1 has the Void check box cleared, whereas the form in Figure 13-2 has the box checked and has a large stamp that reads "VOID" across the face of the check. Because the Void check box could easily be missed as the user navigates from record to record, the form was designed with the stamp as a visual cue for the user to see.

By definition, a check box, option button, or toggle button can be only either true or false, giving the controls either a positive or negative state. Additionally, because of their unusually small size, they may be very easily overlooked. Using additional visual cues, such as the "VOID" stamp, will make the controls more effective. This is especially vital for important information such as whether a check is void or not.

This check box serves two functions. As with a real checkbook in which you would mark a check as voided, you can do the same in the Check Writer sample program. On the Check form, the Void check box is bound to a field also named Void. This is used to store whether the current check record is voided in the table. In this respect, the control is no different from another bound control. Figure 13-3 shows how the form looks in Design view. Selecting the check box marks the record as being voided. The second purpose is in the After Update event of the check box. The code found here displays the "VOID" stamp across the check to indicate that the check has been voided.

The code in Listing 13-1 shows the After Update event of the Void check box. It determines if the transaction type is a check and what the value of the check box is. The "VOID" stamp becomes visible if the transaction is a check and the Void field is True. This is done in the code by initiating a With statement and referencing the CodeContextObject property. This refers to the object that the current code is being executed from. In this case, it is the Check Writer form. This eliminates the need to explicitly refer to each control.

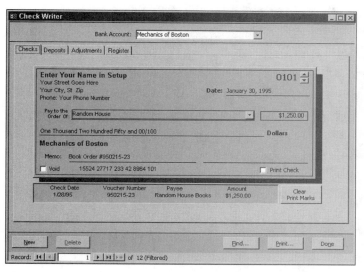

Figure 13-1
A view of the Check Writer form with the Void check box cleared

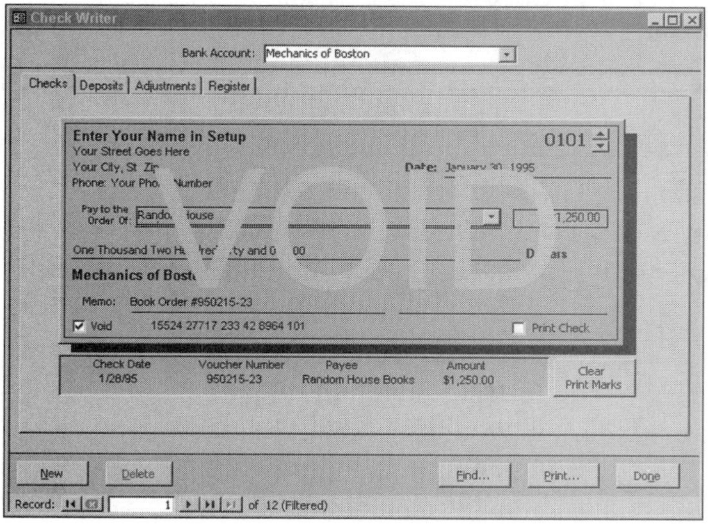

Figure 13-2
A view of the Check Writer form with the Void check box selected and the "VOID" stamp visible

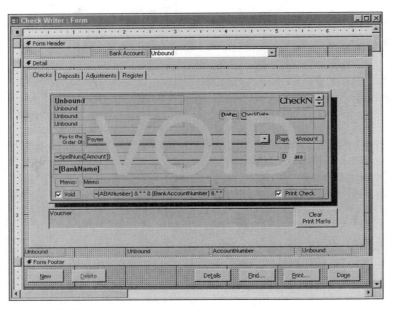

Figure 13-3
*The Design view of the Check Writer form showing the check box and the
"VOID" stamp*

Listing 13-1
After Update Event for the Void Check Box

```
Private Sub Void_AfterUpdate()
On Error GoTo Check_Writer_Update_Messages_Err


    With CodeContextObject
        If (.[TransType] = "Check" And (.Void = False Or
        IsNull(.Void))) Then
            .[Void Stamp].Visible = False
        End If
        If (.[TransType] = "Check" And (.Void = True And Not
        IsNull(.Void))) Then
            .[Void Stamp].Visible = True
        End If
    End With
```

```
Check_Writer_Update_Messages_Exit:
    Exit Sub

Check_Writer_Update_Messages_Err:
    MsgBox Error$
    Resume Check_Writer_Update_Messages_Exit
End Sub
```

The code uses two If Then statements. Both of them work the same way. Each determines the transaction type of the record. This is done because the void status applies only to checks and not to deposits or adjustments. In the first condition, if the transaction is a check and the Void field equals False or is null, then the "VOID" stamp's visible property is set to False. This means it will not be displayed. The second If Then statement checks for the check transaction but checks for a True value, verifies that the field is not null in the Void field, and sets the "VOID" stamp's visible property to True. This causes the stamp to be displayed. The following is the code in the After Update event of the Void check box.

A key point to remember when using this technique is that whether it is a visual cue such as the "VOID" stamp or for another reason, as you navigate from record to record, the status of that particular field may change. Because the value may change, the form must respond accordingly. One record may be voided and the next may not be. It is therefore vitally important to check the status and have the form display correctly the visual cue as you move from record to record. This is done in the form's On Current event. Reviewing the code in the On Current event, you will see the exact same code as in the After Update event of the Void check box. As the user moves from record to record, the On Current event will fire and check the transaction and the Void field. The "VOID" stamp will display appropriately.

This particular example displays a visual cue. You could use the same technique and different code for other purposes. For example, you could have a field named Locked, and you could have code that locks the form based on a particular field. Your creativity is the key to the many ways these controls and techniques can be used.

Programming Option Group Controls

What if you want to have more than a simple True or False value available? This individuality of a check box can be limiting. For instance, you may want the user to choose one of six different values instead of just two. This is where an option group would work. Whereas a check box can be tied to a single field and then be only either a True/False value, an option group gives you more flexibility.

Toggle buttons, option buttons, or check box controls can be used separately or as part of a group, as shown in Figure 13-4. The top half of the figure shows two sets of controls. The controls change state when they are active and inactive. When used independently, these controls can represent a two-state Yes/No or True/False data type. When used as a group, these controls become a single entity of an option group in which each option selected now represents a numbered value.

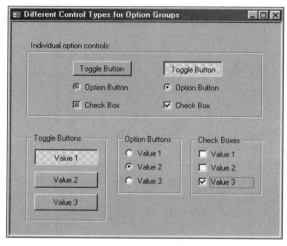

Figure 13-4
Examples of an option group and the different control types

The bottom half of Figure 13-4 shows three separate option groups. In this example, each option group has only three choices. You could just as easily have four, five, or more. The option group, as a whole, can have only one value associated with it and is usually bound to a single field. Each of the option groups in the example are toggled between one of the three choices. These controls can be very useful and effective when you need to provide several options but tie the selection value to a stored field and have an action produced. The Check Writer program provides many examples of option groups, two of which are presented below.

An option group functions as just that — a group. Within the option group, you can have any number of values to select from. However, you can not select multiple items in the option group. The group can hold or store only a single value returned by the different options.

Figure 13-5 shows the form yCheck Print Dialog. This form is opened when you click the Print button on the Check Writer form. This is what the user would see when printing out a check. Several options and conditions are available based on the choices. This works in the following way. The user clicks the Print button on the Check Writer form. The Print dialog box opens and the user is presented with options, the first of which is Check Type. There are three toggle buttons that alternate between a check stock that has the check on top, on the bottom, or a continuous sheet of checks.

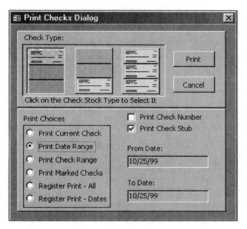

Figure 13-5
The Print Checks dialog for the Check Writer with two option groups

Under Check Type is the Print Choices selection. This lets the user choose between printing the current check, a range of checks based on the date, a range of checks by check number, checks marked for printing, or printing the register for all transactions or for a specific date selection. Notice that as you change from one option to the next in the Print Choices section, additional controls appear and disappear to prompt the user for more input. In addition, the user can choose whether to print check numbers on the printout and whether to print the check stub. Then when the selections have all been made, clicking the Print button will initiate the printing of the selected check(s) or register.

Two separate option groups are being used on this form. The first is under Check Type, where toggle buttons are used to indicate which style of checks to use. The second group uses option buttons where there are six different print choices from which to select. Changing the print choices to either Print Date Range or Register Print – Dates will cause two fields to appear on the form: From Date and To Date. Moving to another print choice causes the controls to disappear.

Notice the use of pictures on the toggle buttons. In the Check Writer sample, bitmap images of check styles were created and placed on the buttons. Adding images to buttons is an excellent way to make a form and interface more user friendly.

Listing 13-2
The After Update of the Option Group for Print Choices

```
Private Sub Type_of_Print_AfterUpdate()
  Me![From Check].Visible = False
  Me![To Check].Visible = False
  Me![From Check Text].Visible = False
  Me![To Check Text].Visible = False
  Me![From Date].Visible = False
  Me![To Date].Visible = False
  Me![From Date Text].Visible = False
  Me![To Date Text].Visible = False
  If Me![Type of Print] = 2 Or Me![Type of Print] = 6 Then
    Me![From Date].Visible = True
    Me![To Date].Visible = True
    Me![From Date Text].Visible = True
    Me![To Date Text].Visible = True
  End If
  If Me![Type of Print] = 3 Then
    Me![From Check].Visible = True
    Me![To Check].Visible = True
    Me![From Check Text].Visible = True
    Me![To Check Text].Visible = True
  End If

End Sub
```

The code in Listing 13-2 illustrates this use of the option group. One technique used in this listing is that the initial lines of code are setting several controls' Visible property to False. When you use the Print Dialog form, as you make certain choices in the option group for Print Choices, additional controls appear and disappear. These conditional controls are set to be invisible in the first eight lines of code. Why? To "reset" the interface as you move from option to option.

The reason is to avoid extensive lines of code to determine which option was last selected, thereby avoiding writing additional code to handle turning off the last set of options that were activated. This is done by simply setting all of the controls to be invisible that could be affected by any of the choices. This way, it is irrelevant what the previous value selected was; then, the remaining code determines what the current value selected is and proceeds from there.

20 Min. To Go

Working with Combo and List Boxes

The combo box and list box are the only Access controls that allow you to see multiple columns (or fields) of data in a single listing. These two can be very useful because of this feature. Figure 13-6 shows a combo box used in the Check Writer form. At the top of the form is a combo box that lists the available bank accounts that can be selected. Clicking on the drop down arrow shows a listing of the Bank Name, Account Type, and Account Number. This example also illustrates how a combo box can be extended beyond a simple selection control. Upon selecting a different bank account, the form is updated to display only transaction records that apply only to that account.

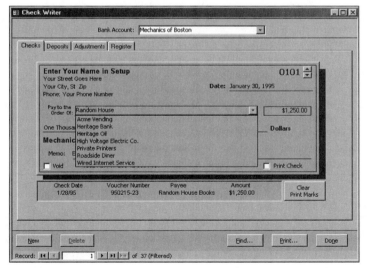

Figure 13-6
A Combo Box used in the Check Writer form

Part III—Saturday Afternoon
Session 13

Understanding the differences between combo boxes and list boxes

Table 13-1 is a comparison of combo and list boxes and their related features. Figure 13-7 is an example of a form with combo boxes and a list box.

Table 13-1
Combo Box and List Box Feature Comparison

Feature	Combo Box	List Box
Size/Space	When not selected by the user, compresses down to the height of a single field.	Has the size and dimensions that you assign. Displays more than one row of information and is always open.
Typing	Allows for "fill-in-as-you type" feature. For instance, as you type in **A**, it will go to the first instance of A in the column. If you then type in **B**, the first instance of AB comes up. This will continue until no more matches can be made	Typing a letter will bring you to the first item that starts with that letter. If you type in **A**, the focus will move to the first instance of A. If you then type in **B**, the focus moves to the first instance of B, disregarding the previously typed A.
Choice	You can choose from the list or enter a value not in the listing, depending on which setting you choose in the Limit to List property	You can select only the items in the list.
Selection	Allows for only one selection.	Gives you different levels of selection, from a single selection to multiple selections.

Basic elements of combo boxes and list boxes

Both the combo box and list box are powerful controls in that they are able to display more than just a single field of data. You can define multiple columns for a single record or row and bind that to a particular field. Understanding the properties available to you will greatly increase the usefulness of these controls.

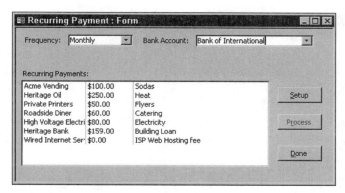

Figure 13-7
An example of a form with combo boxes and a list box

Figures 13-8 and 13-9 show the property sheet dialog box for a combo box and a list box, respectively. Notice that in addition to the universal properties such as Name and Control Source, these two controls also have the following properties shown in Table 13-2. It is important that you have a solid understanding of these properties, as they will dramatically affect how your controls work, especially because, as the examples will show, you can programmatically set these properties and greatly affect the appearance and function of the control.

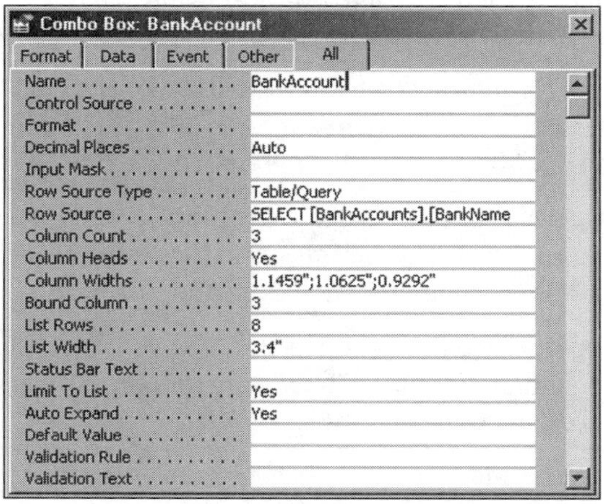

Figure 13-8
Property sheet dialog box for a sample combo box

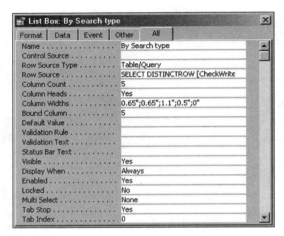

Figure 13-9
Property sheet dialog box for a sample list box

Table 13-2
Key Properties for List Boxes and Combo Boxes

Property	Description
Row Source Type	This property indicates how data will be provided to the Row Source. You can choose between three standard settings.
Table/Query (including SQL statements):	This property indicates whether the data for the control is from an existing table, query, or an explicit SQL statement. The name or SQL statement is entered in the Row Source.
Value List	This property indicates that the data for the list is specified in the Row Source. Choose this option when you want to give options that are limited and static.
Field List	This property indicates that the data for the control is a list of field names from a table, query, or SQL statement used in conjunction with the Row Source.
Row Source	This property indicates the name of a table, query, or the SQL statement to use for populating the list information.

Property	Description
Column Count	This property indicates how many columns to display in the listing. The key point tember in regards to referencing the columns with VBA is that the number of the columns is zero-based. This means the first column is considered 0, the next is considered 1, and so on.
Column Heads	This property is a Yes/No value that sets whether the column names (or field names) will be displayed as headers in the list.
Column Widths	This property allows you to have varying widths for each column.
Bound Column	This property indicates which column's data should be stored once the row has been selected. A field can be bound to both the combo box or list box.

In addition to the common properties listed in Table 13-2 that list boxes and combo boxes share, each has some properties that are unique only to that interface. A combo box has the following additional properties associated with it (Table 13-3).

Table 13-3
Additional Properties for Combo Boxes

Property	Description
List Rows	A value representing the number of rows of the list to show when the combo box is activated.
List Width	A separate value from the Width property of the control. The List Width can be narrower or wider than the actual width of the control. This would be set in conjunction to the Column Widths property. Note that unless you specify the column widths, the default value of the control width is used. This means that if you have multiple columns and want to have them wide enough to adequately display the information, it will be ignored. Your columns will be truncated unless they are set in this property.
Limit To List	A Yes/No value that determines if the item entered must match an existing item in the list or if other entries can be entered and accepted.

Although Access uses a zero-based numbering system when referencing the columns in VBA code, when referencing the bound column, it is zero- based. This means that if you want to reference the first column in the Bound Column property of the control, you would enter 1. To reference the same column in code, you would enter 0.

A list box has one additional property associated with it: Multi Select, a property that indicates whether to allow multiple selections. There are three possible settings: None, Simple, or Extended:

None	No multiple selections can be made
Simple	Multiple selections are allowed. Clicking on the row or pressing the Space bar on the keyboard selects and deselects a row.
Extended	Multiple selections are allowed. You select rows by clicking on the row while pressing the Shift key. You can extend the selection by clicking the first row and using the mouse or arrow keys to select contiguous rows. Additionally, holding down the Ctrl key and clicking a row allows you to select or deselect that row.

Populating the controls

By referencing the Row Source Type and Row Source property of either the combo box or list box in your VBA code, you can affect the information it displays. This gives you the ability to dynamically change the data source listed, the order (sorting), and which fields or columns to list.

For this example, refer to Figure 13-10, which shows the yCheck Search Dialog form that opens when you click the Find button on the Check Writer screen.

The yCheck Search Dialog form allows you to choose different types of searches based on the criteria. The Type of Search section lists five different options. Notice how the option group in this instance is used to control the display of the list box. As you change the type of search to do (e.g., "Checks By Check Number" to "Checks By Payee"), the list box changes its display. You then scroll up and down until the desired row or record is displayed. Double-clicking will close the yCheck Search Dialog dialog form and open the selected record. You can also select the desired record with a single click and click the OK button, which will also close the form and go to the selected transaction.

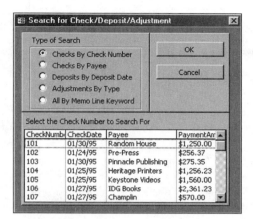

Figure 13-10
The yCheck Search Dialog form showing an option group and list box

This operates by changing the Row Source property of the list box, depending on which option is chosen for the search type (option group). Also notice that the type of information is not only changing, but the column widths also change to accommodate the differences in the information displayed. This example illustrates the dramatic effects gained by manipulating the Row Source and Column Widths properties programmatically.

The following is a partial code listing of the processes that occur in the After Update event of the option group and how it affects the list box display.

Listing 13-3
After Update Event of the Type of Search Option Group

```
Private Sub Type_of_Search_AfterUpdate()
    Me!Keyword.Visible = False
    With Me
      ![By Search type].RowSource = ""
      Select Case ![Type of search]
        Case 1
          Forms![Check Writer].TabControl.Pages("Checks").SetFocus
          ![Search Text].caption = "Select the Check Number to Search For        "
          ![By Search Type].RowSource = ""
          ![By Search Type].ColumnCount = 5
          ![By Search Type].ColumnWidths = ".65 in;.65 in;1.1 in;0.5 in;0 in"
          ![By Search Type].BoundColumn = 5
          ![By Search Type].RowSource = "SELECT [CheckNumber], [CheckDate], & _
             [CheckWriter].Payee, [PaymentAmount],[TransID] AS Amount FROM & _
```

Continued

Listing 13-3 *Continued*

```
        [CheckWriter] WHERE (([TransType]='Check') and [AccountNumber]= & _
        [Forms]![Check Writer]![BankAccountNumber]) ORDER BY [CheckNumber]"
    Case 2
      Forms![Check Writer].TabControl.Pages("Checks").SetFocus
      ![Search Text].caption = "Select the Payee Record to Search For    "
      ![By Search Type].RowSource = ""
      ![By Search Type].ColumnCount = 5
      ![By Search Type].ColumnWidths = "1.1 in;.65 in;.5 in;.65 in;0 in"
      ![By Search Type].BoundColumn = 5
      ![By Search Type].RowSource = "ChecksByPayee"
```

This snippet of code performs several tasks. In this case, the example shows the code for values 1 and 2 and for the options "Checks By Check Number" and "Checks By Payee," as they appear in the form. These are the values of the options in the option group. Analyzing the code, you will see that the settings for the list box are based on the case value. The code changes the Caption property of the label control to correctly describe the type of search. From there, the number of columns is set to five in the Column Count property.

In conjunction with the Column Count, the Column Widths are set to display the data appropriately, varying the width size as needed. Note that in this case, the *bound column* — the column that has its information saved to the field — does not change. It is not required that you keep the same bound column. As a matter of practice, you may find it easier to keep the bound column the same within a given control even when changing the row source. Finally, the Row Source is updated. In the first case, the source is set to a SQL string. In the second, you will see that it refers to a query ("ChecksByPayee") instead.

 Changing any of the properties above causes the control to be reset and requeried for each change. This can cause major performance problems each time you set a property, especially if you are using a complex query or the source tables are large. Therefore, the trick is to set the Row Source **to be a blank value. As the control is requeried, because there is no** Row Source, **it will requery faster. This is done with the following line of code:**

```
![By Search type].RowSource = ""
```

Then, after setting all the other properties, set the Row Source **property with the query name or SQL string you wish to use.**

You have seen in the last case how you can use an option group to change the display of a list box. The following examples from the Check Writer sample program takes the concept further and illustrates some simple ways that you can create dynamic, interactive forms.

The following example uses the After Update event of a combo box to affect the data and the form display. The Check Writer form's Bank Account combo box changes or filters records for the form based on the selection the user chooses. This is shown in the following code, Listing 13-4.

Listing 13-4
The After Update Event of the Bank Account Combo Box

```
On Error GoTo Check_Writer_Change_Account_Err
 Dim curconn As ADODB.Connection
 Dim BankTB As New ADODB.RecordSet, Response As Integer

    Set curconn = CurrentProject.Connection
    Set BankTB = New ADODB.RecordSet
    BankTB.Open "SELECT * FROM BankAccounts WHERE_
    [BankAccountNumber] = """" & _
                Me!BankAccount & """", curconn, adOpenForwardOnly
    With Me
        .BankName = BankTB!BankName
        .BankAccountNumber = BankTB!BankAccountNumber
        .ABANumber = BankTB!ABANumber
        If .TabControl.value <> 0 Then
            .TabControl.Pages(0).SetFocus
        Else
            TabControl_Change
        End If
    End With
    BankTB.Close
    Set BankTB = Nothing

Check_Writer_Change_Account_Exit:
    Exit Sub

Check_Writer_Change_Account_Err:
    MsgBox Error$
    Resume Check_Writer_Change_Account_Exit

End Sub
```

This is a simple but very significant code listing. In this case, the form is being set to filter for check transactions only for a particular bank account. Without having to do a filter on the form, we have set it up so that with a simple selection from a combo box, the user is changing the record source for the entire form. This is an extremely user-friendly way of setting up filters for your forms. With a minimum of code and without the user having to go through menu items, you can filter the records on a form.

Handling items not in the list

One of the most versatile properties of the combo box is its ability to handle nonlisted items. The property Limit to List and the event On Not In List work together to dictate how the control handles instances where the text entered in the combo box does not match the list.

The Payee combo box of the Check Writer form has been set up to illustrate how you can give the end user the ability to update the listing as new information is encountered. In this example, the Payee combo box allows you to select from a pre-existing list of payees. The property Limit to List has been set to No, which allows the user to enter a name that is not listed.

However, to provide a more robust interface, the property in our example has been set to Yes to force only listed items to be selected. In addition, the code shown in Listing 13-5 was added to the On Not In List event that will run when a value that is not listed has been entered. The code will prompt the user to see if he/she wishes to add the nonlisted payee to the listing for future use. If No is returned, the code ends. Otherwise, if Yes is returned, it will add the record.

Listing 13-5
The On Not In List event code for the Payee combo box

```
Private Sub Payee_NotInList(NewData As String, Response As
Integer)
    Dim CurConn         As ADODB.Connection
    Dim PayeeTB         As New ADODB.RecordSet
    Dim MSGString       As String

    MSGString = "'" & NewData & "' is not a choice in the list."
    MSGString = MSGString & vbcr & vblf &  "Add to list?"

    If MsgBox(MSGString, vbQuestion + vbYesNo, _
        "Not in list") = vbNo Then
```

```
        Response = acDataErrDisplay
    Else
        Set CurConn = CurrentProject.Connection
        Set PayeeTB.ActiveConnection = CurConn
        PayeeTB.CursorType = adOpenKeyset
        PayeeTB.LockType = adLockOptimistic
        PayeeTB.Source = "Payees"
        PayeeTB.Open options:=adCmdTable

        With PayeeTB
            .AddNew
                .Fields("Payees") = NewData
            .Update
        End With
        Response = acDataErrAdded
    End If

Set PayeeTB = Nothing

End Sub
```

The previous code listing involves a very simple situation in which the Payees table consists of a single field. In most cases, your tables will have more fields, including some that may require input from the user before the record can be created. You may wish to expand this example even further by opening up a data entry form for the user to populate the entire record and then updating the list.

**10 Min.
To Go**

Selecting and handling multiple choices

Unlike a combo box or an option group, a list box has the unique ability to allow for multiple selections, or what Access refers to as the MultiSelect property. The MultiSelect property can have one of three different variations: None, Simple, or Extended. The difference between Simple and Extended is that with Simple, the user selects the row by clicking the mouse. Extended allows you to select records that you want by using the Shift or Ctrl key and clicking on each. You can select a contiguous group of rows by clicking the first and last row while holding down the Shift key. The Ctrl key will allow you to select rows in any order you wish.

The Recurring Payments module has a list box that is set up with the MultiSelect property set to Extended, as shown in Figure 13-11. The code in the On Click event of the Process button will cycle through all of the selected rows and create checks for each record selected.

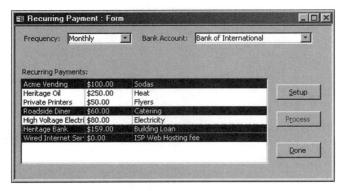

Figure 13-11
The Recurring Payments form with a MultiSelect list box

You should be aware of several key properties when dealing with the MultiSelect property.

ListCount	An integer value indicating the total number of items in the list box.
ListIndex	A zero-based value assigned to each row. You can use this to determine which row is selected.
SelectedProperty	A property that you can use to determine if a particular item in the list box is selected. A True/False value indicates whether a row is selected.
ItemsSelected	A collection of variants that indicate the row of items selected in a list box. This collection is used with other properties to allow you to retrieve data from specific rows and columns in the list box.

These properties are also available for a combo box.

On the Recurring Payments form, the user can set up multiple recurring payments. First, each payment that would be considered a recurring payment must be set up. This works by clicking on the Setup button. The user is then presented with a form in which to create new payment listings. Each payment must be entered and set up here first, before it can be used on the Recurring Payments form. When the time comes for the checks to be created, the user simply selects from the Recurring Payments list box and marks the items to be processed. Once all of the items have been marked, clicking the Process button creates the checks.

You will see that the code for referencing the columns refers to a variable, varitem. Remember that referring to a particular column requires you to pass the row and the column because you are referring to a row that is represented by varitem.

Listing 13-6
The On Click Event for the Process Button

```
Private Sub btnProcess_Click()
    Dim CurConn        As ADODB.Connection
    Dim CheckTB        As New ADODB.Recordset
    Dim MSGString      As String

    On Error GoTo btnProcess_Error

'Verify items selected
    If Me.Recurring_Payments.ItemsSelected.Count = 0 Then
        MsgBox "Please select checks to process.", vbCritical, _
            "No checks selected."
        Me.Recurring_Payments.SetFocus
        GoTo btnProcess_Exit
    End If

'Verify Bank Account Selected
    If IsNull(Me.BankAccount) Then
        MsgBox "Please select a Bank Account", vbCritical, "No Bank Account"
        Me.BankAccount.SetFocus
        GoTo btnProcess_Exit
    End If
    Set CurConn = CurrentProject.Connection
    Set CheckTB.ActiveConnection = CurConn

    CheckTB.CursorType = adOpenKeyset
    CheckTB.LockType = adLockOptimistic
    CheckTB.Source = "CheckWriter"
    CheckTB.Open options:=adCmdTable
```

Continued

Listing 13-6 *Continued*

```
'Open recordset for the Check Writer table and write new checks
    With CheckTB
        'Start loop to process all items selected in the
        'Recurring Payments list box
        For Each varItem In Me.Recurring_Payments.ItemsSelected
            .AddNew
            .Fields("TransType") = "Check"
            .Fields("AccountNumber") = Me.BankAccount
            .Fields("CheckNumber") = CheckNum()
            .Fields("CheckDate") = Date
            .Fields("Payee") = Me.Recurring_Payments.Column(1, varItem)
            .Fields("PaymentAmount") = Me.Recurring_Payments.Column(2, varItem)
            .Fields("Memo") = Me.Recurring_Payments.Column(3, varItem)
            .Fields("Voucher") = "Payee: " & Me.Recurring_Payments.Column & _
                (1, varItem) & "  Amount: " & Format(Me.Recurring_Payments. & _
                Column(2, varItem), "Currency") & "  Date: " & Date & vbCr & _
                vbLf & Me.Recurring_Payments.Column(3, varItem)
            .Update
        Next varItem
    End With
```

Listing 13-6 is the partial listing of the On Click event code for the Process button. The code starts by first declaring the variables for the procedure. Next, the code does standard checks to verify that items have indeed been selected and that a bank account was selected. Then the code starts processing the selections. The "CheckTB" recordset is opened using ADO code. We are opening a recordset based on the Check Writer table, since this is where the data will be populated. A loop is initiated and it goes through all of the items in the ItemSelected collection. For each of the rows retrieved from the collection, the check information is populated. This first saves the transaction as a check, then saves the account number and date. The Payee, Amount, and Memo fields are populated by referring to the other columns in the list box.

Information is concatenated into the Voucher field. This is done by building a string and setting the field to it:

```
.Fields("Voucher") = "Payee: " & Me.Recurring_Payments.Column & _
(1, varItem) & "  Amount: " & Format(Me.Recurring_Payments. & _
Column(2, varItem), "Currency") & "  Date: " & Date & vbCr & _
vbLf & Me.Recurring_Payments.Column(3, varItem)
```

This example uses the ItemsSelected property to process the selected rows. Alternatively, you could use the ListCount, ListIndex, and SelectedProperty to loop through and check each value to determine if a particular row was selected.

Concatenating strings

In the last section, you were introduced to a piece of code that concatenated or built a string. This string was then used to populate the Voucher field of the check, thereby eliminating the need to retype the data in the string. Concatenation is a technique that you should master. It allows you to build a string of separate pieces of data that you can then store in a field. Additionally, you can use it to build SQL statement strings or text strings for message box displays.

The key component of concatenation is the ampersand (&) or the plus (+) sign. You can use these to join two separate statements together. The key difference between the two operators is that the plus operator can only join text data together. The ampersand allows you to join text data as well as nontext data. In addition, the ampersand converts nontext data to text.

If you must use the plus operator for nontext data, you can convert the data to a text format. For example, the function CStr() **would convert the string to a text data type.**

```
= "Today's Date Is: " + Cstr(Date())
```

The following are two examples of concatenating two strings of data. The first takes the First Name and Second Name strings and creates a resultant Names string that is a single text string. Note that three items are actually being added together in the example: First Name, a space, and Last Name. The reason that a space must be added is because no spaces are automatically added when you concatenate. You must take proper spacing into consideration. Otherwise, the example's resultant could have been "JohnDoe" with no spaces.

```
[First Name] = John
[Last Name] = Doe
Concatenate: [First Name] & " " & [Last Name]

Resultant: "John Doe"
```

The next example starts like the previous example but is a little more sophisticated. It joins several strings of text and field references, including calling a function.

```
[First Name] = John
[Last Name] = Doe
[Amount] = 3,299.50
```

```
Concatenate: "Pay To: " & [First Name] & " " & [Last Name] & _
             "    " & Format$(Date(),"mm/dd/yyyy") & "    " & _
             Format$([Amount], "Currency")"
```

```
Resultant:   "Pay To: John Doe 11/09/1999    $3,299.50"
```

On the Check Writer form, there is a Create Check Stub button on the bottom. The code in Listing 13-7 builds a string of text by concatenating several pieces of data into the Voucher string. This is first done by determining if the Voucher field is empty. If it is, the code then sets the voucher. If the existing Voucher field is not blank, then the user is prompted with a message box of whether to overwrite the existing stub information. If the response is Yes, then the code overwrites the existing stub with the concatenated string of data. The concatenated string is the following line:

```
Me![Voucher] = "Pay To: " & Me![Payee] & "    " & _
             Me![CheckDate] & "    " & Format$(Me![Amount], _
             "Currency")
```

Listing 13-7
The On Click Event Code of the Create Check Stub button

```
Private Sub CreateCheckStub_Click()
  Dim Response As Integer
  If IsNull(Me![Voucher]) Then
        Me![Voucher] = "Pay To: " & Me![Payee] & "    " & _
        Me![CheckDate] & "    " & Format$(Me![Amount], "Currency")
     Else
        Response = MsgBox("Do you want to overwrite the Check
Stub?", 36, "Create Stub")
        If Response = vbYes Then
            Me![Voucher] = "Pay To: " & Me![Payee] & "    " & _
            Me![CheckDate] & "    " & Format$(Me![Amount], _
            "Currency")
        End If
     End If
End Sub
```

Done!

REVIEW

In this chapter, you learned about the check box, option group, combo box, and list box controls. You also learned how to programmatically manipulate the information displayed and associate events to the controls. The following topics were covered:

- Populating the controls
- Using code to change the row source properties of the combo box and list box
- Handling items not in the list
- Writing code to handle instances in which the text entered in the combo box is not an item in the list
- Selecting and handling multiple choices
- Using the list box to choose multiple selections
- Creating a dynamic form using these controls and going beyond data entry
- Using the controls to change the look, operation, and function of forms
- Concatenating data together to build a string

QUIZ YOURSELF

1. Which interface would be the most appropriate to use in the following situation?

    a. You wish to have a Posted field and lock the form on records that are marked as Posted and unlock the form for records that are not. (See "Handling True/False Selections with a Check Box.")

    b. You want the user to be able to select multiple items on a list. (See "Basic elements of combo boxes and list boxes.")

    c. You want a control that lists multiple items. You want to have the first column be bound to a field called ItemNumber, and you want the user to be able to type in a partial item number and have it pull up the closest match. (See "Understanding the differences between combo boxes and list boxes.")

2. Which main characteristic differentiates a combo box from a list box? (See "Basic elements of combo boxes and list boxes.")

3. The `Item Not In List` property is available for which control? Detail the general steps you would take to handle a situation where the item was not in the list. (See "Handling items not in the list.")

Programming Subforms and Continuous Forms

Session Checklist

✔ Understanding subforms

✔ Creating subforms

✔ Specifying the subform control's form

✔ Linking master and child forms

✔ Referencing controls in subforms

**30 Min.
To Go**

Subforms give you great flexibility in displaying and entering data, especially when using data found in more than one table and with one-to-many relationships. Continuous forms let you display many records at the same time from one table and still use editing- and data-searching techniques as well as calculated columns and totals. In this session, you will see several examples of how to use subforms and continuous forms to display data.

What is a Subform?

A *subform* is simply a form within a form. It lets you use data from a second form within another form. For example, in the Check Writer example, the main Check Writer form displays the check register in a subform in a continuous form view. A *subform control* is simply a container for displaying another form. The form view displayed within the subform control depends on the view of the form used in the subform.

There are three basic types of form views:

- **Datasheets.** Display multiple records using one line per record
- **Forms.** Display one record on a form
- **Continuous forms.** Display multiple records on a form

Creating a Subform

Any of these form views can be displayed within a subform. There is no difference when creating the subform control. Figure 14-1 shows the Bank Accounts form. This form displays one record at a time. The Check Writer form in your CheckWriter2000.mdb example file is a tabbed dialog box that displays several tabs, including one with a continuous subform.

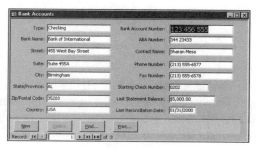

Figure 14-1
The Bank Accounts form

Suppose you want to display the bank accounts information in this tabbed dialog box. The best way would be to add a new tab and a subform. Including a subform on your form enables you to display your data in multiple formats. Figure 14-2 shows this process. First a new tab is added to the end of the Check Writer form. Then, a subform control is added to the tab page.

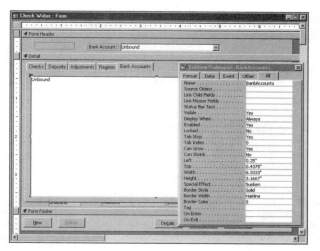

Figure 14-2
Adding a subform to a form

You can add a subform to any form, and you can add more than one subform to a form. A subform can even contain a subform, but you are limited to two levels deep.

Selecting the subform's control Source Object

Once you place a subform control onto a form, you must tell the control which form will be displayed within it. To do this, you use the Source Object property. In this example, select the Bank Accounts form from the list that is displayed of all forms in the control's Source Object property. The Bank Accounts form displays controls used to store data for each bank account.

Once you select the Source Object, the form is displayed within the Subform control. You can see this is Figure 14-3.

You can edit the form if you want and change anything by working through the Subform control.

Remember, if this form is used by another subform or displayed by itself in another part of your application, changing it here will change it every other place it is used. You are not working with a copy, but the original version of the form.

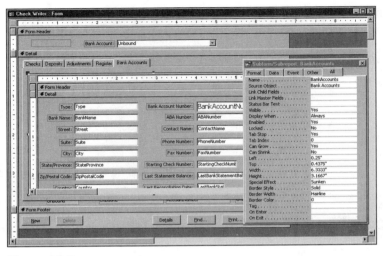

Figure 14-3
Selecting the Subform control's Source Object property

**20 Min.
To Go**

Once you have set the Source Object property of the subform, you may be done if all you want to do is display the form. However, you can perform many other functions with subforms. One function is to limit the records displayed in the subform to match a record displayed in the main form.

You might want to link the Bank Accounts form displayed in the subform to the combo box displayed in the main Check Writer form.

Linking the subform to the main form record

When you create a subform, you can link the main form to it by a common field or expression. The subform will then display only records that are related to the main form.

When you create a subform, if Microsoft Access finds a predefined relationship or a match between a primary key and foreign keys, the Link Child Fields and the Link Master Fields properties of the subforms show the field names that define the link. You should verify the validity of an automatic link. If the main form is based on a query, or if neither of the conditions just listed is true, Access cannot match the fields automatically to create a link.

The Link Child Fields and Link Master Fields property settings must have the same number of fields and must represent data of the same type. In this example, as you can see in Figure 14-4, the BankAccountNumber field is found in both the Check Writer and Bank Accounts forms. Although the data must match, the names of the fields can differ. For example, the BankAccountNumber field in the subform could be linked to the Account Number field in the Check Writer form since they contain the same value.

In this example, the relationship will be a one-to-one relationship, as the Bank Accounts form displays only one record at a time.

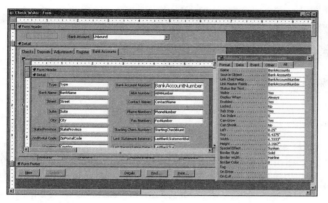

Figure 14-4
Linking the subform to the main form

When you select a bank account from the combo box in the main form, you are changing the displayed bank account. As the BankAccountNumber field changes in the main form, an internal filter in the subform control is applied to only display records where the BankAccountNumber in the Check Writer or Check Register value matches the value of BankAccountNumber

Working with Continuous Form Subforms

The greatest advantage of subforms is their ability to show the one-to-many relationship. The main form usually represents the *one* part of the relationship; the subform represents the *many* part. An example of this is found in the Check Register form. The form zCheck Register is a continuous form, as shown in Figure 14-5.

You can see in the property window that Default View is set to Continuous Forms. Notice that the detail section contains two rows of controls. This is one of the benefits of a form over a datasheet. A datasheet is limited to one row of largely unformatted data. The continuous form can contain controls with different background colors and fonts, combo boxes, check boxes, and even command buttons

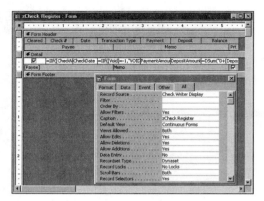

Figure 14-5
Building a continuous form

When you use the form as a subform, you simply embed it within a form just as you do with a datasheet or form view. Figure 14-6 shows this form within the Register tab of the Check Writer form. Notice that there is also an unbound OLE object frame containing the image of the ledger. This is just used as a background and does not affect the subform control.

In Figure 14-6, you can see that the Source Object property of the subform control is set to the form zCheck Register and the common field AccountNumber is used as the Link Master Fields and Link Child Field properties.

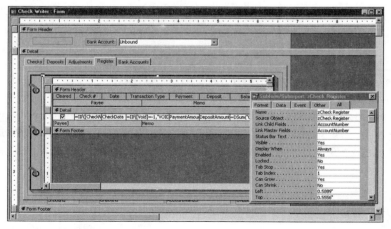

Figure 14-6
Linking the subform control to the main form

When this form is run, all of the records in the continuous form are displayed from the selected bank account. This is filtered by the link to the Account Number field. Without this link, all of the records in the Check Writer table would be displayed.

Referencing controls in subforms

The Check Register form is one of the more interesting forms in the application, as it includes some unique calculations in the controls. As you can see in Figures 14-5 and 14-6, there are several calculated controls.

The Check Register displays data from the Check Writer table, which includes check, deposit, and adjustment data. Each is a little different. The Check # control contains a formula that displays a check number if the line is a check, and if it is a deposit or adjustment, it displays a blank. It does this by checking for the value of the check number and if it is 0, it assumes it is not a check.

```
=IIf([Check Number]=0," ",[Check Number])
```

The transaction type is set to either Check, Deposit, or one of an unlimited user-defined set of adjustments. If the transaction is a check and is Void, then the word VOID is placed in front of the transaction type to indicate that it is not included in any totals:

```
=IIf([Void]=-1,"VOID-" & [Trans Type],[Trans Type])
```

The last calculated control named Balance calculates a running total for the check register. This uses a calculation that looks at the transaction ID (TransID) field and sums all of the records for the current transaction and all previous transactions.

```
=DSum("0+[Deposit Amount]-[Payment Amount]","Check Register
Display","[TransIDTransID] <=Forms![Check Register]![zCheck
Register].Form![TransID] and Void <> Yes")
```

The calculation must start with 0+ because if it doesn't, then the calculation will fail as there is no starting point.

Notice that the calculation uses the reference for the TransID within the subform control's form. This requires a special notation:

```
Forms![Check Register]![zCheck Register].Form![TransID]
```

uses the format:

```
Forms![main form name]![subform control name].Form![subform control]
```

After the subform control is referenced, a `.Form` reference is used to move internal focus to the subform control's form where controls on that form can now be referenced.

Some people might argue that the calculation is in error. Because the calculation uses the TransID field (which is an auto number), it may not group transactions together by date. For example, because the autonumber field increments sequentially, if, after entering all of your checks for the previous week, you realize you forgot one, you can enter the check and enter the date that might be last week. But the transaction will appear with the next batch of transactions because the sort (or DSUM filter) is only by the TransID field. Suppose you want to change that calculation to something else. For example, rather than to display the values in the order of the transaction ID (which is in the order the records were entered), you want to give the user the option to display the records by the transaction date. You could include an option group or a command button on the main form to give the user the option to change the calculation.

While the DSUM calculation sums the data using the last value of TransID, suppose you want to sum it by the latest date and, when the dates are the same, by the TransID. The calculation would change to the following:

```
=DSum('0+[DepositAmount]-[PaymentAmount]','CheckWriter', "([CheckDate] < _
[Forms]![Check Writer]![zCheck Register].Form![CheckDate] OR [TransID] <= _
[Forms]![Check Writer]![zCheck Register].Form![TransID]) and [CheckDate] = _
[Forms]![Check Writer]![zCheck Register].Form![CheckDate] and          " _
[AccountNumber]=[Forms]![Check Writer]![BankAccount] and Void <> True')"
```

If you wanted to create an option group to allow the user to change the calculations, you could build the option group in the main form and then use the `AfterUpdate` event of the option group to trigger the change. Figure 14-7 shows this option button control built and the Visual Basic program to change the calculation. Also notice that `OrderByOn` was used to allow the `OrderBy` property specified in each block of code to be used.

Done!

You would reference totals the same way. If you had an example where you wanted to sum a field for all the displayed lines in a continuous form, you would add a control with a SUM operator in the footer of the subform. You can then reference this total and display it in the main form using this format:

```
=Forms!mainformname!subformcontrol.Form!sumcontrolname
```

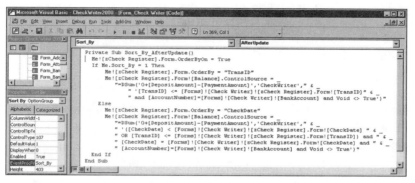

Figure 14-7
Changing a subform control's value from a main form

REVIEW

In this session, you learned about subforms, which allow you to display a form within a form. Using subforms, you can display one record or many records using a datasheet or continuous form view. The following topics were covered:

- A subform is simply a form within a form.

- You can create a subform control on any form and specify another form using the subform control's Source Object property.

- You can link a subform to a main form using the Link Child Fields and Link Master Fields properties.

- To have the subform control automatically fill in the linking properties, you must have single field relationships already specified.

- Using continuous forms allows you to display one-to-many relationships.

- You can reference controls in the subform's form by adding the .Form control reference after the subform control.

In the next session, you will learn how to program tabbed controls.

Quiz Yourself

1. Define the term subform. (See "What Is a Subform?")

2. Name the three types of forms that can be displayed with a subform. (See "What Is a Subform?")

3. Which property allows the subform control to display another form? (See "Selecting the subform's control Source Object.")

4. Which properties allow you to link a subform and a main form? (See "Linking the Subform to the main form record.")

5. Which type of data do you need to create a link between a form and subform? (See "Linking the subform to the main form record.")

6. How do you reference a control on a subform? (See "Referencing controls in subforms.")

Programming Tabbed Controls

Session Checklist

**30 Min.
To Go**

✔ Using tabbed controls

✔ Using tabbed controls vs. using multipage forms

✔ Programming tabbed controls

You have no doubt noticed the increased use of tabbed controls in many applications. The Microsoft Office Suite, as well as the Windows operating system's ubiquitous use of tabbed controls in recent incarnations, indicates both their popularity and, more importantly, their effectiveness. Using tabbed controls in your applications can improve the user's experience and enhance your application in many ways. Programming the controls will allow you to expand the capabilities of a form and, in turn, your application.

Why Use Tabbed Controls?

Why have tabbed controls gained so much popularity? Foremost, tabbed controls are user friendly. Users have become accustomed to seeing them and they are now a Windows standard. You can set them up to group information or functions in an organized and logical manner. This can allow you to make effective use of space on a form.

In addition to their inherent ease of use, tabbed controls are simple to program and you can manipulate them in many different ways. From a developmental viewpoint, tabbed controls give the programmer an excellent tool. You can manipulate a tabbed control's pages, the look of the tabbed control itself, and its properties. All of these features explain why tabbed controls have become so popular and effective, as you can see in Figure 15-1 — the main Check Writer form of the sample Check Writer program.

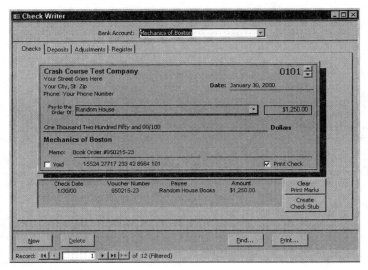

Figure 15-1
View of the Check Writer form illustrating the look of a tabbed control

There are many reasons to use tabbed controls, ranging from aesthetics to functionality. Whether you want to standardize a "look and feel" for your program or to increase functionality by segregating your data and controls, tabbed controls are a great tool for your programming toolbox. Use a tabbed control in any of the following situations:

- To incorporate a standard Windows "look and feel."
- To break up your data into logical groups or functions, each on its own tab.

- To make effective use of desktop space.
- If you have numerous controls that simply will not all fit on a single form, to tie the controls to the same record source so that you do not have to create multiple separate forms.

You can, of course, use tabbed controls in other ways. With a few exceptions, you are limited only by your creativity in regards to their use. You can perform many tasks by using controls, but some limitations also exist. The following lists are not necessarily pros and cons, but rather, features and limitations of tabbed controls.

Features:

- *Use multirow capability*. You can set the Multi Row property setting to choose the number of tabbed rows you wish to use.
- *Control the form's appearance*. The tabbed control can be "morphed" from Tabs, Buttons, or None. Use the None setting if you want to create a multi-page form with little programming required.
- *Use graphics on the tabs*. You can display both a bitmap picture and text on the tabs. Remember that visual cues such as graphics or icons can enhance the user's experience.
- *Control the display of pages*. You can programmatically control the display of the tabs during runtime. This allows you to hide and unhide pages. Use this feature if you wish to make certain data or functions on specific pages accessible under different circumstances.
- *Order the pages*. You can programmatically control how the pages are ordered.
- *Layer controls*. You can place additional controls on top of a tabbed control. This lets you "float" a control on top that will be visible on all of the pages and not just one.

Limitations:

- *Add or delete pages during runtime*: Although you can hide or unhide pages during runtime, you can not add or delete pages. You can add or delete pages only in Design view.
- *Nest tabbed controls*: You cannot embed one tabbed control within another. You are only able to "float" it.
- *Change the text orientation*: You cannot change the orientation of the text. You can have the text on the tabs only horizontally.

Tabbed Controls Versus Multipage Forms

Tabbed controls are really a variation on a multipage form. You may be familiar with this concept from earlier versions of Access or from other applications. A *multipage form* is one in which you use a page break to split a single form into multiple sections. The reason for this is to extend the area available on the form because you are limited in the area that you can display on the screen. Remember, a well-designed form does not cram too many controls in one area. You should space controls apart appropriately for readability, functionality, and aesthetics.

Using multiple page breaks allows you split a form into different sections. A tabbed control is an extension of this concept. It simplifies the process of creating a single form that can be tied to a single record source much easier to develop and manipulate. In addition, because you are using the form in this manner, it then gives you more room to work with. Figure 15-2 illustrates the Check Writer form designed using page breaks rather than a tabbed control. Note the page break controls (a line of dots) on the lefthand side above the second and third checks.

You can still use multipage forms to create a single form that contains a lot of controls. However, using a tabbed control is a better alternative for several reasons.

First, a tabbed control is a container for multiple pages. Each page is its own separate entity and has properties pertaining to it as well as controls that are a part of that particular collection. At the same time, the controls and properties can be referenced as if they were a part of the form. Thus, each control that is part of the page collection of the tabbed control is also a part of the form's collection as well. This unique situation makes it tremendously easy to put controls on a page of a tabbed control and bind it to a field from the form's record source. You can also reference all the controls as if they were right on the form itself and not as if they were embedded within another control.

Second, if you were to set up a multipage form using page breaks, you would need to program navigation buttons to move from page to page. Multipage forms have no built-in navigation buttons to do this. This can be a major task if you have a large form and need to account for differences going from one page view to another. The tabbed control eliminates the need for this by giving you two means of moving from one page to the next using tabs or buttons.

In addition, on a multipage form, you must make sure you design each section correctly to prevent a "jumping" effect caused by differences in the section sizes and in placement of common controls from one page to the next. Otherwise, controls and the page will seemingly move about because not everything is positioned or sized properly.

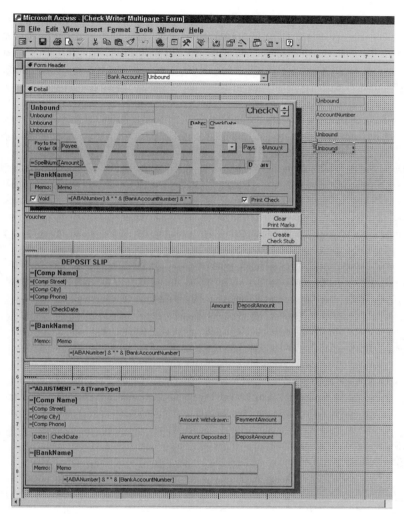

Figure 15-2
The Check Writer form using page breaks to create a multipage form

Third, a form's length is limited to only 22 inches. This is a major problem in Access 2.0 and Access 95. How do you create a single form that has room for multiple controls that exceeds 22 inches if you were to place them all? The solution in prior versions was to use subforms. A tabbed control makes the size limitation a moot point. You can have numerous pages in a tabbed control that, if put together, would easily extend past 22 inches.

All in all, tabbed controls are simply the descendents of multipage forms. This does not make multipage forms entirely useless. You may find that creating a multipage form for simple situations is a better solution than using a tabbed control. However, there are few instances where a tabbed control would not be a better solution than a multipage form.

**20 Min.
To Go**

Programming a Tabbed Control

Programming a tabbed control can extend the functionality of the control several times over. Once you understand which properties can be manipulated and how they can be manipulated, you can affect a tabbed control during runtime and create a more powerful interface.

A tabbed control can be viewed as a container that holds the controls for a particular page. Each page is then a collection of controls that are on that page. The advantage of this is that the controls on the page are also a part of the collection of controls on the form. You can reference the controls on the page just as you would a control on a form. In this manner, working with the controls on your tabbed control can be viewed as working with any other control on a form.

Tabbed control properties and methods

As with any Access control, you can programmatically affect many properties of a given control. Tabbed controls are no different from any other. Table 15-1 lists the properties that pertain to tabbed controls.

Table 15-1
Tabbed Control Properties

Property Name	Function	Set at Runtime
MultiRow	Allows you to have multiple rows of tabs. The default is No. If you set this property to No and the tabs exceed the width of the control, Access adds a scroll bar and truncates the widths as necessary.	No
Style	Allows you to choose between Tab, Buttons, or None.	Yes

Property Name	Function	Set at Runtime
TabFixedHeight	Allows you to choose the height of the tabs. If the value is set to 0, the height will be high enough to display the caption and picture.	Yes
TabFixedWidth	Allows you to choose the width of each tab. If you set the value to 0, each tab will be wide enough for its contents. If there are multiple rows of tabs, the width of the tab will be adjusted so that each row's total width is equal to the control width.	Yes
Picture	Allows you to display a bitmap graphic alongside the text of the caption on a particular tab. If you want only the graphic, you can enter in a space for the caption text.	No
On Change	Allows you to set and assign a macro or code that is processed when the user changes from tab to tab. Especially useful when you want to run code that reacts to going from tab to tab.	No
Page Index	Allows you to indicate the position of the tab or page in relation to all of the tabs.	Yes
Visible (tabbed control page)	Allows you to hide and unhide a particular tab or page of the tabbed control.	Yes

Tabbed control styles

Tabbed controls provide three different styles that you can choose from: Buttons, Tabs, or None. The default is Tabs. This lets you choose how the tab will look. Figures 15-3, 15-4, and 15-5 illustrate how the same tabbed form of the Check Writer program looks with the three different styles. The default style of tabs gives you the standard tabbed control look in Figure 15-3. The Buttons style uses buttons in place of the tabs as shown in Figure 15-4. Selecting None for the style gives you the look shown in Figure 15-5.

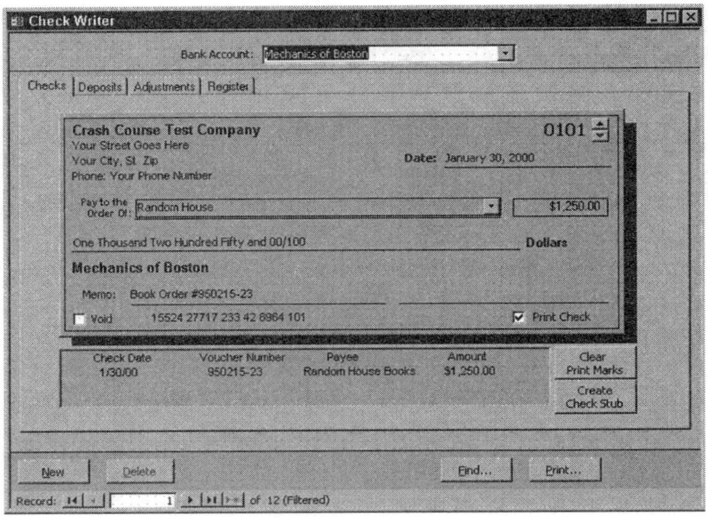

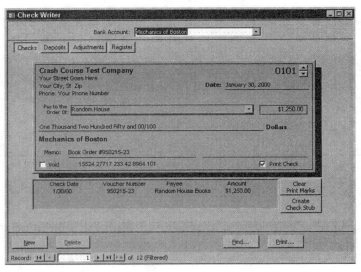

Figure 15-3
The Check Writer form with tabs

Figure 15-4
The Check Writer form using buttons for navigating

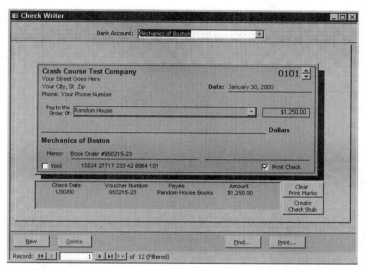

Figure 15-5
The Check Writer form with the style property set to None

Picking the style type is primarily an aesthetic choice; however, sometimes one style is preferable over the other regardless of the look. If you are designing a tabbed control with multiple pages, using the Tabs style is the best choice. The look is clean and the operation is intuitive for the end user. This is especially true if you are using the multirow property to have more than one row of tabs. Multirowed buttons would look cluttered and messy.

Sometimes you may want to use the Buttons option. If your design calls for only two or three pages, using buttons to navigate the forms may be a better choice. In this case, it may be just as intuitive and aesthetically pleasing to use buttons in place of the tabs.

At first, selecting None as the style may seem to be a redundant choice considering this is, after all, a tabbed control. However, there are times you may wish to set up multiple pages without any tabs or buttons. One excellent example is when creating a wizard-like interface. In the case of a wizard form such as AddAccountWizard, a tabbed control is used to set up each page of the wizard. Because a wizard has a specific order in which the information must be presented, there is no need to give the user free access to move from page to page randomly.

Giving such freedom in a wizard would present problems if the user went through the wizard in the wrong order. Specific buttons to move forward and backwards are provided as the means of navigating from one page to the next. This lets you add in conditional checks at each point to make sure that the data entered on a page is valid. In this manner, it is again better to remove all tabs and buttons as navigational tools. More importantly, using a tabbed control to set up the wizard makes designing the form easier.

Session 25 contains more information on creating wizard-type forms.

Changing the style programmatically

One nice trick is to use code to change the style programmatically during runtime, for instance, if certain users of the program should have access only to the Deposits page of the form and no other page. You do not want the user to be able to create checks or view the check register. When you open the form Check Writer Limited Functionality, you are prompted to enter one of two IDs: Supervisor or User. If you enter Supervisor, you will see the Check Writer form as you normally would. All of the tabs are present. If you enter User, you will see only the Deposit page of the tab. Note also that no tabs appear at all.

If you view the same form in Design view, you will see that it is identical to the Check Writer form except for the code in the On Open event that determines the user and his or her access level. If the user enters an ID of User, then only the Deposits page of the tabbed control is displayed. In addition, the tabbed control is set to display None as the style. This prevents the user from seeing and accessing different pages. If the ID entered is Supervisor, then you would see the form as you normally do, with all of the tabs visible.

The code for changing the look of the tab is very straightforward. It is simply a matter of setting the tab's Style property. You can have one of three settings: Tabs (0), Buttons (1), or None (2). You can view this at the end of the On Open event's code, as seen here:

```
If InputBox("Please enter in either Supervisor or User", "Log In") = "User" Then
        Me.TabControl.Style = 2
        Me.TabControl.Pages(1).SetFocus
End If
Me.TabControl.Visible = True
```

The beginning of the code has a line that sets the tabbed control to not visible. This is only so that the user does not initially see the form open with all of the tabs and then see it disappear after he/she has entered the logon ID. The code provides prompts for an ID by using the InputBox function. If the entry is for the

ID of User, the tabs are turned off by setting the style to 2. The focus is then set to the tabbed control's page 1. Note that the pages are indexed starting from zero as the starting page.

Showing and hiding pages

Another excellent technique is to make the individual pages of the tabbed control visible and not visible. This allows you incredible control over how the tabbed control appears as well as access to specific tab pages. In this case, rather than hiding all of the tabs, only specific ones are hidden. This can be done by setting the visible property of the page. On the bottom of the form Check Writer Limited Functionality, a new button, Hide Tabs, has been created. This button lets the user enter the name of the tab and the code and then hides that particular tab page. The code works in the following manner.

```
Private Sub btnHideTabs_Click()
    Dim TabName As String

    TabName = InputBox("Enter the tab name you wish to hide.", "Hide Tabs")

    With Me.TabControl
        .Pages(0).Visible = True
        .Pages(1).Visible = True
        .Pages(2).Visible = True
        .Pages(3).Visible = True
    End With

    Select Case TabName

        Case "Checks"
            Me.TabControl.Pages("Checks").Visible = False

        Case "Deposits"
            Me.TabControl.Pages("Deposits").Visible = False
        Case "Adjustments"
            Me.TabControl.Pages("Adjustments").Visible = False
        Case "Register"
            Me.TabControl.Pages("Register").Visible = False
        Case Else
            MsgBox "No valid tab name entered.", vbCritical, "Tab Name Error"
    End Select

End Sub
```

First, all of the tabs are set to visible. The code then uses the InputBox function to let the user enter a tab name. A Select Case statement is used to determine which tab to make not visible. Note that in this example, the control name of the tab page is used rather than the index page number.

Using either technique to limit access to specific tabs can provide security. Of course, the two types of security are very simplistic. However, coupled with other techniques, they can be an important element of a fully secured application.

Using the On Change event

Often, you will want to affect an event as the user goes from tab to tab. This is where the On Change event of the tabbed control comes into use. For example, in the Check Writer form, as the user moves from tab to tab, the On Change event is run. Because each tab of the form is set for different types of transactions, as the user moves from tab to tab, only those records that pertain to the particular tab that they are on is displayed. Thus, when you are on the tab for checks, you see only check transactions. When you are on the tab for deposits, you see only deposits, and so on. The code for the tabbed control's On Change event in the Check Writer form follows.

```
Private Sub TabControl_Change()
Dim CurConn As ADODB.Connection
Dim CheckTB As New ADODB.RecordSet
Dim FindCrit As String

    Set CurConn = CurrentProject.Connection

    On Error GoTo ErrorHandler
    With Me
        Select Case .TabControl.value
            Case 0 'Checks
                .Filter = "[TransType] = 'Check'"
                .FilterOn = True
                .Requery
            Case 1 'Deposits
                .Filter = "[TransType] = 'Deposit'"
                .FilterOn = True
                .Requery
            Case 2 'Adjustments
                .Filter = "[TransType] <> 'Deposit' AND [TransType] <> 'Check'"
                .FilterOn = True
                .Requery
            Case 3 'Register
                DoCmd.RunCommand acCmdSaveRecord
                .zCheck_Register.Requery
                If Not IsNull(.[TransID]) Then
                    .zCheck_Register.SetFocus
                    .[zCheck Register].Form![TransID].Enabled = True
                    .[zCheck Register].Form![TransID].SetFocus
                    DoCmd.FindRecord Forms! _
                        [Check Writer Limited Functionality]![TransID]
                End If
```

```
                .[zCheck Register].Form![Memo].SetFocus
                If (Not IsNull(.[TransID])) Then
                    .zCheck_Register.Form![TransID].Enabled = False
                End If
        End Select
        Select Case Me.TabControl.value
            Case 0, 1, 2
                .NavigationButtons = True
                .New.Visible = True
                .Delete.Visible = True
                .btnDetails.Visible = False
                'Move to the matching Check Writer item pointed to in Register
                If IsNull(![TransID]) Then
                    DoCmd.GoToRecord acActiveDataObject, , acLast
                Else
                    FindCrit = "TransID = " & Me![TransID]
                    Set CheckTB = Forms![Check Writer Limited Functionality] _
                        .RecordsetClone
                    CheckTB.Find FindCrit
                    If Not CheckTB.EOF Then
                        Forms![Check Writer Limited Functionality].Bookmark = _
                            CheckTB.Bookmark
                    End If
                    CheckTB.Close
                    Set CheckTB = Nothing
                End If

            Case 3
                .NavigationButtons = False
                .New.Visible = False
                .Delete.Visible = False
                .btnDetails.Visible = True
        End Select
    End With
    GoTo Done

ErrorHandler:
    If Err.Number = 2105 Then
        New_Click
        Resume Next
    End If
Done:
End Sub
```

The code uses two Select Case statements to affect changes to the tabbed control and the information it displays. Each statement checks for the page that the control is on. The first is used to change records to be filtered for that particular tab. So for the Checks tab, which has an index of 0, the filter is set to display only transactions of checks. For the Deposits tab, which has an index of 1, the filter is set to display only deposit transactions. This is done for each of the four tabs.

Done!

The second Select Case`select case` statement turns the additional navigation buttons to visible. It then checks to see if a particular Trans ID has been entered in the Trans ID field and moves to that record. This is done for instances where a particular record has been selected in the Check Register. Otherwise, the last record is selected. If the tab is the Register tab, then the Delete and New navigation buttons are set to be not visible.

REVIEW

Tabbed controls can be extremely useful in creating a user-friendly interface. From a developmental standpoint, they are also very easy controls to set up and manipulate.

A tabbed control is unique in that it can be viewed as a container for pages on a form. Each page in turn has its own properties that can be manipulated and is a collection for controls that are on that page or tab. At the same time, the controls on the page are also a part of the control collection for the form.

Understanding the properties of a tabbed control lets you affect it programmatically. You can change its looks by choosing the style. You can also affect changes as you move from tab to tab to reflect information of the particular tab you are on.

You can control many aspects of tabs. Tabbed controls are very versatile. You will no doubt use them often in designing forms.

QUIZ YOURSELF

1. Why are tabbed controls so effective? (See "Why Use Tabbed Controls?")
2. If you wanted to make a particular button on the main form visible and not visible when you move from page 0 to page 1, what technique would you use? (See "Programming a Tabbed Control.")
3. You can determine which page of the tab you are on by referencing which property? (See "Programming a Tabbed Control.")
4. Can tabbed controls contain a subform? (See "Programming a Tabbed Control.")
5. What technique can you use to make some tabs or pages visible and others not visible? (See "Programming a Tabbed Control.")

SESSION

Message Boxes and Error-Handling Programs and Techniques

Session Checklist

✔ Using the Access Message Box function

✔ Understanding different types of errors

✔ Handling errors

✔ Understanding the Error and Err collections

I n this session you will learn about two of the most frequently used elements of application programming: communicating with the user using the message box and handling of errors.

**30 Min.
To Go**

The Message Box Function

Probably one of the most commonly used functions is the MsgBox function. It is frequently used because it provides an easy way for VBA code to communicate with the user. Not only does it display a message, but it can also return a selection from the user. The selection is limited to a predefined set of buttons, but in most cases, these buttons are all you need. The syntax of this function follows:

YNTAX ▶

```
MsgBox(prompt[, buttons] [, title] [, helpfile, context])
```

When called, it displays the string expression "prompt" in a dialog box. This string expression can be up to 1,024 characters and can include the string constant vbCRLF to start a new line.

The buttons parameter is an optional numeric expression that does more than just display a set of buttons. It also determines the icon that will be displayed, which button will be the default button, and the modality of the message box. When a form opens as a modal form, you must first close the form before you can move focus to another object.

The list of button sets are shown in Table 16-1. You can use the value or, to make your code more readable, use the constants.

Table 16-1

MsgBox Button Values and Constants

Value	Button Set	Constant
0	OK	VbOKOnly
1	OK, Cancel	VbOKCancel
2	Abort, Retry, Ignore	vbAbortRetryIgnore
3	Yes, No, Cancel	VbYesNoCancel
4	Yes, No	VbYesNo
5	Retry, Cancel	VbRetryCancel
6 – 15	Not used	

To choose an icon, you add another value to the button value. Note that these values represent bits in a binary number. This allows them to be added and to be mutually exclusive of each other. Icon values are shown in Table 16-2.

Table 16-2

MsgBox Icon Values and Constants

Value	Icon	Constant	Image
0	No icon		
16	Critical message	VbCritical	⊗
32	Warning query	VbQuestion	?
48	Warning message	VbExclamation	⚠

Value	Icon	Constant	Image
64	Information message	VbInformation	
80, 96, 112, 128, 144, 160, 176, 192, 208, 224, 240	Not used		

You can also select which button is the default by adding another number to the Button argument. Table 16-3 shows the values for the button defaults.

Table 16-3
Constants for Setting Button Defaults

Value	Button is default	Constant
0	First button	vbDefaultButton1
256	Second button	vbDefaultButton2
512	Third button	vbDefaultButton3
768	Fourth button	vbDefaultButton4

By default, the message box is "Application" modal, which means the user must respond to the message box before continuing within the current application. If you add a value of 4096 (the constant is vbSystemModal), then the message box will be "System" modal, where all applications are suspended until the user responds to the message box.

A few other options are also available, as shown in Table 16-4.

Table 16-4
Values and Constants for Other MsgBox Options

Value	Action	Constant
16384	Adds a Help button to the message box	vbMsgBoxHelpButton
65536	Makes the message box window the foreground window	VbMsgBoxSetForeground

Continued

Table 16-4 *Continued*

Value	Action	Constant
524288	Right-aligns the text	`vbMsgBoxRight`
1048576	Makes text appear as right-to-left reading on Hebrew and Arabic systems	`vbMsgBoxRtlReading`

So as an example, let's say you want a Yes/No button combination with a Help button and a Warning icon, and you want the No button to be the default. The button value should be:

```
VbYesNo + VbExclamation + vbDefaultButton2 + vbMsgBoxHelpButton
= 4 + 48 + 256 + 16384 = 16,692
```

The optional `Title` argument is a string expression displayed in the title bar of the dialog box. When this is omitted, the application name is displayed in the title bar.

If you display a Help button, you should enter values for the two parameters `HelpFile` and `Context`. The `HelpFile` is a string expression that contains the name of the Help file. The `Context` argument is a numeric expression that is the help context number assigned to the appropriate help topic. Without a Help button, pressing the F1 button will have the same effect. Pressing the Help button will call the Microsoft Help Workshop or Microsoft HTML Help Workshop application. It will load the custom Help file specified by the HelpFile string, and display the Help topic specified by the Context parameter. Refer to the Microsoft Access online Help topics "HelpContextID, HelpFile Properties" to get more information. Pressing the Help button will not cause the MsgBox to close or return a value.

The `MsgBox` function can return a value that represents the button pressed. The return values are listed in Table 16-5.

Table 16-5
MsgBox Return Values and Constants

Value	Description	Constant
1	OK	`vbOK`
2	Cancel	`vbCancel`
3	Abort	`vbAbort`

Value	Description	Constant
4	Retry	vbRetry
5	Ignore	vbIgnore
6	Yes	vbYes
7	No	vbNo

As an example of how to use the Msgbox function, refer to Listing 16-1. This subroutine comes from the form "Bank Accounts Unbound" in the sample Check Writer application. The subroutine is called when the form is closed or unloaded. If the control FlagEdited is True, then the user has changed or entered data on the form and did not save the data. So if FlagEdited is true, a message box appears that reads "Do you want to save your changes?" The function is called with the vbYesNoCancel value set for the buttons, so three buttons are displayed: Yes, No, and Cancel. The function returns a value for the user selection and it is assigned to the variable Answer. If Answer contains the value associated with the Cancel button, then the Cancel variable is set to true and the form does not close. If Answer contains the value associated with the Yes button, then the function uf_SaveRecord is called to save the data. Otherwise, the No button must have been pressed, so the form continues to close.

Listing 16-1
Example of Using the MsgBox Function

```
Private Sub Form_Unload(Cancel As Integer)
Dim Answer As Integer
    If Me.FlagEdited Then
        Answer = MsgBox("Do you want to save your changes?", _
            vbYesNoCancel)
        If Answer = vbCancel Then Cancel = True
        If Answer = vbYes Then uf_SaveRecord Me
    End If
End Sub
```

There will probably be 100 calls to the MsgBox function within an application. Be sure to use the powerful features that this function provides to communicate with your users.

EZ Extensions from Database Creations, Inc., includes a customizable message box that can be used to replace the Access message box. It is compatible with the Access message box, plus it provides for the use of user-defined icons, allows different fonts and font sizes to be used, allows text alignment to be changed, and can be further customized by the user to include different font colors, background colors, and so on.

Errors

20 Min. To Go

Assuming you get past the syntax checking using the VBA Editor and you also get past the errors that Access will find when you compile your application, the only remaining errors that can occur will occur at runtime. Runtime errors occur for many reasons. When they do occur, one of following will happen:

- A fatal error will occur and the application will crash.
- An untrapped error will occur and the Access error dialog box will appear.
- A handled error will occur and your code will take care of the problem.
- An unknown application error will occur that will not cause an Access error.

Types of errors

A fatal error is a nonrecoverable error that will crash an application. This error generally occurs as a result of an operation outside the Access environment, so Access cannot handle it, and therefore, your code will not be able to handle it. Fatal errors generally occur when a Windows API is called. Windows API calls are those calls you make from your application that call a procedure in a Windows library. An example of this type of call may be retrieving the screen resolution. You have to go to Windows to get this kind of information. Since we cannot do much about fatal errors in our Access VBA program, let's concentrate on the types of errors we can control.

The Access error dialog box will appear for untrapped errors. (See Figure 16-1.) This can be good for development because problems can be traced to the specific line of code that caused the error. By pressing the Debug button, the VBA window will open and highlight the guilty line of code. But this is not the kind of reaction you generally want with your applications and end users. Therefore, having an error handler and making it a handled error can sometimes not only alert the user of a problem, but may also even prevent the user from worrying about the problem by having the code either work around the error or correct the problem.

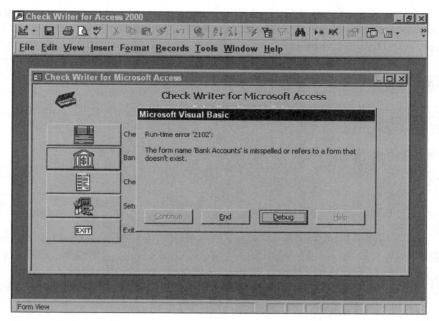

Figure 16-1
The Access error dialog box

The last type of error is the unknown application error. This is a logic error in the code. No error notification will occur since the program is working the way it was coded. The problem is that the code is performing the wrong function. This could be the hardest type of error to discover. There are two ways to handle an unknown application error:

- Test, test, test.
- Check the results programmatically by redundantly checking the results.

As a simple example to show how results can be checked, imagine a spreadsheet of numbers. Create a column that contains a subtotal on each row that is the sum of all the numbers in a given row. Then total the subtotals to get the total for all the numbers. Now to check that result, create a new row that sums the numbers in each column with a subtotal for each column. The total of these subtotals should equal the first total. If it doesn't, you have an error condition and should take some action.

Since this type of error checking is very application-specific, it cannot be discussed in general terms. The Check Writer sample contains many application specific error checking code that is described throughout this book. This session will deal with the errors that Access can detect.

The elements of error handling

Access 2000 and ADO provide four basic programming elements for error handling. These include the following:

- The Errors collection
- The Err object
- VBA Error statements
- The Error event

When Access detects an error, most of the time an object is created for the error. The two types of error objects in Access are based on whether the error was detected by ADO or Access. The Errors collection is part of the ADO object model. The Err object is part of the Access object model. In addition to these two elements, Access has an Error event that gets triggered when an error occurs with a form or report.

The Errors collection

When an error occurs in an ADO object, an Error object is created in the Errors collection of the Connection object. These are referred to as data access errors. When an error occurs, the collection is cleared and the new set of objects is put into the collection. While the collection exists only for one error event, the event could generate several errors. Each of these errors is stored in the Errors collection. The Errors collection is an object of the Connection object, not ADO.

The Errors collection has one property, Count, which contains the number of errors or error objects. It has a value of 0 if there are no errors. There are a few properties of each Error object. These include Description, HelpContext, HelpFile, Number, and Source. When there are multiple errors, the lowest-level error is the first object in the collection and the highest-level error is the last object in the collection.

When an ADO error occurs, the VBA `Err` object contains the error number for the first object in the `Errors` collection. You need to check the `Errors` collection to see whether additional ADO errors have occurred. See Listing 16-2 later in this session for an example.

The Err object

The `Err` object is created by VBA. When an error occurs, information about that error is stored in the `Err` object, which contains information about only one error at a time. When an error occurs, the `Err` object is cleared and updated to include information about that most recent error.

The `Err` object has several properties, including `Number` and `Description`. The `Err` object also has two methods: `Clear` to clear information from the `Err` object, and `Raise` to simulate an error.

When an error occurs relative to the Jet database engine or ADO, you need to refer to the `Errors` collection to get more information.

VBA error statements

There are two basic VBA statements for handling errors: `On Error` and `Resume`. The `On Error` statement enables or disables error handling. There are three forms of the `On Error` statement:

- On Error GoTo *label*
- On Error GoTo 0
- On Error Resume Next

The `On Error GoTo `*label* statement enables an error-handling routine. The label should be the label for the error-handling routine. When this statement is executed, error handling is immediately enabled. When an error then occurs, execution goes to the line specified by the *label* argument, which should be at the beginning of the error-handling routine.

To disable error handling, use the `On Error GoTo 0` statement. This statement also resets the properties of the `Err` object.

The `On Error Resume Next` statement ignores the line that causes an error and continues execution with the line following the line that caused the error. No error-handling routine is called. This statement is useful if you want to ignore errors or if you want to check the values of the `Err` object immediately after a line at which you anticipate an error will occur, and handle the error within the procedure rather than in an error handler.

You return to the main procedure from an error handler using the `Resume` statement. If you do not want to resume execution in case of an error, the `Resume` statement is not necessary. All you need to do is exit the procedure.

As with the `On Error` statement, there are three forms of the `Resume` statement:

- Resume or Resume 0
- Resume Next
- Resume *label*

The `Resume` or `Resume 0` statement returns execution to the line at which the error occurred. This statement is used typically when the user must make a correction. This might occur if you prompt the user for the name of a file to open, and the user enters a filename that doesn't exist. You can then force the execution of the code back to the point where the filename is requested.

When your error handler corrects or works around the problem that caused the error, the `Resume Next` statement is used. It returns execution to the line immediately following the line at which the error occurred.

If you need to continue execution at some other place besides the line that caused the error or the line after the line that caused the error, then you should use the `Resume label` statement. It returns execution to the line specified by the *label* argument.

The Error event

**10 Min.
To Go**

Access provides for an `Error` event with forms and reports. This give you a nice way to trap an error when VBA code is not running. This event is triggered when an error occurs on a form or report. You need to create an event procedure for the `On Error` event to trap these errors. The procedure would look like one of the following depending on whether it was a form or report.

```
Private Sub Form_Error(DataErr As Integer, Response As Integer)
'Insert error handler here
End Sub
```

```
Private Sub Report_Error(DataErr As Integer, Response As Integer)
'Insert error handler here
End Sub
```

These subroutines have two arguments: `DataErr` and `Response`. `DataErr` is the error code returned by the `Err` object when an error occurs. Note that the `Err` object isn't populated with information after the event occurs. You need to use the `DataErr` argument to determine which error occurred. The second argument Response should contain either one of the following constants:

AcDataErrContinue Ignore the error and continue without displaying the default Access error message.

AcDataErrDisplay   Display the default Access error message. (This is the default.)

When you use AcDataErrContinue, you can then supply a custom error message or handler in place of the default error message.

Error-handling procedures

There are obviously numerous ways to deal with errors within forms, reports, and code. Each form and report, as well as each function and subroutine, can and probably should have an error-handling routine. It is usual to see a good part of the development effort devoted to error handling. As you look through the various components in our example Check Writer application, you will see numerous instances of error-handling routines.

Probably the most common routine is shown in Listing 16-2.

Listing 16-2
Error-Handler Structure

```
Function SampleCode
'Dim statements here

    On Error goto ErrorHandler
    'insert functional code here
    Exit Function

ErrorHandler:
    'error handler code here
    Msgbox err.description
    'either enter a resume statement here or
        ' nothing and let the function end

End Function
```

The On Error statement enables the error handler and if an error occurs, execution will continue on the line after the label ErrorHandler. This label could be any valid VBA label. The error-handler code would then deal with the error and then either resume execution back in the body of the procedure or just exit the function or subroutine. The inclusion of the Msgbox statement in the error handler is a typical way of informing the user of what happened.

When an error occurs in a called function or subroutine that doesn't have an enabled error handler, VBA will return to the calling procedure looking for an enabled error handler. This process will proceed up the calling tree until one is found or, if not, execution will stop with an Access error message displayed.

Creating an error-handling routine

When an error occurs within an application, you have a few choices:

- Ignore the error and resume execution.
- Programmatically correct the problem causing the error and resume execution.
- Request that the user correct the problem and resume execution.
- Inform the user of the problem and continue execution.
- Inform the user of the problem and stop execution.

For this session, we will create a section of a generic error handler that informs the user of the problem. We will do this by exploring the Error and Err objects that contain the information about the error.

Listing 16-3 contains an error handler that can be used in a procedure that deals with an ADO connection. When an error occurs, the code following the label ErrorHandler runs and first checks to see if the Error object contains any items. If it does, then it checks to see if the error is the same as the Err object; if so, then the error was an ADO error and the variable strMessage will contain the descriptions of all the errors in the Errors collection. If it is not an ADO error, then the error is from VBA and the single Err.Description value will be displayed. This error handler is used in the form "Bank Accounts Unbound" in our sample application.

Listing 16-3
General Error Handler

```
Dim cnn As New ADODB.Connection
Dim errX As ADODB.Error
```

```
Dim strMessage As String

    On Error goto ErrorHandler

    'insert code here

    GoTo Done

ErrorHandler:
    If cnn.Errors.Count > 0 Then
      If err.Number = cnn.Errors.Item(0).Number Then
        'error is an ADO Connection Error
        For Each errX In cnn.Errors
          strMessage = strMessage & err.Description & vbCrLf
        Next
        MsgBox strMessage, , "ADO Error Handler"
      End If
    Else
        'error is a VBA Error
        MsgBox err.Description, , "VBA Error Handler"
    End If
Done:
```

Other Ideas

In designing your application, there are many other ways that you can expand its capabilities. However, a full discussion is beyond the scope of this book. Consider the following ideas to get you started:

- Create a user-defined error. If something goes wrong with data within your application or an operation the user has chosen, you can use the Raise method of the Err object to cause an error to occur and run your standard error handler. The range 513–65535 is available for user-defined errors and is used with the Raise method as an argument.

- Create a standard error handler called from multiple procedures.

- Record errors in a log. Create a table to store errors as they occur. You can then keep a history of errors for further refinement of your application design or to see trends with problems.

Done!

- Instead of just displaying an error message, provide for a printed problem report that could get forwarded to the appropriate technical support group. Or automatically e-mail an error message to a technical support organization.

REVIEW

In this session, you learned about the MsgBox function as well as how to handle error conditions in an application. The following points were discussed:

- One of the most commonly used functions is the MsgBox function. It provides an easy way for your VBA code to communicate with the user both by displaying a message and by returning a decision by the user.
- Having an error handler can alert the user of a problem and prevent the application from crashing.
- Error handlers can also take some action to either work around the error or correct the problem and prevent any user intervention.
- You should devote a good part of your development effort to handling errors.

QUIZ YOURSELF

1. Why is the MsgBox function one of the most commonly used functions? (See "The Message Box Function.")
2. What four possible things might happen when a runtime error occurs? (See "Errors.")
3. When and why do fatal errors occur? (See "Types of errors.")
4. How would you reduce the likelihood of an application error? (See "Types of errors.")
5. What are the two different types of error objects? When is each type used? (See "The elements of error handling.")

1. True or false: A Switchboard is a type of menu system.

2. True or false: The Switchboard Manager must be used to create a switchboard.

3. True or false: You can create a custom menu bar by using the Access 2000 Commandbar object or by creating a macro.

4. True or false: `KeyUp`, `KeyDown`, and `KeyRight` are all three types of keyboard events.

5. Which of the following is/are true for unbound forms?

    a. They do not have a constant connection and open view of the underlying data.

    b. They retrieve one record at a time.

    c. They improve performance.

    d. Record changes are under control of code.

    e. All of the above.

6. True or false: When you use unbound forms Access automatically handles record locking.

7. List three functions you need to include on an unbound form to make it functional.

8. List two reasons why you would not want to use unbound forms.

9. When is it preferable to use an option group over a checkbox?

10. True or false: A ComboBox allows you to have multiple selections.

11. Which properties are unique to combo and list boxes?

    a. Controlsource

    b. rowsource

    c. font size

    d. after update

    e. column width

    f. bound column

    g. multi selection

12. You want to run code that occurs when a user selects an item that is not listed. What event do you use?

    a. After Update

    b. Before Update

    c. In List

    d. Not In List

13. What are the three different types of form views?

14. True or false: A subform must be linked to a main form.

15. Name the most compelling reason to use a continuous form instead of a datasheet.

16. What are the properties that are used to link data between a subform to a form?

17. List three reasons why you should use a tabbed control.

18. To run a procedure as the user changes from tab to tab, you would use which event?

    a. After Update

    b. On Click

    c. On Change

    d. On Tab Click

19. True or false: You can only set the Visible property for the tab control as a whole.

20. What are the three types of tab styles you can use?

PART

IV

Saturday
Evening

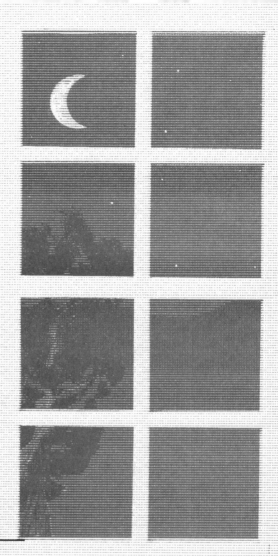

Importing and Exporting Data

Session Checklist

✔ Importing and exporting data

✔ Creating import/export specifications

✔ Programming an import interface

✔ Programming an export interface

**30 Min.
To Go**

It is becoming standard and important that applications be able to communicate with one another in some way. One of the main functions of any database program is its ability to import and export data. Fortunately, Access has a powerful built-in wizard that walks you through doing an import or export. Plus with the power of VBA, you can design interfaces to give your end users a more intuitive means of processing external data.

Importing and Exporting

Access's built-in import and export capabilities are powerful, flexible, and simple to use. You can import and export with another database, spreadsheet, or a SQL database that supports ODBC. In fact, Access allows you to directly import or export to numerous popular "off the shelf" databases and spreadsheets. Access also allows you to import and export with standard text files, further expanding its flexibility. Table 17-1 lists the formats from which you can import and export.

Table 17-1
File Formats That Access Supports

Data Source	Version/Format
Microsoft Access databases	2.0, 7.0/95, 8.0/97, 9.0/2000
Microsoft Access Project	9.0/2000
dBase	III, III+, IV, and 5 7.0 — Linking requires Borland Database Engine 4.x or later
Paradox	3.x, 4.x, 5.0 8.0 — Linking requires Borland Database Engine 4.x or later
Microsoft Excel Spreadsheet	3.0, 4.0, 5.0, 7.0/95, 8.0/97, 9.0/2000
Lotus 1-2-3 Spreadsheet	.wks, .wk1, .wk2, .wk3, and .wk4
Microsoft Exchange	All versions
Delimited text files	All character sets
Fixed-width text files	All character sets
HTML	(for lists), 3.x (lists and tables) SQL tables, Microsoft FoxPro, and all other data sources that support ODBC Visual FoxPro 2.x, 3.0, 5.0, and 6.x (only for import)

Importing data

With Access, you can do two types of importing: a true import, where the data is copied into the database, versus linking the table. In an actual import of the data, the information is copied into the existing database and becomes a part of the database. This can be either an import where the data becomes a new table or the data is appended to an existing table. A linked table means the information remains external and is never truly incorporated into the database.

Which method is the best? The answer depends on several factors that you should take into account. You should import the data into the database in the following situations:

- Performance is key. Local tables provide the best performance. Access is optimized to work with local data in an Access format.
- The incoming data need not be shared with other database applications. The data from the table will not be accessed from other external applications.
- The information contained in the table is not updated frequently, or this is a one-time update of the data.
- You are converting from one format to another and will no longer need to maintain the older (legacy) format.

Consider using Access's linking feature in the following situations:

- Your application structure has the data tables in a separate database from the application database.
- You need to be able to update and keep the original data available to other applications.
- The information is frequently updated from other applications.
- The file size of the database exceeds the 1GB capacity of Access's limit for local tables.

Issues of importing data

Importing data is actually a very simple process. The complexity lies not in bringing the data into Access, but rather, with making sure the data gets updated properly in the local tables. Importing data can be broken into the following major steps.

1. Organize the data.
2. Format the data.
3. Map the data.
4. Append the records.

Let's take a closer look at each of these steps:

Organizing the data to import

How you gather and organize the data depends on which database platform you use. If the database is another Access database, you can either export an entire table or parts of the table. Should you need to export a part of a table, you can use a query and export the results of the query. You can also pull information from multiple tables into a single query and use that resultant. What information you gather and from which tables you gather that information totally depends on what you need to import into the current database. Therefore, start with a listing of information or data that you need to import and then gather that from the appropriate tables. Once the information has been gathered together, you will need to format it.

Formatting the import data

Because of Access's ability to read many different types of file formats, the first step in importing data is to get the data file in a format that Access can read. This depends on the external program from which the data is coming.

If you are working with other Access databases, you don't need to convert the data. Even if the data is coming from another database, Access can read directly from such sources as FoxPro, dBase, and Paradox. In addition, it can read directly from spreadsheet programs like Excel and Lotus.

What if you are coming from a nonstandard platform? For instance, you are using a legacy MS-DOS-based system, a mainframe, or a once-popular-but-presently-obscure format, like Btrieve. In these cases, you will need to output the data into a format that Access can read. In most cases, this means exporting the data from the external application into a text file.

Text files can have many different formats, but they fall into two essential groups: delimited and fixed-width. In a *delimited text file*, the fields are separated by some character and individual records are each on a line. Separator characters ("delimiters") can be any of the following standard ones such as a comma, semicolon, space, or tab. Additionally, nonstandard text formats sometimes use other characters that can be defined. With a delimited file, it is unnecessary to define the field widths, as seen in Figure 17-1. Each line is considered a separate record and as you read the line from left to right, each instance of the delimiter indicates a new field.

A *fixed-width file* does not use any type of delimiter to separate the fields. In this format, the records are also each on a separate line. However, the text file is formatted so that the widths of the fields are defined as part of the file. Simply put, the data is formatted so that the fields are lined up in a columnar structure. Figure 17-2 shows an example. The figure contains data that is identical to the data shown in Figure 17-1 but in a fixed-width format. The column widths determine the size of the fields, and the data for that field must fit within the column.

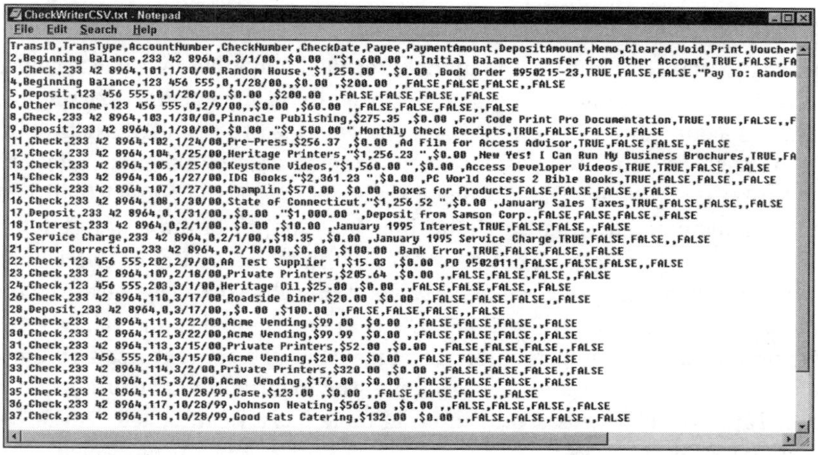

CheckWriterCSV.txt - Notepad

File Edit Search Help

```
TransID,TransType,AccountNumber,CheckNumber,CheckDate,Payee,PaymentAmount,DepositAmount,Memo,Cleared,Void,Print,Voucher
2,Beginning Balance,233 42 8964,0,3/1/00,,$0.00 ,"$1,600.00 ",Initial Balance Transfer from Other Account,TRUE,FALSE,FA
3,Check,233 42 8964,101,1/30/00,Random House,"$1,250.00 ",$0.00 ,Book Order #950215-23,TRUE,FALSE,FALSE,"Pay To: Random
4,Beginning Balance,123 456 555,0,1/28/00,,$0.00 ,$200.00 ,,FALSE,FALSE,FALSE,,FALSE
5,Deposit,123 456 555,0,1/28/00,,$0.00 ,$200.00 ,,FALSE,FALSE,FALSE,,FALSE
6,Other Income,123 456 555,0,2/9/00,,$0.00 ,$60.00 ,,FALSE,FALSE,FALSE,,FALSE
8,Check,233 42 8964,103,1/30/00,Pinnacle Publishing,$275.35 ,$0.00 ,For Code Print Pro Documentation,TRUE,TRUE,FALSE,,F
9,Deposit,233 42 8964,0,1/30/00,,$0.00 ,"$9,500.00 ",Monthly Check Receipts,TRUE,FALSE,FALSE,,FALSE
11,Check,233 42 8964,102,1/24/00,Pre-Press,$256.37 ,$0.00 ,Ad Film for Access Advisor,TRUE,FALSE,FALSE,,FALSE
12,Check,233 42 8964,104,1/25/00,Heritage Printers,"$1,256.23 ",$0.00 ,New Yes! I Can Run My Business Brochures,TRUE,FA
13,Check,233 42 8964,105,1/25/00,Keystone Videos,"$1,560.00 ",$0.00 ,Access Developer Videos,TRUE,TRUE,FALSE,,FALSE
14,Check,233 42 8964,106,1/27/00,IDG Books,"$2,361.23 ",$0.00 ,PC World Access 2 Bible Books,TRUE,FALSE,FALSE,,FALSE
15,Check,233 42 8964,107,1/27/00,Champlin,$570.00 ,$0.00 ,Boxes for Products,FALSE,FALSE,FALSE,,FALSE
16,Check,233 42 8964,108,1/30/00,State of Connecticut,"$1,256.52 ",$0.00 ,January Sales Taxes,TRUE,FALSE,FALSE,,FALSE
17,Deposit,233 42 8964,0,1/31/00,,$0.00 ,"$1,000.00 ",Deposit from Samson Corp.,FALSE,FALSE,FALSE,,FALSE
18,Interest,233 42 8964,0,2/1/00,,$0.00 ,$10.00 ,January 1995 Interest,TRUE,FALSE,FALSE,,FALSE
19,Service Charge,233 42 8964,0,2/1/00,,$18.35 ,$0.00 ,January 1995 Service Charge,TRUE,FALSE,FALSE,,FALSE
21,Error Correction,233 42 8964,0,2/18/00,,$0.00 ,$100.00 ,Bank Error,TRUE,FALSE,FALSE,,FALSE
22,Check,123 456 555,202,2/9/00,AA Test Supplier 1,$15.03 ,$0.00 ,PO 95020111,FALSE,FALSE,FALSE,,FALSE
23,Check,233 42 8964,109,2/18/00,Private Printers,$205.64 ,$0.00 ,,FALSE,FALSE,FALSE,,FALSE
24,Check,123 456 555,203,3/1/00,Heritage Oil,$25.00 ,$0.00 ,,FALSE,FALSE,FALSE,,FALSE
26,Check,233 42 8964,110,3/17/00,Roadside Diner,$20.00 ,$0.00 ,,FALSE,FALSE,FALSE,,FALSE
28,Deposit,233 42 8964,0,3/17/00,,$0.00 ,$100.00 ,,FALSE,FALSE,FALSE,,FALSE
29,Check,233 42 8964,111,3/22/00,Acme Vending,$99.00 ,$0.00 ,,FALSE,FALSE,FALSE,,FALSE
30,Check,233 42 8964,112,3/22/00,Acme Vending,$99.99 ,$0.00 ,,FALSE,FALSE,FALSE,,FALSE
31,Check,233 42 8964,113,3/15/00,Private Printers,$52.00 ,$0.00 ,,FALSE,FALSE,FALSE,,FALSE
32,Check,123 456 555,204,3/15/00,Acme Vending,$20.00 ,$0.00 ,,FALSE,FALSE,FALSE,,FALSE
33,Check,233 42 8964,114,3/2/00,Private Printers,$320.00 ,$0.00 ,,FALSE,FALSE,FALSE,,FALSE
34,Check,233 42 8964,115,3/2/00,Acme Vending,$176.00 ,$0.00 ,,FALSE,FALSE,FALSE,,FALSE
35,Check,233 42 8964,116,10/28/99,Case,$123.00 ,$0.00 ,,FALSE,FALSE,FALSE,,FALSE
36,Check,233 42 8964,117,10/28/99,Johnson Heating,$565.00 ,$0.00 ,,FALSE,FALSE,FALSE,,FALSE
37,Check,233 42 8964,118,10/28/99,Good Eats Catering,$132.00 ,$0.00 ,,FALSE,FALSE,FALSE,,FALSE
```

Figure 17-1

A sample of a delimited text file. This file uses a comma to separate the fields. Note the first line contains the field names.

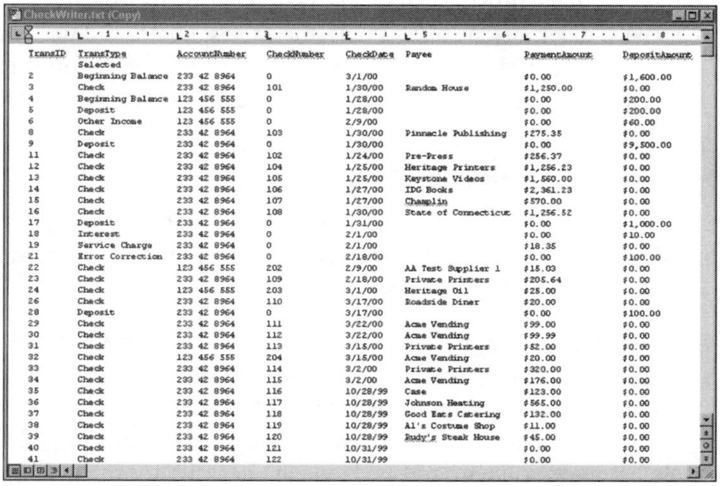

CheckWriter.txt (Copy)

TransID	TransType Selected	AccountNumber	CheckNumber	CheckDate	Payee	PaymentAmount	DepositAmount
2	Beginning Balance	233 42 8964	0	3/1/00		$0.00	$1,600.00
3	Check	233 42 8964	101	1/30/00	Random House	$1,250.00	$0.00
4	Beginning Balance	123 456 555	0	1/28/00		$0.00	$200.00
5	Deposit	123 456 555	0	1/28/00		$0.00	$200.00
6	Other Income	123 456 555	0	2/9/00		$0.00	$60.00
8	Check	233 42 8964	103	1/30/00	Pinnacle Publishing	$275.35	$0.00
9	Deposit	233 42 8964	0	1/30/00		$0.00	$9,500.00
11	Check	233 42 8964	102	1/24/00	Pre-Press	$256.37	$0.00
12	Check	233 42 8964	104	1/25/00	Heritage Printers	$1,256.23	$0.00
13	Check	233 42 8964	105	1/25/00	Keystone Videos	$1,560.00	$0.00
14	Check	233 42 8964	106	1/27/00	IDG Books	$2,361.23	$0.00
15	Check	233 42 8964	107	1/27/00	Champlin	$570.00	$0.00
16	Check	233 42 8964	108	1/30/00	State of Connecticut	$1,256.52	$0.00
17	Deposit	233 42 8964	0	1/31/00		$0.00	$1,000.00
18	Interest	233 42 8964	0	2/1/00		$0.00	$10.00
19	Service Charge	233 42 8964	0	2/1/00		$18.35	$0.00
21	Error Correction	233 42 8964	0	2/18/00		$0.00	$100.00
22	Check	123 456 555	202	2/9/00	AA Test Supplier 1	$15.03	$0.00
23	Check	233 42 8964	109	2/18/00	Private Printers	$205.64	$0.00
24	Check	123 456 555	203	3/1/00	Heritage Oil	$25.00	$0.00
26	Check	233 42 8964	110	3/17/00	Roadside Diner	$20.00	$0.00
28	Deposit	233 42 8964	0	3/17/00		$0.00	$100.00
29	Check	233 42 8964	111	3/22/00	Acme Vending	$99.00	$0.00
30	Check	233 42 8964	112	3/22/00	Acme Vending	$99.99	$0.00
31	Check	233 42 8964	113	3/15/00	Private Printers	$52.00	$0.00
32	Check	123 456 555	204	3/15/00	Acme Vending	$20.00	$0.00
33	Check	233 42 8964	114	3/2/00	Private Printers	$320.00	$0.00
34	Check	233 42 8964	115	3/2/00	Acme Vending	$176.00	$0.00
35	Check	233 42 8964	116	10/28/99	Case	$123.00	$0.00
36	Check	233 42 8964	117	10/28/99	Johnson Heating	$565.00	$0.00
37	Check	233 42 8964	118	10/28/99	Good Eats Catering	$132.00	$0.00
38	Check	233 42 8964	119	10/28/99	Al's Costume Shop	$11.00	$0.00
39	Check	233 42 8964	120	10/28/99	Rudy's Steak House	$45.00	$0.00
40	Check	233 42 8964	121	10/31/99		$0.00	$0.00
41	Check	233 42 8964	122	10/31/99		$0.00	$0.00

Figure 17-2

A sample of a fixed-width text file. Notice the columnar formatting of the text. Each column indicates a separate field.

Mapping the data

Mapping is the process of matching up field for field and table for table. Obviously, if the information you are importing does not need to be appended to existing tables, this issue is moot. However, in most cases you will need to populate existing tables.

There are three issues to consider when mapping data to existing tables: matching, definition, and order. The first involves matching up the correct fields and tables. This requires knowing the definition, function, or purpose of a field and table. Just imagine the old school book exercise in which you have two columns of names and identifiers and you need to match up the correct names from one column to the correct identifier in another column. The fields and tables from your external source may have different names, but the content itself will match up to existing fields and tables. For example, the external table may refer to a field as "PayToName" whereas your internal table has a field named "Payee." The function of each in both cases is the name of the "Pay To" or "Payee" on a check transaction.

The second issue to consider during the mapping process is field definition. This goes one step deeper into the structure of the fields and tables. In this step, you are going beyond the superficial names of the fields and need to compare the fields' data types, length, and other characteristics. You must take great pains to make sure that you properly reconcile the definition of the fields and tables. Compare a list of each field's definitions on both sides and make sure that you are bringing the information across correctly. The following is a list of some of the field properties you should take into consideration during an import.

Data type	Number, text, date, etc.
Field length	Reconcile differences in field size or risk losing data.
Validation rules	Make sure you consider any validation rules that apply to the field.

The final step in mapping is the order in which the information is imported and updated. Your database is most likely a normalized relational database. This means that you have table relationships established and, thus, your data must be populated in a specific order. For example, you would most likely want to update the BankAccounts table before you import and update the Check Writer table. The reason is that the Check Writer table has a foreign key that ties back to the BankAccounts table. Therefore, you must update in the proper order. If you have enforced referential integrity in your relationships, you will get errors if you attempt an import in the wrong order. This is because referential integrity requires that the parent record exist before you can create a record that references it.

Consider the following points as you perform your data import:

- Update lookup tables first. Even if you have not established a relationship, it's good practice to update the lookup tables first.
- Update parent tables before you update any child tables.
- If you are importing a table that has an autonumber field as your primary key, make sure that when you append to the table, the numbers are not automatically renumbered by Access. If they are renumbered, there will be a rippling effect in that related information will need to be updated accordingly as well.

**20 Min.
To Go**

Appending the data

Once you gather the data, get it in a format that Access can recognize and read. Once you have outlined how the data will be mapped, the actual process of appending or writing the imported data is fairly painless and straightforward. You do, however, have two different approaches to take in importing the data into your database: Using queries or using ADO. The methodology is discussed further later in this session.

Issues related to exporting data

The process for exporting data is almost identical to that of importing data. It requires similar steps in that you must organize the data to export, format, and map it accordingly, and finally, export or write it to the external file. Again, because Access supports popular database and spreadsheet applications, you can export to many formats directly. In addition, as with the import function, you can export to both SQL ODBC-compliant databases or to text files.

1. Collect the data.
2. Format the data.
3. Map the data.
4. Export the records.

Let's look closer at each of these steps.

Collecting the data to export

You can use either a query or VBA code to process the existing data and create a recordset with the information you wish to process in the export procedure. Access allows you to export the data in various formats. The formats supported for an export are the same as those supported for data importing. See Table 17-1.

Formatting the export data

As with importing, Access supports many formats when exporting. Which format you export to depends on the external program to which you are exporting. Again, you can choose to export to another Access database, other databases such as dBase and Paradox, any that support ODBC, or to common spreadsheet programs like Excel and Lotus.

Mapping the data

In mapping the data to be exported, you must consider the same factors as during an import. This is especially true of situations where you are exporting to a text file. You will need to set up every aspect of the export file.

In many cases, you do not have control over external programs and must export your data to follow a specific format set by that program. In these cases, you will need to map your data as part of the export process. Start by first matching the data, field for field and table for table. Make sure that you give the exported file the correct field names as defined by the structure of the external program. One of the nice features of Access is the ability to define the first line of the text file as the field names.

You then need to make sure that the field definitions are correct. Define text fields appropriately and, in many cases, you may need to convert or redefine your fields' basic properties. Neither the delimited nor fixed-width formats contain information about the field definitions. You must format the information appropriately prior to writing the text file. Make sure to check the following properties:

Data type	Number, text, date, etc.
Field length	Reconcile differences in field size or risk losing data.
Validation rules	Make sure you consider any validation rules that apply to the field.

The order in which you export the information may also be important. Should the external program you export to require the data to be formatted in a specific order. You will need to take that into consideration as part of the export process.

Import/Export Processes

Access has several ways in which to import and export data. Which process you use depends on how much control you wish to give the end user. For a quick and easy setup, you can use the Access Import/Export wizard to do the work for you. However, if you wish to create your own interface, you will want to use some of the built-in methods available and write the appropriate code to process it.

Import/export specification

Access has a very useful feature that allows you to create importing and exporting specifications for text files. This is a great utility in that you can create a single specification that you can use over and over. You can use this on both delimited or fixed-width text files.

When would you use the specification file?

- You want to automate the import/export process.
- You wish to import the information from multiple text files to the same tables.
- You wish to export the data to the same text file.

An import or export specification is stored with a default name: `filename_ImportSpec` or `filename_ExportSpec`. The specification is stored in the database and is an Access system object. To create a specification file, you can use either of the Import Text or Export Text wizards. The wizard creates a listing of information that is critical to the import or export process, such as the format of the file, field mappings, field properties, and so on. Initiate the import wizard by selecting Get External Data from the File menu and then choosing Import. Once you select a text file, the wizard will open. There is an Advanced button in the lower left of the screen. Clicking the Advanced button will open up the form shown in Figure 17-3.

You can use the wizard only on text files where the specific format of the file is not known. Access databases and other recognized standard formats do not allow you to use import/export specifications.

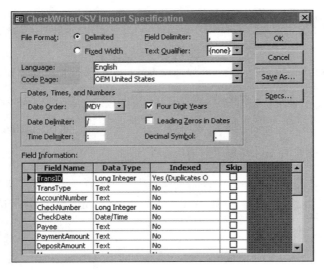

Figure 17-3
Clicking the Advanced button in the Access Import/Export wizard opens the Import Specification dialog box.

Looking at the figure, notice that the main information for how the file is formatted is displayed. There are check boxes that indicate the file format (Delimited or Fixed Width). Choosing Delimited will enable Field Delimiter and Text Qualifier fields. The Field Delimiter field allows you to choose which character is the delimiter character. The Text Qualifier field defines whether text strings are enclosed with a single or double quote or no quotes at all. You can also indicate which language and code page to use. The Code Page option lets you choose the character set to use. Additionally, you can also define how date and time fields are formatted to ensure proper reading of the files. Set the order in which the days, months, and years will be arranged and indicate if the data includes four-digit years. You can also enter the delimiter character for both date and time data types.

This is very important if you are importing information from different countries, as the standard month, day, year format common to the U.S. is different from the day, month, year format of many European countries.

When you have selected the File Format options, you can then start to enter in the field information. Enter a field separately on each line. Start by entering the field name. In many of the files you export or import, the first line can be used to store the field names. You can enter this information manually and define the field properties in the File Format options. Enter the name of the field followed by its data type, such as text, currency, number, and so forth. You can then determine if the field should be an indexed field. This indicates to Access whether an index of that field should be created during the import.

As an alternative to creating a specification file within Access, you can also define a file type by creating a Schema.ini file. This is a very advanced technique for automating the import/export process. A Schema.ini file operates by providing Access with the specifics of a particular data source. In this manner, you can provide a detailed specification file for all parameters of the data source. Creating a Schema.ini file is an advanced technique you will want to learn later; however, its creation and use is beyond the scope of this session.

Methods for importing and exporting

Once the main pieces of information are obtained, the Start Import button (see Figure 17-4) initiates the import process. In reviewing the code (shown in Listing 17-1), you will see that the import is done using one of three Access methods: `TransferDatabase`, `TransferSpreadsheet`, or `TransferText`. You can use these methods for importing and exporting to and from Access.

The TransferDatabase method

SYNTAX ▶ `TransferDatabase` allows you to import or export. The method has the following syntax:

```
DoCmd.TransferDatabase [transfertype], databasetype, databasename[,
objecttype], source, destination[, structureonly][, saveloginid]
```

Its arguments are defined as the following. Note that when using the `TransferDatabase` method for importing tables, a new table is created with the data. This method does not append the data to an existing table.

Transfertype	Can be one of the three constants: acExport, acImport, or acLink
Databasetype	The name of the type of databases that Access recognizes: Microsoft Access Jet 2.x Jet 3.x dBase III dBase IV dBase 5 Paradox 3.x Paradox 4.x Paradox 5.x Paradox 7.x ODBC databases
Databasename	The full name and path of the file
ObjectType	One of the following constants: acTable acQuery acForm acReport acMacro acModule acDataAccessPage acServerView acDiagram acStoredProcedure
Source	The name of the object to be imported
Destination	The name of the object in the destination file
Structureonly	A Boolean value of whether to import just the structure or the data and its structure
Saveloginid	A Boolean value of whether to save the login identification and password for connecting to ODBC databases

The Transferspreadsheet method

SYNTAX ▶

The Transferspreadsheet method allows you to import or export from standard spreadsheet files that Access supports.

```
DoCmd.TransferSpreadsheet [transfertype][, spreadsheettype],
tablename, filename[, hasfieldnames][, range]
```

Transfertype	Can be one of the three constants: acExport, acImport, or acLink
Spreadsheettype	The name of the type of databases that Access recognizes:
	acSpreadsheetTypeExcel3
	acSpreadsheetTypeExcel4
	acSpreadsheetTypeExcel5
	acSpreadsheetTypeExcel7
	acSpreadsheetTypeExcel8
	acSpreadsheetTypeExcel9
	acSpreadsheetTypeLotusWK1
	acSpreadsheetTypeLotusWK3
	acSpreadsheetTypeLotusWK4
	acSpreadsheetTypeLotusWJ2—Japanese version only
Tablename	The name of the Access table you want to import the data into or the table name of that which you want to export the data from
Filename	The full name and path of the file
Hasfieldnames	A Boolean value to indicate whether the first row of the spreadsheet contains the field names
Range	An expression indicating the cell rows to import. This is only an import option.

The TransferText method

SYNTAX ▶

TransferText is the method to import from text or HTML files.

```
DoCmd.TransferText [transfertype][, specificationname], tablename,
filename[, hasfieldnames][, HTMLtablename][, codepage]
```

Transfertype	Can be one of the following constants:
	acExportFixed
	acExportHTML
	acExportMerge
	acImportDelim
	acImportFixed

```
                              acImportHTML
                              acLinkDelim
                              acLinkFixed
                              acLinkHTML
```

Specificationname	The name of an import or export specification file you have created in Access
Tablename	The name of the Access table you want to import the data into or the table name of that which you want to export the data from
Filename	The full name and path of the file
Hasfieldnames	A Boolean value to indicate whether the first row of the spreadsheet contains the field names
Htmltablename	The name of the table or listing in an HTML file to which you wish to import or link
Codepage	A value indicating the character set to use

**10 Min.
To Go**

Creating an Import Interface

Certainly, you can let your application use the built-in Import wizard that Access provides. However, to provide a better experience for the end user, you will want to create an interface form for this purpose. The need for the end user to understand all of the intricacies of file formats can be overcome with a good form design. This gives you more control over which files are imported and how the data of the files are processed.

Parts of an import interface

All import utility interfaces share similar basic characteristics. Figure 17-4 shows an example of a simple import form. This import utility allows Check Writer users to import information from external sources into the program. You open this form by clicking the Import button on the main menu. This form illustrates the necessary components needed in a basic import form. The user is prompted for the information to import ("Payee Listing," "Bank Account Information," or "Bank Transactions"). Next, the ability to select which file to import from is provided. The Open File button allows the user to select which file to import. The file's path and name is then entered into the text box. Alternatively, the user can manually enter the path and filename directly into the text box. Once the filename has been entered, clicking on Start Import will process the data.

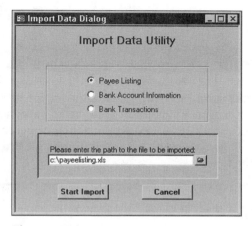

Figure 17-4
The import utility used to allow data import in the Check Writer program

In reviewing the Import Data Dialog box, the basic components of an import are evident. An option group lets the user choose the type of information to import. There is an entry for the file's path and name and a button to initiate the import process.

This is an oversimplified example, but all of the basic components of an import utility are present. In your application of this interface design, you may add more advanced features. For instance, you can expand it further to allow the user control over which fields from the data file to import. This example imports all of the information and uses the code and import specification to selectively remove unnecessary information.

Initiating and completing the import process

The above methods are all illustrated in the import example. Once the main parameters are obtained about which data to import and which file to import from, clicking the Start Import button initiates the process. In reviewing the code, the following steps occur. The code first verifies that all the necessary parameters needed are being provided. Then it determines which data is being imported: payee, bank account, or transactions. This is done with a select case statement that references the ChooseDataType option group on the form. Next, the code analyzes the file selected and bases the import on which type of format the file is in: Access, Excel, or text file. Once the format has been determined, the import is done using the appropriate Access method: `TransferDatabase`, `TransferSpreadsheet`, or `TransferText`.

The entire import process occurs in the `On Click` event of the `StartImport` Button. The first initial import occurs for the Payees table. The code in this example illustrates several points. First, the code verifies that all the necessary information to do the import has been provided. Next, it starts the import by using a `Select Case` statement to determine which data type is being imported. This can be seen in Listing 17-1. In the first `Case`, Payee information is processed. You will see another nested `Select Case` statement. It's used to determine which file type and, therefore, which of the three methods to use for importing.

Listing 17-1
The following lists the code in the On Click event of the Start Import button.

```
Private Sub StartImportButton_Click()
    Dim curconn         As ADODB.Connection
    Dim TransTB         As New ADODB.RecordSet
    Dim PayeeTB         As New ADODB.RecordSet

    Dim strtablename    As String

    On Error GoTo StartImportBtn_Err

'check that type was selected
    If IsNull(Me.ChooseDataType) Then
        MsgBox "You must select a data type.", vbExclamation, "Error"
        Me.ChooseDataType.SetFocus
        GoTo StartImportBtn_Exit
    End If

'check a filename was entered
    If IsNull(Me.ChooseDataType) Then
        MsgBox "You must enter the path and filename.", vbExclamation, "Error"
        Me.File1.SetFocus
        GoTo StartImportBtn_Exit
    End If

'if new table was checked, verify tablename entered
    If Me.Newtable = True And IsNull(Me.tablename) Then
        MsgBox "You must enter the new filename.", vbExclamation, "Error"
        Me.tablename.SetFocus
        GoTo StartImportBtn_Exit
    End If

'turn on the hourglass
    DoCmd.Hourglass True
'turn off warnings
    DoCmd.SetWarnings False
```

```
'determine what information to import
    Select Case Me.ChooseDataType
        Case 1 'payees

            'if new table then set the variable for the new table name
            If Me.Newtable = True Then
                strtablename = Me.tablename
            Else
                strtablename = "Payees"
            End If

            'determine the type of file
            'this is done by examining the last file extension
            Select Case Right$(Me.File1, 3)
                Case "mdb" 'Access database
                    If Me.Newtable = True Then
                        DoCmd.TransferDatabase acImport, "Microsoft Access",
Me.File1, acTable, "Payees", strtablename
                    Else
                        DoCmd.TransferDatabase acImport, "Microsoft Access",
Me.File1, acTable, "Payees", "temptable"
                        'initiate ADO recordset to loop through the data

                        With PayeeTB
                            Set curconn = CurrentProject.Connection
                            Set PayeeTB.ActiveConnection = curconn

                            .CursorType = adOpenKeyset
                            .LockType = adLockOptimistic
                            .Source = "Payees"
                            .Open options:=adCmdTable
                        End With

                        With TransTB
                            Set TransTB.ActiveConnection = curconn

                            .CursorType = adOpenForwardOnly
                            .CursorLocation = adUseClient
                            .LockType = adLockBatchOptimistic
                            .Source = "temptable"
                            .Open options:=adCmdTable
                        End With

                        'create ADO recordset to append the new data
                        Do Until TransTB.EOF
                            PayeeTB.AddNew
                                PayeeTB![Payees] = TransTB![Payees]
                            PayeeTB.Update

                            TransTB.MoveNext
                        Loop
```

Continued

Listing 17-1 *Continued*

```
                        PayeeTB.Close
                        Set PayeeTB = Nothing

                        TransTB.Close
                        Set TransTB = Nothing
                   End If

                   DoCmd.DeleteObject acTable, "temptable"

              Case "xls", "xl*"  'Excel spreadsheet
                   If Me.Newtable = True Then
                        DoCmd.TransferSpreadsheet acImport,
acSpreadsheetTypeExcel97, strtablename, Me.File1, True
                   Else
                        DoCmd.TransferSpreadsheet acImport,
acSpreadsheetTypeExcel97, "Payees", Me.File1, True
                   End If

              Case "txt", "csv"  'text file
                   If Me.Newtable = True Then
                        DoCmd.TransferText acImportDelim, "delimitedpayees",
strtablename, Me.File1
                   Else
                        DoCmd.TransferText acImportDelim, "delimitedpayees",
"Payees", Me.File1
                   End If
         End Select

    Case 2 'bank accounts
         'if new table then set the variable for the new table name
         If Me.Newtable = True Then
              strtablename = Me.tablename
         Else
              strtablename = "BankAccounts"
         End If

         Select Case Right$(Me.File1, 3)
              Case "mdb"  'Access database
                   If Me.Newtable = True Then
                        DoCmd.TransferDatabase acImport, "Microsoft Access",
Me.File1, acTable, "BankAccounts", strtablename
                   Else
                        DoCmd.RunSQL "INSERT INTO BankAccounts SELECT " &
strtablename & ".* FROM " & strtablename & ";"
                        DoCmd.DeleteObject acTable, strtablename
                   End If

              Case "xls", "xl*"  'Excel spreadsheet
                   If Me.Newtable = True Then
```

```
                        DoCmd.TransferSpreadsheet acImport,
acSpreadsheetTypeExcel97, strtablename, Me.File1, True
                    Else
                        DoCmd.TransferSpreadsheet acImport,
acSpreadsheetTypeExcel97, "BankAccounts", Me.File1, True
                    End If

            Case "txt", "csv" 'text file
                    If Me.Newtable = True Then
                        DoCmd.TransferText acImportDelim, "delimitedbankacct",
strtablename, Me.File1
                    Else
                        DoCmd.TransferText acImportDelim, "delimitedbankacct",
"BankAccounts", Me.File1
                    End If
            End Select

        Case 3 'bank transactions
            'if new table then set the variable for the new table name
            If Me.Newtable = True Then
                strtablename = Me.tablename
            Else
                strtablename = "CheckWriter"
            End If

            Select Case Right$(Me.File1, 3)
                Case "mdb" 'Access database
                    If Me.Newtable = True Then
                        DoCmd.TransferDatabase acImport, "Microsoft Access",
Me.File1, acTable, "CheckWriter", "CheckWriter"
                    Else
                        DoCmd.RunSQL "INSERT INTO CheckWriter SELECT " &
strtablename & ".* FROM " & strtablename & ";"
                        DoCmd.DeleteObject acTable, strtablename
                    End If

                Case "xls", "xl*" 'Excel spreadsheet
                    If Me.Newtable = True Then
                        DoCmd.TransferSpreadsheet acImport,
acSpreadsheetTypeExcel97, strtablename, Me.File1, True
                    Else
                        DoCmd.TransferSpreadsheet acImport,
acSpreadsheetTypeExcel97, "CheckWriter", Me.File1, True
                    End If

                Case "txt", "csv" 'text file
                    If Me.Newtable = True Then
                        DoCmd.TransferText acImportDelim, "delimitedtrans",
strtablename, Me.File1, True
                    Else
```

Continued

Listing 17-1 *Continued*

```
                        DoCmd.TransferText acImportDelim, "delimitedtrans",
    "CheckWriter", Me.File1, True
                    End If
            End Select
      End Select

'display message that import is completed
    MsgBox "Import Completed.", vbExclamation, "Import Status"


StartImportBtn_Exit:
    DoCmd.SetWarnings True
    DoCmd.Hourglass False
    Exit Sub

'Error messages
StartImportBtn_Err:
    MsgBox "An Error occurred while importing", vbCritical, "Import Error"

    DoCmd.SetWarnings True
    DoCmd.Hourglass False
    Echo True
    Application.Echo True
    DoCmd.Close acForm, "ImportPatients"

End Sub
```

In addition, there is another process going on. On the form, the user is given the option of importing the table as a new table or importing into existing tables. In the first instance, importing is done from an Access database as the source. The `TransferDatabase` method when used to import tables will import the entire table. There is no way to import just the data using this method. Therefore, this code imports the table in and then uses a VBA code to process it. The code in this case is used to process the payees' information. It opens up two recordsets. The first is for the imported table and the second is for the local Payees table. It then loops through the newly imported table, and for each record, it creates a new record for that payee in the Payees table. The import table for the Bank Accounts table uses an append query instead.

Note that in the `TransferText` method, lines of code used for each reference import specification files that have been set up in advance. To view the specifications, select the Get External menu item and select Import, then click the Advance button and click Specs. This gives a listing of all the available specification files. To view one, select it and open it.

Once the import has been completed, any temporary tables are then deleted and a message that the import was successful is displayed. The example should give you an idea of how many places you can affect the data during the import process. You can do it during the creation of the import specification. It can be manipulated once it is in a table. You can do it during the append query or through VBA code during the ADO updates.

Creating an Export Interface

You can create an export interface similar to an import interface. The goal is again to either simplify the export process or give more control over the export of the data. You can perform the export using the same techniques as the import.

Parts of an export interface

The ExportChecks form in the Check Writer database is an example of an export interface. The main elements are all represented, as shown in Figure 17-5. An option group allows you to select what type of information is being exported: Payee Listing, Bank Account Information, or Bank Transactions. Note that choosing Bank Transactions will make visible additional options from which to choose. The user would select which account and the date range of the transactions he or she wishes to process. All of the available transactions are then listed.

The user then has the option of selectively choosing which records to export. This is an example of providing a multilevel selection. The user can choose which type of data, specific groups of records such as by bank account and with a date range, as well as which records from that data source to export. Once the records have been selected and the filename and path is entered, the Start button is clicked and the export process is finally initiated. Similar to the import, the what, where, and how must be collected. Any export interface will require input regarding which information is to be exported, which of the records will be imported, where it will be exported to, and how.

Coding the export procedure

The Start button's On Click event (see Listing 17-2) on the Export form starts the export process by verifying that the necessary components have been supplied. The user must select the type of data to export, which records to export, and where to export to.

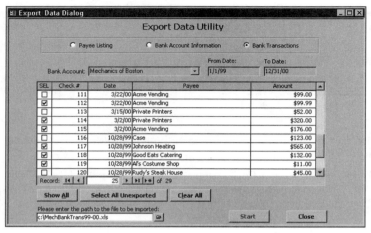

Figure 17-5
Example of the Export utility in the Check Writer database

Listing 17-2
The code listing for the On Click event of the Start Export button.

```
Private Sub StartExportButton_Click()

    Dim curconn         As ADODB.Connection
    Dim TransTB         As New ADODB.RecordSet
    Dim ExportTB        As New ADODB.RecordSet

    Dim filetype        As String
    Dim strtablename    As String

     On Error GoTo StartExportBtn_Err

'check for path and filename
    If IsNull(Me.File1) Then
        MsgBox "You must enter in the path and filename.", vbCritical, "Error"
        Me.File1.SetFocus
        GoTo StartExportButton_Exit
    End If

'make sure an extension is entered
    If Left(Right$(Me.File1, 4), 1) <> "." Then
        MsgBox "You must enter in an extension for the filename.", vbCritical,
"Error"
        Me.File1.SetFocus
        GoTo StartExportButton_Exit
    End If
```

```
'check for selected records
    Select Case Me.SelectType
        Case 1
            If DCount("[Selected]", "[Payees]", "[Selected] = True") = 0 Then
                MsgBox "You have not selected any Payee records to export.",
vbCritical, "Error"
                GoTo StartExportButton_Exit
            End If
        Case 2
            If DCount("[Selected]", "[BankAccounts]", "[Selected] = True") = 0
Then
                MsgBox "You have not selected any Bank Account records to
export.", vbCritical, "Error"
                GoTo StartExportButton_Exit
            End If
        Case 3
            If DCount("[Selected]", "[CheckWriter]", "[Selected] = True") = 0
Then
                MsgBox "You have not selected any Payee records to export.",
vbCritical, "Error"
                GoTo StartExportButton_Exit
            End If
    End Select


'get extension and determine file type
    filetype = Right$(Me.File1, 3)

    DoCmd.Hourglass False

'turn off warnings to avoid prompts for updates
    DoCmd.SetWarnings False

    If Right$(Me.File1, 3) = "mdb" Then
        strtablename = Me.tablename
    End If

'exports selected records to separate table and initiates method

    Select Case Me.SelectType
        Case 1
            DoCmd.OpenQuery "ExportPayeesQuery"

            Select Case filetype
                Case "mdb" 'Access database
                    DoCmd.TransferDatabase acExport, "Microsoft Access",
Me.File1, acTable, "Payees", tablename
                Case "xls", "xl*" 'Excel spreadsheet
                    DoCmd.TransferSpreadsheet acExport, acSpreadsheetTypeExcel9,
strtablename, Me.File1, True
                Case "txt", "csv" 'text file
```

Continued

Listing 17-2 *Continued*

```
DoCmd.TransferText acExportDelim, "delimitedpayees", "ExportedPayees", Me.File1,
True
                End Select
        Case 2
                DoCmd.OpenQuery "ExportBankAccountsQuery"

                Select Case filetype
                        Case "mdb"  'Access database
                                DoCmd.TransferDatabase acExport, "Microsoft Access",
Me.File1, acTable, "BankAccounts", strtablename
                        Case "xls", "xl*"  'Excel spreadsheet
                                DoCmd.TransferSpreadsheet acExport, acSpreadsheetTypeExcel9,
tablename, Me.File1, True
                        Case "txt", "csv"  'text file
                                DoCmd.TransferText acExportDelim, "delimitedBankAcct",
"ExportedBankAccounts", Me.File1, True
                End Select


        Case 3
                DoCmd.OpenQuery "ExportTransactionQuery"

                Select Case filetype
                        Case "mdb"  'Access database
                                DoCmd.TransferDatabase acExport, "Microsoft Access",
Me.File1, acTable, "CheckWriter", strtablename
                        Case "xls", "xl*"  'Excel spreadsheet
                                DoCmd.TransferSpreadsheet acExport, acSpreadsheetTypeExcel9,
tablename, Me.File1, True
                        Case "txt", "csv"  'text file
                                DoCmd.TransferText acExportDelim, "delimitedtrans",
"ExportedCheckWriterTrans", Me.File1, True
                End Select

    End Select

    MsgBox "Export Completed Successfully.", vbExclamation, "Error"

StartExportButton_Exit:
    DoCmd.Hourglass False
    DoCmd.SetWarnings True

    Exit Sub

StartExportButton_Err:

    MsgBox "An error has occured during the export process.", vbCritical,
"Error"
    GoTo StartExportButton_Exit

End Sub
```

The usual verification is done. Note that the code uses a `Dcount` function to quickly count whether any records have been selected for each of the data types. An error message is presented if no records have been selected. Additionally, also note that if the extension is .MDB for an Access database, the system checks for a valid table name to be entered. The code then starts a `Select Case` statement to determine the type of data being processed. For each one, a make-table query is run. This is done to create a new query for just the selected data. Next, a nested `Select Case` statement is used to determine which format to export to. This is based on what is entered for the filename and its extension. Then, the appropriate code is used to export the data using one of these three methods: `TransferDatabase`, `TransferSpreadsheet`, or `TransferText`. The syntax for the methods is similar to doing an import. Refer to the section on the import methods for the full syntax.

Done!

As with the import example, you have a lot of control over several aspects of the export process. You can manipulate the data at several points: with the specification files, during the queries to export the selected records, or during the export.

REVIEW

Importing and exporting is a means of extending your programs' communication with other programs and the information they can process. You have learned the general issues behind importing and exporting data. More advanced imports and exports may require further considerations. However, they all follow the same logic of the general techniques shown in this session.

The basic logic is as follows:

Importing:

1. Organize the data.
2. Format the data.
3. Map the data.
4. Append the records.

Exporting:

1. Collect the data.
2. Format the data.

3. Map the data.

4. Export the records.

You also learned the significance of import/export specifications and how to set them up within the Access Import wizard. Now you know how to create a user-friendly interface to simplify a sometimes complicated process.

Quiz Yourself

1. What is the general order you should follow when performing an import or an export? Why is the order important? (See "Importing and Exporting.")

2. Does Access allow you to export only to databases? Explain the limits, if any, that Access imposes on importing and exporting. (See "Importing and Exporting.")

3. Where in Access do you set up import/export specifications? (See "Import/export specification.")

4. What are the three VBA methods that Access provides for doing imports and exports? (See "Methods for importing and exporting.")

Techniques to Improve the Speed of an Application

Session Checklist

✔ Tuning your computer hardware for maximum performance

✔ Increasing performance dramatically by keeping your code
in a compiled state

✔ Compacting your database

✔ Creating .MDE databases for better performance

✔ Organizing your database into referenced libraries

✔ Improving the absolute speed of your database

✔ Improving the perceived speed of your database

**30 Min.
To Go**

hen you create an application, you want it to run as fast as possible. Sometimes, applications run slowly because they are processing hundreds of thousands of records; other applications run slowly because they are poorly written. The larger your database becomes, the slower it will invariably run. While sloppy programming practices can be ignored with small databases, they will make the performance of an application unacceptable with larger ones. You should employ good programming techniques with the smallest databases and make speed a priority in all of your applications. This chapter will teach you several techniques for making Access applications run faster.

Hardware and Memory

The published minimum RAM requirement for a computer to run Access 2000 on Windows 95 is 16MB RAM plus 8MB for each Office product run simultaneously — with an emphasis on minimum. On a Windows NT machine, the published minimum is 32MB of RAM plus 8MB for each Office product run simultaneously. If you are going to do serious development with Access 2000, you should have at least 64MB of RAM or, preferably, 128MB especially on Windows NT.

Memory is actually more important than the processor speed. Increasing your memory from 64MB to 128MB can easily double or triple the speed of your application, while changing the processor by 100 MHz and keeping the memory the same will make little difference.

Understanding the Compiled State

If your application contains even one line of VBA code, it is incredibly important that you understand what compilation is and what it means for an application to be in a compiled state. There are actually two types of code in Access: the code that you write in the Visual Basic window and the code that Microsoft Access can understand and execute.

Before a procedure of VBA code that you have written can be executed, the code must be run through a compiler to put it in a form that Access can understand. Access actually lacks a true compiler and instead converts the code into precompiled code and then uses an interpreter to run the code. The code in the converted form is known as compiled code, or as being in a compiled state.

If a procedure is run that is not in a compiled state, the procedure must first be compiled and then the compiled code is passed to the interpreter for execution. In reality, this does not happen at the procedure level, but at the module level; when you call a procedure, the module containing the procedure and all modules that have procedures referenced in the called procedure are loaded and compiled. You can manually compile your code, or you can let Access compile it for you on the fly. It takes time to compile the code, however, so the performance of your application will suffer if you let Access compile each time you run your code.

In addition to the time it takes for Access to compile your code at runtime, decompiled programs use considerably more memory than code that is compiled. When your application is completely compiled, only the compiled code is loaded into memory when a procedure is called. If you run an application that is in a decompiled state, Access loads the decompiled code and generates the compiled code as needed. Access does not unload the decompiled code as it compiles, so you are left with two versions of the same code in memory.

Putting your application's code into a compiled state

There is only one way to put your entire application into a compiled state: choose Compile from the Debug menu on the Modules toolbar. The Compile menu item will be followed by the internal project name, as shown in Figure 18-1. To access the Debug menu, you must have a module open.

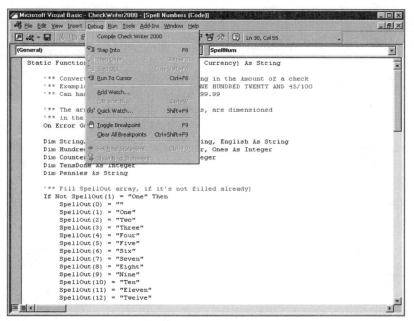

Figure 18-1
Compiling a program

The internal project name is the filename used when you first create the Microsoft Access database file. You can change the internal project name by selecting the project name Properties option from the Tools menu in the Visual Basic window. The project name will precede the text Properties at the bottom of the menu. Changing the internal project name will cause the database to decompile.

It can take a long time to compile complex or large applications with a lot of VBA code. You should close your application after performing compiling. To compile all your modules, Access needs to load every single one of them into memory. All this code stays in memory until you close down Access.

In previous versions of Access, there used to be a Compile button on the Visual Basic toolbar.

Losing the compiled state

In previous versions of Access, changing any code would decompile the entire application. In Access 2000, only portions of code affected by certain changes are put into a decompiled state — not the entire application.

The following will cause portions of your code to be decompiled:

- Modifying a form, report, control, or module containing code. (If you don't save the modified object, your application is preserved in its previous state.)

- Adding a new form, report, control, or module. (This includes adding new code behind an existing form.)

- Deleting or renaming a form, report, control, or module.

If you modify objects such as reports or forms at runtime through VBA code, portions of your application are put into a decompiled state when the objects are modified. (Wizards often do this.)

If your application creates objects such as reports or forms on the fly, portions of your application are put into a decompiled state when the objects are created. (Wizards often do this as well.)

Using the undocumented/decompile option

Sometimes, you will find that no matter what you do, your database will not stay compiled. You may start your program only to see an error that Access can't find a project or library. You may get a compile error when you know there are no code problems or syntax errors. To fix a database that won't stay compiled and compile your database, you must run an undocumented startup command-line option called /decompile. You may have seen many of the command-line options such as /nostartup, /cmd, and /compact. This starts Access 2000 in a special way and when a database is opened, saves all VBA modules as text. This works with module objects and all the code behind forms and reports.

Decompiling is very different than the database simply being in an uncompiled state. An uncompiled state is when any module is not compiled. The undocumented decompile command forces a decompile of every module in the database and additionally cleans up code within the database. Nothing else in Microsoft Access cleans up a database better than this command.

To decompile the database, choose Run from the Windows Start menu and type **msaccess /decompile**, as shown in Figure 18-2. You will be asked to select the database file you want to open. When you do this, hold the Shift key down so any Startup options in autoexec macros are not run when the database is opened. This would potentially allow module code to be executed in your database and it would first have to compile the code before it would run. This is important because, if Access begins to compile your database, the decompile option doesn't work. You won't know it didn't work; it simply will not fix any of the type of problems an uncompiled database displays.

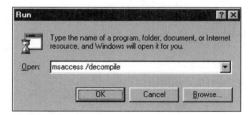

Figure 18-2
Decompiling a program

Access appears to start as usual. When you open your database, you will simply see the Access database container. This means the decompile is done. Immediately exit Access 2000 after it finishes decompiling and then start Access normally.

After you exit Access, you can restart Access normally. You can then open your database and open any module to enter the Visual Basic Editor window. You can also open any form with VBA code behind it and display the code window. Then select the Compile *projectname* option. After the database compiles, you should close the module and return to the database container.

Compacting a database after compiling it

Any time you compile your database, you should also compact it. From the database container, select Tools ⇨ Database Utilities ⇨ Compact and Repair Database. After you complete this, Access will run these procedures much faster than usual and your database will be at least half the size it was before you decompiled it.

An interface for detecting a decompiled database and automatically recompiling

It is very important to make sure that a database is always in a compiled state. Your customers may make simple or even complex changes to your application and then complain because their system is running slowly. While some of your customers may be serious developers, many customers who make changes to Access databases do not know about compilation or compacting.

To see if your database is compiled, you can open the Visual Basic window for any module, display the Debug window, and type **? IsCompiled()**, as shown in Figure 18-3. If the database is compiled, it will display True. If it is in a decompiled state, it will display False, as shown in Figure 18-3.

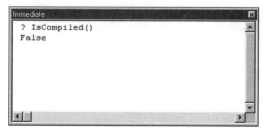

Figure 18-3
Checking to see if a database file is in a compiled state

To solve the problem of a database being uncompiled, you can create an interface that automatically detects if the database is not in a compiled state and then gives the user the option of compiling the application. This code is run each time the database is opened. The user still has to manually compact the database, but the hard part is compiling. Figure 18-4 shows the message that is automatically displayed if the database is decompiled.

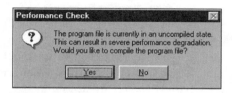

Figure 18-4
A dialog box to help the user compile your application

The code in Listing 18-1 uses the Access 2000 built-in `IsCompiled` function to determine the compiled state of the application. If the application is not compiled, the `MsgBox` is displayed as shown in Figure 18-3. Users have two choices. If they are still testing, they may not want to compile yet because it takes some time, and they may want to test some other things without caring if their application runs fast. If they want to compile, they simply have to press the Yes button.

Listing 18-1
VBA module to detect and automatically compile an application

---

```
Dim MsgTxt As String
If Not IsCompiled() Then
MsgTxt = "The program file is currently in a decompiled state" & _
     vbCrLf
MsgTxt = MsgTxt & "This can result in severe performance problems." & _
  vbCrLf MsgTxt = MsgTxt & "Would you like to compile the program file?"
  Response = MsgBox(MsgTxt, vbYesNo+vbQuestion, "Performance Check")
  If Response = vbYes Then
    'You could display a message box that tells the user to be patient while _
    'the database is compiled
    DoCmd.Echo False    'Stop screen display to eliminate seeing the module _
      open and close
    DoCmd.OpenModule "anymodulename"    'Open any module you have in the
      database
    DoCmd.SelectObject acModule, "anymodulename"  'You must select the module _
                                       'after you open it
    RunCommand (acCmdCompileAndSaveAllModules) 'This command does the compile _
                                    'and save
```

Continued

**20 Min.
To Go**

Listing 18-1 *Continued*

```
        DoCmd.Close acModule, "anymodulename"        'Close the module after the _
                                                     'compile and save is done
        DoCmd.Echo True       'Start screen display again
    MsgTxt = "            The program file has been compiled" &  vbCrLf
    MsgTxt = MsgTxt & "You should now select Tools | Database Utilities | Compact
    Database" & vbCrLf
    MsgTxt = MsgTxt & "from the menu above the database container. "
        Response = MsgBox(MsgTxt, vbInformation, "Compile Completed Successfully")
      End If
End If
```

Although there is no easy way to automatically compact the open program file, the user can be instructed to simply select Tools ⇨ Database Utilities ⇨ Compact and Repair Database. When the program database is open, this also reruns the startup or Autoexec macro file after compacting the database.

Creating and Distributing .MDE Files

One way to ensure that your application's code is always compiled, is to distribute your database as an .MDE file. When you save your database as an .MDE file, Access compiles all code modules (including form modules), removes all editable source code, and compacts the database. The new .MDE file contains no source code but continues to work because it does contain a compiled copy of all of your code.

Not only is this a great way to secure your source code, but it also allows you to distribute databases that are smaller (because they contain no source code) and always keep their modules in a compiled state. Because the code is always in a compiled state, less memory is used by the application and there is no performance penalty for code being compiled at runtime.

In addition to not being able to view existing code because it is all compiled, the following restrictions apply:

- You cannot view, modify, or create forms, reports, or modules in Design view.

- You cannot add, delete, or change references to object libraries or databases.

- You cannot change your database's VBA project name using the Options dialog box.

- You cannot import or export forms, reports, or modules. Note, however, that tables, queries, and macros can be imported from or exported to non-.MDE databases.

- Because of these restrictions, it may not be possible to distribute your application as an .MDE file. For example, if your application creates forms at runtime, you would not be able to distribute the database as an .MDE file.

There is no way to convert an .MDE file back into a normal database file. Always save and keep a copy of the original database! When you need to change the application, you must open the normal database and then create a new .MDE before distribution. If you delete your original database, you will be unable to access any of your objects in Design view.

There are some prerequisites to meet before you can save a database as an .MDE file. First, if security is turned on, the user creating the .MDE file must have all applicable rights to the database. In addition, if the database is replicated, you must remove all replication system tables and properties before saving the .MDE file. Finally, you must save all databases or add-ins in the chain of references as .MDE files, or your database will be unable to use them.

You should first close the database if it is currently opened. If you do not close the current database, Access will attempt to close it for you, prompting you to save changes where applicable. When working with a shared database, all users must close the database, as Access needs exclusive rights to work with the database.

Select <u>T</u>ools ➪ <u>D</u>atabase Utilities and then click Make .MDE File, as shown in Figure 18-5.

If the database is closed and no database is open, specify the database you want to save as an .MDE file in the Database To Save As .MDE dialog box, and then click Make .MDE.

If you had a database open when you selected Make .MDE File, this step is skipped and Access assumes you want to use the previously opened database. If you wish to use a different database, you will need to cancel creating the .MDE file, close the database, and select Make .MDE File again. At that time, you will be asked for the database to save as an .MDE file.

In the Database to Save as .MDE dialog box, specify a name, drive, and folder for the database. Do not attempt to save the .MDE file with the same filename as the original database.

Do not delete or overwrite your original database! As stated previously, there is no way to convert an .MDE file to a normal database, and you cannot edit any objects in an .MDE file. If you delete or otherwise lose your original database, you will never again be able to access any of the objects in the design environment.

Part IV–Saturday Evening
Session 18

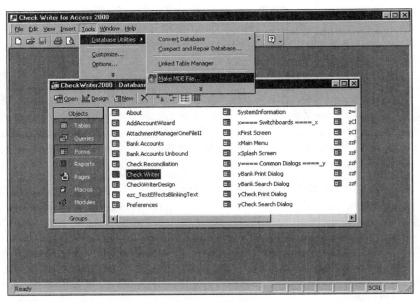

Figure 18-5
Saving your database as an .MDE file

Organizing Commonly Used Code Into a Library

After your application is finished and ready for distribution, you may want to consider putting commonly used code that is never modified by an end user into a library database.

A *library database* is an external Access program database that is referenced from your application database. A little overhead is incurred by having to call code from the library rather than accessing it directly in the parent application, but the benefit is that the library code will never be put into a decompiled state — even if your application creates or modifies objects on the fly or your users add new objects or modify existing objects.

This technique can greatly increase an application's performance and keep the performance consistent over periods of time. Most importantly, it separates the database file into two smaller databases, and the smaller the database, the faster it runs.

The first step of referencing procedures in an external database is to create the external database with all its modules just as you would an ordinary Access database.

Any procedures that you declare as Private are not made available to the calling application, so plan carefully what you want and don't want to expose to other databases.

After you have created the second database and created or exported its objects (forms, reports, modules), you can create a reference from the main program file to the referenced database (the database your users will run).

To create a reference, first open any module in your main application database in Design view. When you have a module in Design view, there will be a new command available from the Tools menu called References, as shown in Figure 18-6.

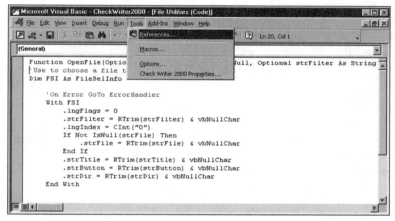

Figure 18-6
Selecting the References option

After you select Tools ⇨ References, you will see the References dialog box (see Figure 18-7). In the References dialog box, you specify all the references your application needs for using OLE automation or for using other Access databases as library databases.

When making a reference to another Access database as opposed to an OLE server created with another development tool such as Visual Basic 6.0, you will probably need to browse for the database. Use the Browse dialog box as though you were going to open the external database.

After you have selected the external Access database, it shows up in the References dialog box with a check mark to indicate that it is referenced.

To remove a reference, access the References dialog box again and clear the referenced item by selecting its check box. After you have made all the references you need to make, click the OK button.

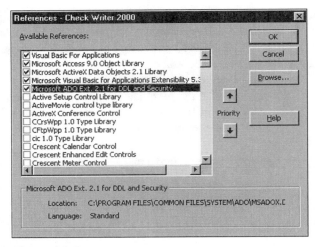

Figure 18-7
Viewing and selecting references

After a database is referenced, you can call the procedures in the referenced database as though they existed in your application database. No matter what happens in your application database to cause code to decompile, the referenced database always stays in a compiled state unless it is opened and modified directly using Access.

Improving Absolute Speed

When discussing an application's performance, the word *performance* is usually synonymous with speed. In software development, there are actually two different types of speed: absolute and perceived. *Absolute speed* refers to the actual speed at which your application performs a function, such as how long it takes to run a certain query.

Perceived speed is the phenomenon of an end user actually perceiving one application to be faster than another application — even though it may indeed be slower — because of visual feedback provided to the user while the application is performing a task. Absolute speed items can be measured in units of time; perceived speed cannot.

Some of the most important items for increasing actual speed are the following:

- Keeping your application in a compiled state
- Organizing your procedures into "smart" modules

- Opening databases exclusively
- Compacting your databases regularly

You should always open a database exclusively in a single-user environment. If your application is a standalone application (nothing is shared over a network), opening the database in exclusive mode can really boost performance. If your application is run on a network and shared by multiple users, you will not be able to open the database exclusively. (Actually, the first user can open it exclusively, but then no other user can access the database thereafter.)

The preferred method for running an application in a network environment is to run Microsoft Access and the main program .MDB file locally on each workstation and link to a shared database containing the data on the server. If your application is used in this manner, you can open and run the code database exclusively, but everyone can share the data files.

To open a database exclusively, select Open Exclusive from the Open command button after selecting a file in the Open dialog box, as shown in Figure 18-8.

Figure 18-8
Opening a database exclusively

All of the preceding methods are excellent (and necessary) ways to help keep your applications running at their optimum performance level, but these are not the only ways you can increase the absolute speed of your application. Almost every area of development, from forms to modules, can be optimized to give your application maximum absolute speed.

Minimizing form and report complexity and size

One of the key elements to achieving better performance from your forms and reports is reducing their complexity and size. To reduce a form or report's complexity and size:

- Minimize the number of objects on a form or report. The fewer objects used, the less resources needed to display and process the form or report.

- Reduce the use of subforms. When a subform is loaded, two forms are in memory — the parent form and the subform. Use a list box or a combo box in place of a subform whenever possible.

- Use labels instead of text boxes for hidden fields; text boxes use more resources than labels do. Hidden fields are often used as an alternative to creating variables to store information. You cannot write a value directly to a label like you can to a text box, but you can write to the label's caption property like this: Label1.Caption = "MyValue".

- Move some code from a form's module into a standard module. This enables the form to load faster because the code doesn't need to be loaded into memory. If the procedures you move to a normal module are referenced by any procedures executed upon loading a form (such as in the Form Load event), moving the procedures will not help because they are loaded anyway as part of the potential call tree of the executed procedure. A call tree is the potential chain of commands where one module calls another which calls another.

- Don't overlap controls on a form or report.

- Place related groups of controls on form pages. If only one page is shown at a time, Access does not need to generate all the controls at the same time.

- Use light forms whenever possible. Light forms have no code module attached to them, so they load and display considerably faster than forms with code modules.

- Use a query that returns a limited result set for a form or report's Record Source rather than using a table. The less data returned for the Record Source, the faster the form or report loads. In addition, return only those fields actually used by the form or report.

Using bitmaps on forms and reports

Bitmaps on forms and reports make an application look attractive and also help convey the purpose of the form or report (like in a wizard). Graphics are always resource-intensive, so you should use the fewest number of graphic objects on your forms and reports as possible. This helps minimize form and report load time, increase print speed, and reduce the resources used by your application.

Often you will display pictures that a user never changes and that are not bound to a database. Examples of such pictures are your company logo on a switchboard or static images in a wizard. When you want to display an image such as this, you have two choices.

If the image will never change and you don't need to activate it in Form Design view, use an Image control. Image controls use fewer resources and display faster. If you need the image to be a linked or embedded OLE object that you can edit, use an unbound object frame. You can convert OLE images in unbound object frames.

If you have an image in an unbound object frame that you no longer need to edit, you can convert the unbound object frame into an Image control by selecting Change To Image from the Format menu.

When you have forms that contain unbound OLE objects, you should close the forms when they are not in use to free resources. Also avoid using bitmaps with many colors — they take considerably more resources and are slower to paint than a bitmap of the same size with fewer colors.

If you want to display an unbound OLE object but don't want the user to be able to activate it, set its Enabled property to False.

**10 Min.
To Go**

Getting the most from your modules

Consider reducing the number of modules and procedures in your application by consolidating them whenever possible. There is a small memory overhead incurred for each module and procedure you use, so consolidating them may free up some memory.

Using appropriate data types

You should always explicitly declare variables using the Dim function rather than arbitrarily assigning values to variables that have not been Dim'ed. To assure that all variables in your application are explicitly declared before they are used in a procedure, select Tools⫐Options from the Database Container window and then set the Require Variable Declarations option on the Modules tab.

Use integers and long integers rather than singles and doubles when possible. Integers and long integers use less memory and they take less time to process than singles and doubles. Table 18-1 shows the relative speed of the different numeric data types available in Access.

Table 18-1
Data Types and Their Mathematical Processing Speed

Data Type	Relative Processing Speed
Integer/Long	Fastest
Single/Double	Next to fastest
Currency	Next to slowest
Variant	Slowest

In addition to using integers and long integers whenever possible, you should also use integer math rather than precision math when applicable. For example, to divide one long integer by another long integer, you could use the following statement:

```
x = Long1 / Long2
```

This statement is a standard math function that uses floating-point math. The same function could be performed using integer math with the following statement:

```
x = Long1 \ Long2
```

Of course, integer math isn't always applicable. It is, however, commonly applied when returning a percentage. For example, you could return a percentage with the following precision math formula:

```
x = Total / Value
```

However, you could perform the same function using integer math by first multiplying the total by 100 and then using integer math like this:

```
x = (Total * 100) \ Value
```

You should also use string functions ($) where applicable. When you are manipulating variables that are of type String, use the string functions (for example, Str$()) as opposed to their variant counterparts (Str()). If you are working with variants, use the nonstring functions. Using string functions when working with strings is faster because Access doesn't need to perform type conversions on the variables.

When you need to return a substring by using Mid$(), you can omit the third parameter to have the entire length of the string returned. For example, to return a substring that starts at the second character of a string and returns all remaining characters, you would use a statement like this:

```
szReturn = Mid$(szMyString, 2)
```

When using arrays, use dynamic arrays with the Erase and ReDim statements to reclaim memory. By dynamically adjusting the size of the arrays, you can ensure that only the amount of memory needed for the array is allocated.

In addition to using optimized variables, consider using constants when applicable. Constants can make your code much easier to read and will not slow your application if you compile your code before executing it.

Writing faster routines

You can speed up your procedures in a number of ways by optimizing the routines they contain. If you keep performance issues in mind as you develop, you will be able to find and take advantage of situations like those discussed here.

Some Access functions perform similar processes but vary greatly in the time they take to execute. You probably use one or more of these regularly and knowing the most efficient way to perform these routines can greatly affect your application's speed:

- For/Next statements are faster than Select Case statements.
- The IIF() function is much slower than a standard set of If/Then/Else statements.
- The With and For Each functions accelerate manipulating multiple objects and/or their properties.
- Change a variable with Not instead of using an If/Then statement. (For example, use x = Not(y) instead of If y = true then x= false.)
- Instead of comparing a variable to the value True, use the value of t he variable. (For example, instead of saying If X = True Then . . ., say If X Then . . ..)
- Use the Requery method instead of the Requery action. The method is significantly faster than the action.
- When using OLE automation, resolve references when your application is compiled rather than resolve them at runtime using the GetObject or CreateObject functions.

Using control variables

When referencing controls on a form in code, there are some very slow ways and some very fast ways to use references to form objects. The slowest possible way is to reference each control explicitly. This requires Access to sequentially search for the form name, starting with the first form name in the database and continuing until it finds the form name in the forms list (msysObjects table). If the form name starts with a z, this can take a long time if there are many forms in the database. For example:

```
Forms![Check Writer]![Bank Account Number] = something
Forms![Check Writer]![Bank Account Name] = something
Forms![Check Writer]![Payee] = something
```

If the code is in a class module behind the Check Writer form, you could use the Me reference. The Me reference refers to the open object (forms or reports) and substitutes for Forms![formname]. This is much faster because it can go right to the form name. For example:

```
Me!Bank Account Number] = something
Me![Bank Account Name] = something
Me![Check Writer]![Payee] = something
```

If your code is not stored behind the form but is in a module procedure, you can use a control variable like the following:

```
Dim frm as Form
set frm = Forms![Check Writer]
frm![Bank Account Number] = something
frm![Bank Account Name] = something
frm!Check Writer]![Payee] = something
```

This way, the form name is looked up only once. An even faster way is to use the With construct. For example:

```
With Forms![Check Writer]
  ![Bank Account Number] = something
  ![Bank Account Name] = something
  !Check Writer]![Payee] = something
End With
```

You can then reference the variable rather than reference the actual control. Of course, if you don't need to set values in the control but rather use values from a control, you should simply create a variable to contain the value rather than the reference to the control.

Improving Perceived Speed

Perceived speed is how fast your application appears to run to the end user. Many techniques can increase the perceived speed of your applications. Perceived speed usually involves supplying visual feedback to the user while the computer is busy performing some operation, such as constantly updating a percent meter when Access is busy processing data.

Loading and keeping forms hidden

If there are forms that are displayed often, consider hiding them rather than closing them. To hide a form, set its Visible property to False. When you need to display the form again, set its Visible property back to True. Forms that remain loaded consume memory, but they display more quickly than forms that must be loaded each time they are viewed. In addition, if you are *morphing* a form or report (changing the way the form or report looks by changing form and control properties), keep the form hidden until all changes are made so that the user doesn't have to watch the changes take place.

Using the hourglass

When your application needs to perform a task that may take a while, use the hourglass. The hourglass cursor shows the user that the computer is not locked up but is merely busy. To turn on the hourglass cursor, use the Hourglass method like this:

```
DoCmd.Hourglass True
```

To turn the hourglass back to the default cursor, use the method like this:

```
DoCmd.Hourglass False
```

Using the percent meter

In addition to using the hourglass, you should consider using the percent meter when performing looping routines in a procedure. The percent meter gives constant visual feedback that your application is busy, and it shows the user in no uncertain terms where it is in the current process. The following code demonstrates using the percent meter in a loop to show the meter, starting at 0 percent and expanding to 100 percent, 1 percent at a time:

```
Dim iCount As Integer, iCount2 As Long
Dim Result As Integer
Result = SysCmd(acSysCmdInitMeter, "Running through loop", 100)
For iCount = 1 To 100
    Result = SysCmd(acSysCmdUpdateMeter, iCount)
    For iCount2 = 1 To 50000: Next iCount2 ' This creates a pause
                                           'so the meter is readable
Next iCount
Result = SysCmd(acSysCmdRemoveMeter)
```

The first step for using the percent meter is initializing the meter. You initialize it by calling the SysCmd function like this:

```
Result = SysCmd(acSysCmdInitMeter, "Running through loop", 100)
```

The acSysCmdInitMeter in this line is an Access constant that tells the function that you are initializing the meter. The second parameter is the text you want to appear to the left of the meter. Finally, the last value is the maximum value of the meter (in this case, 100 percent). You can set this value to anything you want. For example, if you were iterating through a loop of 504 records, you could set this value to 504. Then you could pass the record count at any given time to the SysCmd function; Access decides what percentage the meter should show filled.

After the meter has been initialized, you can pass a value to it to update the meter. To update the meter, you call the SysCmd function again and pass it the acSysCmdUpdateMeter constant and the new update meter value. Remember, the value that you pass the function is not necessarily the percent displayed by the meter. When the loop is completed, run SysCmd(acSysCmdRemoveMeter) to remove the meter from the status bar.

Done!

REVIEW

In this chapter, you learned about ways to make your application run faster by keeping it compiled or by using a variety of techniques to increase the speed in which it runs. The following topics were covered:

- Tuning your computer hardware for maximum performance
- Increasing performance dramatically by keeping your code in a compiled state

- Compacting your database
- Creating .MDE databases for better performance
- Organizing your database into referenced libraries
- Using techniques to improve the absolute speed of your database
- Using techniques to improve perceived speed using the hourglass and progress meter

In the next chapter, you will learn how to create animated splash screens, about boxes, and startup screens.

QUIZ YOURSELF

1. What is the optimum amount of memory you need to run Microsoft Access 2000? (See "Hardware and Memory.")

2. Why would you want to compile your program? (See "Understanding the Compiled State.")

3. How do you compile your Access database file? (See "Putting your application's code into a compiled state.")

4. Should you compact your database after compiling it? (See "Compacting a database after compiling it.")

5. What are the advantages of creating an .MDE file? (See "Creating and Distributing .MDE Files.")

6. Why should you split your database files into libraries? (See "Organizing Commonly Used Code into a Library.")

7. What are several techniques for improving the absolute speed of an application? (See "Improving Absolute Speed.")

8. How can you display the hourglass and a progress meter when you run long processes? (See "Improving Perceived Speed.")

Creating Animated Splash Screens, About Boxes, and Startup Screens

Session Checklist

✔ Displaying startup screens

✔ Examining common startup dialog boxes

✔ Creating basic types of startup forms

✔ Getting Access to open and close the dialog boxes

✔ Adding animation

30 Min. To Go

Nearly every professional application uses startup forms and they are important for many reasons. You may be running processes when you first open your database or application that take a long time to load, and you want to keep your customers' attention. You may want to make sure they see that they have loaded the latest version of your software. If your customers need to link to data stored in a separate database, you may want to make sure they are aware of what data file they are attached to and that they are working with the correct database. All of these items can be presented to users by way of a friendly, informational screen.

The more information your system displays, the more it will help alleviate the number of errors that are likely to be introduced during subsequent processes. If you can consistently present usable information to the operator of your system, you are more likely to be successful. In this session, you will learn how to create three basic types of informational screens:

- Splash screens
- About boxes
- First screens

Creating a Splash Screen

A *splash screen* is a form that is displayed for a few seconds and then disappears. It is normally displayed when the user first opens the application, and it is used for two main reasons:

- To display information about the application, such as the name, version, and registration information
- To provide the user with something to look at while the application loads

Figure 19-1 shows a typical splash screen. This is the form xSplashScreen found in the Check Writer example database.

Figure 19-1
The Check Writer splash screen

You create the splash screen form like any other form. Figure 19-2 shows the design of the splash screen form used in the Check Writer application. Notice the components used on this form. There is a company logo, a product logo, and several text and label controls used to display information about the program. When creating your own splash screen form, you can link to or embed your logos or other graphics to the form.

You can also add a background image to the form or any other information you may want users to see when they first start the application.

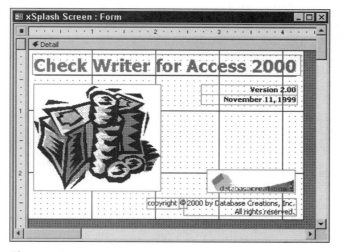

Figure 19-2
The Design view of the Check Writer splash screen

When creating the form, consider its size. Pop-up forms will always appear on top of other forms. Also, splash screens are not maximized to the full screen as other forms may be. For this reason, you will want to create a form large enough to display all the information you plan to place on the form.

Don't set the form to Modal since you want other processes to continue running while the form is displayed. When a form is set as modal, you cannot click or select anything in another window until the modal form is closed.

Figure 19-3 shows the property sheet for xSplash Screen. The form is set to Pop-up, while scroll bars, navigation buttons, and record selectors have all been disabled. This is because you don't want the user to have interaction with this form since it is used only for display purposes.

Figure 19-3
The property sheet for xSplash Screen

Starting a form automatically when a database is opened

Once you have added the objects and controls to the form, you need to let Access know how the form should be opened. Since it is being used as a splash screen, you will want Access to display this form first when the application starts. There are a few ways you can do this:

- Set the form as the startup display form
- Call the form from the startup display form
- Open the form from an autoexec macro

If you use the `Startup` **property, make sure you do not have any Autoexec macros. These will affect which form displays first when the application opens.**

Setting the form as the startup display form

To set the form as the startup display form, follow these steps:

1. Open the Tools menu in Access.

2. Choose Startup. The Startup dialog box is displayed, as shown in
   Figure 19-4.

Startup   ? ✕

Application Title: Display Form/Page:
Check Writer for Access 2000   xSplash Screen   ▾   [OK]

Application Icon: ☑ Display Database Window   [Cancel]
[   ] [...]   ☑ Display Status Bar
                                                                       [Advanced >>]
Menu Bar: Shortcut Menu Bar:
(default)   ▾   (default)   ▾

☑ Allow Full Menus   ☑ Allow Built-in Toolbars
☑ Allow Default Shortcut Menus   ☑ Allow Toolbar/Menu Changes

Figure 19-4
The Startup dialog box

3. Select the form you want to use as a splash screen in the Display Form:
   field. This box displays all forms in the current database. The dialog box
   also allows you to control other options displayed when the application
   opens, such as showing the database window, toolbars, and status bar.

**20 Min.
To Go**

Calling the form from the startup display form

You can also call the splash screen from another form set as the startup display
form. You accomplish this by opening the other form and adding code to the On
Load event as shown below. As this form loads, it will open the splash screen form
as well.

```
Private Sub Form_Load()
    DoCmd.OpenForm "xSplash Screen"
End Sub
```

Using an Autoexec macro to open the splash screen

Prior versions of Access used the Autoexec macro to carry out an *action* or series of
actions when a database first opens. When you open a database, Access looks for a
macro named Autoexec and, if it finds one, runs it automatically.

To create an Autoexec macro, create a macro containing the actions you want
to run when you open the database, and then save the macro with the name
Autoexec. An example of an Autoexec macro used to open a splash screen is
shown in Figure 19-5.

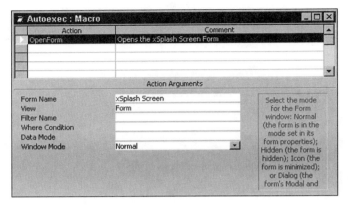

Figure 19-5
An Autoexec macro

 In earlier versions of Access, Autoexec macros were commonly used to control startup options. Current versions of Access use the Startup Display form to set startup options.

Using Timer events

Since splash screens are displayed on screen only for a few seconds, you need to tell Access how long to display the splash screen and what to do after it is closed. In some cases, you may also want to kick off other events while the splash screen is open. You can use a Timer event to do this.

By running a macro or event procedure when a Timer event occurs, you can control what Microsoft Access does at every timer interval. For example, you might want to open other forms, run macros, or control any animation used in your splash screen.

Figure 19-6 shows the property sheet for xSplash Screen with the Timer Interval and On Timer selections displayed. You can adjust the time period by changing the value of Timer Interval. This can also be done programmatically with the statement

```
Me.TimerInterval = x
```

where x represents the number of milliseconds. There are a thousand milliseconds in a second. To set each update of the form to 5 seconds, enter 5,000 in the previous statement or in the Timer Interval property field.

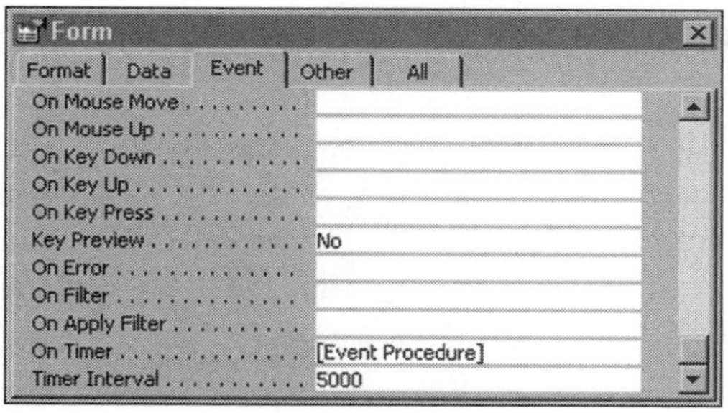

Figure 19-6
Setting Timer events

The On Timer property is used to set what happens once the form is displayed for the selected timer interval. Looking at the following code behind the event, notice that when the timer interval is reached, the form named AttachmentManagerOneFileII is opened and the xSplash Screen form is closed.

```
Private Sub Form_Timer()
Numtime=Numtime+1
Select case Numtime
Case 3
    DoCmd.OpenForm "AttachmentManagerOneFileII", acNormal, , , , , "Startup"
    DoCmd.Close acForm, "xSplash Screen"
 End Select
End Sub
```

> **Setting the timer interval to 0 prevents the timer event from executing.**

Suppose you wanted to kick off the previous events at different time intervals. You can accomplish this by adding an On Load event and changing the On Timer event code to the following:

```
Private Sub Form_Load()
Dim NumTime As Integer
NumTime = 0
End Sub

Private Sub Form_Timer()
    NumTime = NumTime + 1
    If NumTime = 1 Then
        DoCmd.OpenForm "AttachmentManagerOneFileII", acNormal, , , , , "Startup"
    End If
    If NumTime = 3 Then
```

```
        DoCmd.Close acForm, "xSplash Screen"
        End
End Sub
```

The code in the Form_Load event sets the timer interval, named NumTime, to 0. The Form_Timer event is then used to control the action that takes place when the timer reaches a certain interval. NumTime=NumTime + 1 tells Access to increment the timer by 1. When the interval reaches 1, the AttachmentManagerOneFileII form is opened. When it reaches 3, the xSplash Screen form is closed.

Adding animation to a splash screen

You can create more interesting splash screens by adding animation to the form. The form named xSplash Screen Animated found in the Check Writer sample database uses some simple animation techniques to enhance the form. The design of this form is shown in Figure 19-7.

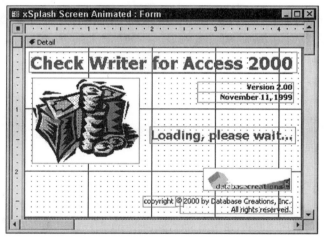

Figure 19-7
A design of an animated splash screen

In this form, the text "Loading, please wait..." blinks on the screen while the form loads. This is done by adding the code shown in Listing 19-1 to the On Timer event of the form.

Listing 19-1
Code for blinking text

```
Option Compare Database    'Use database order for string comparisons
Option Explicit
Dim NumTime As Integer

Private Sub Form_Load()
    Me.TimerInterval = 400
End Sub
Private Sub Form_Timer()
   NumTime = NumTime + 1
   If Me.Title.Visible = True Then
      Me.Title.Visible = False
   Else
      Me.Title.Visible = True
   End If
   If NumTime = 8 Then
   DoCmd.Close
   End If

End Sub
```

The text that blinks is set as a label object named Title. The If statement in the Form_Timer event turns the display of the label on and off, which gives it the appearance of blinking. You can set how fast the text blinks by setting the Timer Interval property. In this example, the interval is set to 400, which means the text will appear and disappear or "blink" about every half a second. Once the timer interval reaches 8, the form closes.

Creating an About Box

One of the standard interfaces you will find in most software is an About box. This form is often displayed by selecting an option from the Help menu, or by clicking on a picture, logo, or hidden area of the screen.

The About box used for the Check Writer form is shown in Figure 19-8. This represents a typical type of About box used in standard applications. The name of the application is displayed, the version number, copyright information, and the names of the developers.

About boxes are normally set as a pop-up, modal type of form. This is because the form is generally used to display basic information about the application, and you will want the user to exit the form before anything else can be done within the application.

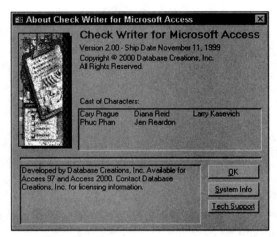

Figure 19-8
The Check Writer About box

Adding functionality to the About box

In addition to displaying basic information about the application, you can also add additional functionality to the form. This includes adding buttons to open other forms, setting hyperlinks, and adding sound to the form.

Notice that the Check Writer About box contains three buttons. The OK button is simply used to close the form, while the System Information button opens the `SystemInformation` form. This form is used to display information about the user's operating system and version of Access.

The button labeled Tech Support is actually a hyperlink that, when pressed, opens a URL that allows the user to get technical support on the application.

Setting a hyperlink is simple. Just add the URL to the `Hyperlink Address` prop-erty of the command button, as shown in Figure 19-9.

Command Button: Tech Support

Format	Data	Event	Other	All

Name	Tech Support
Caption	&Tech Support
Picture	(none)
Picture Type	Embedded
Transparent	No
Default	No
Cancel	No
Auto Repeat	No
Status Bar Text	
Hyperlink Address	http://www.databasecreations.com
Hyperlink SubAddress	
Visible	Yes

Figure 19-9
Adding a hyperlink

Note

If using hyperlinks and connection to a remote URL is required, make sure the user has a browser installed and is able to estab-lish a connection to the URL, as well as sufficient access rights to display the hyperlinked page. If you anticipate that some users may not have a browser installed or a connection config-ured, you may need to provide them with additional functionality to establish the connection to the hyperlinked document.

Notice also that the first character of text on each button is underlined. This is because an Access key has been set for each button. When you assign an access key to the button, pressing the Alt key plus the underlined character moves the focus to the button. You can set the access key to any character of the button's `Caption` property. This is done by adding an ampersand (&) character to the left of the character you want to use as the access key. Figure 19-9 displays the access key used for the Tech Support button.

Don't use the same character as an access key for more than one button or control on the same form. When the same access key is assigned to multiple buttons, pressing the Alt + access key combination will select the first button in the tab order. However, this may not be the button the user wanted.

Adding sound to the About box

You can add some extra pizzazz to your About box by playing a sound clip when the form opens. This is done by inserting a sound clip onto the form. The exact location and size doesn't really matter, as you can set its size when the form is opened. Notice in Figure 19-10 the sound clip in the design of the About Box form, as represented by a sound icon.

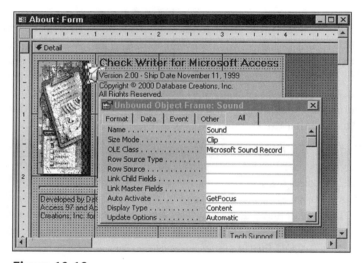

Figure 19-10
Adding a sound clip to a form

In addition to adding the sound clip, you will also need to enable the object by setting its Enabled property to Yes and change the Auto-Activate property to Get Focus. Finally, you will need to set focus on the control, which you do in the Form Open event.

Figure 19-11 shows the form's On Load event. Notice the code added for the sound file named Sound. First, the focus is set to this object. This is necessary to get the sound to play. Then, the width and height of the object is set to 0. This is done so the sound icon is not displayed on the form when it opens.

The sound will not play if you set its Visible **property to No.**

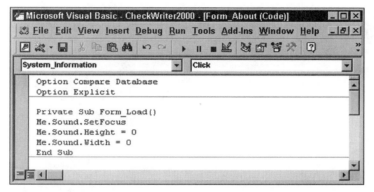

Figure 19-11
Setting the On Load event to play the sound clip

Creating a First Screen

A First Screen form is the form that appears the first time you run an application. It is often used to guide new users through the installation or setup of the application. It may also be used to provide a guided tour, demo, or tutorial.

As you can see in Figure 19-12, the First Screen form for the Check Writer application, named xFirst Screen, gives the user basic instructions on the system. It consists of several label fields, a text box, a button, a check box, and one unbound object used to display a graphic.

The Continue button is used to close the xFirst Screen form and open the next form to be displayed. This could be the application's main menu, tutorial, or demo form.

Checking the value to display the first screen

The check box labeled "Don't show this screen again" allows users to decide if they want to continue displaying the first screen each time the application is opened. If they choose not to have the screen displayed, the first screen will be bypassed when the application starts. This is typically done by adding code to the On Open event of the First Screen form to check to see if the user has selected not to view the form at startup.

In the Check Writer application, the On Unload event of the Attachment-ManagerOneFileII form is used to open the First Screen form. This code is shown in Listing 19-2.

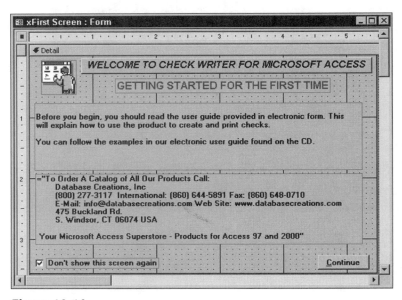

Figure 19-12
The design of the First Screen form

Listing 19-2
Opening the First Screen form in the On Unload event

```
Private Sub Form_Unload(Cancel As Integer)

    If Me.OpenArgs = "Startup" Then
        If LinkErrors Then
            If MsgBox("There are errors with your linked tables." & vbCrLf & _
                "Are you sure you want to exit?", vbExclamation + vbYesNo, _
                "Check Writer - Attachment Manager") = vbYes Then
                DoCmd.Quit
            Else
```

```
               Cancel = True
           End If
       Else
           'everything is OK on startup
           DoCmd.OpenForm "xFirst Screen"
       End If
   End If
```

Notice that this code opens the First Screen form regardless of whether the user selects not to view the form. To control whether the form should open based on the user's selections, there is code behind the On Open event of the xFirst Screen form that checks to see what the user selected:

```
Private Sub Form_Open(Cancel As Integer)
  If Me.First_Time Then ContinueButton_Click
End Sub
```

The xFirst Screen form is bound to the table named First Time. This table consists of one field named First_Time. When the First Screen form opens, the value of the First_Time field is checked. If the value of the field is True (the user does not want the First Screen form displayed), the form is closed. This is done by programmatically pressing the command button on the form named ContinueButton, which is the button on the form used to close the form.

Storing the value to display the screen

Done!

Since users have control over whether the First Screen form is displayed, you will need some way to store their selection so the application can determine whether the form should be opened. Since the form is bound to the table First Time, you can store a value in a field in this table. The First Time table contains one field and one record. The application checks the value of the field to determine whether to display the form.

In the Check Writer application, the value is stored in the First_Time field. This field is represented on the form by the check box labeled "Don't show this screen again." If the user selects this box, the value of this field is updated to True. So the next time the application is started, the First Screen form checks the value of this field and if it is true, the form will immediately be closed. Otherwise, the form will continue to be opened each time the application is started until the user selects otherwise.

Make sure you set the value of the First_Time field to False if you want the First Screen form to open when the user first starts the application.

REVIEW

In this session, you learned about some of the different types of forms used in applications. You also learned how to control the display of these forms, as well as some techniques for adding advanced functionality to the form, such as animation and sound.

QUIZ YOURSELF

1. Which event can you use to control actions performed within a form? (See "Using Timer events.")

2. How can you control whether a form is displayed based on a user's selection? (See "Creating a First Screen," "Checking the value to display the first screen," "Storing the value to display the screen.")

3. How can you add sound to a form or a control on the form? (See "Adding functionality to the About box," "Adding sound to the About box.")

4. How can you set a hyperlink to a button on a form? (See "Adding functionality to the About box.")

Creating Help Systems

Session Checklist

✔ Understanding the Help Viewer

✔ Authoring help topics

✔ Using help-authoring tools

✔ Assigning help topic IDs

✔ Calling help from forms and controls

**30 Min.
To Go**

Help systems are a fundamental component of any application. Many developers omit this critical component because they either lack the skills involved in creating one, or they do not have the time. Learning how to develop a great help system and how to integrate it will provide a real boost to the success of your application. In this session, you will learn how to integrate a help system into your application.

Understanding the Help Viewer

The Help Viewer displays the files that make up the help system. Pressing the F1 key is the quickest way to display the Help Viewer. You can also display it by choosing Help from the menu bar. Figure 20-1 shows the Help Viewer for the Check Writer system.

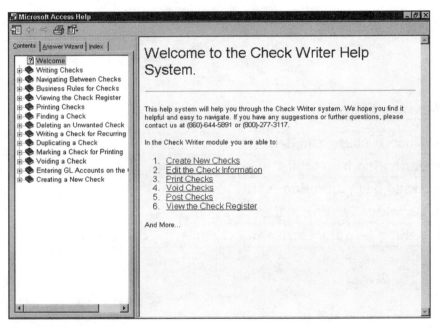

Figure 20-1
Displaying the Help Viewer on the Check Writer form

The Help Viewer displays when you press F1 anywhere on the Check Writer form. Or, you can choose Help ➪ What's This? from the Help menu.

The Help Viewer includes three components:

- The Topic pane
- The Navigation pane
- The toolbar

The Topic pane is where the text for the help item displays. The Navigation pane displays to the left of the Topic pane and includes the Contents tab. The

Contents tab lists all of the topics that are included in the help system. The toolbar displays at the top of the viewer and includes buttons for the following:

- Displaying or hiding the Navigation pane
- Moving forward or backward between previously viewed topics
- Printing a displayed topic
- Setting options for displaying the Help Viewer

The Contents tab displays in a tree-like format. An Open button and a book icon display next to each high-level topic. To see the subtopics available for a high-level topic, you click the Open button. When you click the Open button, it changes to a Close button, the book icon changes to an open book icon, and one or more subtopics display below the high-level item.

A question-mark icon displays next to each subtopic. When you select a subtopic, the help topic information for that subtopic displays in the Topic pane.

Creating a Help System

Building a help system requires not only a significant amount of labor, but also a tremendous amount of planning and creativity. Before you can begin writing the help contents, you need to define a list of all of the important features and functions of the application and organize them into an outline format. Creating the outline is a lot like creating an outline before you write a paper or book. The order of the items should coincide with the flow of the application. After you have completed the help system, this outline should look very similar to its table of contents.

Once the outline for your help system is complete, you can create the topic information that will display for each topic. You create the help content for each topic in HTML format. The content for each topic is stored in a separate HTML file.

 You can use Microsoft Word or any authoring tool that can create HTML files.

HTML format provides the ability to be very creative in authoring help topics. In addition to textual content, you can also add graphics, sounds, animated images, or anything else that will give users the information they need. Figure 20-2 shows the HTML file for the Writing A Check topic in Microsoft Word.

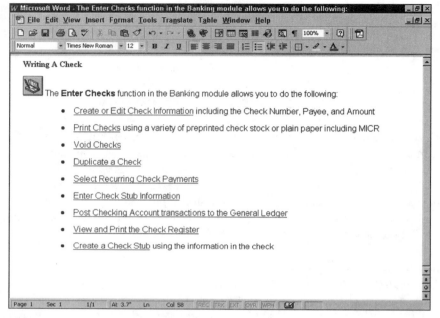

Figure 20-2
Creating a help topic using Microsoft Word

The Writing Checks topic includes some informational text along with a graphic and several hotspots. The hotspots display as underlined colored text. When you move the cursor over a hotspot, the cursor changes to a hand. The hand cursor indicates that if you click on the hotspot, you can jump to the related topic to which the hotspot refers.

To bundle all of the help topic files into a format that can be accessed from the Help Viewer, you need a help-authoring tool. Help-authoring tools perform the following functions:

- Compile all of the topic files into a single help file (.CHM) that you can distribute with your application

- Create a table of contents, index, and full-text search utility

- Provide an interface to the Windows HtmlHelp API so that you can integrate the help system into your application

Numerous help-authoring tools are available for creating help systems. The developer version of Microsoft Access 2000 includes the HTML Help Workshop. Two other popular tools are Doc-2-Help and RoboHelp. For a list of other available tools, look for information on HTML help in Microsoft's Web site (`http://www.microsoft.com/`).

The specifics on how to create a help system using these help-authoring tools is outside the scope of this book. A lot is involved in using these tools effectively, and the process varies with each tool. In fact, entire books are available on the vast array of tips and techniques that these tools can provide to help you implement really professional help systems. "The Official Microsoft HTML Help Authoring Kit" published by Microsoft Press is a good one to try.

**20 Min.
To Go**

Defining Help Topic IDs

For the purposes of this session, however, you need to understand how to use the help-authoring tool to set up HtmlHelp application programming interface (API) properties. The HtmlHelp API properties tell applications how to access the help system's topics. In this session, the HtmlHelp API properties will be set up using the HTML Help Workshop.

Creating the header file

An application retrieves a help topic from a help system by passing the topic ID. Each topic in the help system must have a unique topic ID. To assign a topic ID to each topic, you create a header file. A *header file* is just a special type of text file that contains data in a predefined format. Figure 20-3 shows the header file for the Check Writer help system.

The Check Writer.h file contains the header information for the Check Writer help system. You can use Notepad to create the file, or you can use any application that can create a text file.

Each line in the file assigns a unique ID to a help topic. The syntax for the entries in the header file is:

```
#define     <symbolic name>      <ID>
```

The entries in the header file are like a program. You use the #define command to execute the assignment statement. The symbolic name is just a descriptive name that you use to refer to a topic and must be all alpha characters and contain no spaces. The ID is the numeric identifier that you use to refer to the topic. Each ID in the header file must be unique.

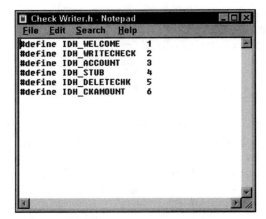

Figure 20-3
Creating the help system's header file

It is a good idea to create the entries in ID order to make it easier for others to work with the file later. Also, if you increment each ID by a multiplier of 10, 100, or even 1,000, it will be easier to insert a topic ID later.

Adding the header file to the help project

Once you have created the header file containing the topic IDs, you need to incorporate the file into your help project. To add the file to the help project, follow these steps.

1. Open the HTML Help Workshop.
2. Open the help project file (.HHP) for your help system.
3. Click the HtmlHelp API Information button in the HTML Help Workshop. The HtmlHelp API Information dialog box displays, as shown in Figure 20-4.
4. Click the Header filer button on the Map page of the HtmlHelp API dialog box. The Include File dialog box displays.
5. Use the Browse button to select the name of the header file you created. Then click the OK button. The header file name displays on the Map tab.

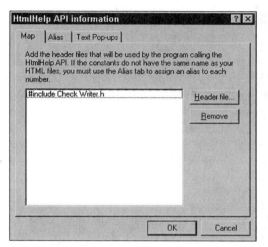

Figure 20-4
Including a header file for the help system

If you prefix the symbolic ID with "IDH", the HTML Help Workshop will automatically verify that the topic exists in your help project when you compile it.

The header file is used to assign topic IDs for your help system. Now the help system needs to know which topic file, or HTML file, is associated with each topic ID. To map the topic IDs to HTML files, follow these steps.

1. Select the Alias tab of the HtmlHelp API dialog box, shown in Figure 20-5.

2. Click the Add button on the Alias tab. The Alias dialog box displays, as shown in Figure 20-6.

3. In the first field of the Alias tab, enter the first symbolic ID you created in the header file.

4. Pick the name of the HTML topic file that you want to use for the symbolic ID. Then click the OK button. The Alias string displays on the Alias tab.

5. Enter the alias definitions for each of the symbolic IDs you created in the header file.

6. When you have finished creating the alias definitions, click the OK button on the Alias tab to save them.

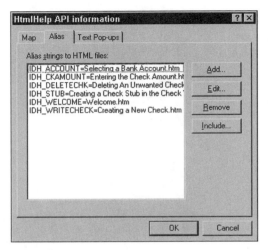

Figure 20-5
Mapping the IDs to HTML files

Figure 20-6
Adding an HtmlHelp API alias

Be sure to save and compile the help project whenever you make any changes.

Testing HtmlHelp API definitions

The HTML Help Workshop provides a facility for testing your HtmlHelp API mappings. You can use this facility to make sure that your symbolic IDs are mapped to the proper help topic. To test each topic ID, follow these steps.

1. Choose Test ⇨ HtmlHelp API from the HTML Help Workshop menu. The Test HtmlHelp API dialog box displays, as shown in Figure 20-7.

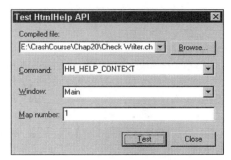

Figure 20-7
Testing the HtmlHelp API definitions

2. Use the Browse button to select the name of your compiled help file if it was not automatically selected. Select HH_HELP_CONTEXT for the command. Enter the topic ID you want to test in the Map Number field.

3. Click the Test button. The Help Viewer opens displaying the help topic that corresponds to the topic ID you entered in the Test HtmlHelp API dialog box.

If the Help Viewer did not display the right topic or did not display any topic, check the following list to troubleshoot your topic error.

*   Is the correct header file selected on the Map tab of the HtmlHelp API?
*   Did you enter the correct symbolic ID for the HTML file you selected on the Alias tab of the HtmlHelp API?
*   Does the symbolic ID on the Alias tab match the one in the mapped header file?
*   Did you save and recompile your project?

Now that you have tested your HtmlHelp API definitions, you are ready to link the help system to your Access application.

**10 Min.
To Go**

Connecting the Help File to an Access Application

Once you have a help file in good working order, it is easy to link it up to an Access application. You can display general help for forms or specific help topics that relate to fields, command buttons, and menu items.

Specifying help for a form

Each form contains two help properties: HelpFile and HelpContextID. You use the HelpFile property to set the source for all of the help topics you want to display for the form. The HelpContextID contains the topic ID to use for general form help.

To set the HelpFile property, enter the path and filename of the compiled help (.CHM) file that you want to use for the form. Figure 20-8 shows the help settings for the Check Writer form.

The Check Writer form is connected to the CheckWriter.chm file. If you do not specify a path name for the help file, Access looks in the application's folder for the specified filename.

It is always a good idea to avoid hard-coding path names in any application.

The Check Writer form's HelpContextID is set to 1. The HelpContextID settings that you can use come from the topic IDs you assigned in the HtmlHelp API dialog box in the help system.

For the form's HelpContextID, you should use a topic ID that corresponds to general help about the form. Topic ID 1 in the Check Writer help system corresponds to the Welcome help topic. When the user presses F1 on the form, the Help Viewer displays the Welcome help topic.

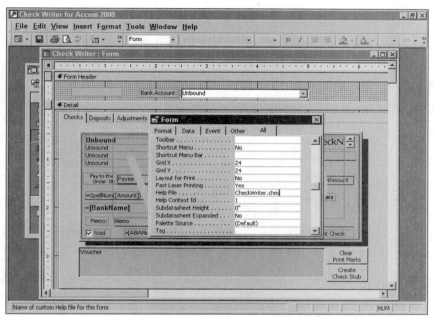

Figure 20-8
Integrating help for a form

Displaying help topics for controls

You can display a help topic for an individual control on a form. When the control has focus, the user can press F1 to display the help topic that describes the active control. To link a control to a help topic, you set the control's HelpContextID. The help file used for control-level help is the one you entered for the form's HelpFile property. The IDs that you can link to are the ones you entered in the help file's header file.

When you are setting up help for the controls on a form, you need to have the contents of the help file's header file handy. An easy way to do this is to tile the header file and Access design windows together on the screen, as shown in Figure 20-9.

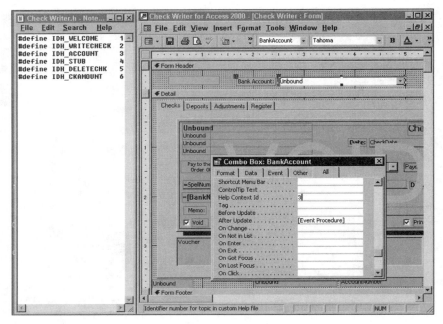

Figure 20-9
Setting up control-level help for a form

When setting HelpContextIDs for radio buttons and option buttons, be sure to set the HelpContextID for the labels as well. Some users may click the label instead of the control itself. This way, the appropriate help topic will display regardless of where the user clicks.

If your help file does not include specific help for a control on the form, you can leave its HelpContextID set to 0 (the default). When the user requests help on the control, the form's general help topic will display.

 Don't forget to set the form's HelpContextID. **If the form's** HelpContextID **is 0, Microsoft Access help will display for form-level help and for any control with** HelpContextIDs **set to 0.**

Testing custom help

After linking the help system to the controls in the form, you should test the form's help connections. Figure 20-10 shows the help topic that displays when you press F1 on the Bank Account field in the Check Writer form.

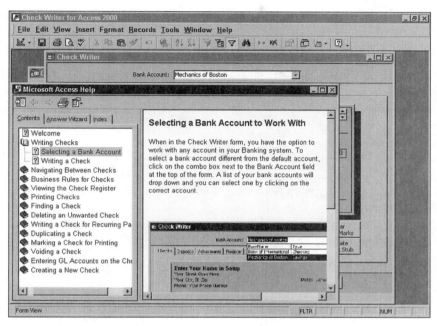

Figure 20-10
Testing a form's custom help

Done!

To test the help system links, open the form. Then select and press F1 for each control on the form. Check to make sure the correct help topic displays for each control. Form-level help should display for controls with no specific `HelpContextID` setting.

REVIEW

A truly professional application includes a well-constructed, thorough help system. The users of your application will experience a much greater sense of ease as they begin to use the application if they know they can get quick and accurate help instantly. A good help system reduces the amount of time you will spend performing technical support and increases the usability of the application.

- Access applications display help using the Windows Help Viewer.
- Help topics are created in HTML format.
- You need a help-authoring tool like HTML Help Workshop to build a help system.

- The HtmlHelp API allows applications to display individual help topics from a help system.
- You can display help for an Access form by setting the help properties for the form and its controls.

QUIZ YOURSELF

1. Name the three components of the Help Viewer. (See "Understanding the Help Viewer.")

2. Identify the first step in creating a help system. (See "Creating a Help System.")

3. Name the utility that allows applications to display a help system. (See "Defining Help Topic IDs.")

4. What is the purpose of the help system header file? (See "Creating the header file.")

5. Name the two help properties you use in an Access form to display help. (See "Connecting the Help File to an Access Application.")

6. Name the source of the list of topic IDs that you can use in a form. (See "Displaying help topics for controls.")

PART

IV

Saturday Evening

1. What are the five parameters for the `MsgBox` function?
2. True or false: The buttons parameter of the `MsgBox` function also determines the icon to be displayed.
3. Describe the difference between application modal and system modal as it pertains to the message box function.
4. Which of the following statements is/are correct?
    a. Error handling is enabled with the `On Error Goto 0` statement.
    b. The `Resume 0` statement disables error handling.
    c. The `Resume Next` statement returns execution to the line immediately following the line at which the error occurred.
    d. All of the above.
    e. None of the above.
5. List some of the types of file formats are you able to import or export.
6. What are the four basic steps in doing an import?
7. What is a Import/Export Specification and where would you set it up?
8. List the methods available for transferring data.
9. What is more important for improving the speed of Microsoft Access — memory or a faster processor?
10. Name three ways to lose the compiled state.
11. What is the name of the undocumented command that can greatly speed up an Access program and clean up your database file at the same time?

12. What are three things you cannot do with a .MDE database file?

13. True or false: A splash screen is a type of menu system.

14. True or false: When a form is modal, the user cannot select anything in another window until the modal form is closed.

15. True or false: An AutoRun macro is used to carry out an action or series of actions when a database first opens.

16. True or false: Setting a timer event to 0 stops the timer event from executing.

17. The _____ pane displays the text for the help item.

18. True or false: You create the content for the help topics in HTML format.

19. A help-authoring tool performs all but which one of the following features?

    a. Compiling all of the topic files into a single help file (.CHM).

    b. Creating a table of contents, index, and full-text search utility.

    c. Providing an interface to the Windows HtmlHelp API.

    d. Inserting the topic IDs into the forms and fields in your application.

20. Which property is used to connect a control to a help file?

    a. HelpContextID

    b. OnHelp

    c. OnKeyDown

    d. Caption

☑ Friday

☑ Saturday

 **Sunday**

PART

V

Sunday Morning

Creating Search Dialog Box Forms

Session Checklist

✔ Understanding dialog boxes

✔ Creating a search dialog box

✔ Changing the searchable items

✔ Finding the selected item in the form

✔ Calling a search dialog box form

**30 Min.
To Go**

While Microsoft Access contains several built-in techniques to search for data, each technique requires that users understand their complexities. A search dialog box allows users to quickly select a method to view data, select a desired record, and display the record on any underlying data entry form. While you may think that users can easily place the cursor on a field and press the binocular toolbar button, this method is simply not obvious or intuitive. Expecting users to use the Query by Form view is even less likely if they have little or no experience with Microsoft Access but just want to run an Access application. Since many Access applications hide some or all of the Microsoft Access interface, a programmed search dialog box is essential.

Understanding Dialog Boxes

Pop-up dialog boxes are a major part of any application, as they help control the flow from one area of an application to another and provide the user with many options that otherwise would take hours of coding or manual intervention. By creating innovative dialog boxes that give the user many choices, you simplify an application and increase intuitiveness. Allowing the user to easily move from one selection to another decreases training costs and increases the user's productivity.

Figure 21-1 shows the yCheck Search dialog box for the Check Writer form.

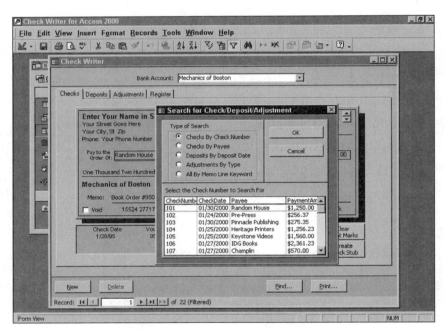

Figure 21-1
Using a dialog box to search for a record

Clicking the Find button on the Check Writer form displays the yCheck Search dialog box, which includes an option group labeled Type of Search and a list box that shows the items available to search in the Check Writer form. The Type of Search option group includes seven different search options. When the user clicks on one of the options, the contents of the list box change to reflect the type of information corresponding to the Type of Search option. For example, the Checks by Check Number option lists all of the checks in the Check Writer sorted by check number. The Deposits by Deposit Date option, on the other hand, lists all of the deposits in the Check Writer sorted by deposit date. When the user selects an item in the list box and clicks the OK button, the dialog box closes and the Check Writer form displays the record that the user selected in the dialog box list box.

While data entry forms and dialog boxes are both forms, dialog boxes have some unique characteristics. Most significantly, dialog boxes are generally not bound to any data source. Since their job is simply to guide you from one form to another, or from one record to another, they do not need a data source of their own. The controls on the dialog box are all that you need to determine where to go next.

Some of the other properties unique to dialog boxes include the following:

Auto Resize	Yes (True) — Dialog box resizes to size of controls within
Auto Center	Yes (True) — Dialog box is displayed in the center of the screen
Pop Up	Yes (True) — Form pops up on top of all other windows
Modal	Yes (True) — User cannot select another window until dialog box is closed
Border Style	Dialog — Displays a nonresizable thick border
Control Box	Yes (True) — Displays the Control Menu box in the upper left corner
Min Max Buttons	None — Hides the Minimize and Maximize buttons
Close Button	Yes (True) — Displays the Close button (Control box must be Yes)

While these are the traditional dialog box settings, you may not always want to use them. Figure 21-2 shows the settings for the yCheck Search dialog box.

The Pop Up setting forces the dialog box to display in front of any other displayed window. However, if your dialog box displays another window while the dialog box is still open (a Print Preview window, for example), the dialog box will remain stuck in front of the other window. If you use the Pop Up property, you must either close the dialog box before displaying another window, or, if you need to keep the dialog box open for some reason, you can hide it.

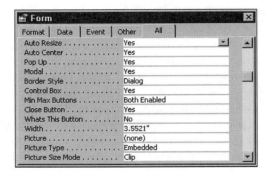

Figure 21-2
Setting the properties for a dialog box

Modal dialog boxes are being used less and less frequently. The concept of Windows and event-driven programming is to let the users decide what they want to do and when they want to do it. Unless you absolutely need to guide users down a specific navigation path and not let them out of the dialog box until they perform some action or close the dialog box, you should avoid the modal setting.

Dialog boxes in the past have always used a thick, nonsizable border to indicate that they were modal dialog boxes. However, with today's choices of screen resolutions and a definite move to give the user more freedom of the environment, dialog boxes are showing up with a resizable thin border rather than the dialog border style.

The Auto Center property works in conjunction with the Pop Up property to force the dialog box to appear in the center of the screen. While the Auto Center dialog box can always be moved, it will reopen in a centered position. The only reason to use this property is when vastly different resolutions may be encountered and dialog boxes (which are often smaller than data entry forms) may be moved to a corner of a larger screen resolution. When the application is opened in a smaller resolution, a dialog box could appear partially off the screen and in some cases, become inaccessible.

20 Min. To Go

Creating Search Dialog Boxes

The first step in building a search dialog box is to create a form — just like you would create a normal data entry form. Then set the form's AutoResize, AutoCenter, PopUp properties, and so on, so that it displays as a dialog box .

Then you can add controls to the dialog box. A typical search dialog box, like yCheck, includes the following controls:

- An option group for selecting the type of search
- A list box or combo box for displaying the searchable items
- A set of command buttons to process or cancel the dialog box

You should set one of the option buttons as the default so that when the dialog box opens, one of the options is already selected and the list box displays the corresponding set of items. Figure 21-3 shows setting the default option for the Type of Search option group. You can create as many different options as you want. You are limited only by physical space on the screen. You can always switch the option group to a combo box if you need unlimited options.

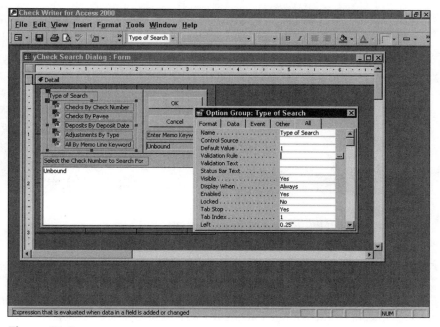

Figure 21-3
Setting the default search option

If you have five search options or fewer, option buttons are the most visual and intuitive choice to use. If you have more than five options, it may be more practical to use a combo box.

After setting the default search option, be sure that you set the `RowSource` for the list box to match the default search option. This way, when the form opens, the list box will automatically display the correct items for the selected search type. Figure 21-4 shows the RowSource property setting for the list box in the `yCheck` Search dialog box.

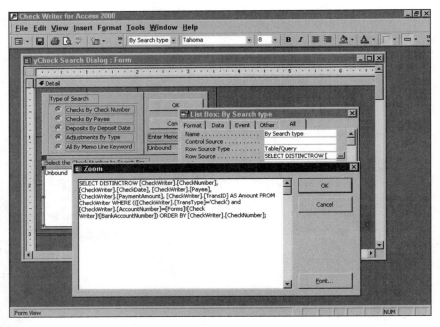

Figure 21-4
Setting the default list box RowSource property

Changing the list box items

Each time the user selects a different search option, the contents of the list box change. To change the contents of the list box, you use the `AfterUpdate` event of the option group. Figure 21-5 shows the `AfterUpdate` event for the Type of Search option group.

The `Type_Of_Search_AfterUpdate` event includes a `Case` statement for evaluating the option the user selected. Each branch in the `Case` statement includes the same types of statements, but the values that the statements set change depending on the selected type of search.

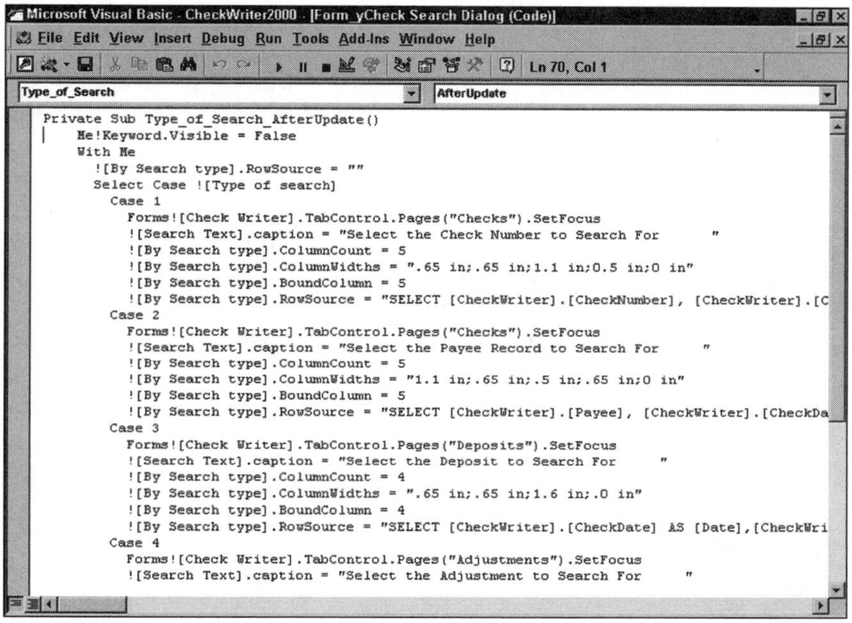

Figure 21-5
Changing the contents of the list box.

Using the statement before the `Case` statement `[By Search Type].RowSource = ""`, however, may be the most important technique you learn in this session. This statement sets the `RowSource` property of the combo box to null. This is mandatory because if the row source is set to a valid data source, the data source is requeried each time other properties are set, such as `ColumnCount`, `ColumnWidths`, or `BoundColumn`. If your combo box row source returns 100,000 records, you could wait a long time, as the combo box must retrieve the data four times — once when the row source is set, and each time one of the three properties are set.

The first statement in each branch of the `Case` statement changes the active page in the Check Writer form's tab control. The tab control page in the Check Writer form must be in sync with the type of search the user selected in the search dialog box. For example, if the user chooses to search for a deposit by deposit date, you must change Check Writer's active tab to the Deposits tab.

The second statement sets the caption for the search dialog box's list box. The caption displays instructions appropriate to the type of search. For example, selecting the option Deposits by Deposit Date displays the caption "Select the Deposit to search for."

The next three lines of code set the properties for the list box columns:

ColumnCount	Number of columns in the combo box
ColumnWidths	Width of each column
BoundColumn	Column containing the key field (TransID)

Notice that the ColumnWidth **for the last column (**TransID**) in each** Case **statement is set to 0. Setting the** ColumnWidth **to 0 makes the column hidden in the list box. The last column in each** Case **statement is also the** BoundColumn**. Even though the column is hidden, you can still access its value through the** BoundColumn **property.**

The last statement in each Case statement sets the RowSource property for the list box. This statement uses a SQL SELECT statement to retrieve the values to display in the list box columns and also specifies the sort order for the list box rows.

See Session 7 to review the information on creating SQL statements.

10 Min. To Go

Finding the selected record

When the user selects a record in the search dialog list box and clicks the OK button, the selected record displays in the data entry form. The code for the OK button uses the BoundColumn property of the search dialog list box to locate the record in the data entry form's record source. There are two different methods that professional programmers use to find the record:

- Place the cursor in the key field of the calling form and use the FindRecord method.
- Use the RecordsetClone method and Bookmark property to find the record.

The FindRecord method can be used only if the form's RecordSource uses a single-field key and the form includes a control bound to the key field. You can always add a hidden field or use a concatenated key, but generally, you want to use this method only on single-field keys.

Searching on an indexed field provides superior performance to searching on a nonindexed field. Nonindexed field searches require Access to use a slow sequential search from the first to last record in the table.

Figure 21-6 shows the `OK_Click` event procedure for the `yCheck` Search dialog box. The code first checks to make sure a list box item was selected. The value of the list box is null if no record was selected. Only four statements are needed to find the record. First, the calling form is selected using the `SelectObject` command. Next, the cursor is placed on the key field (TransID) using the `SetFocus` method. The `FindRecord` command is then used to position the record pointer to the correct record, and last, the search dialog box is closed.

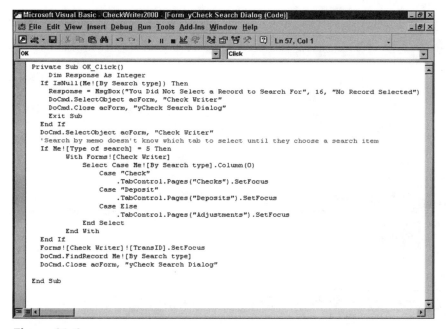

Figure 21-6
Using the FindRecord method to locate a record

The `Bookmark` method shown in Listing 21-1 is quicker and more versatile. The `RecordsetClone` method makes a copy of the recordset used in the Check Writer form. The `FindFirst` method searches the cloned recordset for the first record that meets the specified criteria. An object's bookmark property contains a value that uniquely identifies each record for the object. If a match is found, then the form's record pointer jumps to the bookmark that matches the cloned recordset's bookmark value.

Listing 21-1
Using the Bookmark method to locate a record

```
Public Sub OK_Click()
    Dim SearchCrit As String, GetData As DAO.RecordSet
    SearchCrit = "TransID = " & Me![By Search type]
    Set GetData = Forms![Check Writer].RecordsetClone
    'Perform the search
    GetData.FindFirst SearchCrit
    If Not GetData.NoMatch Then
        'Synchronize the form's recordpointer to the current
        'recordset item
        Forms![Check Writer].Bookmark = GetData.Bookmark
    End If
    GetData.Close
    'Return to calling form
    DoCmd.SelectObject acForm, "Check Writer"
    DoCmd.Close acForm, "yCheck Search Dialog"

End Sub
```

The `GetData` **recordset in the** `OK_Click` **event is declared as a DAO recordset. The** `FindFirst` **method is not available in ADO.**

Opening the Search Dialog Box From the Form

You can add a command button to the data entry form to open the dialog box you want to use for the search. Figure 21-7 shows the Find command button for the Check Writer form.

The Find command button in the Check Writer form uses an event procedure for its `OnClick` event to open the search dialog box. The code for the `Find_OnClick` event to open the yCheck Search dialog box is very simple:

```
DoCmd.OpenForm "yCheck Search Dialog", acNormal, , , acEdit
```

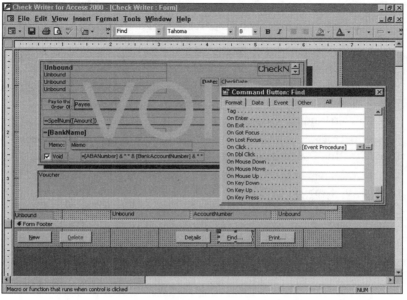

Figure 21-7
Using a button to open the search dialog box

REVIEW

Search dialog boxes provide your users with a flexible tool for searching for a record. Each form in your application can have its own search dialog box, each with its own set of search criteria. This session covered the following topics:

- Dialog boxes provide an intuitive way for the user to move from one area of the application to another.
- Dialog boxes usually have no data source.
- Modal dialog boxes force the user to make a selection before moving to another form.
- Setting the RowSource property for a list box changes the items that display in the list box.
- You can use either the FindRecord or the Bookmark methods to synchronize the selected record in the search dialog box with the data entry form.
- You use a command button on the data entry form to open its search dialog box.

QUIZ YOURSELF

1. Which property makes a dialog box display on top of any other form? (See "Understanding Dialog Boxes.")

2. Which property rquiresthe user to either make a selection from the dialog box or close it before he or she can move to any other form? (See "Understanding Dialog Boxes.")

3. Name the three most common types of controls used in dialog boxes. (See "Creating Dialog Boxes.")

4. Which statement is mandatory when writing event procedures that change the RowSource property for a list box or combo box? (See "Changing the list box items.")

5. Which property and setting make a list box column invisible? (See "Changing the list box items.")

6. What does the Recordsetclone method do? (See "Finding the selected record.")

Session Checklist

✔ Dialog Box Design

✔ Creating a search dialog box

✔ Designing a print dialog box

✔ Programming reports

**30 Min.
To Go**

While data entry and display forms are critical to handling data in any application, dialog boxes are just as important to handle selecting options (menu navigation), searching, printing, and other nondata-type information. Data entry forms and dialog boxes are both forms, and they share many common features and controls. Properly designed, dialog boxes can make a system more usable and make their users more productive.

Basic Dialog Box Design

While dialog boxes use forms as a starting point, none of them generally use bound forms. This means that there is no bound data source such as a table or query behind a dialog box. A dialog box is displayed with no predetermined selections, or possibly some default selections ready for users to select their options so that the program can then proceed. Some dialog boxes (we call them Smart Dialogs) may save the last set of options chosen and maintain a table for these options. You can do this programatically on the OnOpen event of the form, or you can do it through a bound selection. It simply depends on your data model.

Generally, dialog boxes have some specific properties that differ from data entry forms. These may include the following:

Auto Resize	Yes (True) — Dialog box resizes to size of controls it contains
Auto Center	Yes (True) — Dialog box is displayed in the center of the screen
Pop Up	Yes (True) — Dialog box pops up on top of all other windows
Modal	Yes (True) — User cannot select another window until dialog box is closed
Border Style	Dialog — A nonresizable thick border
Control Box	Yes (True) — Displays the Control Menu box in the upper left corner
Min Max Buttons	None — Hides the Minimize and Maximize buttons
Close Button	Yes (True) — Displays the Close button (Control Box must be Yes)

The Pop Up setting is great to force the dialog box in front of any other displayed window, but if you then display another window while the dialog box is open such as a Print Preview window, the Print Preview window is forced behind the dialog box and effectively hidden. Of course in that case, you might actually hide the dialog box before displaying the Print Preview window.

The modal property is becoming less and less used. *Modal* means that the focus is set to the form and the user cannot click on other forms until the modal form is closed. Windows and event-driven programming allow users to decide what they want to do and when they want to do it. Unless you absolutely need to guide users down a specific navigation path and keep them in the dialog box until they perform a task in the dialog box or close it, you should avoid the modal setting.

Dialog boxes in the past have always used a thick, nonsizable border to indicate that they were modal dialog boxes. However, with today's choices of screen resolution and a definite move to give user more freedom of their environment, dialog boxes are showing up with a resizable thin border rather than the dialog border style.

The Auto Center property works in conjunction with the Pop Up property to force the dialog box to appear in the center of the screen. While an autocentered dialog box can always be moved, it will reopen in a centered position. The only reason to use the Auto Center property is when vastly different resolutions may be encountered and a dialog box (which is often smaller than a data entry form) may be moved to a corner of a larger screen resolution. When the application is opened in a lower resolution, the dialog box could appear partially off the screen and in some cases, be inaccessible.

Creating and Using Search Dialog Boxes

A search dialog box allows the user to quickly select a method to view data, select a desired record, and display the record on any underlying data entry form. While Microsoft Access contains several built-in ways to search for data, each requires that users understand the complexities of using them. While you may think that users can easily place their cursor on a field and press the binocular toolbar button, it simply is not intuitive. Expecting an operator to use the Query by Form view is even less likely if they have little or no experience with Microsoft Access but just want to run an Access-based application. Since many Access-based applications hide some or all of the Microsoft Access interface, a programmed search dialog is essential. The simple search dialog shown in Figure 22-1 illustrates use of several simple controls:

- Option Group and Option Buttons
- Drop Down Combo Box to Display Records in the original Data Entry Form
- Optional Buttons to Search or Cancel

When you click on the Find button on the Check Writer form, a dialog opens. The Type of Search is defaulted to Checks By Check Number. The list box below is filled with the preprogrammed data fields in the desired order. This example has five options or types of searches to choose from. You can create as many different options as you want. You are only limited by physical space. You can always switch the option group to a combo box if you need unlimited options. If you only have a few options, the option buttons are the most visual and easiest to select for the user.

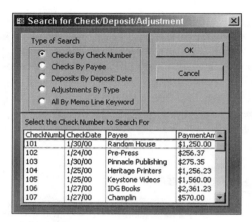

Figure 22-1
Sample of the Search Dialog in the Check Writer program. Note the use of the Option Groups, Buttons, and Combo Boxes.

Once the user double clicks the desired record, the code in the On Click event of the OK button is run. The code does some verification to make sure a record was selected or that the user is not on a new record. It then selects the Check Writer form. It then, based on the type of search, moves to the appropriate tab page. This is done using a Select Case statement. Finally, the focus is moved to the Trans ID field on the Check Writer form which is the key field of the underlying table. The FindRecord method is used to move to the specified record.

You'll notice that the code in the On Double Click **event of the list box actually calls the code in the** On Click **event of the OK button. This is a nice technique to use that reduces the amount of time required to code. The same effect is desired whether the user clicks on the record and clicks OK or double clicks the record.**

Displaying the Search Dialog box form

From the main form you can add a button or some other method of opening the dialog box you want to use in your searches. In Figure 22-1, there was a "Find..." button on the Check Writer form. The code to open the yCheck Search Dialog form is very simple. The code below is found in the OnClick event of the Find button on the main Check Writer form.

```
DoCmd.OpenForm "yCheck Search Dialog", A_NORMAL, , , A_EDIT
```

Building a Search dialog box

Each time a different option is selected, the properties of the list box in the dialog box are changed. This is known as changing a property at runtime and is a common programming technique. While this example will show you specifcally how to change the properties of a list or combo box, these techniques can be used to change other objects such as tabs, subform links, or even text box captions or values.

Designing and working with list boxes and combo boxes is detailed in Session 13.

The first step is to create a form and use the desired dialog box options. As you can see in Figure 22-2, the dialog box contains an option group and list box. If you open the form in design view, you will notice that the list box control is unbound as the data selected is not bound to any table field. Initially, you will see that the properties that fill the combo box with data are null. Until a Type of Search is chosen or a default type retrieved or set, there is no reason to waste time or resources filling the combo box. All of the properties of the combo box are set in the After Update event of the Type of Search option group.

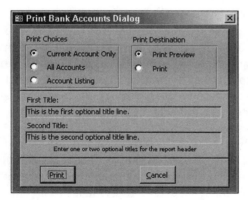

Figure 22-2
The form yBank Print Dialog illustrates the basic controls needed for a Print Dialog.

Setting list box properties

The AfterUpdate event of the option group sets the settings for all of the controls on the dialog form. Refer to Session 13 for a full discussion on how this code works. Based on the chosen option, the After Update event will set the rowsource of the list box to display the appropriate records.

The line of code: [By Search Type].RowSource = "" sets the RowSource property of the list box to null. This is mandatory because if the row source is set to a valid data source, the data source is requeried each time other properties are set such as the ColumnCount, ColumnWidths, or BoundColumn. If your list box row source returns 100,000 records, you could wait a long time as the list box must retrieve the data four times – once when the row source is set and each time one of the three properties are set.

The other lines of code set the various properties for each selection including the text caption and:

**20 Min.
To Go**

ColumnCount	Number of columns in the Combo Box
ColumnWidths	Width of each eolumn (if 0, then column is hidden)
BoundColumn	Column containing the key field (Trans ID)

Finding and displaying the selected record

Once the dialog box is displayed and the user selects a record in the list box, you can take the value of the list box and use it to find the record in the original calling form. There are two approaches to finding the record. One way this can be done is by placing the cursor in the key field of the calling form and using the FindRecord method to navigate to the record. The second method uses a recordset clone of the calling form and searches for the record using ADO code and finding the Bookmark of the record.

The FindRecord method can only be used if the form or underlying data source uses a single field key and a control that is bound to the key field appears on the form. You can always add a hidden field or use a concatenated key but generally you only want to use this method on single field keys. It also helps to use an indexed field, as a non-indexed field would create a slow sequential search from the first to last record. Listing 22-1 shows the use of the FindRecord method in the On Click event of the Bank Search dialog box's OK button.

Listing 22-1

Using the FindRecord method: the On Click event of the OK button on the yBank Search Dialog form

```
Private Sub OK_Click()
 On Error GoTo ResetBank
  Dim Response As Integer

  If IsNull(Me![By Search type]) Then
    Response = MsgBox("You Did Not Select a Record to Search For",
    16, "No Record Selected")
    DoCmd.SelectObject acForm, "Bank Accounts"
    DoCmd.Close acForm, "yBank Search Dialog"
    Exit Sub
  End If
  If IsNull(Forms![Bank Accounts]![BankAccountNumber]) Then
    Response = MsgBox("You Cannot Search from a New Record", 16,
    "New Record Search Disallowed")
    DoCmd.SelectObject acForm, "Bank Accounts"
    DoCmd.Close acForm, "yBank Search Dialog"
    Exit Sub
  End If
  If Trim$(Me![By Search type]) = Trim$(Forms![Bank
  Accounts]![BankAccountNumber]) Then
    DoCmd.SelectObject acForm, "Bank Accounts"
    DoCmd.Close acForm, "yBank Search Dialog"
    Exit Sub
  End If
  DoCmd.SelectObject acForm, "Bank Accounts"
  DoCmd.GoToControl Forms![Bank Accounts]![BankAccountNumber].Name
  DoCmd.FindRecord Me![By Search type]
  DoCmd.GoToControl Forms![Bank Accounts]![Type].Name
  SendKeys "{ESC}"
  DoCmd.Close acForm, "yBank Search Dialog"
ResetBank:
  MsgBox ("Error Occured" & Error(Err))
  Exit Sub

End Sub
```

Part V—Sunday Morning
Session 22

As you can see in the code, it first checks to make sure a record has been selected. The value of the list box is null if no record has been selected. Only four statements are needed to find the record. First the calling form is selected using the SelectObject command. Next the cursor is placed on the key field (TransID) using the SetFocus method. The FindRecord command is then used to position the record pointer to the correct record and then the search dialog is closed.

The Bookmark method shown in Listing 22-2 is quicker and more versatile. A variable named GetData is created to contain the form's RecordsetClone. A string variable named Criteria is used to store the search string [TransID] = "somevalue" where somevalue is the value of the selected items TransID field from the list box. The FindFirst method is used to position the Bookmark to the right record and then the form is synchronized with the bookmark moving the form to the selected record. The Check Writer form is then selected and the search dialog closed.

Listing 22-2

Using the Bookmark method: the On Click event of the OK button on the yCheck Search Dialog form

---

```
Private Sub OK_Click()
    Dim Response          As Integer
    Dim rst               As New ADODB.RecordSet
    Dim checkbookmark     As Variant


    If IsNull(Me![By Search type]) Then
        Response = MsgBox("You Did Not Select a Record to Search
        For", 16, "No Record Selected")
        DoCmd.SelectObject acForm, "Check Writer"
        DoCmd.Close acForm, "yCheck Search Dialog"
        Exit Sub
    End If
    If IsNull(Forms![Check Writer]![TransID]) Then
        Response = MsgBox("You Cannot Search from a New Record", 16,
        "New Record Search Disallowed")
        DoCmd.SelectObject acForm, "Check Writer"
        DoCmd.Close acForm, "yCheck Search Dialog"
        Exit Sub
    End If
```

```
        If Trim$(Me![By Search type]) = Trim$(Forms![Check
    Writer]![TransID]) Then
          DoCmd.SelectObject acForm, "Check Writer"
          DoCmd.Close acForm, "yCheck Search Dialog"
          Exit Sub
        End If
        DoCmd.SelectObject acForm, "Check Writer"
        'Search by memo don't know which tab to select until they
        choose a search item
        If Me![Type of search] = 5 Then
              With Forms![Check Writer]
                  Select Case Me![By Search type].Column(0)
                      Case "Check"
                          .TabControl.Pages("Checks").SetFocus
                      Case "Deposit"
                          .TabControl.Pages("Deposits").SetFocus
                      Case Else
                          .TabControl.Pages("Adjustments").SetFocus
                  End Select
              End With
        End If

    'set recordsetclone
        With rst
            DoCmd.SelectObject acForm, "Check Writer"

            Dim frmname As Form

            frmname = Forms![Check Writer].Form
            rst.Open Forms(frmname).RecordsetClone

            rst.Find "[TransID] = " & Me.By_Search_Type, ,
            adSearchForward

            checkbookmark = rst.Bookmark

            rst.Close
```

Continued

Listing 22-2　　　　　　　　　　　　　　　　　　　　　　　　*Continued*

```
     Set rst = Nothing
   End With

   Forms![Check Writer].Bookmark = checkbookmark
   DoCmd.Close acForm, "yCheck Search Dialog"

End Sub
```

Creating and Using Print Dialog Boxes

Print dialogs let you control what and how a user prints reports in their system. While Microsoft Access provides a print button for data sheets, forms, and reports and a very good report writer, the average user spends too much time manipulating report record sources to print the desired data.

When you create a report using Microsoft Access, you are only creating a template for data to flow through. While the report object produces all of the great formatting and calculations that make a report a report, the data that is passed to the report is critical to accurate reporting.

Each report has a single Record Source. This record source can be a table, query, or a SQL statement. By using a query, you can work with an optimized SQL statement. More importantly, you can enable communication between the query, your report, and an intuitive dialog box. This way, you simply run the report and let the dialog box and query work together to pass the desired data to the report. A simple report dialog box form was illustrated in Figure 22-2, and a more complex one is shown in Figure 22-3.

As you can see in the dialog box form, there are just a few controls. Two option groups are available. One to choose the type of check stock to print to and the second to control which records are printed. The two text boxes allow the user to enter optional titles to be printed in the report if entered. Finally, the From Date and To Date fields are used by the query to limit the selection to records where the Last Purchase Date field is between the From Date and To Date entered.

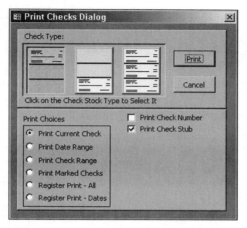

Figure 22-3
The form "yCheck Print Dialog" is a more sophisticated print dialog form

Displaying the Print dialog box form

From the main form you can add a button or some other method of opening the dialog box you want to use in your printing. In the figure shown previously, there was a "Print..." button on the Supplier form. The code to open the yBank Print Dialog form is very simple. The code below is found in the `OnClick` event of the Print button on the main Suppliers form.

```
DoCmd.OpenForm " yCheck Print Dialog", A_NORMAL, , , A_EDIT
```

Building a Print dialog box

The Print Dialog example used is fairly simple. The technique to learn here is the communication between the dialog box form, the report, and how the data is filtered for the report.

The first step is to create a form and use the desired dialog box options. As you can see in Figure 22-2, there are two option groups and option buttons, several unbound text boxes, two command buttons, and associated label controls. This is the "yBank Accounts Print Dialog" form.

The option buttons are used strictly to store the selections for the records to be printed (current or all) and the print destination. The Print button contains the logic to use these values. The values in the First Title and Second Title fields are used by the Report itself while the From Date and To Date values are used to communicate with the query which in turn affects the report's record source.

Interfacing queries with Print dialog forms

The "yBank Print Dialog" is a very simple example of a print dialog form. A more complex example is the "yCheck Print Dialog" in Figure 22-3. In this print dialog, depending on the choices the user makes, different records are printed in the report. The code shown below uses the `OpenReport` method and passes a SQL `WHERE` statement as one of the arguments to limit the data selection. For example, there is code to filter for those records whose value in the CheckDate field is between the FromDate and ToDate entered in the yCheck Print Dialog form. The following line of code is taken from the `On Click` event of the OK button.

```
DoCmd.OpenReport RptName, acNormal, , "[AccountNumber]=Forms![Check Writer] _
    ![BankAccount] And [TransType]='" & TxnSel & "' AND [CheckDate] >= _
    Forms![yCheck Print Dialog]![From Date] And [CheckDate] <= _
    Forms![yCheck Print Dialog]![To Date]"
```

This way when the report is run and the criteria argument used, the report will look at the values entered in the print dialog form and use it to select records. Many applications require the user to open the query and enter the values they want to use in the query. Other applications use parameter queries which pop up when the query is run. Neither are acceptable in professional applications. You want to allow the user to control their application from a user interface not the programming environment. This gives the user a sense of control and flexibility.

An alternative approach to this is to open the report and then set the `RecordSource` of the report. You can do this by setting the `recordsource` for report after you run the `OpenReport`. For example, if you want to run the Bank Account report and have it list just checking transactions, you can have the following line of code. This would go after an `OpenReport` method. The code sets the recordsource with a SQL string.

```
Reports![Bank Accounts].RecordSource = "SELECT * FROM [Bank Accounts] WHERE_
[Type] = 'Checking'"
```

The above line of code uses a SQL string as the recordsource and sets the report to print only records that are Checking accounts types.

You could also substitute the name of a table or query.

```
Reports![Bank Accounts].RecordSource = Bank Accounts
```

Although it is more convenient to use the Criteria argument of the OpenReport method, there are reasons to set the report's recordset programmatically. You may need to print a complex report. One which does a lot of calculations or involves multiple complex queries such as a Union Query. It is much easier to create the query and then set it to reference the controls on the print dialog than to programmatically build the SQL string to use as the criteria argument. In this case it is easier to use a query and set it programmatically.

Printing reports from the dialog box

The report is printed after the code first hides the modal print dialog. This way if the report is printed as a Print Preview, it will not appear behind the modal dialog. The value of the Type of Output option group is checked. The ReportDest variable is set to acPreview if the Print Preview choice is selected or acNormal is the Print choice is selected.

Finally, the OpenReport method is used to print the report. If we look at the form "yBank Print Dialog", a variable, ReportDest, is used to select the second parameter print destination while a filter is also passed to the report if the current record is being printed using the value of the current Bank Account field. In the form, "yCheck Print Dialog" the OpenReport does not use a variable for the print type because all of the printing will be sent directly to the printer.

> **Remember, that the report filter created here and the criteria in the query are not mutually exclusive. If you select the current record only and the Last Purchase Date does not fit within the date parameters from the print dialog you will see no records in the report.**

Interfacing reports with Print dialog forms

Print dialog forms and reports can "communicate" further with each other in many ways. By referencing controls on the dialog form, the report can display information that the user either enters in or is set programmatically.

For example, in the "yBank Print Dialog" there are two text boxes that lets the user enter in two optional report titles. The report in Figure 22-4 uses the FirstTitle and SecondTitle fields in the "yBank Print Dialog" form when printing the report. The titles are simply calculated text boxes that refer to the values in the dialog form and are displayed. If you look at the control source of the two controls on the report, you will see that they are set to reference the controls on the print dialog. The two controls on the report have the following lines for the controlsource.

```
=[Forms]![yBank Print Dialog]![First Title]
=[Forms]![yBank Print Dialog]![Second Title]
```

A simple but very effective technique.

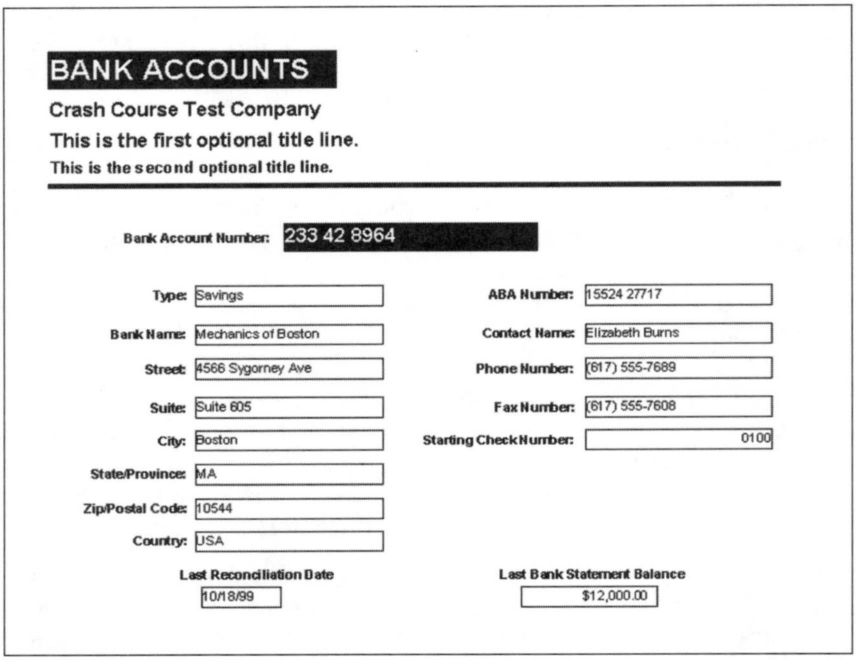

BANK ACCOUNTS

Crash Course Test Company
This is the first optional title line.
This is the second optional title line.

Bank Account Number: 233 42 8964

Type: Savings	ABA Number: 15524 27717	
Bank Name: Mechanics of Boston	Contact Name: Elizabeth Burns	
Street: 4566 Sygorney Ave	Phone Number: (617) 555-7689	
Suite: Suite 605	Fax Number: (617) 555-7608	
City: Boston	Starting Check Number: 0100	
State/Province: MA		
Zip/Postal Code: 10544		
Country: USA		

Last Reconciliation Date
10/18/99

Last Bank Statement Balance
$12,000.00

Figure 22-4
The report "Bank Account" shows the two additional title fields. These refer to the two text box controls on the print dialog form.

While this example is simplistic, there is no limit to this technique. You can reference form values in reports, queries, and modules and even other forms. You can prompt the user for information as well as setting visible or invisible controls with information that you pull in from a setup table. Set controls on the open form and then reference them from the report. Just remember that to reference the controls the form that they are on must remain opened. Therefore you may at times want to set the form to Visible = False which would leave the form open but hidden from the user. Then you can still reference the controls from the report. This technique is quick and easy to design. Most of all, it lets you reference information more easily.

Programming Reports

Up to this point, you have been introduced to a few techniques used to affect a report programmatically. You have seen ways to change the records that the report will display. You have also seen an example of how to place information on the report itself from the form. Access has a tremendously powerful reporting module. You have created reports up to this point. However, you may not have used the events available in reports to program them. There are several features and properties of a report that can be program and will enhance your reporting capabilities.

Report sections

In order to understand programming a report is very important to understand report section and how they interact with the report and with each other. Any report has the following sections, Report Header and Footer, Page Header and Footer, and the Detail section. Access allows you to create sections in addition to the standard sections mention previously and you can set these sections in the Grouping and Sorting property sheet.

- The Report Header and Footer section prints at the beginning and the end of the report repsecively. The Report Header goes before the Page Header section. You can use this to print a logo or company information or use it as a cover page for the report. The Report Footer is the last section of the report. It however prints before the Page Footer on the last page of the report. Use this section to display the report totals.

- The Page Header section appears at the top of each page. It appears after the Report Header on the first page and is present on each page that follows. This section is ideal for displaying column headings or other information you wish to appear at the top of each page such as page numbers.. The Page Footer section appears at the bottom of each page. You can setup calculated fields to display page totals in this section or page numbers.

- The Detail section is where the main body of information is displayed for the report. This section is on every page and is repeated for each record. This is where your information would be displayed, repeating each record.

Depending on how you setup additional sections, they will go before or after the Detail section and will display and group records that you set to show in that section.

**10 Min.
To Go**

Section events

Each section has innate events that you can use to run code on. The following list details the events available to you for each section of any given report.

On Format   The On Format event allows you to set a macro or event procedure to the section. Access will execute the section when it formats the particular section.

On Print   Assign a macro or event procedure to a section's On Print event. The macro or code is run when Access starts printing the section or displaying it in Preview.

On Retreat   A macro or event procedure that is run when after Access processes the On Format and before the On Print. This event is only executed in an instance when Access must backup or move back to the previous page when a particular section will not fit on the page. This event is important if you are using the option of Keep Together. The code is processed during the backing up. Then the On Format is run again.

Report events

Every report created in Access has the following events available that can contain code. These events can make running reports seamless and can help to fully integrate into your application.

On Open   A macro or VBA code that Access runs when the report is run either in Print or Print Preview. This precedes all other events. Put code in here to close or hide open forms or other open reports. In addition if you want to programmatically set controls on a report you can do so here.

On Close   Macro or code that is run when the report is closed. This is also activated when you close out of a Print Preview. Enter code here that will make hidden forms or reports visible or update records. For instance, you can have code that marks a particular record as having been printed. The code would go in this section so it can be fired off when the user closes the report.

On Activate   This event occurs when the report receives the focus during a Print Preview. You can write code that displays a custom menu for the user during preview.

`On Deactivate`	This event is fired when the preview report loses the focus. You can turn off any custom menus or toolbars that were available during the preview.
`On No Data`	This event is activated when the report's recordsource contains no data. Most likely you would have code in here that displays a message indicating no data was available and closes the report.
`On Page`	A macro or event procedure that is executed after the On Format event has been executed for a section but prior to the printing of that section.
`On Error`	Use this event to enter a macro or VBA code to display proper error messages in response to any errors encountered in running the report.

Learning to program a report will increase the effectiveness of a report as well as expanding the reports. To view examples of how a report can be manipulated programmatically, look at the Check Register report.

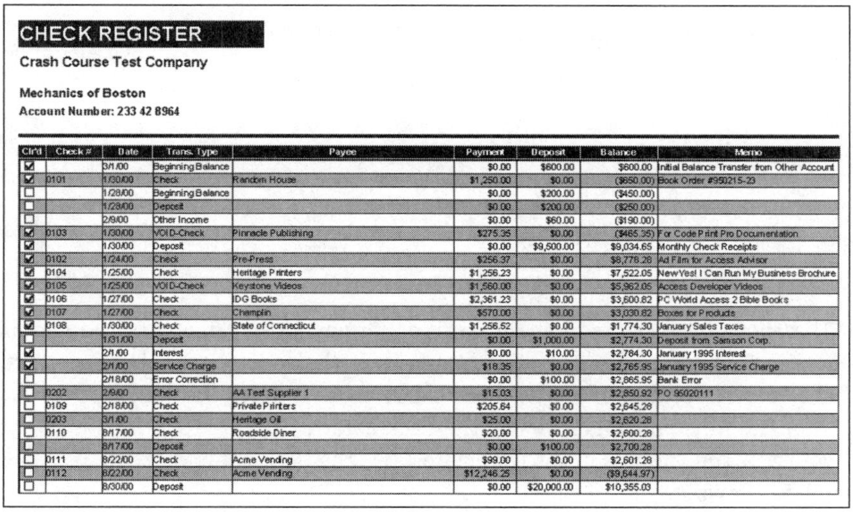

CHECK REGISTER

Crash Course Test Company

Mechanics of Boston

Account Number: 233 42 8964

Clr'd	Check #	Date	Trans. Type	Payee	Payment	Deposit	Balance	Memo
☑		3/1/00	Beginning Balance		$0.00	$600.00	$600.00	Initial Balance Transfer from Other Account
☑	0101	1/30/00	Check	Random House	$1,250.00	$0.00	($650.00)	Book Order #950215-23
☐		1/28/00	Beginning Balance		$0.00	$200.00	($450.00)	
☐		1/28/00	Deposit		$0.00	$200.00	($250.00)	
☐		2/9/00	Other Income		$0.00	$60.00	($190.00)	
☑	0103	1/30/00	VOID-Check	Pinnacle Publishing	$275.35	$0.00	($465.35)	For Code Print Pro Documentation
☑		1/30/00	Deposit		$0.00	$9,500.00	$9,034.65	Monthly Check Receipts
☑	0102	1/24/00	Check	Pre-Press	$256.37	$0.00	$8,778.28	Ad Film for Access Advisor
☑	0104	1/25/00	Check	Heritage Printers	$1,256.23	$0.00	$7,522.05	NewYes! I Can Run My Business Brochure
☑	0105	1/25/00	VOID-Check	Keystone Videos	$1,560.00	$0.00	$5,962.05	Access Developer Videos
☑	0106	1/27/00	Check	IDG Books	$2,361.23	$0.00	$3,600.82	PC World Access 2 Bible Books
☑	0107	1/27/00	Check	Champlin	$570.00	$0.00	$3,030.82	Boxes for Products
☑	0108	1/30/00	Check	State of Connecticut	$1,256.52	$0.00	$1,774.30	January Sales Taxes
☐		1/31/00	Deposit		$0.00	$1,000.00	$2,774.30	Deposit from Samson Corp.
☑		2/1/00	Interest		$0.00	$10.00	$2,784.30	January 1995 Interest
☑		2/1/00	Service Charge		$18.35	$0.00	$2,765.95	January 1995 Service Charge
☐		2/18/00	Error Correction		$0.00	$100.00	$2,865.95	Bank Error
☐	0202	2/9/00	Check	AA Test Supplier 1	$15.03	$0.00	$2,850.92	PO 95020111
☐	0109	2/18/00	Check	Private Printers	$205.64	$0.00	$2,645.28	
☐	0203	3/1/00	Check	Heritage Oil	$25.00	$0.00	$2,620.28	
☐	0110	8/17/00	Check	Roadside Diner	$20.00	$0.00	$2,600.28	
☐		8/17/00	Deposit		$0.00	$100.00	$2,700.28	
☐	0111	8/22/00	Check	Acme Vending	$99.00	$0.00	$2,601.28	
☐	0112	8/22/00	Check	Acme Vending	$12,246.25	$0.00	($9,644.97)	
☐		8/30/00	Deposit		$0.00	$20,000.00	$10,355.03	

Figure 22-5

The report "Check Register" illustrates how programming the report can accomplish some very sophisticated visual effects.

The Check Register makes use of several events in the report. When you run the report, you will see that the lines are printed with alternating background colors to make it easier to see. This is done by setting the background color of the text boxes on the report (to do the check box a box was drawn behind the check box itself). The first line of code that is necessary to do this is in the On Format event of the Page Header. This one line of code sets a hidden field, "backgroundsetting". This field is used to hold whether or not the background should be white (0) or grey (-1).

Rather than using a field to hold the value, a global variable for the report could have been declared. However, in this example a text box was used so that you can turn on the Visible **setting and see how its value changes from −1 to 0 during the format and printing.**

The code which then handles turning the background from white to grey is done in the event of the Detail section. This code was placed in this section since it was the detail information that will be affected. The following code appears in the event.

```
Dim x As Integer   'used to count through the columns

If Me.backgroundsetting = 0 Then
    For x = 1 To 9 Step 1
        Me("column" & x).BackColor = 16777215
    Next x
Else
    For x = 1 To 9 Step 1
        Me("column" & x).BackColor = 12632256
    Next x
End If

Me.backgroundsetting = Abs(Me.backgroundsetting) + (-1)
```

The above code works in the following manner. It first dimensions a variable that will be used for the For Next loops. Then the code checks the current status of the "backgroundsetting" text box. If the value is zero, then it loops through each of the nine controls and sets the back color to 16777215, which is the value of white. If the value is other than zero (-1), the back color is set to 12632256, which is the value of light grey.

The final line of code does a very neat trick. Since the values can only be true (-1) or false (0), the code takes the absolute value of the current value and adds a negative one to it. You may have to recall some elementary math but doing this saves you from having to set the value twice, once for the negative instance and another for the positive.

The code declares a variable x that will be used to count through the columns. If you look at the properties for each of the text boxes, you will see that the names are set to "column1", "column2", "column3", etc. The reason for this is to save some programming time. Rather than writing several lines of code to set the values of each control, we can do a loop instead. This is an excellent technique to use when you have many controls that you want to affect programmatically.

You are not limited to just making superficial types of changes to a report pro-grammatically. You can do calculations and process data via code rather than doing it at the query or report level. For instance to calculate the running balance as each transaction is displayed, the original report uses a Dsum function shown below.

```
=DSum("0+[DepositAmount]-[PaymentAmount]","CheckWriter","[TransID] <= _
    [Reports]![Check Register]![Trans ID] and _
    [Forms]![Check Writer]![BankAccount]=[AccountNumber] and Void <> Yes")
```

Alternatively, you can set a variable via code and in the On Format event of the Detail section keep adding to that variable. If you review the report, "Check Register 2" you will see how this is done. A public variable is declared. Then in the On Format event of the Report Header, the value for the variable, runningbalance is set to zero. The code is placed here since we want this value to run across multi-ple pages. If you had set it in the On Format event of the Page Header, it would get reset whenever a new page is started. Review the code in the On Format event of the Detail section. You will see the following line of code at the end of the listing.

```
runningbalance = runningbalance + Nz([DepositAmount]) - Nz([PaymentAmount])
```

Of course this is a simplistic example. You could also do it without any program-ming at all by using the Running Sum property. The emphasis in this session is that you are not limited to using queries to calculate and manipulate your data. In many cases, to create fast printing reports, you may want to do calculations via code if they prove to be faster.

The above examples have focused on the On Format event of the report method. What about the On Print? When is it appropriate to use code in this event? Well, if you wanted to track if a report had ever been printed, you can write code to track such an event. Open up a recordset, move to the record that you are currently print-ing and set the field for "printed" to True. This can be seen in the report, "Check Print – Bottom". The code in the On Print event of the Detail section opens up a recordset and finds the transaction by searching for the ID. Once it finds the record it then marks it as Printed.

Done!

REVIEW

This session has exposed you to four main topics:

- basic dialog design
- search dialogs
- print dialogs
- programming reports

Having explored these topics, you should be able to design effective dialog boxes. More importantly you can create powerful search dialog boxes that gives your users searching capabilities. In addition, you can design and program print dialog boxes that can either limit or expand the options available to your end user.

Many of the techniques you have learned in previous sessions coupled with the basic understanding of which report events are available should allow you to program more effective reports. The goal in discussing programming reports was primarily to illustrate that you can do two things in regards to programming reports; affect the display and manipulate the data. Using code to change how a report looks can expand the report's features by giving you more dynamic reports. You can hide and display controls according to settings or a particular field's contents. In addition, you can also do calculations or pull in data from a source other than the report's recordsource. This gives your report tremendous power because it frees you from displaying only the data in from the recordsource of the report.

QUIZ YOURSELF

1. What are the basic characteristics of a dialog box? (See "Basic Dialog Box Design.")

2. What is the significance of the properties Modal and Pop ? (See "Basic Dialog Box Design.")

3. What two methods can be used in a Search Dialog to go to the selected record? What are the significance of using either method over the other? (See "Finding and displaying the selected record.")

4. What are some of the basic controls you would want to put on a Print Dialog? (See "Building a Print dialog box.")

5. What command is the easiest to use in running the report from the Print Dialog via VBA code? (See "Printing reports from the dialog box.")

6. What are the main sections of a report? What events are associated with each section? (See "Programming Reports.")

7. If you wanted to put in a message displayed only when an error occurs which event would you use? (See "Programming Reports.")

Packaging Your Application

Session Checklist

✔ Understanding application architecture for a complete application

✔ Structuring your VBA code and dealing with compilation

✔ Using the Program file configuration

✔ Learning considerations for .MDE files

✔ Using runtime

**30 Min.
To Go**

I n this session, you will learn how to prepare your application to deploy to your users. Obviously, there are many considerations, such as the media you will create the installation on, the destination computer's environment, and so on. This session will present the relevant topics from several perspectives.

Application Architecture

Assuming you have created the tables, forms, reports, and so on that make up your application, you probably need to include some additional items that you normally find in other professionally designed software that handle the general program functionality. Preceding sessions have touched on some of these, but let's put them into perspective as a whole.

In addition to the custom and unique functions required for an application, you need to include items from the following categories:

- Startup forms and About boxes (Refer to Session 19.)
- Switchboard or menu systems (Refer to Session 11.)
- Security (Refer to Session 28.)
- Error handling (Refer to Session 16.)
- Help (Refer to Session 20.)
- Support

All the items listed have been discussed at some point except for the support item. The category of functions that should be included can be one or more of the following:

- Technical support
- Preference management
- Archiving
- Backup
- Repair
- Compaction
- System information

The technical support screen

Providing a pop-up form usually called from the About box or the Help pull-down menu can give frustrated users an easier way of contacting the right organization to help them with their problem. List phone numbers, fax numbers, e-mail addresses, and/or Web addresses where users can get technical support.

Preference management

The use of the word *preferences* in the context of this function includes more than just preferences. Information about the application, user, organization, etc. needs to be handled as well. You can hardcode this type of information, but this doesn't make the application flexible, easy to maintain, or user-configurable.

You generally create preferences when building your application. You might not allow users to have any control over system preferences such as the version or copyright, but you would let them select how an application may run. For example, each user may want to search for data differently or have a different default value.

Preferences can be one of three types:

1. System
2. Default
3. User

The System preferences are those that exist only once and are common to all users. Preferences such as the license information, security options, startup options, and so on, fall into this category. Default preferences are preferences that may be different from user to user. If a set of preferences has not been established for a particular user, then the Default preferences are used. User preferences are duplicates of the Default preferences but set to a specific user. You might have a file location that is user-dependent, a form color, a report heading, etc. Just as users can have specific security options, with preferences, they can have specific options to control the way the application works.

Preferences are usually stored in a separate table either locally on a client machine, on a server, or a combination of both. There are generally two different schemes for handling preferences: the single-record method, or the multiple-record method. With the single- record method, you create a field for each preference and have only one record in the table. You might actually use a record for each user if you provide for independent preferences by user.

In the multiple-record method, there is a record for each preference. This method has the advantage of not requiring a table design change when you want to add a preference. The disadvantage is that every preference value is stored as a text value instead of as a specific field type. In most cases, a preference stored as a string value is fine, but if you need to store a preference as numeric, date/time, OLE object, or another type, then the single-record method is better.

In our example application, the Check Writer, there is a preferences table as shown in Figure 23-1. This shows an example of the single-record method. In Figure 23-2, the same preferences are shown in a datasheet view using the multiple-record method.

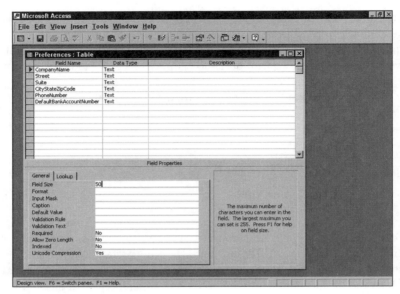

Figure 23-1
The Design view of the single-record preference table

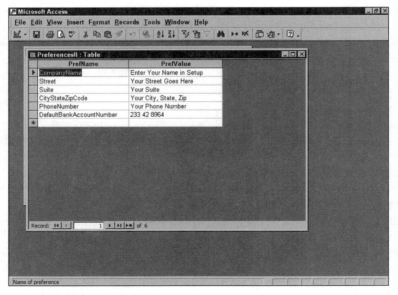

Figure 23-2
The Datasheet view of the multiple-record preference table

You can access the data in these tables directly using your own code or functions just like you would retrieve normal table data. It is a good idea to have a function to set and retrieve preference values. This makes it easy to reference them on forms, reports, and within code. In the sample application, there is a module called `PreferenceFunctions` that contains two functions `GetPref` and `SetPref`, which can be used to retrieve and set preferences from either type of preference table. The code listing for these functions is covered in the section Conditional Compiling later in this session. Conditional compiler constants were used to handle the two different types of tables from the same function code base.

Using the `GetPref` function requires that you simply pass a preference name to the function. The value of the preference will then be returned. The returning value type is a variant because its type may vary. If there is an error or if the preference doesn't exist, a null value is returned. Here is an example of a call to this function:

```
StrCompanyName = GetPref("CompanyName")
```

Using the `SetPref` function is a little more involved. First, if the preference exists, its value will be replaced. If the preference does not exist, then the preference will be added. If there are no errors, a True value will be returned by the function to indicate the successful setting of the preference.

The arguments of the `SetPref` function are the following:

1. The name of the preference (`String`)
2. The value of the preference (`Variant`)
3. The ADO data type, which is used only when creating a new preference (default value is `adWChar`)
4. The size of the field (default value is 255)

Arguments 3 and 4 are used only for the single-record method. Here is an example of a call to this function:

```
BlnSuccess = SetPref("Report Header","The Acme Corporation", adWChar, 100)
```

Archiving

Archiving is the process of moving data records from the active database to a separate database. Usually, the records moved are deleted from the active database. This cuts down on the number of records in the application database. This has significant benefits:

- The size of data tables are reduced, improving performance in loading forms, running queries, running reports, etc.

- The time to load forms and set values to controls is reduced.
- The number of items the user has to choose from in list and combo boxes is reduced, saving time and effort.
- The disk requirements for file storage are reduced.
- The time to do backups and the size of the media is reduced.

Archiving has far-reaching benefits that save time and money and help you maintain a better performing application while safeguarding data that you may need later.

Backup

If you have ever had an Access database that was corrupted beyond repair, you will understand the importance of backing up your database. You can manually make a copy of your program file once, and unless you make changes to it, the copy can be stored safely. However, assuming you properly split your program and data files, the data file is changed every time you use your application. You should include some means of creating a backup.

Repair

The Repair function allows the user to choose an .MDB file and repair it. Occasionally, you may need to repair an Access database. Repairing is necessary because data files can occasionally become fragmented or corrupted. You cannot select to repair the program database you are currently using. You can repair the database as long as it is not used exclusively and no attached tables are in use by bound forms. You cannot repair a database that is in use by other users.

Compaction

The Compact function will compact a selected .MDB file. If you delete tables, your database can become fragmented and use disk space inefficiently. Compacting the database makes a copy of the database, rearranging how the database file is stored on disk. This defragments your database and saves file space. It is important to automate this process somehow or at least give your users a way to compact their databases once in a while. You cannot select to compact the database you are currently using. You also cannot compact a database that is in use by other users.

The System Information screen

You should include a System Information screen to display information that would
be useful to the user and the technical support person trying to solve a problem.
Helpful information to include on a system information screen includes the following: the version of Access running; the initialization file for Access; the name and
location of the current program .MDB file; the location of Access; the location of
any attached data files; the program version; the current user; and the system date
and time.

This should be a purely informational screen that requires no action from the
user except to press OK to close the form. This is usually displayed from an About
box or other utility form to allow the developer to help the user debug any envi-
ronmental problems. A sample System Information screen is shown in Figure 23-3.
This form is included in the sample Check Writer application.

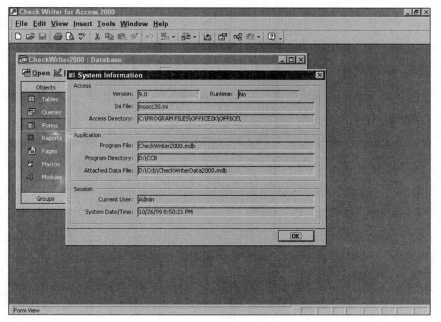

Figure 23-3
The System Information screen

The code for this form is shown in Listing 23-1. Everything happens on the
Form_Load event. The listing is broken down into sections: Access information,

application information, and session information. The Access information is derived by using the SysCmd function. Application information comes from the object CurrentProject and from looking at the MsysObjects table. The MsysObjects table is used to see how many attached tables there are. If there is only one, then the file for the attached tables is displayed. If there is more than one, then a message "Use the Attachment Manager" is displayed. If there is none, then a message saying there are no attached tables is displayed. Session information is pulled from the CurrentUser function and the Now function.

Listing 23-1
The System Information screen form load subroutine

```
Private Sub Form_Load()

  On Error GoTo ErrorHandler

  With Me
    'Access information
    .AccessVer = SysCmd(acSysCmdAccessVer)
    .RunTime = IIf(SysCmd(acSysCmdRuntime), "Yes", "No")
    .IniFile = SysCmd(SYSCMD_INIFILE)
    .AccessDir = SysCmd(SYSCMD_ACCESSDIR)

    'Application information
    .ProgramFile = CurrentProject.Name
    .ProgramDirectory = CurrentProject.Path
    If DCount("Database", "MsysObjects", "Type = 6") > 0 Then
      If DCount("Database", "MsysObjects", "Database <> " & Chr(34) & _
      DLookup("Database", "MsysObjects", "Type = 6") & Chr(34)) = 0 Then
        .AttachedTo = DLookup("Database", "MsysObjects", "Type = 6")
      Else
        .AttachedTo = "Multiple files, use Attachment Manager"
      End If
    Else
      .AttachedTo = "No attached tables"
    End If

    'Session information
    .User = CurrentUser()
    .SystemDateTime = Now()

  End With
  GoTo Done

ErrorHandler:
    MsgBox err.Description
Done:

End Sub
```

Using this type of form, you could display even more information that would be useful for technical support purposes.

EZ Access Developer Suite from Database Creations, Inc., contains powerful and flexible interfaces that handle all the functions previously described, including a Preference Manager, Archive Manager, File Utilities, and System Information Screen. The CD contains a demo of this product.

VBA Code

**20 Min.
To Go**

Your VBA code can be handled in a number of different ways. This includes the methods for compiling as well as how the code is structured. The methods in general affect maintainability and performance.

Compiling

As discussed in previous sessions, your VBA code is stored within a Visual Basic project. For your code to execute, it must be compiled. Microsoft Access stores the code in two states: the source code version and the compiled version. Whenever the source code is changed, the compiled version is deleted. Access will compile the necessary modules when they are used if they are not in a compiled state. This is not the preferred method since it is nice to know if there are compilation errors before you attempt to execute the code. You can compile the project using the Debug ➪ Compile Project pull-down menu selection when in the VBA window.

Compile options

Choosing Options from the Tools menu in the VBA window gives you some control over how Access compiles. Making this selection displays the window, as shown in Figure 23-4. In the lower right corner of the General tab, you will find two options for compilation:

- **Compile On Demand.** Limits what Access will compile when a form is opened. Only those functions that are used will be compiled.

- **Background Compile.** Will compile any uncompiled code when Access's processes are not busy.

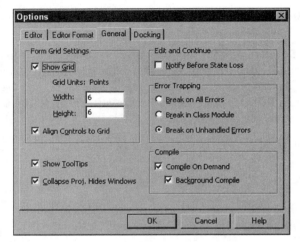

Figure 23-4
Compiler options

It is always best to compile an application completely before delivering it to a user.

The IsCompiled property

You can check the status of the compiled state of a project by looking at the IsCompiled property of the Application object. This property returns a Boolean value indicating whether the project is in a compiled state. It is True (-1) if the project is in a compiled state. It is False (0) when the project has never been fully compiled, if a module has been added, edited, or deleted, or if a module hasn't been saved in a compiled state.

Conditional compiling

Sometimes certain code may not apply to a specific environment. For example, you might have an application that will run differently in Access 97 or Access 2000. Or maybe some code is applicable to Windows NT and some other code is applicable to Windows 98. Other reasons include debugging statements and localizing an application for different languages. To have one code base that can run in different environments, Access and VBA provides a concept called *conditional compilation*.

You use conditional compilation to run blocks of code selectively. To do this, you need:

1. A conditional compiler constant identified with #Const
2. An #If... #Then... #Else directive (they can be nested)

As an example of using compiler constants can be found in the module PreferenceFunctions, which is part of the sample Check Writer application. The code for this module is shown in Listing 23-2. As previously discussed, there are two methods of dealing with preferences: the single-record and the multiple-record methods. The module is coded to work with either of these methods, and the selection of the method is handled with compiler constants.

Listing 23-2
The Preference functions

```
'Prior to using these functions you must set the type of preference
' system you will be using and include the appropriate table

#Const PreferenceSystem = 1 '1 = single record. 2 = multiple record
#If PreferenceSystem = 1 Then
  Const PrefTable As String = "Preferences"
#Else
  Const PrefTable As String = "PreferencesII"
#End If

Public Function GetPref(strPrefName As String) As Variant
'Function returns the preference data for the preference name
'  or null if preference cannot be determined
Dim rst As ADODB.Recordset

  On Error GoTo ErrorHandler
  Set rst = New ADODB.Recordset
  rst.ActiveConnection = CurrentProject.Connection
  rst.CursorType = adOpenKeyset

  #If PreferenceSystem = 1 Then
    rst.Open "Select * from " & PrefTable
    If rst.RecordCount = 1 Then
      GetPref = rst(strPrefName)
    Else
      GetPref = Null
    End If
  #End If

  #If PreferenceSystem = 2 Then
```

Continued

Listing 23-2 *Continued*

```
        rst.Open "Select * from " & PrefTable & " Where PrefName = " & Chr(34) &
strPrefName & Chr(34)
    If rst.RecordCount = 1 Then
      GetPref = rst!PrefValue
    Else
      GetPref = Null
    End If
  #End If

  GoTo Done
ErrorHandler:
  GetPref = Null
Done:
End Function

Public Function SetPref(strPrefName As String, varPrefValue As Variant, Optional
strPrefType = "adWChar", Optional lngPrefSize = 255) As Boolean
Dim varX As Variant
'Function sets preference data for the preference name
'  A new preference will be created if it doesn't exist
'  If it exists the previous value will be replaced
'The arguments are as follows:
' strPrefName is the name of the preference
' varPrefData is the value of the preference
' strPrefType is the ADO data type that is used only when creating a new
preference
'    This argument is optional and will default to a string type
'Function returns a True if preference was successfully set or a false if there
was a problem
#If PreferenceSystem = 1 Then
Dim rst As ADODB.Recordset
Dim cat As New ADOX.Catalog
Dim tbl As New ADOX.Table
Dim col As New ADOX.Column

  On Error GoTo ErrorHandler
  Set rst = New ADODB.Recordset
  rst.ActiveConnection = CurrentProject.Connection
  rst.Open PrefTable, , adOpenKeyset, adLockPessimistic, adCmdTable

  'Do check to see if field exists
  On Error Resume Next
  varX = rst(strPrefName)
  rst.Close
  If Err.Number = 3265 Then
  'Field does not exist, create new field
    On Error GoTo ErrorHandler
    cat.ActiveConnection = CurrentProject.Connection
```

```
      col.Name = strPrefName
      col.Type = strPrefType
      col.DefinedSize = lngPrefSize
      cat.Tables(PrefTable).Columns.Append col
      Set cat = Nothing
    End If

    'Change value of Field
    On Error GoTo ErrorHandler
    rst.Open PrefTable, , adOpenKeyset, adLockPessimistic, adCmdTable
    rst(strPrefName) = varPrefValue
    rst.Update

#End If

#If PreferenceSystem = 2 Then
Dim rst As ADODB.Recordset

    On Error GoTo ErrorHandler
    Set rst = New ADODB.Recordset
    rst.ActiveConnection = CurrentProject.Connection
    rst.Open PrefTable, , adOpenKeyset, adLockPessimistic, adCmdTable
    rst.Find ("PrefName = '" & strPrefName & "'")
    If rst.EOF Then
      'add new preference
      rst.AddNew
      rst!PrefName = strPrefName
      rst!PrefValue = varPrefValue
      rst.Update
    Else
      'preference exists
      rst!PrefValue = varPrefValue
      rst.Update
    End If
#End If

  SetPref = True
  GoTo Done
ErrorHandler:
  SetPref = False
Done:
End Function
```

The first section of the code in Listing 23-2 contains the general declarations section. The constant PreferenceSystem is used to determine the Preference method. A value of 1 is used for the single-record method, and a value of 2 is used for the multiple-record method. Note that the value of the constant PrefTable is set to a different table name based on the compiler constant PreferenceSystem. This is done with the #If, #Then, #Else, #Endif directives.

Both the functions GetPref and SetPref contain the #If, #Then, #Else, #Endif directives that determine the method used to handle preferences. When the compiler processes the code, only the code appropriate to the preference method is compiled and used.

Conditional compiler constants are always private to the module in which they appear. It is not possible to create public compiler constants using the #Const directive. To define public compiler constants, use the Project Properties window and enter them in the Conditional Compilation Arguments field on the General tab.

VBA defines constants for use with the #If...Then...#Else directive without defining them with the #Const directive. These constants are global in scope and apply to all modules in a project.

Constant	Description
Vba6	True if VBA version 6.0
Win16	True indicates that the development environment is 16-bit
Win32	True indicates that the development environment is 32-bit
Mac	True indicates that the development environment is Macintosh

Decompiling

Just like you can compile an application, you can also decompile an application. This is not something that is normally done, but it has sometimes been found to correct some peculiar errors with Access. These errors occasionallyoccur when a new library reference is added or the operating system has changed. You can decompile the entire project in one of two ways:

1. Change the name of the project.
2. Use the /decompile command line option when starting Access.

Module structure

Access and VBA provide the ability to have multiple modules within a database or project. Each module can have one or more functions or subroutines as well as globally declared constants and variables. You might first choose to put all your code into one module. The problem with doing that is whenever a single function is needed in that module, the whole module is loaded into memory. This may adversely affect the performance of your application.

On the other hand, if each function is in a separate module, every time a new function is called, Access will be stopping the application to load the new module. The best method is to break your functions and subroutines into logical groups that make sense to load at the same time. If functions are related, put them into the same module. If a function calls another function, put them both into the same module. Another good rule is to keep public declarations and variables in a separate module.

Program File Configuration

10 Min. To Go

You can control the behavior of Access and your application by configuring various options and properties. The following sections describe several of these options and properties.

Startup options

Access provides various startup options that control how an application runs, which you can access by choosing Tools ⇨ Startup. These can be also set using VBA and ADO. These properties are defined by Microsoft Access and aren't automatically recognized by the Jet database engine.

When the property is set for the first time, you must create the property and append it to the `Properties` collection of the object to which it applies. Once the property is in the collection, you can set it in the same manner as any ADO property. When the property is set for the first time in the user interface, it is added to the `Properties` collection and you can set it without appending it. When writing code to set these properties, include error-handling code to verify that the property you are setting already exists in the `Properties` collection.

> **Note**
> **When you create a property, you must correctly define its** Type **before you append it to the** Properties **collection.**

The following list contains some Microsoft Access defined properties that apply to the Application object: `AppTitle`, `AppIcon`, `StartupShowDBWindow`, `StartupShowStatusBar`, `AllowShortcutMenus`, `AllowFullMenus`,

AllowBuiltInToolbars, AllowToolbarChanges, AllowBreakIntoCode, AllowSpecialKeys, Replicable, and ReplicationConflictFunction.

Startup procedures

You have three choices for starting your VBA code to run when a database is opened:

1. Use the command line argument /x *macro*, which runs the specified macro when the application starts. Have this macro call a VBA procedure.
2. Use the macro named AutoExec, which automatically runs when Access starts.
3. Set the Display Form/Page entry on the Startup dialog box available from the Tools menu. The code in the OnLoad or OnOpen event of this form will then be run when the form automatically opens when Access starts.

Compacting

Compaction of a database file will significantly affect performance. You must provide provisions within your application to perform this important function.

What is compacting?

You compact an Access database to remove deleted objects that are still taking file space. When you delete data or objects in an Access database, the file can become fragmented and use disk space inefficiently. Compacting the database makes a copy of the file and rearranges how the file is stored on your disk. This optimizes the performance of the database. If you distribute your application such that data is in a separate file from your application and you have protected your application from being changed, compacting won't be necessary on the application. Before distributing your application, be sure to compact it.

Compaction requires exclusive access by the program doing the compaction. In other words, you cannot have other users using the database file while it is being compacted. This is one of the shortcomings of Access versus a database management system like SQL Server which allows users to use the database while the file is being compacted or backed up.

How to compact programmatically

You can compact a database using VBA and ADO/JRO by using the `CompactDatabase` method. This method copies and compacts a closed database and gives you several options. These options include changing its version, collating order, using encryption, and more. The syntax is

```
JetEngine.CompactDatabase(SourceConnection, DestConnection)
```

where `SourceConnection` is a string value specifying a connection to the source database to be compacted. The `SourceConnection` must be closed. `DestConnection` is a string value specifying a connection to the destination database to be created by the compaction. You will get an error if the `DestConnection` already exists or if another file with that name already exists. It is not possible to do a compaction of the same database, that is, one in which the source database and destination database are the same.

.MDE files

Access provides for a special type of database file that prevents users from viewing the code and design of forms and reports. This is an .MDE file. You might want to consider distributing your application in this format.

What is an .MDE file?

An .MDE file is a copy of an .MDB file, with all source code removed and only compiled code included. It is used for distribution of applications to users who have no need to modify the code. By not having the source code, it is smaller than the .MDB file. It has other benefits in addition to being a smaller file: it remains compiled, it prevents users from viewing or changing the code modules, and it prevents changes to forms and reports.

The .MDE property

There is an `MDE` property that you can use to determine whether a database has been saved as an .MDE file. When a database is saved as an .MDE file, Access adds the `MDE` property to the database and sets it to the `String` value "T".

 The `MDE` property doesn't exist in a database that is not an .MDE file. Trying to determine this property will cause an error in an .MDB file.

How to create an .MDE file

You can change a database to an .MDE file by choosing Tools ⇨ Database Utilities ⇨ Make .MDE File. When you create an .MDE file, Access does the following:

- Removes all editable source code
- Compiles all modules
- Compacts the database

Be sure to save a copy of your original database to maintain the source code.

Runtime

With the Office Developer Edition, Microsoft has provided a means of distributing Access applications without the user having purchased Access. This is a great way of deploying an application to hundreds or thousands of users without purchasing that many copies of Access. Although this has a big advantage, there is a price to pay. Namely, the runtime version of Access has limitations. These limitations basically prevent the runtime version from being used by itself. As a developer, you need to know these limitations and provide the functionality you need in your application to replace these missing functions. Here is a list of the functions not included in the runtime version:

- Database window is hidden
- Macro and Module windows are hidden
- No design views are available
- Menu items are limited — only menu items you include
- No built-it toolbars — only custom toolbars that you include
- No Access help files — only help files you create
- No built-in error handling — Access runtime crashes if you haven't included error handling
- Some key combinations aren't enabled. These are generally those related to the database window, design views, menu items, help items, and error handling.

Done!

The use of a setup or installation program is covered in Session 24. This is one way to specify when runtime is to be used.

REVIEW

In this session, you learned how to make your application ready for your users. Based on the application and the users' needs, you learned how to configure your application to work in the correct and optimum environment.

- A complete application includes startup forms, an About box, a switchboard or menu system, security, error handling, a help system, and support.
- A support system includes technical support, preference management, archiving, backup, repair, compaction, and system information.
- There are two different schemes for handling preferences: the single-record method and the multiple-record method. There are advantages and disadvantages to each.
- The Compact function will defragment your database, save file space, and improve performance of your database.
- An .MDE file contains only compiled code and is useful for distribution of applications by developers to users who have no need to modify the code.
- The runtime version of Access has limitations that prevent the runtime version from being used by itself. You need to know these limitations and provide the functionality you need in your application.

QUIZ YOURSELF

1. What are the two different schemes for handling preferences? List the advantages and disadvantages of each. (See "Preference management.")
2. List the five benefits of archiving. (See "Archiving.")
3. What are the restrictions on repairing a database? (See "Repair.")
4. What type of information is displayed on a System Information screen? (See "The System Information screen.)

5. What method is used to compact a database programmatically? (See "Compacting.")

6. What are the characteristics of the .MDE property? (See ".MDE files.")

7. List the Access functions not included in the Access runtime version. (See "Runtime.")

Creating Setup Routines Using Office Developer Edition or Third-Party Programs

Session Checklist

✔ Why you need a setup program

✔ Uses for a setup program

✔ The Package and Deployment Wizard

✔ Third-party programs

**30 Min.
To Go**

Most of the time you will be distributing your application using a setup program of some sort. This is characteristic of just about all software. With the architecture of Windows-based operating systems, it is generally necessary to be sure your application will run within the operating system, as well as have the operating environment aware of your program. In this session, you will learn about the process of installing your software on a computer.

Why Do You Need a Setup Program?

Unless your program is a single database file without reference to any other files, you should have a setup or installation program. More than likely, your application is split into more than one database, one for data and the other for the program.

If this is the case, you must make sure that the links from one to the other database will work based on where a user puts your application. A setup program can help you make sure this is not a problem.

Also, you have most likely used a reference, library, ActiveX control, help file, or similar item in your application. If these add-ins are not installed on the user's computer in the correct location, your application will crash when it first starts up. The setup program will properly handle the installation of add-ins on a user's computer.

Another reason for using a setup program involves creating desktop shortcuts, menu items, and including icons for the shortcuts. Without these, the user will be forced to start Access first, then search for the application using the Open dialog box. This is not only inefficient, but frustrating for the user as well.

Setup programs will also contain compressed versions of your files, so distribution of the code will require less storage. This makes it more efficient for storage on a CD or for deployment over a network or the Internet.

If you are going to distribute your application with Access Runtime, a lot of files, registry entries, etc. would need to be installed. Using the setup program provided with Office 2000 Professional makes including Runtime an easy process.

Finally, setup programs provide for including readme files, license agreements, other technical support information, and the ability to remove the application through an uninstall program.

Using the Package and Deployment Wizard

The Package and Deployment Wizard included with Microsoft Office 2000 Developer provides a means of creating a setup program that will work with Access 2000, Access 2000 Runtime, and Microsoft Data Engine (MSDE)-based applications. You can create a setup program that is contained on a floppy disk or that is Web-based, and everything in between, including network-based setup programs and CDs.

The process of distributing an application with the Package and Deployment Wizard is shown in Figure 24-1. There are four major steps:

1. Creating a package
2. Deploying a package
3. Installing a package
4. Testing a package

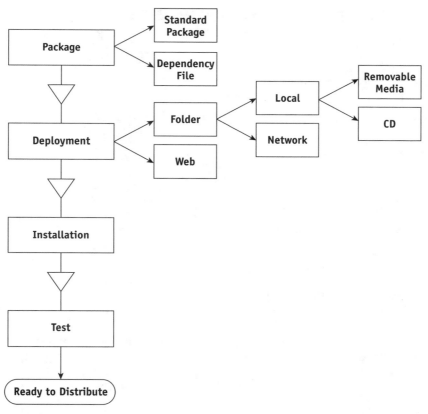

Figure 24-1
The process of distributing an application

Installing the Package and Deployment Wizard

The Package and Deployment Wizard is installed as a VBA add-in. To install the wizard, you need to be in the VBA window. From the Add-Ins menu, choose Add-In Manager. You should see the window shown in Figure 24-2. Several add-ins come with the Access 2000 Developer Edition. These are shown in the dialog box that appears. Choose the VBA Package and Deployment Wizard by double-clicking that entry in the list. Click OK. The wizard is now installed.

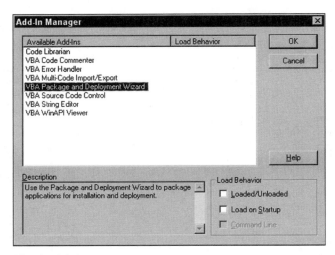

Figure 24-2
Installing the VBA Package and Deployment Wizard

To start the wizard, open the Add-Ins menu again, as shown in Figure 24-3, and choose Package and Deployment Wizard, which now shows up on the menu.

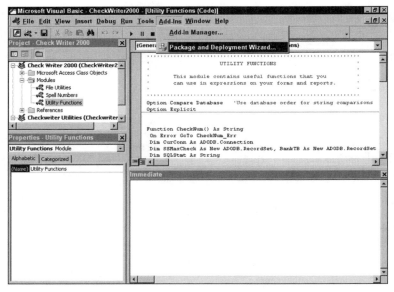

Figure 24-3
Starting the Package and Deployment Wizard

Creating a package

The main screen of the wizard is shown in Figure 24-4. To create a package, press the Package button. If there are any previously saved scripts, you will be prompted to select one.

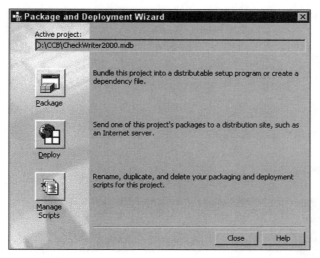

Figure 24-4
The Package and Deployment Wizard main menu

If you choose not to use a previously saved script, the next step in packaging an application is to select the package type. (See Figure 24-5.) There are two types of packages available: Standard Setup Package and Dependency File. The standard setup package creates a package that can be installed using the Setup.exe program that is self-contained and executed during installation. The dependency file is generally used when you use another setup program. This option creates a list of all the components needed for your application.

In Figure 24-6, you see the next step in the process. Here you specify where you want the package to be located. If files already exist in the local or network folder, you will be prompted to overwrite the files.

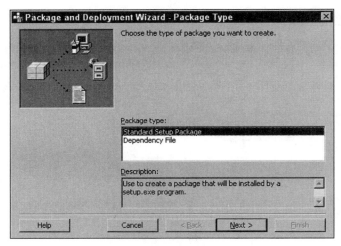

Figure 24-5
Selecting the package type

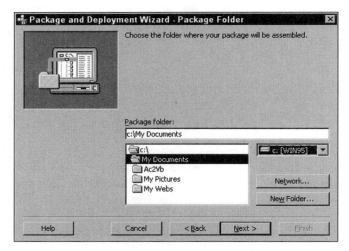

Figure 24-6
Choosing the package target location

You can include additional files in addition to those listed by the wizard in the next step. In Figure 24-7, a list of files to be included in the package is provided. You can either remove a file listed by clearing the check box or add a file by pressing the Add button. In addition, Access Runtime and the related files would be included when the Include Access Runtime check box is selected.

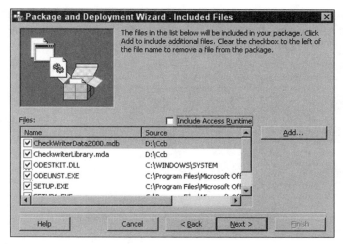

Figure 24-7
Included files

**20 Min.
To Go**

In Figure 24-8, you are given the option to create a single cab file or multiple cab files. A *cab file* is a compressed container file, also referred to as a cabinet file. The elements required for installing and setting up your application are compiled together by the wizard into a cab file. Use a single cab file for network installations or CD installations. Use multiple cabs when using floppy disks.

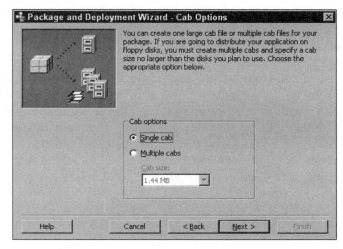

Figure 24-8
Cab options

The wizard takes you to another step, as shown in Figure 24-9. Here you enter the title of the application and a command to run when the installation is completed. This could be the application itself, a tutorial, or another program.

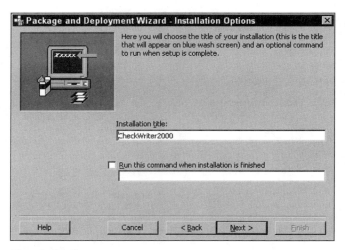

Figure 24-9
Installation options

One of the features of running a setup program is the ability to add menu items to the Windows Start menu. In Figure 24-10, you see the next step of the wizard. Here you can create groups and items to include in each group. The Properties button gives you the ability to modify the Name, Target, and Start In path for the selected menu item or shortcut.

You can choose the location to store your files. The wizard will set the installation location to a default value based on the type of file. Changing the value in the Install Location column can modify this location. You can enter an absolute path or use the several predefined folder variables that provide variable locations determined at the time the setup program runs. These predefined variables are shown in Table 24-1 and refer to the paths at the time the setup program runs.

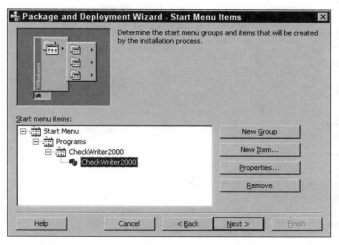

Figure 24-10
Start Menu items

Table 24-1
Predefined Variables for Installation Locations

Variable	Description
$(AppPath)	This is the path specified by the user where the application files are stored.
$(WinPath)	This is the path on the computer where Windows is installed (e.g., C:\Windows).
$(WinSysPath)	This is the path to the systems folder usually located under the Windows folder (e.g., C:\Windows\System).
$(ProgramFiles)	This is the path where application files are normally stored (e.g., C:\Program Files)
$(CommonFiles)	This is the path where common files are normally stored (e.g., C:\ProgramFiles\Common Files).

You can use a combination of predefined folder variables and absolute folder names. For example, if you want to store your help files in a separate directory under your application, use the following file location: $(AppPath)/AppName/ HelpFiles.

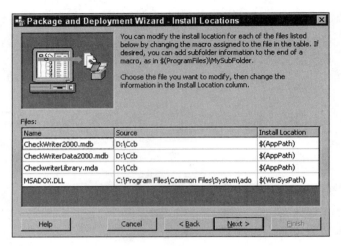

Figure 24-11
Installation locations

The next step of the wizard allows you to specify files as being shared. Sharing a file means that another application can use the file. This type of file will not be removed when the current application is being uninstalled.

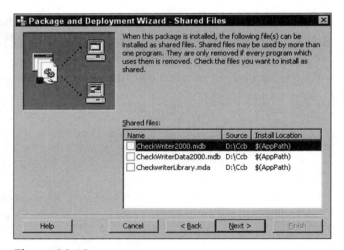

Figure 24-12
Choosing shared files

For the last step, you specify the name you want to use to save the settings you just created. The saved settings are stored in a script and can be loaded, modified if necessary, and used again. For those scripts saved, when you start the wizard, it will prompt you for the name of the saved script you want to use.

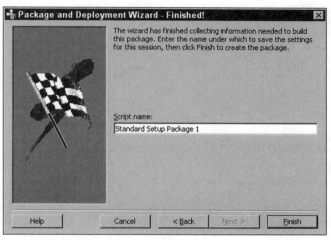

Figure 24-13
Saving package settings and creating the package

After pressing the Finish button, the wizard creates the package and then displays a message box with information about the cab file for your application, a batch that will allow you to recreate the cab file in case you make changes to some of the files. Also, if you choose to install Access Runtime, the location of the runtime files for this application will be displayed.

Deployment

The deployment part of the wizard takes the cab files created in the packaging step and creates an executable file that users can use to install the application. The executable file is created in a folder that you specify or on a Web site, depending on the deployment method you choose. To begin the deployment process, click the Deploy button on the main screen of the wizard. (See Figure 24-4.) The next step is shown in Figure 24-14. Here you choose the package that you want to deploy.

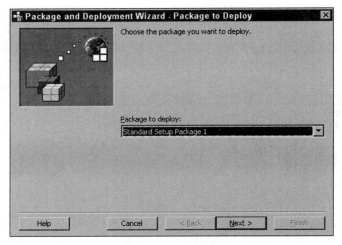

Figure 24-14
Choosing the package to deploy

In the next step, you choose to deploy to a folder or to a Web site (Figure 24-15). Choose Folder to create the setup program for removable media, a hard disk, or a network location. Choose Web Publishing to send the setup program to a URL.

If you chose a folder in the previous step, then the next step is to select a folder in which to store the setup program (Figure 24-16).

The final step is to enter a name under which to save the settings. This will allow you to use the settings again. Click the Finish button as shown in Figure 24-17, and the deployment will occur. After the wizard creates the setup program, a message dialog box will appear indicating what occurred and the location of the setup program and cab file(s).

If you chose to deploy to the Web and not a folder, you will see the screen as shown in Figure 24-18. Here, you choose the URL where you want to send the files and also the publishing protocol you will be using.

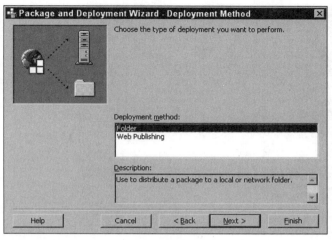

Figure 24-15
Choosing the Deployment method

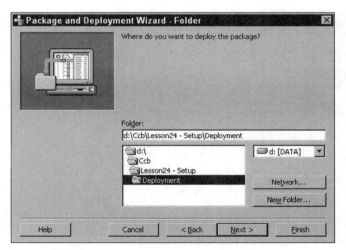

Figure 24-16
Choosing the deployment location

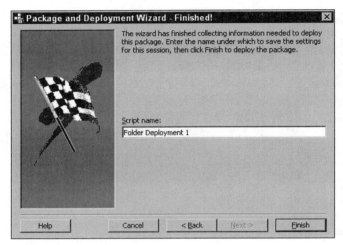

Figure 24-17
Saving the deployment script and deploying the Application

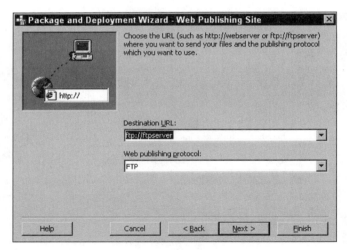

Figure 24-18
Web deployment

**10 Min.
To Go**

Installing and testing

Before delivering the application to the user, you should run through the installation program and test the results of the installation. For the same reasons you test your application for bugs, you should also test the setup program and verify that the setup program does its job properly. A lot of problems can occur since computer environments vary significantly. A lot of variables are associated with the computer hardware, operating systems, and other applications that may be loaded.

To run the setup program, locate the Setup.exe file as created in the deployment step. Execute the Setup.exe file and follow the prompts and screens to install the application.

> **The Check Writer sample application file has a setup program on the CD that was created by the Package and Deployment Wizard. Run the Setup.exe file located in the root directory of the CD.**

You should test the setup program and test the application in a variety of operating environments to ensure that the programs will work properly for your users. While the number of combinations of processors, speed, memory, operating system, and other variables are almost unlimited, it would be wise to at least choose a few different environments to test the application.

Considerations for Using a Setup Program

Generally, a setup program needs to be aware of the environment on which it is installing the software. Based on the configuration of the computer and other installed software, some different actions may be necessary by the setup program.

General considerations

Since the application you are developing is written in Access, you do need to consider the implications of running the application on a machine that has more than one version of Access or the wrong version of Access. Checking the registry entries to see which versions are installed best accomplishes this. You cannot perform this check within your application, since that would imply that the correct version of Access exists and was loaded for the application to run. Therefore, you must perform this check within the setup program or set the menu shortcut properties to point to the correct version of Access to run. The problem is simplified if you include the Runtime version, since the setup program should install Access runtime and correctly create the menu shortcuts.

Considerations when using the Package and Deployment Wizard

If you are including Access Runtime, the distribution sets are quite large and will be at least 160MB. This prohibits the use of floppy disks.

Microsoft Internet Explorer (IE) version 5.0 or later is required when using Access 2000 data pages. IE 5.0 will be installed as part of the setup program. IE will not be the default browser unless a previous version of IE existed on the target computer.

 You can customize the Package and Deployment Wizard using Visual Basic 6.0 by modifying the Setup1.vbp program. Refer to Microsoft documentation for more information.

Third Party Programs

The Package and Deployment Wizard has other options as well. These options are programs created by third parties. The two most popular third party vendors are Wise Solutions, Inc., and InstallShield Software Corporation.

Wise Solutions, Inc., located in Canton, Michigan, produces several installation programs that have various features depending on which type of installation you need to perform. A brief list follows:

- Wise for Windows Installer
- InstallBuilder
- InstallManager
- InstallMaster
- InstallMaker
- InstallAnywhere

InstallShield Software Corporation, located in Schaumburg, Illinois, also provides several installation programs. Their products include:

- InstallShield Professional 2000
- InstallShield
- DemoShield
- InstallFromTheWeb
- PackageForTheWeb
- WebUpdate

Done!

REVIEW

In this session you learned about distributing your application using a setup program. You learned that a setup program will insure that your application willl run within the operating system, as well as make the operating system aware of your application.

- You should have a setup program to handle the multitude of files your application requires. These files include attached data files, references, libraries, ActiveX controls, help files, etc.

- Other reasons for using a setup program include creating desktop shortcuts and menu items, including icons, compressing files, including Access Runtime, including readme files, license agreements, other technical support information, and the ability to remove the application through an uninstall program.

- The Package and Deployment Wizard included with Microsoft Office 2000 Developer provides a means of creating a setup program that will work with Access 2000, Access 2000 Runtime, and MSDE-based applications.

- The process of distributing an application with the Package and Deployment Wizard consists of these four major steps: Create a package, deploy the package, install the package, and test the package.

- The Package and Deployment Wizard is installed as a VBA add-in.

- You should test the setup program and test the application in a variety of operating environments to ensure that the programs will work properly for your users.

- There are other options to the Package and Deployment Wizard: programs created by third parties.

QUIZ YOURSELF

1. List the reasons why you need a setup program. (See "Why Do You Need a Setup Program?")

2. What are the four steps to distributing an application with the Package and Deployment Wizard? (See "Using the Package and Deployment Wizard.")

3. What is the difference between a standard setup package and a dependency file? (See "Creating a package.")

4. Under what circumstances would you use multiple cab files? (See "Creating a package.")

5. How would you specify loading your application files in the folder normally used for program files? (See "Creating a package.")

6. What does the deployment part of the wizard do? (See "Deployment.")

7. What are some of the variables affecting the installation of an application on a user's computer? (See "Installing and testing.")

Programming Wizard-Type Forms for Easier Processing

Session Checklist

✔ Understanding wizards

✔ Understanding the structure of a wizard

✔ Creating a generic wizard

✔ Looking at a sample wizard

**30 Min.
To Go**

Wizards are used throughout Access and other commercial software to make the software easier to use and, in particular, to help users accomplish an activity. In this session, you will learn about wizards and you will look at a sample wizard created for the Check Writer application.

What Is a Wizard?

Microsoft Access has several built-in wizards to guide users through various steps to accomplish a task. These wizards provide a step-by-step user interface with navigational buttons to go back a step, move forward to the next step, cancel the operation, or finish the operation.

Here are some pointers to remember when designing your wizard:

- Use the wizard to step through a process.
- Each page of the wizard should be a step toward completing the process.
- The order of the steps should make sense.
- Keep buttons, fonts, and controls consistent between pages.
- Keep pages uncluttered.
- Use defaults as much as possible to simplify user input.

The Structure of a Wizard

Wizards can be created in a variety of ways with different Access objects. For example, you can use a single form, with page controls to separate the pages of the wizard. Or, you can use a main form with subforms for each page. You might also see a separate form for each page of the wizard. You will need to decide which is the best approach to take. In this session, we will use a different approach than those just mentioned. We will use a Tab control on a single form, with each page on the Tab control being a page in our wizard. This approach has the following advantages:

- The entire wizard is contained within one Access object, a form.
- The Tab control provides properties and methods that will simplify coding. For example, you can set focus to a page, hide a page, etc.
- The tabs on the Tab control can be shown or made invisible depending on your needs. They can even be buttons.
- There needs to be only one set of navigation buttons.

The normal navigation buttons that a wizard requires are Next, Back, Cancel, and Finish. These won't be on the tab control but instead, on the main form. It is also common, but not necessary, to have a graphic on the left side of a wizard page. With our structure, you have a choice of putting one graphic on the main form, or different graphics on each page. This affects the size of the tab control. The tab control takes up most of the main form's area if it includes the graphics, or just part of the main form if the main form has the graphic. For the example we will be using, we will have only one graphic. This will also save memory requirements.

Creating a Generic Wizard

Before exploring the wizard that is included in the CheckWriter application, let's look at a template for a generic wizard, which can be the starting point for creating any wizard with the tab control scheme.

 The Generic Wizard template is located on the CD-ROM accompanying this book in the file GenericWizard.MDB.

The Generic Wizard template contains general controls and layout so you can add your own unique controls to the wizard. Navigation buttons are included with all the code to move through the wizard. The wizard is based on pages, so you move from one page to the next or back. The template is shown in Design view in Figure 25-1.

Figure 25-1
Design view of the Wizard template

In this figure, you can see the graphic, the tab control, and the navigation buttons. The control software for the template will control which page is displayed as well as which navigation buttons are enabled or disabled.

The tabs are normally hidden when the form is opened, but in Design view, they are visible to make it easier to work with. On the left side of the form is an unbound object frame for you to add your own graphic. You can add any picture type using one of the standard methods in Access for adding pictures. On the bottom of the form are the four navigational buttons: Cancel, Back, Next, and Finish. These buttons are used to move through the wizard. The check mark on the bottom left portion of the form is normally invisible. It is named "StatusForward" and is used to indicate the direction the wizard is going (forward/backward).

Wizard forms are generally designed with the border style set to dialog box, no scroll bars, and no record selectors.

Here are a few rules for the buttons that apply to the code included with this template:

- The Back button is always disabled on the first page.
- The Finish button is disabled on all pages except the last page.
- The Forward button is always disabled on the last page and may be disabled on a page-by-page basis depending on whether the user has completed the information on a given page.
- The Cancel button is always enabled.

The opening page of the wizard template is shown in Figure 25-2. On this first page, you need to identify the wizard and its purpose.

There are 11 pages built into this template. You can add as many additional pages as you want. Likewise, if you are not going to use all 11 pages in your wizard, you can delete pages or just ignore them.

You can add whatever controls you want to each page. There is code behind the form to control navigation between pages. The code for all the navigation buttons is described in this session, with additional comments on how to modify the code for your own needs. In addition, there is a subroutine for the Form Open event and a general subroutine that is called to change a page.

Figure 25-2
The first page of the Wizard template

**20 Min.
To Go**

The Form Open subroutine

The Form Open subroutine sets the tab style to none so the user doesn't see the tabs. The buttons are initialized and the focus is set to the first page. Listing 25-1 shows the code for this subroutine.

Listing 25-1
The Wizard Form Open Subroutine

```
Private Sub Form_Open(Cancel As Integer)
'set tab style to none
    Me.wzdPages.Style = 2
'initialize buttons and goto first page
    Me.butBack.Enabled = False
    Me.butFinish.Enabled = False
    Me.wzdPages.Pages(0).SetFocus

End Sub
```

With a tab control, you can remove the tabs by setting the style to a value of 2. We do that here because the default view is to show tabs so when in Design view, we can navigate between pages. But when the user initiates the wizard, you generally want control over the sequence of events to prevent skipping steps. The subroutine also disables the Back and Finish buttons. To go to the first page of the wizard, you need to set focus only to page 0. Tab control pages start with 0.

The Next button

The next operation of the wizard is controlled by pressing the Next button. This triggers the code shown in Listing 25-2.

Listing 25-2
The Next Button Click Subroutine

```
Private Sub butNext_Click()
Dim tbc As Control

'set status to forward
    Me.StatusForward = True

 'goto next page
Set tbc = Me!wzdPages
    Me.wzdPages.Pages(tbc + 1).SetFocus

'enable Back button
    Me.butBack.Enabled = True

'if last page disable next button and enable finish button
If tbc = Me.wzdPages.Pages.Count - 1 Then
        Me.butNext.Enabled = False
        Me.butFinish.Enabled = True
        End If

End Sub
```

This code runs when the Next button is pressed and sets focus to the next page. The StatusForward control is set to True to indicate that the direction is currently forward. The control tbc is set to the current page control and is used to move to the next page. The Back button is enabled. If the new current page is the last page, then the Next button is disabled and the Finish button is enabled.

Indirectly, another subroutine runs when the Next button is pressed. This occurs when you change the focus to a different page on the tab control. The On Change event for the tab control runs the code in Listing 25-3:

Listing 25-3
The Wizard Page Change Subroutine

```
Private Sub wzdPages_Change()
'Handles navigation among pages or processing when a page changes
'You can do the following in this subroutine
'   Skip pages
'   Change the order in which the pages are displayed
'   Check for valid entries before proceeding to the next page

If Me.StatusForward Then
    'Navigation in the forward direction
    Select Case Me.wzdPages.Value
        Case 0
        Case 1
        Case 2
        Case 3
        Case 4
        Case 5
        Case 6
        Case 7
        Case 8
        Case 9
        Case 10
    End Select
Else
    'Navigation in the backward direction
    Select Case Me.wzdPages.Value
        Case 0
        Case 1
        Case 2
        Case 3
        Case 4
```

Continued

Listing 25-3 *Continued*

```
            Case 5
            Case 6
            Case 7
            Case 8
            Case 9
            Case 10
        End Select
    End If
End Sub
```

This subroutine is called when the form is loaded, when the Next button is pressed, and when the Back button is pressed. The purpose of this subroutine is to handle the navigation between pages. Depending on the direction and which page is current, error checking can occur to make sure the proper inputs were made in the previous step. If not, you can add code to go back to the previous page and show a message. Since this is a template, no specific code is included for any particular page. The appropriate code would be added for a Case statement depending on the direction and the page number. The value for the Case statement is the new current page number. If you adjust the number of pages from 11 (0–10) in the template, then you would add or delete Case statements here. An example of this subroutine is shown later in this session.

The Back button

The code for the Back button is similar to the Next button. It sets focus to the previous page of the wizard. The control tbc is set to the current page control, and the Next button is enabled. If the new current page is the first page, the Back button is disabled. The Finish button is also disabled and the StatusForward control is set to False to indicate that the direction is currently backwards. The code for the Click event of the Back button is shown in Listing 25-4.

Listing 25-4
The Back Button Click Subroutine

```
Private Sub butBack_Click()
Dim tbc As Control

'set status to back
    Me.StatusForward = False
```

```
'goto previous page and enable next button
    Set tbc = Me!wzdPages
    Me.wzdPages.Pages(tbc - 1).SetFocus
    Me.butNext.Enabled = True

'if first page disable button back button
    If tbc = 0 Then Me.butBack.Enabled = False

'disable finish button
    Me.butFinish.Enabled = False

End Sub
```

The Cancel button

Since you want the user to be able to cancel the wizard at any time, the Cancel button is always enabled. The code behind the Click event is shown in Listing 25-5 and is simply used to close the wizard form. If you need to add any cleanup code before the wizard is closed to undo the selections that the user may have made prior to canceling the wizard, you should add it here.

Listing 25-5
The Cancel Button Click Subroutine

```
Private Sub butCancel_Click()
'Cancel wizard and close form
    DoCmd.Close
End Sub
```

The Finish button

On the last page of the wizard, the Finish button is enabled. The On Click event should start execution of whatever you want the wizard to do. Include a statement to close the wizard form when you are done.

The next session explains how to make a wizard work with Access as an add-in.

**10 Min.
To Go**

An Example Wizard

The Check Writer sample application contains a form that is made from the Wizard template previously described. This wizard is used to create a new bank account. The first screen of this wizard is shown in Figure 25-3.

Figure 25-3
The first page of the New Account Wizard

In Listing 25-6, you will see only those subroutines that have been modified from the template. The subroutines for the four navigation buttons and the Form Open subroutine remain the same as the template. Listing 25-6 contains three procedures that are unique to the New Account Wizard: Form_Load, Finish, and wzdPages_Change.

The Form_Load subroutine initializes the control xDataSource on the form so the wizard can actually use the unbound form utilities described in Session 12. The Finish function calls the Unbound Form function uf_SaveRecord to save the new account record and then closes the wizard form.

Listing 25-6
The New Account Wizard Subroutines

```
Private Sub Form_Load()
'Initialize datasource for the unbound form functions
'Assume the datasource is in the same directory as the application
Me.xDataSource = "Data Source=" & Application.CurrentProject.Path & _
"\CheckWriterData2000.mdb"
```

```
End Sub

Public Function Finish()
    'Call the unbound form save record function
    uf_SaveRecord Me
    DoCmd.Close acForm, Me.Name
End Function

Private Sub wzdPages_Change()
'This Subroutine handles the navigation among pages or
'   processing when a page changes
'You can do the following in this subroutine
'   Skip pages
'   Change the order in which the pages are displayed
'   Check for valid entries before proceeding to the next page

If Me.StatusForward Then
    'Navigation in the forward direction
    Select Case Me.wzdPages.Value
        Case 0
        Case 1
        Case 2
        'Set the control for the type of account based
'on the caption for the option selected
        Me.Type = Me.Controls("TypeLabel" & Trim(str(Me.selType))).caption
        Case 3
            'Prevent the user from staying on this page if
            '   the Bank Account field is null
            If IsNull(Me.BankAccountNumber) Then Me.wzdPages.Pages(2).SetFocus
        Case 4
        Case 5
            'Prevent the user from staying on this page if
            '   the fields on the previous page are null
            If IsNull(Me.ABANumber) Or _
              IsNull(Me.StartingCheckNumber) Then
              Me.wzdPages.Pages(4).SetFocus
            End If
        Case 6
            'Skip this page if the user doesn't have the last statement
            If Me.HaveLastStatement <> 1 Then
              Me.wzdPages.Pages(7).SetFocus
            End If
        Case 7
            'Skip this page if the user has the last statement
            If Me.HaveLastStatement = 1 Then
              Me.wzdPages.Pages(8).SetFocus
            End If
        Case 8
    End Select
Else
```

Continued

Listing 25-6 *Continued*

```
    'Navigation in the backward direction
    Select Case Me.wzdPages.Value
        Case 0
        Case 1
        Case 2
        Case 3
        Case 4
        Case 5
        Case 6
          'Skip this page if the user doesn't have the last statement
          If Me.HaveLastStatement <> 1 Then
            Me.wzdPages.Pages(5).SetFocus
          End If
        Case 7
          'Skip this page if the user has the last statement
          If Me.HaveLastStatement = 1 Then
            Me.wzdPages.Pages(6).SetFocus
          End If
        Case 8
    End Select
  End If
End Sub
```

The wzdPages_Change subroutine is the significant controlling code for the
wizard. First, this wizard only has pages 0 thru 8, so the generic wizard code was
modified to remove the last two pages in the subroutine.

In the forward direction, code runs on pages 2, 3, 5, 6, and 7. Note that the
Case statement for a given page runs as soon as the given page has focus. On page
2, some processing is done based on the selection on page 1. Page 1 contains an
option group, and the control Type is set to the label caption for the respective
option selected. On page 3, the value of BankAccountNumber located on page 2 is
checked. If it is null, then focus returns to page 2 since this is a required field. A
similar check is made on page 5 based on the data on page 4, which is also required.
On page 5 (see Figure 25-4), the user is asked whether he or she has the last bank
statement. If the answer is Yes, then page 6 is displayed (see Figure 25-5); otherwise, page 7 is displayed. This shows an example of how you can conditionally display pages based on user input.

Done!

Figure 25-4
Page 5 of the New Account Wizard

In the backward direction, the only logic is again to skip pages not applicable based on the user selection on page 5.

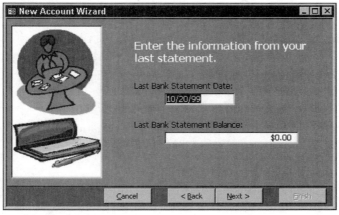

Figure 25-5
Page 6 of the New Account Wizard

REVIEW

In this session, you learned about designing wizards. Wizards provide a step-by-step method to guide users through a process.

- The standard user interface for a wizard includes the Cancel, Back, Next, and Finish buttons.
- Wizards should be designed to step through a process, with each step getting closer to completing the process. The order of the steps should make sense.
- The design of the user interface should be consistent between pages, with pages being uncluttered.
- Using a tab control on a single form with each page on the tab control being a page in your wizard has several advantages: the entire wizard is contained within one Access form, and the tab control provides properties and methods that simplify coding.

QUIZ YOURSELF

1. What are some points to remember when designing your wizard? (See "What Is a Wizard?")

2. What are the different ways of designing a wizard using Access objects, and what are the advantages and disadvantages of each approach? (See "The Structure of a Wizard.")

3. What are the general rules to apply to a wizard's navigation control buttons? (See "Creating a Generic Wizard.")

Using Add-Ins with Your Application

Session Checklist

✔ Using Add-ins

✔ Using the Registry with Access Add-ins

✔ Using the Add-in Manager

✔ Creating a library database

**30 Min.
To Go**

This session provides you with the background to understand how to use Add-ins with Access. Since there are so many possible combinations, levels, and options, the end of the session illustrates only the first step to using a library database as an Add-in.

What are Add-Ins?

Sometimes, there is a lot of confusion about Add-in terminology. You will see menu Add-ins, wizards, builders, libraries, etc. Simply put, an *Access Add-in* is a component thats not part of the basic Microsoft Access product.

Add-ins can be:

1. Provided with Access from Microsoft

2. Purchased from third-party developers

3. Custom designed

Examples of Add-ins provided with Access include control wizards, form wizards, chart wizards, field builders, object libraries, the switchboard manager, the link table manager, the documenter, the performance analyzer, and many, many more. Several Add-ins are available from third parties as well.

Database Creations, Inc., supplies Add-ins as part of their EZ Access Developer Suite and, in particular, the EZ Application Builder. Other vendors include FMS and Black Moshannon Systems. Or you can design your own, as will be discussed later in this session.

In addition to Add-ins coming from different sources, they can be different types. There are two basic types distinguished by the connection that is made to Access. These connections can be either references or the registry.

Add-ins that are connected through references are generally referred to as a library. Reference add-ins generally provide functionality through VBA code as a function call.

Add-ins that are connected through the Registry fall into the categories of wizards, builders, and menu Add-ins. Menu Add-ins are the most obvious since they appear on the Tools menu under Add-Ins. The Add-in Manager is always listed on this submenu. Ironically, the Add-in Manager is an Add-in itself. Most of the menu Add-ins are those provided by third-party vendors or a custom designed component. This doesn't mean that you can create an Add-in that shows up only on this menu. You can also create Add-ins that are initiated in other ways. If an Add-in does not use the Add-in menu, it falls into the category of an Access object wizard.

Wizards exist to assist the user or developer in performing some task. This task could be creating or modifying an Access object, control, or property. For each of these different types of tasks, the Add-ins are generally categorized as the following:

- *Data object wizards.* For tables and queries
- *User interface wizards.* For forms, reports, and data access pages
- *Control wizards.* For creating new objects on forms, reports, or data access pages

- *Property builders.* For setting property values
- *Expression builders.* For creating expressions

To help understand these various categories of wizards and builders, refer to Figure 26-1.

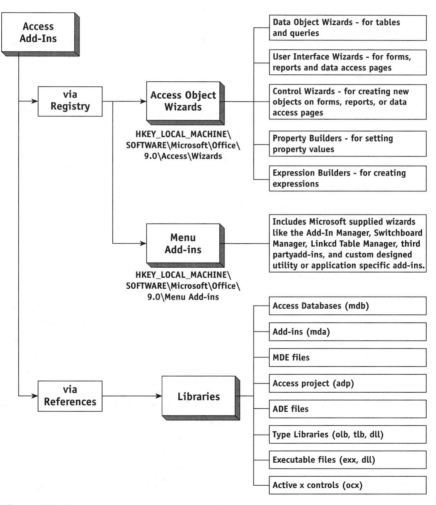

Figure 26-1
The structure of Access add-ins

So where do we go from here? As a programmer, one of the most important elements to understand is how to plug these Add-ins into Access and make them work. The next section discusses the general considerations for add-Ins.

General Add-In Considerations

When dealing with Add-ins you do have to consider various things such as the type of file, making references within the different databases, form properties, and multi-user issues.

File types

Access Add-ins generally use the file extensions .MDA or .MDE. An .MDA file can be opened and the code viewed. The .MDA extension is simply a way to identify an Add-in. The file structure is the same as an .MDB file. In fact, you can still use the extension .MDB for an Add-in if you want. To secure or protect the code, the Add-in should be an .MDE file. This is done using the Tools ⇨ Database Utilities ⇨ Make .MDE file menu item. An .MDE file contains only compiled code, not the source code.

Referring to different databases

When using an Add-in, you will have code in both the main database as well as the Add-in database. To refer to the Add-in database in which code is currently running, use the `CodeProject` or `CodeData` object to return a reference to the Add-in database. If you want to refer to the database that's currently open in Access, use the `CurrentProject` or `CurrentData` object.

The Add-in database can contain any type of object that a regular database can. When you refer to any object, you must be sure that you are referring to it in the correct database. Forms and reports in the Add-in can be bound only to data sources in the Add-in's database. Use an unbound form and ADO code to work around this.

Macros called from the add-in are first checked within the Add-in database. If Access doesn't find the macro there, it will check the current database.

Domain aggregate functions such as Dcount, Dmin, Dmax, **and** Dlookup **always refer to the data in the current database, not the library database.**

General design

It is best to model the interface for an Add-in on those Add-ins that come with Microsoft Access. Users are probably already familiar with this interface, so ease of use will be maximized and training will be minimized.

You can perform a number of tasks to give your Add-in the same appearance as Access Add-ins. These include the following:

- Set the form's `AutoCenter` property to Yes.
- Turn record selectors off.
- Turn scroll bars off, unless they are required.
- Don't use navigation buttons unless you are using a form that has multiple records.
- Place controls consistently on every form.
- Use the dialog mode to prevent the user from moving to the next form until conditions in your code are met.
- Use multipage forms with navigation buttons. This keeps the Add-in within a single form.

See Session 25 for more information on the technique of keeping an Add-in within a single form.

Multiple-user considerations

Add-ins are always opened for shared access, giving multiple users access to the objects in your Add-in. Be aware that if your Add-in needs to write back to its database, you must open the Add-in with read/write permissions.

**20 Min.
To Go**

Wizards

Wizards exist for one primary reason: to guide a user through a series of steps to accomplish a task. As is the case with the built-in wizards that come with Access, the tasks are to build databases, tables, queries, forms, reports, controls, or build values or expressions. A wizard to build a new bank account was shown in

Session 25. Wizards generally use forms, graphics, and helpful text to guide the user through the operation and hide the technical details of what is going on.

Depending on the task to be accomplished, the wizards are categorized as shown in Figure 26-1.

Data object wizards and user interface wizards

Data object and user interface wizards help the user create a new table, query, form, data access page, or report. Access has a number of built-in object wizards, which are available in the New Table, New Query, New Form, New Data Access Page, and New Report dialog boxes. You can create an object wizard that will also appear in one of these dialog boxes. This is accomplished by creating registry entries, which will be covered later in this session.

Control wizards

Control wizards help the user to add either an Access or an ActiveX control to a form, report, or data access page. A control wizard runs when a control in the toolbox is clicked and is dropped onto a form, report, or data access page. The wizard launches only if the control wizards tool in the toolbox is selected.

Builders

Builders are a simpler version of a wizard. Rather than perform a task, a builder usually creates an expression or a single data element. The Expression Builder is built into Access, which is used for several different properties on a form or report. It is typically used for a control source for a control. The Query Builder can be used for the record source of a form. You can also find an Input Mask filter builder, as well as others.

When a builder is available for a particular property, the Build button (the small button with the ellipsis [...]) appears next to that property's name in the property sheet.

Menu Add-Ins

Unlike wizards and builders, menu add-ins go beyond creating expressions, or performing a single task. They generally operate on multiple objects or Access itself. Database Documenter and Performance Analyzer are examples of menu Add-ins.

When a menu Add-in is installed, it is available through the Add-ins submenu of the Tools menu. This provides a means of running the Add-in outside the context of a specific object or property, as the wizards do.

Installing a wizard or menu add-in

Whether you have a wizard or menu Add-in, you have two choices of how to install your Add-in: directly using a setup or installer program, or interactively using the Access Add-in Manager utility. In either case, registry entries are created for each Add-in. A setup program can create the registry entries, or the Add-in Manager can do it. One feature of the Add-in Manager is it can also remove add-ins. Before we look at the mechanics of the Add-in Manager, lets explore which registry entries are required.

Add-In Registry entries

Refer to Figure 26-2, which is the Registry Editor with the key for the menu add-ins expanded. This entry is located under the branch HKEY_LOCAL_MACHINE\SOFTWARE\Microsoft\Office\9.0\Access\Menu Add-ins, which contains all entries that would appear on the Add-in submenu in Access. Only the Add-in Manager is listed here, but you can add your own Add-ins under this branch as well and then have the Add-in appear on the menu.

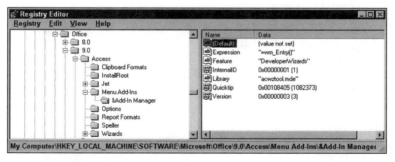

Figure 26-2
A Registry entry for the Add-In Manager

For wizards, the branch in the registry is HKEY_LOCAL_MACHINE\SOFTWARE\Microsoft\Office\9.0\Access\Wizards. This branch and all the default entries are shown in Figure 26-3.

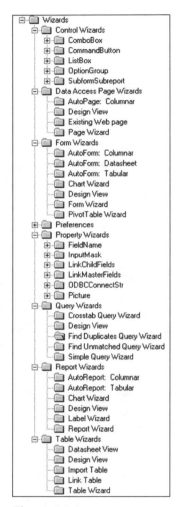

Figure 26-3
Registry entries for the wizards

Placing your entry into any of these folders will make Access aware of your wizard within the context as determined by the folder. For example, you can create your own query wizard and add a key in the folder Query Wizards. Then, when you run Access and create a new query, your wizard will be listed along with the other ones in the same branch. Depending on the type of wizard, registry key values will vary. Refer to the Microsoft documentation for the required entries for each wizard type.

The Add-in Manager utility

To use the Add-in Manager, your Add-in requires two items:

1. Database property entries for Title, Company, and Comments
2. A USysRegInfo table

The database properties Title, Company, and Comments are displayed by the Add-in Manager to let the user know what the add-in is. To set database properties before you install your Add-in, do the following:

1. In the Database window, click Database Properties on the File menu.
2. Click the Summary tab.
3. Enter the values in the Title, Company, and Comments boxes to describe your Add-in.
4. Click OK.

The USysRegInfo table must have specific fields and data, which specify the Windows registry entries that will be created when your Add-in is installed.

 For more information about the UsysRegInfo table see the following article in the Microsoft Knowledge Base: Article ID: Q153858, Title: "INF: How to Create a USysRegInfo Table for Installing Add-ins."

The Add-in Manager is not limited to installing menu add-ins. It can install wizards as well, as long as the registry information is located in the UsysRegInfo table.

The USysRegInfo table is not automatically created for you when you create a new MDA file. The easiest way to create the USysRegInfo table is to import the table from the ACWZLIB.MDE file that ships with Microsoft Access. You then add records to this table to match your Add-in needs. This table contains four fields, as shown in Figure 26-4.

 The USysRegInfo table is a system table and is usually hidden. To view the USysRegInfo table, choose Options on the Tools menu, select the View tab, and then select the System Objects check box.

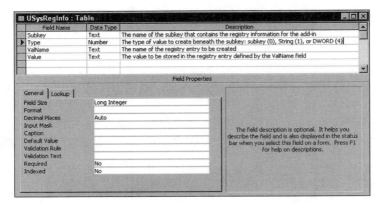

Figure 26-4
The UsysInfoTable structure

Each record in the table is used to describe a subkey or value that is to be added to the registry by the Add-in Manager. Each Add-in requires a minimum of three records, where each record does the following:

1. Creates the subkey for the Add-in
2. Adds the library entry
3. Adds the Expression entry

You can have additional records to store other values in the registry that the Add-in may specifically require. Note that the different types of builders and wizards have different entries.

 The USysReg.doc in the OPG\Appendixes folder on the Office 2000 Developer CD-ROM contains more information about creating the USysRegInfo table.

**10 Min.
To Go**

Library Add-Ins

While Access module objects allow you to share common procedures among other Access objects, library databases allow you to share common procedures among other Access databases. This further reduces redundant code and allows for easier maintenance of the code since it is located in just one place and not several applications. You can also distribute a library database as an .MDE file with the source code protected and distribute the main application open with source code.

A library database is like any other Access database containing tables, queries, forms, data access pages, reports, and modules. You can open it like any other database, but the difference is how the database is loaded.

Functions and subroutines in the library database can be addressed only from the current database if they are declared `Public`. Privately declared procedures are available only within the library database. Also, routines stored in a class module are not available from outside the library database.

Creating a library database

To create a library database, follow these steps.

1. Create the library using forms, modules, and other objects in a new database.
2. Test and debug the library functions.
3. Compile and compact the library database.
4. Rename the library database so it has an extension of .MDA or convert the database to an .MDE file.

Debugging library databases

It's a good idea to test and debug the library functions before you tie a library database into an application, but sometimes this is not possible. In certain cases, you cannot test a library without it being called from an application. Sometimes the library works fine until it is called from an application. The more you can test the library by itself, the easier it will be.

The LoadOnStartup key

The registry entry, LoadOnStartup key, provides a way of having Access load a library database automatically when Access is started. You can add a key called LoadOnStartup to the following tree:

HHEY_LOCAL_MACHINE/SOFTWARE\Microsoft\Office\90\Access\Wizards

The entry for the key is the string value for the path and filename of the library to load. Also enter a data value of "`rw`" for the value.

Using the LoadOnStartup key to load a library causes Access to start more slowly, and the library will occupy memory whether any functions are called or not. Use this feature judiciously.

References

References tell Access where to find a library database. To see the list of references, you need to open the VBA window either by opening a module or by viewing the code for a form or report. Under the Tools menu, there is a References selection. Choosing it will display the References dialog box, as shown in Figure 26-5.

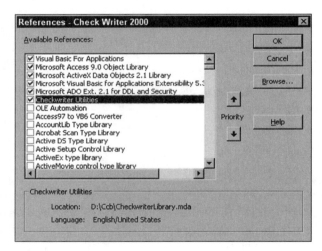

Figure 26-5
The References dialog box

References become invalid if they are relocated. Since they are stored in the referencing database, references are not automatically updated when a library is moved. The reference must be manually or programmatically updated.

Creating a reference

You have two choices for creating a reference: using the References dialog box as shown in Figure 26-5, or programmatically.

Unlike the Registry entries for wizards and menu Add-ins that are established for all databases, references are done on a database-by-database basis. Using the References dialog box at the time you develop an application works fine as long as the references don't move or disappear. It is important in your setup or installation program that the libraries get installed in the correct location and that the version of those libraries are correct. As an extra feature, you can add some code to programmatically add, check, or remove references.

To manually create a reference:

1. Open the VBA window.
2. Choose Tools then References from the pull-down menus.
3. Select the reference you want to add from the available list or press the Browse button to search for a library to reference.
4. Set the priorities of the references. This is important if the same function name is used in more than one library. The reference with the highest priority gets referenced first.

Programmatically working with references

Access contains `Reference` objects that allow you to programmatically work with references.

Working with preferences is beyond the scope of this session; please check the Microsoft documentation for more information about working with references programmatically.

Calling a reference

As long as the function or subroutine in the library database is declared public, you can call the routine just as if it were in the current database. You can optionally use the `Run` method to invoke a library routine. This method gives you the ability to specify the library in which the function is located. This is done be specifying the project name used for the library.

Be aware of naming functions in your library database that may be the same as those in the current database. Access will use the procedure in the current database and not the function in the library database. You can get around this problem by not using the same names or by preceding the function name with the module name like *[ModuleName].FunctionName*.

An Example Library

In our sample application, there is a module that has generic use for unbound forms. This module is named Unbound Form Utilities. Since it is fairly general-purpose and could be used in other databases as well, we made it a library database. The basic steps to do this were as follows:

1. We started development of the module within the application database since we could view the code and debug it easier.

2. After it was tested, we created a new empty database with an .MDA extension and named it CheckWriterLibrary.MDA.

3. We moved the module Unbound Form Utilities from the application database to the new empty library database and deleted it from the application database.

4. With the VBA window open in the application database, we created a reference to the new library database using the Tools ➪ References menu selection. (See Figure 26-5).

5. We compiled both the application and the library databases to verify that there were no errors.

Done!

6. The application was then tested with the library database.

REVIEW

In this session, you have learned about expanding the functionality of Access with add-ins. This can be done at different levels and in various ways. With these capabilities, Access becomes a very customizable program.

- You can get Add-ins with Microsoft Access, purchase them from third-party developers, and have them custom designed.

- There are two basic types of Add-ins distinguished by the connection that is made through either references or the registry.

- The Add-in may contain any type of object that a regular database can, but you must be careful when referring to an object in either the Add-in or the current database.

- The Add-in Manager requires registry information located in a UsysRegInfo table contained within the Add-in.

- References tell Access where to find a library database. Viewing and working with the reference list is done through the VBA window and choosing the Tools ⇨ References menu item.

QUIZ YOURSELF

1. Name the three sources of Add-ins. (See "What are Add-Ins?")

2. What distinguishes the two basic types of Add-ins? (See "What are Add-Ins?")

3. What are the characteristics of the .MDA file type? (See "File types.")

4. What are the two ways of installing an Add-in? (See "Installing a wizard or menu Add-in.")

5. Describe the purpose and the process of creating a UsysRegInfo table. (See "The Add-in Manager utility.")

6. What are the four steps to creating a library database? (See "Creating a library database.")

PART

V

Sunday Morning

1. True or false: You can use the `FindRecord` method with multi-key fields.
2. Setting the _____ property to Yes forces the user to close the dialog box before moving to another form.
3. Which one of the following properties is not typically set for a dialog box?
    a. `PopUp`
    b. `Modal`
    c. `AutoCenter`
    d. `RecordSource`
4. To change the list of items in a find dialog box, which property do you set for the dialog's list box or combo box?
5. List some of the basic features of a Search and Print Dialog.
6. Which of the lines below would be the correct syntax for printing a report via VBA code?
    a. `DoCmd.PrintReport "testreport", acNormal`
    b. `DoCmd.OpenReport acNormal, "testreport"`
    c. `Docmd.OpenReport "testreport, acNormal`
7. Where can you place events on a report?
8. What is the purpose of concatenation?
9. What function provides a means of determining the Access version, runtime, initialization file, and Access directory?
10. True or false: The Background Compile option will compile only those functions that are used.

11. To have one code base that can run in different environments, Access and VBA provides which of the following?

    a. Global constants

    b. Conditional compilation

    c. Preference functions

    d. Decompiling

    e. None of the above

12. List the three choices for starting your VBA code when a database is opened.

13. List at least three reasons to have a setup program.

14. True or false: The Package and Deployment Wizard is installed as an Access Add-in.

15. Which of the following is not true of the Package and Deployment Wizard?

    a. The distribution set is large if you include Access Runtime.

    b. Internet Explorer 5.0 will be installed as part of the distribution set.

    c. You cannot customize the Package and Deployment Wizard.

    d. You can deploy to the Web.

    e. None of the above.

16. What is the best way to deal with having multiple versions of Access on the target machine?

17. List at least three items to consider when designing a wizard.

18. List at least three advantages for using the Tab control in a wizard.

19. True or false: The normal navigation buttons that a wizard requires are Next, Back and Cancel.

20. Which of the following is false?

    a. The Back button is always disabled on the last page.

    b. The Finish button is disabled on all pages except the last page.

    c. The Forward button is always disabled on the last page.

    d. The Forward button may be disabled on a page-by-page basis based depending on whether the user has completed the information on a given page.

    e. The Cancel button is always enabled.

PART

VI

Sunday
Afternoon

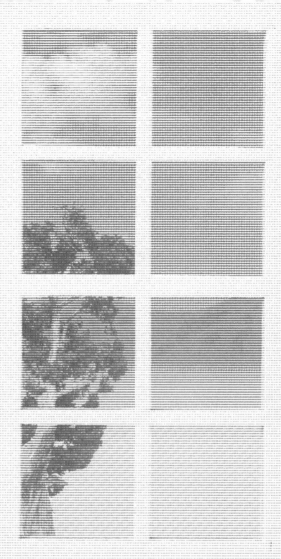

Programming and Using File Attachments

Session Checklist

✔ Defining linked tables

✔ Using linked tables

✔ Using Access-provided tools

✔ Looking at ADO programming features for linked tables

✔ Creating a simple Attachment Manager form for linked tables

**30 Min.
To Go**

I n this session, you will learn about splitting a database into two parts: a front-end and a back-end. The connection between the two are made with attached or linked tables. You will learn how to deal with this connection as well as the functions available for manipulating the connection in VBA.

File Attachments

Access refers to attached tables as *linked tables*. Linking data enables you to read and, in most cases, update data in the external data source without importing. The external data source's format is not altered so that you can continue to use the file with the program that originally created it, but you can also add, delete, or edit its data using Microsoft Access as well. These sources include not only other Access .MDB files, but also Access .ADP, .MDW, .MDA, and .MDE files. Beyond Access, you can connect to Excel, Text, Outlook, Exchange, Paradox, HTML, dBASE, SQL Server, and ODBC data sources.

Application developers commonly keep data tables in a separate file from the program. This technique is referred to as having a front end/back end application. The reasons for using this method are numerous:

- Data files are better managed on a server, while the front-end application runs best on the workstation. This facilitates multi-user access, replication, backups, security, etc.
- Large databases should be handled by a more powerful database management system like SQL Server rather than Microsoft Access.
- Data files might still be maintained by a legacy system.
- Reduced network traffic improves performance.
- Separate files allow independent support and maintenance of the front-end application.

Figure 27-1 shows a typical example of how you might configure linked tables in an application. This figure depicts six different connections. The number of connections could be one or many more than six. The figure shows three different data sources, which could be different because they are located on different servers, relate to different department data, exist as different types of files, or can be separated based on user accessibility. In addition, the figure lists a security data source. This database may contain sensitive information about the security in your application and is therefore separated from the rest of the data. You might also choose to have a separate archive database where historical records are kept. These records cannot change, so backups are not frequently needed. The archived data is accessed only occasionally and is generally read-only.

Another type of linked database could be program configuration data. Such items as preferences, program options, etc. could be stored here. This gives the system administrator some control over the front-end application without actually changing the code or objects in the front-end application.

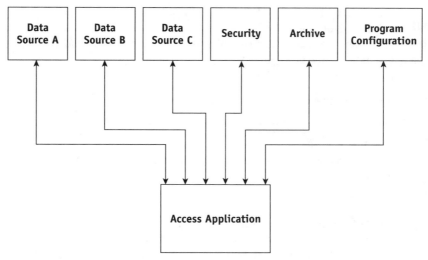

Figure 27-1
An example of linked tables

Basic Principles

You normally create a link to a table in another database by selecting File, Get External Data from the Access menu bar, and then choosing Link Tables. You can also create a link by choosing Tables in the Database window and pressing New. You get a choice of how you want to create the table; one of the options is Link Table.

The File Link dialog box will appear, allowing you to select a file. You can link to an Access data file or other types. The types of data sources you can link to depends on the drivers you installed with Access. If you do not see the data source you are looking for, you may need to rerun the Access setup program and install any missing drivers.

Depending on the type of file you choose from the File Link dialog box, a list of tables contained within the selected file will be displayed. You can choose to link to one or several tables. Access uses different icons to represent linked tables and tables that are stored within the current database. The icon for a linked file contains an arrow pointing to the right. If you delete the icon for a linked table, you delete the link to the table, not the external table itself.

Managing these links can be somewhat tedious, especially if you have many tables and more than one data file. You are not limited to one data source, so tables could come from several different sources. You may also sometimes lose the links if the data source you are linked to is not available. Some causes for this include the following:

- The external data source has moved.
- The server where the external data source is located is down.
- The network is down.
- The user does not have the permissions necessary to access the external data source.
- Share names have changed.

When any of the previous actions occur, you should probably refresh your links. In addition, it is common to want to relink to different data files. This could happen if you have a different set of data files for multiple companies or different projects. When you want to select a different company, you have to respecify the data source to connect to.

Access Tools

In addition to the Table Link Wizard, Access comes with a Database Splitter and a Linked Table Manager. The Database Splitter provides an easy way to move tables from a single .MDB into a front end/back end set of files.

The Linked Table Manager provides a means to look at the links and refresh or change them. Figure 27-2 shows how the Linked Table Manager is started. You choose Tools ➪ Database Utilities ➪ Linked Table Manager.

The interface for the Linked Table Manager is shown in Figure 27-3. The linked tables are listed along with their data sources. You can choose which tables to update and whether to change the location of the linked table.

The Linked Table Manager is adequate for some applications, but it has limitations. With some programming, you can create a robust attachment manager with a lot more features than the Linked Table Manager. This includes making it more suitable for use in a turnkey-type application. We will continue in this session developing a more powerful Attachment Manager.

**20 Min.
To Go**

Figure 27-2
Starting the Linked Table Manager

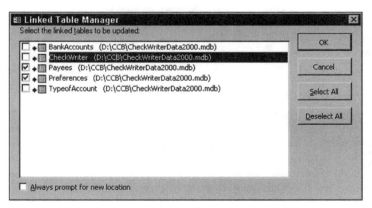

Figure 27-3
The Linked Table Manager interface

Programming Concepts

Working with linked tables requires that VBA code use two different ADO object models:

- ActiveX Data Objects 2.1 (ADODB)
- ADO Extensions 2.1 for DDL and Security (ADOX)

ADODB lets you work with recordsets but not Access table definitions. That is why you also need ADOX to manipulate the table structures. The models perform a variety of other functions as well, but we will concentrate only on those functions needed to work with linked tables.

To use ADOX with your application, you need to establish a reference to the ADOX type library in addition to the ADODB library — which you already should have established since Access 2000 defaults to this library. The description of the ADOX library is "Microsoft ADO Ext. for DDL and Security." The ADOX library file-name is Msadox.dll, and the program ID is ADOX.

You set up references from within the VBA Editor by choosing Tools ➪ References. The resulting dialog box is shown in Figure 27-4.

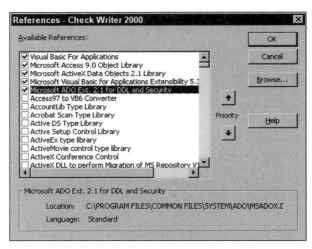

Figure 27-4
The References dialog box

To begin using ADOX for table definitions, the following function can show you the basics. (This function is located in the module Examples in the sample Check

Writer application.) When executed, this function will print in the Immediate window a list of the tables in the current .MDB, along with the table's properties.

To run a function directly in the Visual Basic code window, just move your cursor onto the code within the function and press F5. Note that this does not work in class modules.

Listing 27-1
The ListTableProperties() function

```
'Function prints list of tables and their properties in Immediate window
'using ADOX ActiveX Data Objects
Dim cat As New ADOX.Catalog
Dim tbl As ADOX.Table
Dim i As Integer

    cat.ActiveConnection = CurrentProject.Connection
    For Each tbl In cat.Tables
        Debug.Print tbl.Name; Tab(20), tbl.Type
        For i = 0 To tbl.Properties.Count - 1
        Debug.Print Tab(5); tbl.Properties.Item(i).Name, Tab(50); _
        tbl.Properties.Item(i).Value
        Next
    Next

End Function
```

The ADOX catalog

Referring to the listing for the ListTableProperties function, you first need to define a catalog. A *catalog* contains collections of tables as well as views, users, groups, and procedures. These describe the data source structure or "schema" as it is sometimes referred to.

You create a new ADOX catalog by dimensioning a variable as a New ADOX Catalog, as shown in the statement Dim cat As New ADOX.Catalog.

The catalog has several properties, and the ActiveConnection property must be set to the current project connection. Connections are the means to interface your application to a data source. The statement cat.ActiveConnection= CurrentProject.Connection in the example sets the active connection for the newly created catalog to the connection in the current project. The CurrentProject object has several collections and properties that contain specific objects within the current Access database. In this case, the Connection property returns a reference to the current ActiveX Data Objects (ADO) Connection object and its related properties.

Accessing tables with the catalog

An ADOX catalog contains a Tables collection. Each table in the collection has the following objects: Columns, DateCreated, DateModified, Indexes, Keys, Name, ParentCatalog, Properties, and Type. We are interested in these objects:

- **Name.** The table name.
- **Type.** The type of table. For linked tables, the value for this object is LINK.
- **Properties.** A collection of properties for the table.

The Table Properties collection

For each table in the Tables collection there is a Table Properties collection. Some of these properties relate to providers. ADO accesses data and services from OLE DB providers. For Access, this is the Jet OLDDB provider, so the properties will be a function of this provider.

These properties consist of the following:

- Temporary Table
- Jet OLEDB:Table Validation Text
- Jet OLEDB:Table Validation Rule
- Jet OLEDB:Cache Link Name/Password
- Jet OLEDB:Remote Table Name
- Jet OLEDB:Link Provider String
- Jet OLEDB:Link Datasource
- Jet OLEDB:Exclusive Link
- Jet OLEDB:Create Link
- Jet OLEDB:Table Hidden In Access

When you execute the function in Listing 27-1, you will see a list of tables within the database along with the properties just shown. The basic ones we are interested in as they pertain to linked tables are these:

- Jet OLEDB:Remote Table Name. Contains the name of the table in the remote datasource.
- Jet OLEDB:Link Provider String. A string describing the provider. For Access, this is a blank string.

For Excel, it looks something like `Excel 5.0;HDR=YES;IMEX=2;`
For dBASE, it looks similar to `dBase 5.0;HDR=NO;IMEX=2;`
Each different provider has different formats and parameters. You can include user IDs and passwords in this string as well.

- `Jet OLEDB:Link Datasource`. The path and filename of the external data source.

Linked tables

As you have seen, you can list the tables in a database as well as refer to the linked tables and their properties. You can also change the link's data source. This is the focus of this section since you will often need to reconnect to a data source in another folder, drive, server, or even network domain.

To accomplish this, you actually delete the linked table from the catalog and define a new link. This involves learning a few ADOX methods.

To delete a table, you first need to create a new catalog as you did in the previous section. Then set the connection for that active catalog to the current project connection. Next, execute a `Delete Table` method supplying the name of the table to be deleted and finally, refresh the `Tables` collection. The following code accomplishes all this:

```
Dim cat As New ADOX.Catalog
cat.ActiveConnection = CurrentProject.Connection
cat.Tables.Delete strNameOfTableToBeDeleted
cat.Tables.Refresh
```

With the table removed from the catalog and the Access .MDB, you need to add a new linked table with the same name but connected to a different data source. You set up this operation by dimensioning a new catalog variable, and also dimensioning a new ADOX table variable.

1. For the newly created catalog, set its active connection to the current project connection.
2. Define the new table's parent catalog as the newly created catalog.
3. Name the table and set its properties. These properties include the data source, remote table name, and provider string. If you are reconnecting a previously deleted table, you should temporarily store the values of these properties from the old table so they can be used for the new table.
4. Now set the property `Jet OLEDB:Create Link` to True. This will establish a link when the table is appended to the table's collection.

5. Append the new table to the `Tables` collections. All these operations are
performed in the code in Listing 27-3.

Listing 27-2
Code to link a new table

```
Dim cat As New ADOX.Catalog
Dim tbl As New ADOX.Table

cat.ActiveConnection = CurrentProject.Connection
Set tbl.ParentCatalog = cat
tbl.Name = strTableName
tbl.Properties("Jet OLEDB:Link DataSource") = strDataSource
tbl.Properties("Jet OLEDB:Remote Table Name") = strRemoteTable
tbl.Properties("Jet OLEDB:Link Provider String") = strProvider
tbl.Properties("Jet OLEDB:Create Link") = True
cat.Tables.Append tbl
Set tbl = Nothing
```

If the table that you are connecting to is a Microsoft Access table, you do not have to set the property `Jet OLEDB:Link Provider String.`

The Attachment Manager

In this section, we will create a form that will provide the general functionality
needed in our Check Writer application. The form will be called the "Attachment
Manager" and will provide the following functionality:

- Work with any number of attached tables connected to a single data source.
- Provide for different data sources (e.g., Access, xBase, Excel, ODBC, etc.).
- Check linked tables when the application starts up. If attachments are
  good, then open the next form in the application. If there are errors with
  the attachments, open up the Attachment Manager form for the user to
  select a new file.
- Provide for a user interface when selected from an application's menu system
  that allows the user to change the file to which the tables are attached.
- Display the currently linked tables and information about them.
- Display errors on a table-by-table basis when they cannot be linked.

The form design

The "Attachment Manager" form will be a single form (no subforms) and will rely on only one external function that is used to call the Open File dialog box, which we will cover later on in this session.

You can open the Attachment Manager directly from the database container window as well as from VBA code. When opened from VBA code, if an opening argument string value of "Startup" is passed, then the form will check the currently linked tables to see if there is an error. If not, the form will immediately close so the user doesn't even know what happened. The form will then open the next form for the application. If there is an error with the linked tables, the form will become visible, inform the user of the problem, and provide a means to reconnect to a different file.

When the Attachment Manager is opened without the "Startup" opening argument, the form will display the current status of the tables and provide a dialog box to change the file for the linked tables.

The visual design for this form is based on a main tab control with three tabs. These tabs function as follows (see Figure 27-5):

Tab page 0. List of currently attached tables

Tab page 1. Attach table(s) to file

Tab page 2. List of attached tables and errors

**10 Min.
To Go**

The List of Currently Attached Tables tab contains a list box called ListStatus that lists the currently attached tables along with information about them.

The Attach Table(s) to File tab provides a message to the user as well as an interface to choose a new file.

The List of Attached Tables and Errors tab contains a list box called ErrorList that lists the errors associated with linking the tables.

The code

The list box on the List of Currently Attached Tables tab is filled using a function named FillList. In turn, this function calls the function GetLinkedTables.

> **Refer to the code in the class module of the form**
> AttachmentManagerOneFileII **in the sample application file**
> **Check Writer 2000.mdb.**

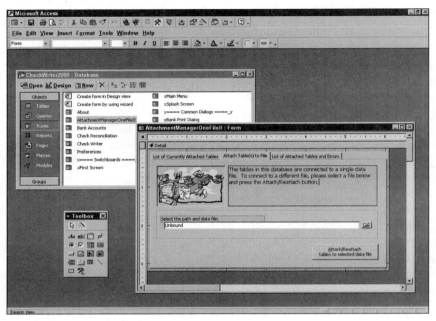

Figure 27-5
Attachment Manager form in Design view

The GetLinkedTables function gets the **ADOX** catalog tables collection information into an array that is used by the form. This form actually uses two arrays:

- LinkedTables. A string array of link information, one entry per table, where:
  LinkedTables(0, x) = Name of table x
  LinkedTables(1, x) = Name of remote table for table x
  LinkedTables(2, x) = Data source for table x
  LinkedTables(3, x) = Type or provider string for table x
  LinkedTables(4, x) = Error message for table x
  LinkedTables(5, x) = New data source for table x

- **LinkedFiles.** A string array of linked files, one entry per file, where:
  LinkedFiles(y) = Data source y

These arrays are public to the functions and subroutines of this form and are used by several of them.

Before the Form Open event even executes, the functions FillList and GetLinkedTables have been executed, the arrays have been initialized, and the list box on page 0 of the tab control has been filled. The processing associated with the form open event is shown in the flowchart in Figure 27-6.

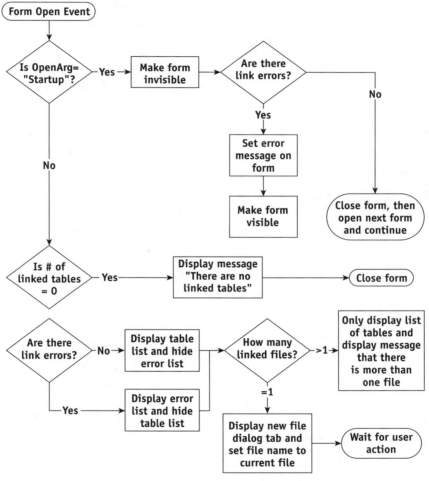

Figure 27-6
Attachment Manager form Open Event processing

Two user buttons are on the form: one to call the File Open dialog box and select a file to attach to, and the second button to actually attach to the data source.

The subroutine `AttachFile1_Click` runs when the user presses the Attach/Reattach button. This function checks for a valid filename and then puts the filename in the array `LinkedTables`, which is used by the function `AttachTable` to link the tables. The `AttachTable` function is called for each table to be linked and returns an error message in the array `LinkedTables` if there is a problem with the link. After the links have been made or attempted to be made, the Boolean variable `LinkErrors` is checked. If a problem exists, the Errors tab is displayed and the list box on that tab is filled with the `FillErrorList` function. If no problem exists, the List of Currently Attached Tables tab is displayed, and the list box is refreshed with the newly attached tables. The user would then simply close the form.

Since the function `AttachTable` does the heart of the work, we have included the listing for that function here. With the prior discussion and examples, you should be able to follow the logic and statements here.

Listing 27-3
The AttachTable function

```
Function AttachTable(strTable As String, strRemoteTable As String, _
    strProvider As String, strDataSource As String) As String
'function attaches table "strTable" to "steRemoteTable" Table in file
'"strDataSource" using "strProvider"

Dim cat As New ADOX.Catalog
Dim tbl As New ADOX.Table

    On Error GoTo ErrorHandler

    cat.ActiveConnection = CurrentProject.Connection
    cat.Tables.Delete strTable
    cat.Tables.Refresh

    Set tbl.ParentCatalog = cat
    tbl.Name = strTable
    tbl.Properties("Jet OLEDB:Link DataSource") = strDataSource
    tbl.Properties("Jet OLEDB:Remote Table Name") = strRemoteTable
    If strProvider <> "Access" Then
        tbl.Properties("Jet OLEDB:Link Provider String") = strProvider
    End If
    tbl.Properties("Jet OLEDB:Create Link") = True
    cat.Tables.Append tbl
    Set tbl = Nothing

    AttachTable = ""

GoTo Done
ErrorHandler:
```

```
    Select Case Err.Number
        Case 3011
            AttachTable = "Could not find the table in " & strDataSource
        Case Else
            AttachTable = Err.Description
    End Select
Done:

End Function
```

There are a few other subroutines in the Attachment Manager form. The `ListStatus_DblClick` subroutine executes when a user double-clicks the table list. This subroutine displays all the information about the table in a message box. A similar function occurs with the `ErrorList_Click` subroutine that runs when the user clicks the error list.

The button near the Filename text box runs a subroutine that displays the Open File dialog box. This is actually handled with the `OpenFile` function located in the module "File Utilities", and the `OpenFile` function calls the API `GetFileInfo` in the Msaccess.exe library. This displays the standard Office 2000 File Open dialog box and after the user chooses a file, it returns the name of the file along with the path.

The last bit of code in the Attachment Manager occurs in the `Form Unload` event. This subroutine runs when the form is closed either programmatically or by the user with the Close window button. No processing is done unless the form was opened with the `Startup` argument. In that case, if link errors still exist, then the user is asked if he or she really wants to exit the application. If the response is Yes, the application will quit; otherwise, the form stays open until no link errors exist.

Operation

To use the Attachment Manager, you must first define your table links within Access as you normally do using the File ⇨ Get External Data ⇨ Link Tables option. With the Attachment Manager, you can then easily change the files that the tables are pointing to, as well as refresh the attachments, and determine which errors if any exist with the attachments.

When you open the Attachment Manager normally, the user will see the Attach Table(s) to File tab and dialog box displaying a message and prompting for a new file. (See Figure 27-7.)

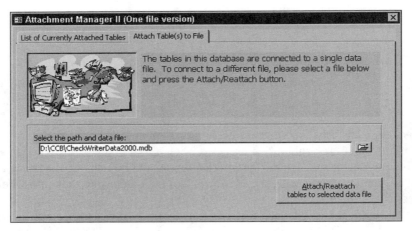

Figure 27-7
The Attachment Manager dialog box

At this point, the user can choose to look at the currently attached files by pressing the List of Currently Attached Tables tab. The linked tables are displayed as shown in Figure 27-8.

Table Name	Remote Table Name	DataSource	Type/Provider String
BankAccounts	BankAccounts	D:\CCB\CheckWriterData2000.mdb	Access
CheckWriter	CheckWriter	D:\CCB\CheckWriterData2000.mdb	Access
Payees	Payees	D:\CCB\CheckWriterData2000.mdb	Access
Preferences	Preferences	D:\CCB\CheckWriterData2000.mdb	Access
TypeofAccount	TypeofAccount	D:\CCB\CheckWriterData2000.mdb	Access

5 attached tables.

Figure 27-8
The List of Currently Attached Tables tab

If more than one file is attached, the only tab that will be displayed is the List of Currently Attached Tables tab, and a message box pops up that says "There is more than one attached file. Cannot process." Double-clicking a particular table in this list will open a message box with more details about the particular table (see Figure 27-9).

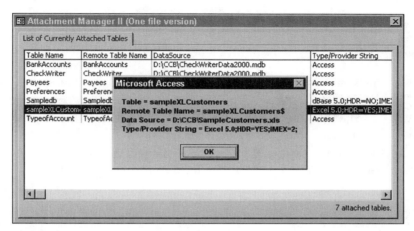

Figure 27-9
Viewing table details

Additional capabilities

Done!

With the Attachment Manager, you have a good starting point for creating a more sophisticated model. Additional features could include the ability to handle more than one attached file, the option to try the current directory automatically if link errors exist, the ability to provide a table-driven system with groups of tables and data sources already stored, and the ability to keep a history of files attached with a name and provide the ability to choose data sources based on the saved name.

REVIEW

In this session, you learned about the front-end and back-end architecture and how the connection between the two are made with attached or linked tables. You also learned how to programmatically manipulate this connection using ADO objects.

- A linked table is a connection to an external data source.
- Linked tables are used for better management of data separate from the front-end application. They can also improve an application's performance.

- ADO programming features for linked tables are based on the ADOX library.
- An ADOX catalog is used to store the table definitions and the link information.

Quiz Yourself

1. What are some of the causes of losing a link to an attached table? (See "Basic Principles.")
2. What are the two ADO object models that allow a programmer to work with linked tables. (See "Programming Concepts.")
3. Which property of the Jet OLEDB provider contains the name of the table in the remote data source? (See "The Table Properties collection.")

Securing Access Databases

Session Checklist

✔ Options for securing an Access database

✔ Share-level security

✔ User-level security

✔ Encryption as a security option

✔ Other considerations for ensuring security

**30 Min.
To Go**

It would be very uncommon to design an application and not be concerned about its security and the data it supports. This session focuses on how to programmatically work with Access security. It is assumed that you have some knowledge of security with Access and also the Access user interface for working with security. If you don't, please refer to Chapter 37 of the Microsoft Access 2000 Bible by Cary N. Prague and Michael R. Irwin published by IDG Books.

An .MDB file on the CD-ROM called Security.MDB contains sample code from this session.

Security Options

Access gives you several options for securing a database. These include some simple options and some more complicated ones. Which option you implement is a function of what your application is, how it is designed, who the users are that will be using the application, where the data is stored, and how complex you want to make it.

You must also consider security from two aspects: the program and the data. Some methods protect the data, while others just protect the program. Table 28-1 summarizes the different methods and the features of each. The table also includes combinations of the methods since you can use more than one method at a time.

Table 28-1
Access Security Methods

Method	Protects Data	Protects Program	Notes
Share level	Good	Good	Gives all users the same password
User level	Better	Better	Can control access user by user
Encryption	Better	Good	Prevents reading data using an external program
.MDE	No	Best	Protects all program code but not data
Share level and encryption	Better	Good	
User level and encryption	Best	Better	
.MDE and encryption	Better	Best	
Share level, encryption, and .MDE	Better	Best	
User level, encryption, and .MDE	Best	Best	Provides the best of both worlds

The next few sections will take each method and describe how to implement it using VBA code.

Share-Level Security

With Access share-level security, the database is secured with a password. To open the database, the user must specify the correct database password. To open a database connection with a password, you need to specify the password in the Open method of the ADO connection, as shown here:

```
Dim cnn As New ADODB.Connection

    cnn.Open "Provider=Microsoft.Jet.OLEDB.4.0;" & _
        "Data Source=C:\nwind.mdb;Jet OLEDB:Database Password=password;"
```

To change a database password, you need to use the JRO object model, not ADOX which is typically used for the Jet database. The Jet and Replication Objects (JRO) object model contains the objects, properties, and methods for creating, modifying, and synchronizing replicas as well as dealing with such things as a database password. Unlike ADO and ADOX, JRO cannot be used with data sources other than Microsoft Jet databases. Changing the password is only possible only when compacting a database. The following listing shows the code needed to change a database password:

```
Dim je As New JRO.JetEngine

    je.CompactDatabase "Data Source=C:\nwind.mdb;", _
        "Data Source=C:\nwind2.mdb;" & _
        "Jet OLEDB:Database Password=newpassword"
```

In the example file Security.MDB, "Database Security Utilities" illustrates the technique for changing a database password based on this listing.

Since you cannot compact a database onto itself, you must compact to a copy of the database. Therefore, you will want to add some code to check to see if the file already exists that you will be compacting to and delete it if it is there. Then, after compacting it, you will want to delete the original database and rename the compacted database to the original name.

User-Level Security

The Access security model consists of workgroups, groups, users, and permissions. The groups and user information is contained within a workgroup file. This file has an .MDW extension. The default filename is System.mdw, but it can be different. Therefore, you can have more than one workgroup file, but only one file can be associated with an application in a given session. Multiple applications can share a single workgroup file as well.

The permission information is stored within the Access database file. This includes assignments of permissions for each object by group or user. Permissions can include from up to eight different types depending on the object being secured. Figure 28-1 shows the User and Group Permissions window, which lists the permissions available.

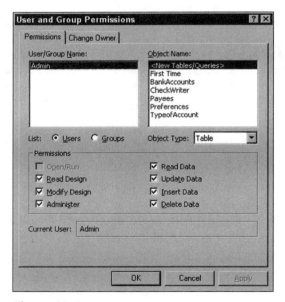

Figure 28-1
The User and Group Permissions window

When designing an application, you may want to provide a different user interface to the security system that provides features, not found in the standard Access security interface. This is particularly true if you distribute your application in the runtime environment since the standard Access security interface is not available. Probably the most common functionality you would need is to have a user change his or her password. In addition, the following list covers the most frequently needed functions to the security system that an administrator handles:

- Change a user password.
- Add a new user.
- Assign a user to a group.
- Remove a user from a group.
- Remove a user.

20 Min. To Go

You can programmatically create groups and assign permissions as well. Since these are not the most commonly needed interfaces and the depth of this session is limited, these functions are not covered here. But with similar techniques as those used in this session, you can provide similar capabilities.

The ADOX security objects

Before starting on the code to perform the common security interfaces, you must understand the security objects with which you will be working. The security objects are contained within the ADOX object model, not the ADO object model. ADOX contains extensions to the ADO model specifically to handle the security information. Figure 28-2 graphically illustrates the model.

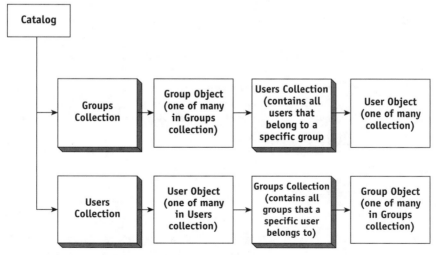

Figure 28-2
The ADOX security object model

Two collections are part of the `Catalog` object: `Groups` and `Users`. These collections, in turn, have an additional collection. The `Groups` collection includes a `Users` collection, and the `Users` collection has a `Groups` collection. This cross-referencing provides the ability to look for users that are part of a group and which groups a user is a member of.

Changing a user password

There are two common functions required for changing a user password: having a user change his/her password and having an administrator change his/her password.

Listing 28-1 shows a function that will prompt the current user for a new password. If successful, the function returns a True value. Otherwise, if there was a problem, the function returns a False value.

Listing 28-1
The Change Current User Password function

```
Public Function ChangeCurrentPassword() As Boolean
Dim cat As ADOX.Catalog
Dim strOldPassword As String
Dim strNewPassword As String

  Set cat = New ADOX.Catalog
  cat.ActiveConnection = CurrentProject.Connection
  strOldPassword = InputBox("Enter your old password", _
  "Password Change for " & CurrentUser())
  strNewPassword = InputBox("Enter your new password", _
  "Password Change for " & CurrentUser())
  If strNewPassword <> InputBox("Reenter your new password", _
  "Password Change for " & CurrentUser()) Then
    MsgBox "Error entering password"
    GoTo Done
  End If
  cat.Users(CurrentUser()).ChangePassword strOldPassword, strNewPassword
  ChangeCurrentPassword = True
  MsgBox "Password successfully changed"
  GoTo Done
ErrorHandler:
  MsgBox Err.Description
  ChangeCurrentPassword = False
Done:
End Function
```

Note that the `CurrentUser()` function is used, which returns the currently active user name. A new ADOX catalog is set first with the current project connection established. The function then prompts the user for the old password, and then twice for the new password. The `ChangePassword` method is then used with the Users collection of the catalog to change the password. If everything completes successfully, the function displays a message saying that the password was successfully changed and then returns a value of True to the calling code. In Listing 28-2, the function is not interactive (no `InputBox` functions), and the passed parameters allow any user password to be changed.

Listing 28-2
the Change User Password function

```
Public Function ChangePassword(strUserName As String, strOldPassword As String,
strNewPassword as string) As Boolean
Dim cat As ADOX.Catalog

  Set cat = New ADOX.Catalog
  cat.ActiveConnection = CurrentProject.Connection
  cat.Users(strUserName).ChangePassword strOldPassword, strNewPassword
  ChangePassword = True
  GoTo Done
ErrorHandler:
  MsgBox Err.Description
  ChangePassword = False
Done:
End Function
```

Adding a new user

The function in Listing 28-3 adds a new user to the workgroup. The required parameters are the user name and the password. The function works by creating a new catalog object and appending the new user name with a password to the Users collection in the catalog. If the function executes without any errors, a value of True is returned; otherwise, a value of False is returned to the calling procedure.

Listing 28-3
The Add User function

```
Public Function AddUser(strUserName As String, strPassword As String) As Boolean
'Adds a new user
Dim cat As ADOX.Catalog

  On Error GoTo ErrorHandler
  Set cat = New ADOX.Catalog
  cat.ActiveConnection = CurrentProject.Connection
  cat.Users.Append strUserName, strPassword
  AddUser = True
```

```
GoTo Done
ErrorHandler:
  MsgBox Err.Description
  AddUser = False
Done:

End Function
```

Assigning a user to a group

To assign a user to an existing group, you need to append the group name to the group's collection of the specific user. Listing 28-4 illustrates how this is done. The function requires two parameters: the user name and the group to which to add the user. If the function executes without any errors, it returns a True value. Otherwise, a False value is returned to the calling procedure.

Listing 28-4
The Assign User to Group function

```
Public Function AssignUserToGroup(strUserName As String, _
strGroupName As String) As Boolean
'Adds a user to an existing group
Dim cat As ADOX.Catalog

  On Error GoTo ErrorHandler
  Set cat = New ADOX.Catalog
  cat.ActiveConnection = CurrentProject.Connection
  cat.Users(strUserName).Groups.Append strGroupName
  AssignUserToGroup = True
GoTo Done
ErrorHandler:
  MsgBox Err.Description
  AssignUserToGroup = False
Done:

End Function
```

Removing a user from a group

Removing a user from a group is similar to adding one: the group name is deleted from the user's group collection. In Listing 28-5, the Delete method is used against the Groups collection for the specified user. If the function executes without any errors, it returns a True value. Otherwise, a False value is returned to the calling procedure.

Listing 28-5
The Remove User from Group function

```
Public Function RemoveUserFromGroup(strUserName As String, strGroupName As
String) As Boolean
'Removes a user from an existing group
Dim cat As ADOX.Catalog

  On Error GoTo ErrorHandler
  Set cat = New ADOX.Catalog
  cat.ActiveConnection = CurrentProject.Connection
  cat.Users(strUserName).Groups.Delete strGroupName
  RemoveUserFromGroup = True
GoTo Done
ErrorHandler:
  MsgBox Err.Description
  RemoveUserFromGroup = False
Done:

End Function
```

Listing 28-6 shows how you would remove a user from the workgroup. This function receives as a parameter the user name to be removed. As with the previous functions, a new catalog object is created with a connection to the current project. By using the `Delete` method for the `Users` collection, a user can be removed. If the function executes without any errors, it returns a True value. Otherwise, a False value is returned to the calling procedure.

Listing 28-6
The Remove User function

```
Public Function RemoveUser(strUserName As String) As Boolean
Dim cat As ADOX.Catalog

  On Error GoTo ErrorHandler
  Set cat = New ADOX.Catalog
  cat.ActiveConnection = CurrentProject.Connection
  cat.Users.Delete strUserName
  RemoveUser = True
GoTo Done
ErrorHandler:
  MsgBox Err.Description
  RemoveUser = False
Done:

End Function
```

Opening a secured database

With security enabled on a database, opening the database using an ADODB connection method requires an ID and password parameter to be passed:

```
Dim cnn As New ADODB.Connection

    cnn.Provider = "Microsoft.Jet.OLEDB.4.0"
    cnn.Properties("Jet OLEDB:System database") = "c:\system.mdw"
    cnn.Open "Data Source=c:\northwind.mdb;User Id=Admin;Password=password;"
```

**10 Min.
To Go**

A Microsoft Jet provider-specific connection property, Jet OLEDB:System database, specifies the workgroup file. Before you can reference provider-specific properties from the Properties collection, you must define which provider you are using. Therefore, the provider is specified first, and then the property for the workgroup file can be specified. Finally, the connection can be opened with the data source, the user ID, and the password.

Encryption

Despite everything that is accomplished with share-level or user-level security, someone can still open an .MDB file with a text editor and read the contents of a file as a series of ASCII characters. This may not mean a lot for code, but for sensitive data, this could be a problem. To overcome this security breech, Access provides for encryption. Encrypting a database compacts the file and makes it indecipherable by any program like a utility program or word processor.

You perform encryption using the JRO compact database method:

```
Dim je As New JRO.JetEngine

    je.CompactDatabase "Provider=Microsoft.Jet.OLEDB.4.0;" & _
        "Data Source=C:\nwind.mdb", _
        "Provider=Microsoft.Jet.OLEDB.4.0;" & _
        "Data Source=C:\nwind2.mdb;" & _
        "Jet OLEDB:Encrypt Database=True"
```

Always back up your files before you do any major file conversion like encrypting or converting to an .MDE.

The encryption method creates a compacted copy of the original database. You will need to add code to check for the existence of a file by the same name. You will also need to add code to rename the file to the original name after it has been encrypted.

.MDE

An option for protecting your application code is to distribute the program as an .MDE file. As discussed in Session 23, an .MDE file is a copy of an .MDB file with all source code removed and only compiled code included. This obviously protects the code since source code is not available. This prevents anyone from going into an object's Design view. It doesn't protect any data, the opening of an object, or the execution of any code. Therefore, it is limited as a security option, but it is important.

 Refer to Session 23 for more information about the .MDE file.

Other Considerations

Beyond specific security features built into Microsoft Access, there are other items that must be considered to be certain that an application and its data are secure. These include such things as file security, hiding the database objects from the user, and disabling various keys that provide access to areas where the user should not go.

File security

With all the security features discussed so far, unless you have operating system protection for your files, someone with access to a database file can simply use Windows to copy, move, replace, or delete files. It is imperative that you consider a method to protect the database application and data using operating system security. Windows 95/98 don't have much security available. Consider Windows NT or Windows 2000 to handle the security that you really need. Discussing the details of a security approach using Windows is outside the scope of this book, but there are many references on the market that can steer you in the right direction. One such reference is *Windows 2000 Server Security for Dummies* (ISBN 0-7645-0470-3), published by IDG Books Worldwide.

Hiding the database window

A good method for maintaining control of the application and data from within Access is to hide the database window. You can do this by selecting Startup Options from the Tools pull-down menu. Figure 28-3 shows the dialog box used to set this option. The option is `Show Database Window`. When unchecked, the database window is hidden. When hidden, the users cannot access the objects. Of course, there are ways to redisplay the database window. The methods to redisplay the database window and the ways to prevent them are discussed in the following two sections.

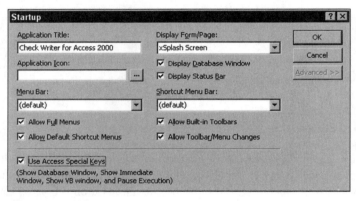

Figure 28-3
The Start-Up Options dialog box

`Startup Show DBWindow` is a property of the database object. To set this property in code, you would execute the code in Listing 28-7. The code in this listing uses an error condition to detect whether the property exists or not. On the line following the "On Error resume next" statement, the property is set to False, but if the property does not exist, an error 3270 occurs. If this is detected, then the property is added with the appropriate value of False.

Listing 28-7
Setting the StartupShowDBWindow property

```
*Dim db As Object
Dim prp As Property

 Set db = CurrentDb
 On Error resume next
```

```
db.Properties("StartupShowDBWindow") = False
If err.Number = 3270 then 'Property not found
  Set prp = db.CreateProperty("StartupShowDBWindow",1, False)
  db.Properties.Append prp
Endif
```

The sample form "Database Security Startup Properties" in the example Security.MDB file illustrates the technique for changing the database properties based on Listings 28-7, 28-8, and 28-9.

Disabling the Bypass key

When a database application is first loaded, execution immediately starts with the command-line argument /x *macro*, the AutoExec macro, and/or the Startup Form set with the database properties. Holding down the Shift key when starting an application will bypass these actions. Doing this could violate security and provide access to objects in your application that you do not want your users to have. Therefore, setting the Allow Bypass Key property to False can prevent the Shift key from stopping the execution of these items. To disable the Bypass Key, you need to set the corresponding database property AllowBypassKey to False. Listing 28-8 shows you how to do this. The error handling in this listing is similar to that described in the Listing 28-7.

Listing 28-8
Setting the AllowBypassKey property

```
Dim db As Object
Dim prp As Property

  Set db = CurrentDb
  On Error resume next
  db.Properties("AllowBypassKey") = False
  If err.Number = 3270 then 'Property not found
    Set prp = db.CreateProperty("AllowBypassKey",1, False)
    db.Properties.Append prp
  Endif
```

Disabling special keys

You can use the AllowSpecialKeys property to prevent the user from gaining access to areas of the application that could violate security. Special keys are listed in the following table. The code to disable the Special Keys is shown in

Listing 28-9. In this code, the property `AllowSpecialKeys` is set or added if it is not there, in a similar fashion to the previous two listings.

Special Key Combination	Action
Alt + F1 (F11)	Displays the database window
Ctrl + F11	Toggles between the custom menu bar and the built-in menu bar
Ctrl + Break	Breaks code execution
Ctrl + G	Displays the immediate window

Listing 28-9
Setting the AllowSpecialKeys property

Done!

```
Dim db As Object
Dim prp As Property

  Set db = CurrentDb
  On Error resume next
  db.Properties("AllowSpecialKeys") = False
  If err.Number = 3270 then 'Property not found
    Set prp = db.CreateProperty("AllowSpecialKeys",1, False)
    db.Properties.Append prp
  Endif
```

All options are sensitive to order, later ones overriding earlier ones.

REVIEW

In this session you learned about the importance of security. The various options for protecting the application and data were discussed. In addition, material and examples were presented that showed you how to programmatically work with Access security.

- Several security options are available, each with its advantages based on the type of application you have, how it is designed, who the users are, and how the data is stored.

- Security options exist to protect the program and the data.
- With Access share-level security, the database is secured with a password that all users use.
- The ADOX object provides the extensions to handle user-level security, while the JRO object provides the methods to handle share-level security.
- Encrypting a database protects the data from being read by a program outside of Access.
- .MDE files primarily protect the program code.
- Other security considerations should be addressed by a developer. These include file security from an operating system perspective, hiding the database window, disabling the bypass key, and disabling other keys that could violate security.

Quiz Yourself

1. What is the best security method to protect data? (See "Security Options.")

2. What is the best security method to protect both the data and the program? (See "Security Options.")

3. In which file are the security permissions stored? (See "User-Level Security.")

4. The Groups and Users collections are part of which object? (See "The ADOX security objects.")

5. What additional precautions should you take beyond using Access security to secure an application? (See "Other Considerations.")

Access and Client/Server

Session Checklist

✔ Understanding client/server architecture

✔ Understanding Microsoft Data Engine (MSDE)

✔ Choosing the right database engine

✔ Working with Access and SQL Server databases

✔ Upsizing an Access database to SQL Server

**30 Min.
To Go**

When you design a database application, you need to understand the needs of the users' current and future environments. An application needs to be flexible enough to easily accommodate users' expanding needs. Access databases can accommodate most small-workgroup environments. However, for environments with large numbers of users or where large volumes of data are processed, you need a true client/server database engine.

Understanding Client/Server Architecture

In a client/server computing environment, two or more network workstations can share a centrally located data source. An application is split into two components: the front end (client component) and the back end (server component). The client component is usually installed on the user's workstation and includes the user-interface functions like switchboards, forms, and reports. The server component is usually located on a network server and stores only the database data. The server database performs functions that are invisible to the user like delivering data to the client to display on a form or report, receiving updated data from the client, and restricting access to its data through database security.

You have already taken steps toward a client/server architecture by using linked Access tables for your application. However, the Access database environment is not a true client/server architecture. Jet, the database engine for Access databases, is called a file server database engine. File server database engines merely move data back and forth between the client and the server. Running an Access query requires Jet to send all of the data for the tables used in the query to the client workstation. The client workstation must then process the query to produce the result.

True client/server database engines do more than simply move data. When you run a query or stored procedure against a client/server database, the server processes the query or stored procedure. The server then simply sends the result to the client. In addition to minimizing traffic on the network, this strategy also makes more efficient use of the client's and the server's processors.

Microsoft Data Engine (MSDE) is a client/server database engine that is included with Access 2000. It is a scaled-down version of Microsoft SQL Server 7.0, optimized to run on the desktop or in a small network environment.

Understanding Microsoft Data Engine

MSDE is a good solution if you are creating an application for a workgroup that consists of a few users today, but it is likely to grow to hundreds or even thousands of users. MSDE is designed using the same database engine as SQL Server 7.0. Databases you build in it are directly portable to SQL Server 7.0.While MSDE is 100 percent compatible with SQL Server 7.0, it does not include all of the SQL Server features.

MSDE runs under Windows 95 or later and Windows NT 4.0 or later. Therefore, you can install MSDE either on a network server, or even on your local workstation. MSDE gives you all the power of SQL Server 7.0 like transaction logging, database recovery, database security, and true client/server-distributed processing right on the desktop.

If the target workgroup for your application includes many users or heavy transaction volumes, you should use SQL Server 7.0 as your database engine instead of MSDE. While MSDE has no limit on the number of simultaneous users, it is optimized for five users. Other limitations include a 2GB database size limit, ability to use up to only two processors, and inability to support all database replication features.

This is one of the primary reasons to use MSDE; however, the developer does not have to be connected to SQL Server 7.0 to develop the application. Both the front end and the database can be developed using Access and MSDE. The back-end database can be easily transferred to SQL Server for user testing and ultimately, for implementation.

Deciding between Jet and MSDE

Since MSDE provides so much power and scalability, it might be tempting to use it with all of your applications. But, as is often the case, with maximum flexibility comes higher complexity. Installing MSDE and maintaining MSDE databases is a lot more complicated than maintaining Jet databases. With Jet databases, once Access is installed, you simply need to install the application's database — Jet is automatically included in Access.

You need to analyze the business environment of the intended workgroup environment before you choose the database for your application. Does the business environment include skilled staff who are capable of maintaining a server database like MSDE? How much memory and disk space do the workstations and server have? Does the application require a solid security system to protect sensitive data? Will there be a large number of users or high volumes of data?

Creating and maintaining an MSDE database is more complicated than creating a Jet database. While MSDE has automatic features for dynamically reconfiguring and recovering from errors, larger databases usually require configuration by a database administrator. On the other hand, damaged Jet databases often cannot be repaired.

While security is optional with Jet databases, MSDE requires database security similar to Windows NT security. Your application will need someone skilled enough to be able to set up user IDs and passwords.

The minimum hardware configuration to run MSDE is a Pentium 166 with 32MB of RAM. Most workstations in the business world today probably easily meet these requirements. If you find that the organization's equipment is closer to the minimum requirements, however, keep in mind that a Jet database generally requires less memory and hard disk space than the same database developed in MSDE.

Determining the number of potential users and the volume of transactions for an application can be unpredictable in some situations. If there will be only a few users and relatively low volumes of data for at least the near future, Jet may be the best solution for the sake of simplicity.

Access includes the Upsizing Wizard to automatically import a Jet database into MSDE.

**20 Min.
To Go**

Using MSDE

Before you can work with an MSDE database, you need to start SQL Server Service Manager. It manages the connections between applications and MSDE databases.

Starting SQL Server Service Manager

To start SQL Server Service Manager, choose Service Manager from the MSDE folder in your Start menu. SQL Server Service Manager displays, as shown in Figure 29-1.

MSDE is not installed automatically when you install Office 2000. You can install it manually from the Office 2000 CD-ROM. See the Office 2000 documentation for information on how to perform the installation.

Figure 29-1
Starting SQL Server Service Manager

To connect to an MSDE database, select MSSQLServer for Services. Then click the Start/Continue button to disable it. When the MSSQLServer service has started, a green arrow displays next to the server in SQL Server Service Manager, and the Pause and Stop buttons become enabled. Figure 29-2 shows the SQL Server Service Manager with MSSQLServer running.

MSSQLServer will start each time you boot up the computer if you select the option Auto-Start service when OS starts.

Figure 29-2
Running the MSSQLServer service

With SQL Server Service Manager running, you can create and connect to MSDE databases. To create an MSDE database from Access, you must first create an Access project.

Understanding projects

You can use an Access project to create and maintain an MSDE database. You can also use an Access project to create the user-interface objects — forms, reports, data access pages, macros, and modules — that get their data from MSDE. The database window for a project looks very similar to the Access database window you are already accustomed to. In fact, creating the user-interface objects is virtually the same as creating them in Access. Figure 29-3 shows the database window for a new project.

Even though you can create the data objects — tables, views, and stored procedures — in a project, the data objects are actually being stored in a separate MSDE database (.MDF) file. The MSDE file is created automatically when you create a new project.

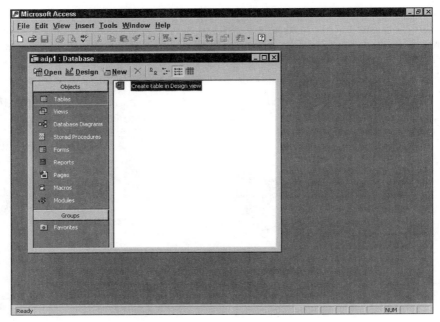

Figure 29-3
Viewing the database window for a project

Views and stored procedures are comparable to Access queries. Views are select queries. Stored procedures are action or parameter queries. Database diagrams are just like relationships in an Access database.

Creating a project

To create an Access project, follow these steps.

1. Start Microsoft Access. Select File ➪ New from the Access menu. The New dialog box displays, as shown in Figure 29-4.

2. Select the Project (New Database) icon and then click the OK button. The File New Database dialog box displays, as shown in Figure 29-5.

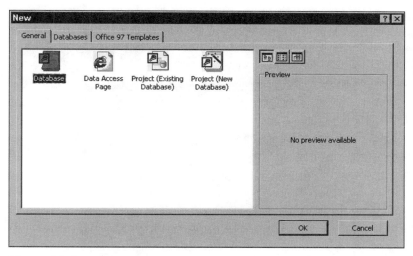

Figure 29-4
The New dialog box

Figure 29-5
The File New Database dialog box

3. Choose a folder for the new project and enter **MyCSProject** for the file-name. Then click the Create button. The Microsoft SQL Server Database Wizard displays, as shown in Figure 29-6.

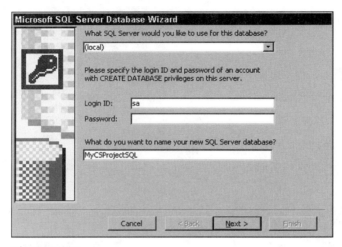

Figure 29-6
The Microsoft SQL Server Database Wizard

4. Enter **(local)** for the server name. Type **sa** for the Login ID. Enter **MyCSProjectSQL** for the database name. Then click the Next button. The final wizard screen displays, as shown in Figure 29-7.

You use (local) when creating an MSDE database on a desktop computer. If you want to create the database on a server on your network, select the server name from the list.

5. Click the Finish button. The Microsoft SQL Server Database Wizard creates the new MSDE database and the new Access project. The Database window for the new project displays.

Creating the new MSDE database and new Access project can take several minutes.

Figure 29-7
The final Microsoft SQL Server Database Wizard screen

Working with data objects in a project is a little different than working with tables and queries in an Access database. But using the project data design tools is really just as easy as creating tables and queries in Access once you get the hang of it.

Creating a table

Creating a table in an Access project is just like creating a table in an Access database. To create a new table, follow these steps.

1. Select the Tables object in the Database container. Then select the "Create table in Design view" item in the Tables object window. The Choose Name dialog box displays.

2. Enter **MyTable** for the new table name. Then click the OK button. The Design view for the new table displays.

Figure 29-8 shows the Design view for the BankAccounts table.

The Design view of an MSDE table displays in a spreadsheet-style format. The first two columns are just like the Access database table design window. The Column Name column is where you enter the names of the fields for the table. The second column contains the datatype for each field. The remaining properties that you can define for each field, or column name, display in the columns to the right of the Datatype column.

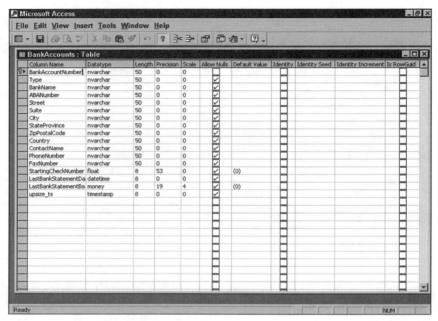

Figure 29-8
The Design view of an MSDE table

Creating a view

Views are like queries in an Access database. You work with views in the View Designer, which works very much like the Access Query Design window. They are used for retrieving rows of data from one or more tables. You can use a view as the record source for a form or as the row source for a combo box. To create a view, follow these steps.

1. Select the Views object. Then select "Create view in designer" in the Views object window. The View Designer opens.

2. To add a table to the View Designer, right-click in the View Designer window. Then select Show Table from the shortcut menu. The Show Table window displays. Expand the Tables item and drag a table to the View Designer window.

3. You can select columns and enter criteria the same way you design queries in an Access database.

Figure 29-9 shows the BankAccountList View in the View Designer. You use the Grid pane (lower section) of the View designer just like the Grid pane of an Access query. However, the rows and columns of the view are pivoted — that is, the column names included in the query are listed as rows in the Grid pane. The table name and criteria for each column are displayed as columns across from each of the column names.

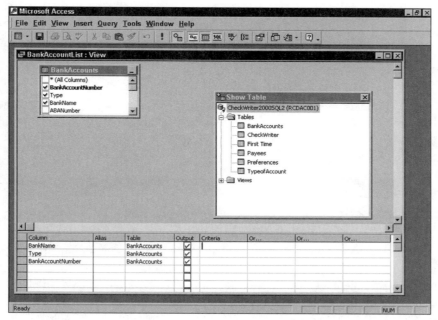

Figure 29-9
Working in the View designer

You cannot use a view to perform Access query actions such as UPDATE, INSERT, or APPEND. Views also cannot receive parameters. You must create a stored procedure for these types of queries.

Creating a stored procedure

A stored procedure is a special type of query that allows you to use commands that update data in the database. Creating a stored procedure is more like writing a VBA procedure than like creating a view or a query. To create a stored procedure, first select the stored procedure's object. Then select "Create procedure in designer." The Stored Procedure design window displays, as shown in Figure 29-10.

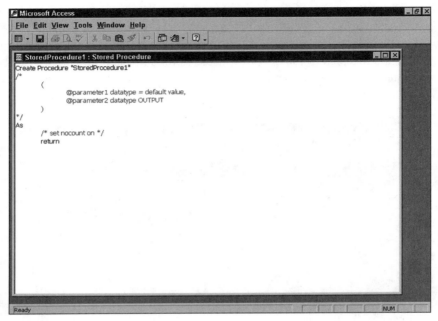

Figure 29-10
Creating a new stored procedure

When the procedure designer opens, it displays a procedure template for the new procedure. The template code is color-coded to assist you in completing the required statements. Commands display in blue text, variable names in black, and comments (indicated between the /* and */ delimiters) in green. As you write the code for your new procedure, you simply replace the supplied variable names with ones that make sense for your procedure. Also replace the commented sections with the code that performs the database update commands.

Figure 29-11 shows the Checks Issued Report stored procedure.

The Checks Issued Report stored procedure receives two datetime parameters: begindate and enddate. The "code" in this procedure is a simple SELECT statement that selects all of the fields from the Check Writer table for the date range specified by the parameters.

Creating the tables, views, and stored procedures for a new SQL Server database can be a time-consuming job. If you are moving an existing Access database to MSDE or SQL Server, you do not have to start from scratch. The Microsoft Access Upsizing Wizard will do most of the work for you.

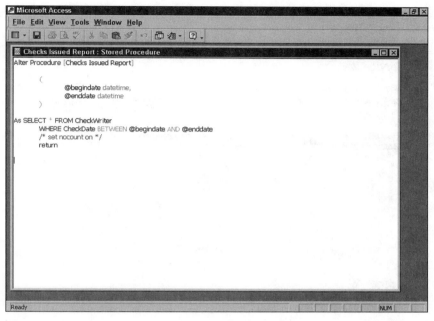

Figure 29-11
Working with stored procedures

Upsizing to MSDE

**10 Min.
To Go**

You can convert an existing Microsoft Access database (.MDB) to a SQL Server database automatically using the Microsoft Access Upsizing Wizard. The Upsizing Wizard creates a new SQL Server database and imports all of the Access database tables. It will import the table structures, indexes, validation rules, defaults, autonumbers, relationships, and — of course — the data, too. At the same time, it will fine-tune the new database structures to take advantage of SQL Server functionality wherever possible. You can also convert the Access application's forms, reports, macros, and modules into a new Microsoft Access project.

Before upsizing, make a backup copy of your Access database.

The following example upsizes the CheckWriter2000 database. To upsize an Access database, follow these steps.

1. Open the Access database that you want to convert. Start SQL Server Service Manager.

2. Select Tools ⇨ Database Utilities ⇨ Upsizing Wizard from the Access menu. The first screen of the Upsizing Wizard displays, as shown in Figure 29-12.

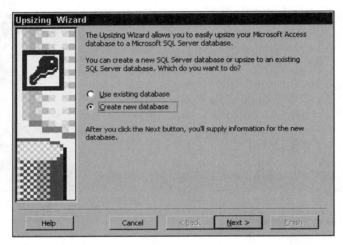

Figure 29-12
The Upsizing Wizard

3. Choose the Create new database option. Then click the Next button. The second Upsizing Wizard screen displays, as shown in Figure 29-13.

4. You use this screen to define the connection information for the new SQL Server database. Type **(local)** as the location for the new SQL Server database. Type **sa** for the Login ID. Type **CheckWriter2000SQL** for the name of the new database. Then click the Next button.

5. Use the next screen, as shown in Figure 29-14, to select the tables to include in the new database. Click the >> button to select all of the tables in the Available Tables list. Then click the Next button.

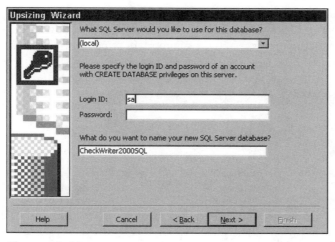

Figure 29-13
Setting up the new SQL Server database

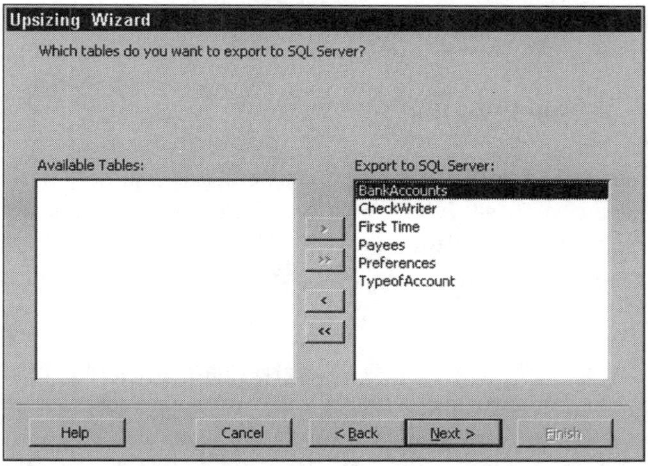

Figure 29-14
Selecting the tables for the new SQL Server database

6. On this screen shown in Figure 29-15, you can take advantage of many SQL Server features such as indexes, validation rules, defaults, relationships, and timestamp fields. Make the appropriate selections. Then click Next to continue.

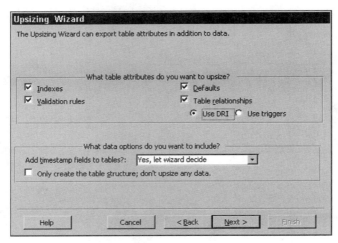

Figure 29-15
Taking advantage of SQL Server features

7. Figure 29-16 shows the screen for creating the new Access project to use with the SQL Server database. Type the path and filename for the new project. Then click the Next button.

8. Click the Finish button on the final Upsizing Wizard screen, shown in Figure 29-17.

It takes several minutes to create the new SQL Server database and Access project. A message box with a progress meter tracks the conversion process while you wait.

When the conversion process is complete, the Upsizing Wizard displays the Upsizing Wizard Report. An example of the report is shown in Figure 29-18. It includes information about how the Access database and application were converted and information about any errors that were encountered.

You can close the Upsizing Wizard Report window when you have finished reviewing it. Then the Upsizing Wizard will automatically load the new Access project.

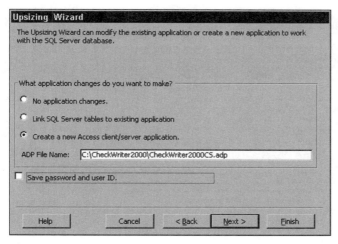

Figure 29-16
Creating the Access project

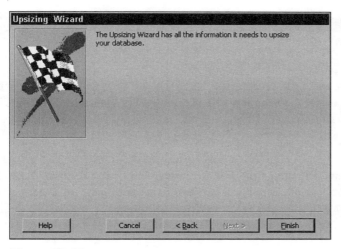

Figure 29-17
The final Upsizing Wizard screen

You can view the Upsizing Wizard Report later. The filename is
the name of your Access application filename with the extension
.SNP (for example, CheckWriter2000.snp).

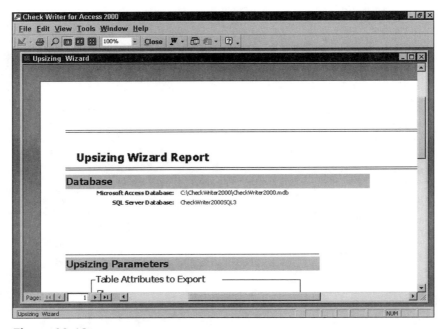

Figure 29-18
Viewing the Upsizing Wizard Report

Done!

When the new project displays, review all of the new objects that the Upsizing Wizard created. You may find, however, that some of the Access queries did not upsize. See the Upsizing Wizard Report for information on the errors that were encountered. You will have to manually create either a view or stored procedure for these.

The CD includes the SQL Server version of the CheckWriter2000 application, which was upsized using the Upsizing Wizard. The project filename is CheckWriter2000.adp.

REVIEW

Using Access and MSDE, you can implement true client/server database applications. MSDE provides virtually all of the functionality and power of SQL Server, yet you can run it on a desktop workstation. This session covered the following topics:

- Client/server databases process queries on the server and send only the result to the application.
- MSDE and SQL Server are examples of true client/server database engines.
- MSDE is a scaled-down version of SQL Server that can run on a desktop computer or on a network server.
- Jet is a file/server database engine that is sufficient for use in smaller, low-volume databases.
- SQL Server views and stored procedures are similar to Access queries.
- Access projects are used to work with MSDE databases.
- The Upsizing Wizard automatically converts an Access database to a client/server application.

QUIZ YOURSELF

1. How do file/server databases differ from client/server databases? (See "Understanding Client/Server Architecture.")
2. Which operating systems can run MSDE? (See "Understanding Microsoft Data Engine.")
3. For which environments is Jet the most practical database solution? (See "Deciding between Jet and MSDE.")
4. What is the purpose of SQL Server Service Manager? (See "Using MSDE.")
5. A project's tables, views, and stored procedures are stored in what type of file? (See "Understanding projects.")
6. Which type of object is used to update a database: a view or a stored procedure? (See "Creating a view.")

Working With The Web

Session Checklist

✔ Creating Web documents in Access

✔ Understanding data access pages

✔ Viewing a data access page in Internet Explorer

✔ Working with groups of data

✔ Using the Access Page Wizard

✔ Working in Page Design view

30 Min. To Go

In the last session, you learned how client/server technology makes efficient use of computing resources. Web computing, however, is becoming a major presence in the business environment today. In this session, you will learn how to use the Web as a database server.

Using Access with the Web

It is easy to publish Access data to the Web. You can create an HTML document for any table, query, form, or report by simply opening the object and then selecting

File⇨Export...Save As Type HTML Documents (.htm). When you create an HTML document this way, however, you are creating a static copy of the data — that is, a read-only snapshot of the data as it existed at that point in time. If you want to provide an updateable Web page or one that displays up-to-the-minute information, you can use a data access page.

Understanding Data Access Pages

Data access pages look a lot like an Access form or report. They are a special type of Web page that you can use to display and update data in an Access database or a SQL Server database. Stored in HTML format, you can view them either in Access or in Internet Explorer 5.0 or later.

Data access pages are stored in the Pages object of the Database container, as shown in Figure 30-1.

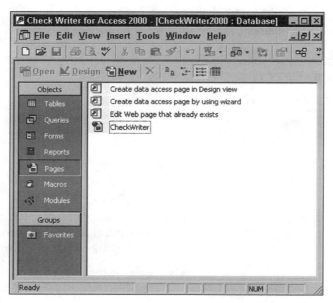

Figure 30-1
The Pages object of the Check Writer database

While you can see a list of the Page objects available in a database, the pages are actually stored in HTML files outside of the database. The names of the pages that you see in the database container are simply pointers to the actual HTML files.

To view a data access page in Access, select the name of the page in the Pages object of the database container. Then click the Open toolbar button. Figure 30-2 illustrates viewing the Check Writer data access page in Access.

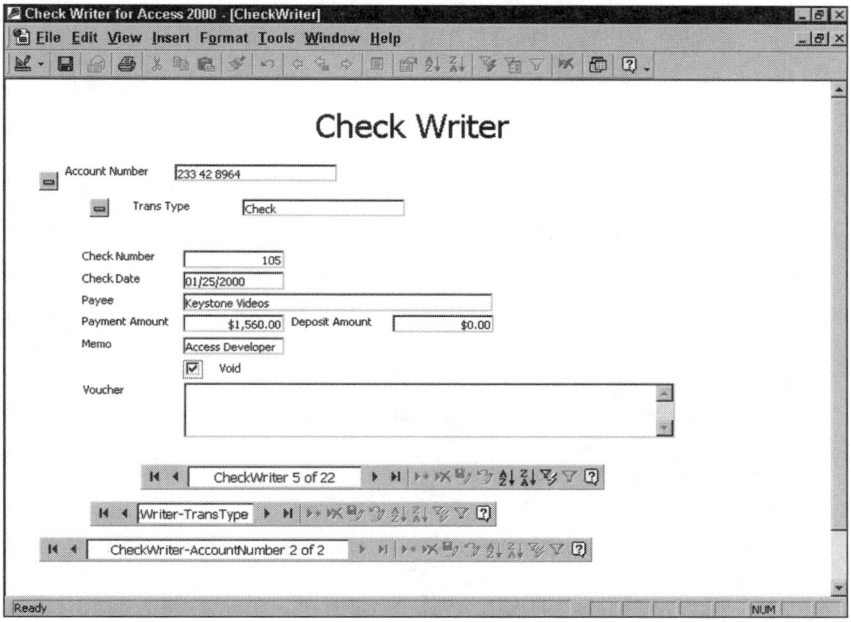

Figure 30-2
Viewing a data access page in Access

Since the data access page is stored as an HTML file, you can view it using Internet Explorer as well. To view the Check Writer data access page in Internet Explorer, simply locate the CheckWriter.htm file in Windows Explorer and open it. The Check Writer data access page (CheckWriter.htm) displays in Internet Explorer, as shown in Figure 30-3.

Even though you need Access to create data access pages, you do not need Access to view or update them. To use data access pages, you need the following:

**20 Min.
To Go**

- Internet Explorer 5.0 or later
- A license for Microsoft Office 2000 or later
- Access to the database that the data access page is linked to. (This could be an Access database or a SQL Server database.)

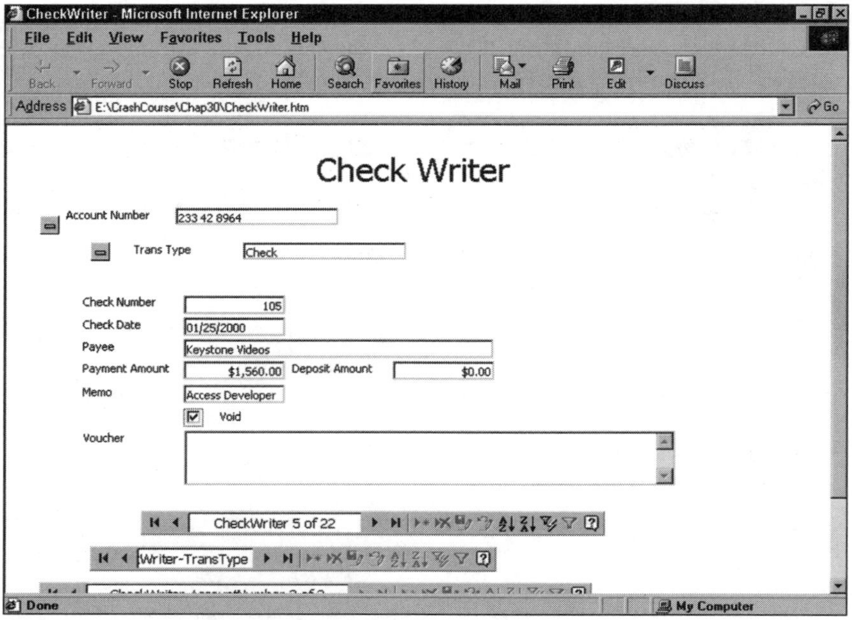

Figure 30-3
Viewing a data access page in Internet Explorer

Working with Data Access Pages

The Check Writer data access page is grouped by bank account number and transaction type. When the page opens, the first bank account number for the Bank Account Number group level displays on the page next to a + button. Figure 30-4 shows how the page looks when it opens.

When you click the + button, it changes to a – button and the Transaction Type grouping displays. The + and – buttons are called expand indicators. You use the *expand indicators* as a toggle to alternately show and hide the detail information for a group.

When the Transaction Type grouping displays, it automatically displays its detail section. The detail section shows the information about the check transaction type, including the check number, check date, payee, amount, etc.

A record navigation toolbar displays at the bottom of each of the sections (bank account number, transaction type, and detail). You can use the Record Navigation toolbar to move from record to record, to sort and filter records, and to get help.

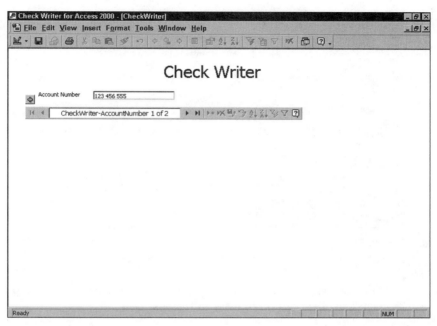

Figure 30-4
Viewing summarized data in a data access page

Each group level can have a different record source. The name of the record source displays on the Record Navigation toolbar.

Creating a data access page

The Page Wizard makes it simple to create a data access page in Access. To create one for the BankAccounts table, follow these steps.

1. Select the Pages object type from the database container.
2. Double-click the "Create data access page by using a wizard" item. The Page Wizard displays.
3. Select the BankAccounts table from the Tables/Queries list. The BankAccounts fields display in the Available Fields list.
4. To select the fields to include, first select a field in the list of available fields, then click the > button. The field displays in the Selected Fields list. As shown in Figure 30-5, select the fields BankAccountNumber, Type, BankName, ABANumber, Street, Suite, City, StateProvince, and ZipPostalCode. Then click the Next button to display the next page.

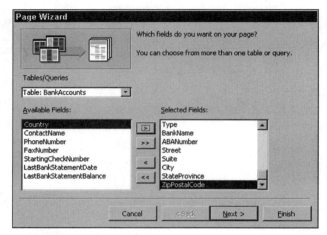

Figure 30-5
Selecting the fields to include on the data access page

5. Double-click the Type field for the grouping level, as shown in Figure 30-6. Then click the Next button to move to the next page.

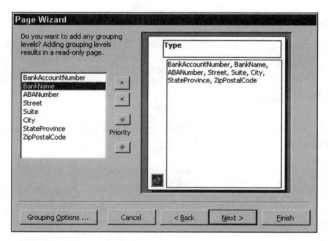

Figure 30-6
Selecting the grouping level for the page

6. Select BankName for the sort order, as shown in Figure 30-7. Then click the Next button to continue.

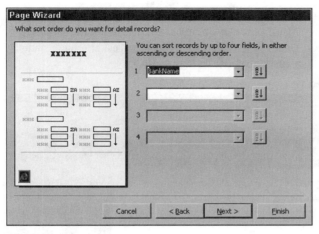

Figure 30-7
Selecting the sort order for the data

7. Type **Bank Account Information** for the page title, as shown in Figure 30-8. Select the Open the page option. Then click the Finish button.

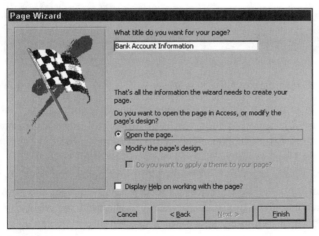

Figure 30-8
Selecting a title for the page

When you click the Finish button, the Page Wizard may take several minutes to complete the page. The wizard processes many steps to create the new Web document for the data access page. When the process completes, the page named Bank Account Information displays, as shown in Figure 30-9.

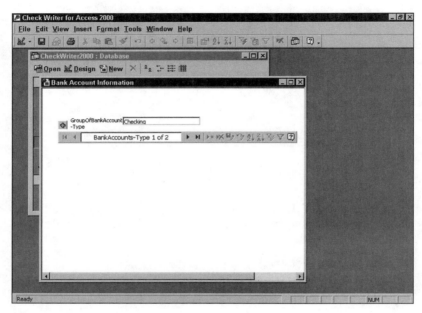

Figure 30-9
The Access Page Wizard displays the new page

The Bank Account Information data access page shows Checking as the first item for the Type group. When you expand the Type group, the detail information for the first Checking-type bank displays. The record navigation toolbar for the bank is disabled because there is only one bank for the Checking type.

The record navigation toolbar for the Type group displays below the detail section's record navigation toolbar. The Type group's record navigation toolbar shows that there is another record in the group. If you move to the next record in the Type group, the Type group heading changes to Savings. When you move to another record in a group, the expand indicator changes to collapsed mode. If you re-expand the Type group, you see the detail information for the Savings type of account.

When you close the new data access page, the Save As Data Access Page dialog box displays. Type **BankAccount.htm** for the filename, as shown in Figure 30-10. Then click the Save button. The new BankAccount data access page is listed on the Pages object tab of the database container.

When you save a data access page, Access creates an HTML document using the filename you specify. This HTML document is the "code" that runs when you display a data access page in Access.

Figure 30-10
Saving a data access page

**10 Min.
To Go**

Modifying a data access page

The Page Wizard gives you a good headstart on creating your first data access page. However, you will probably want to make a few adjustments to the page to create a nice finished product. To modify the BankAccounts data access page, follow these steps.

1. Select the BankAccounts page, then click the Design button on the database container. The Design view of the BankAccounts data access page displays, as shown in Figure 30-11.

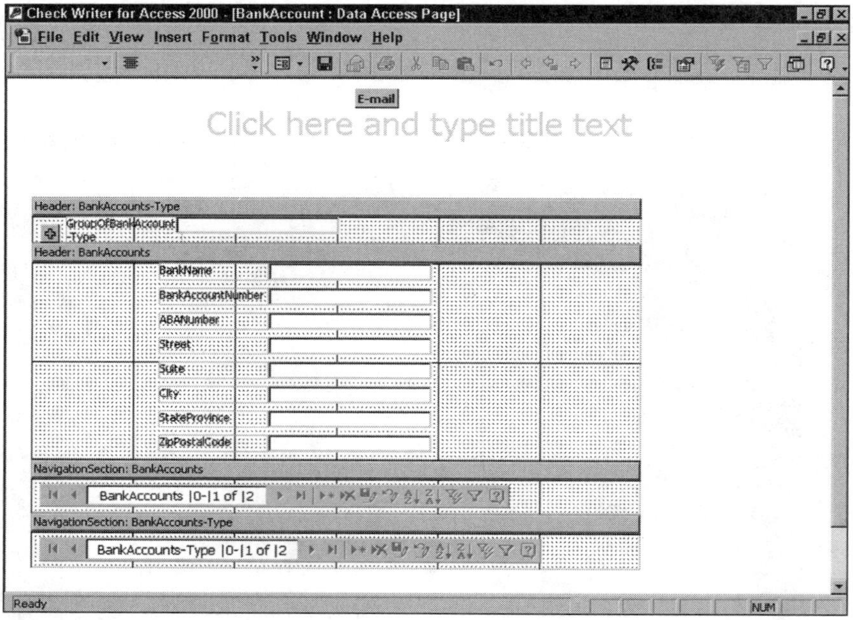

Figure 30-11
The BankAccounts data access page in Design view

2. To create a title for the page, click the section labeled "Click here and type title text." Then type **Bank Accounts** for the title.

3. Widen each of the fields in the BankAccounts detail section and fix up each of the labels.

When the BankAccounts page opens, the Type group displays in unexpanded mode. You can change the Type group to expand automatically when it opens. To modify the default mode of the Type group, follow these steps.

1. Click the Sorting and Grouping button on the Design View toolbar. The Sorting and Grouping dialog box displays, as shown in Figure 30-12.

2. In the Group Record Source area of the dialog box, select the BankAccounts-Type group. In the Group Properties section, set the Expanded By Default property to Yes, then close the Sorting and Grouping dialog box.

3. Your completed page in Design view should look similar to Figure 30-13. You can make any other changes as you see fit.

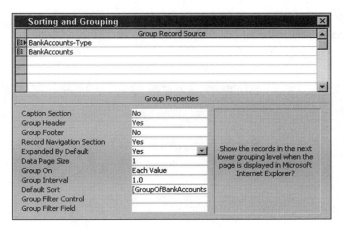

Figure 30-12
Changing the group defaults

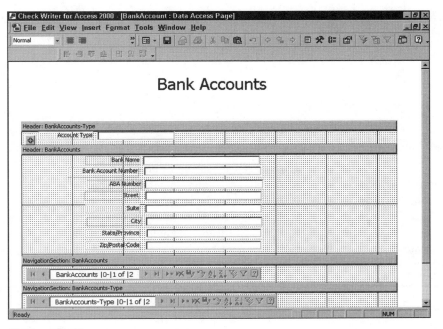

Figure 30-13
Viewing the modifications to the BankAccounts page

4. To view the modified BankAccounts page, close the Design View window. Then click the Open button in the Database container. Figure 30-14 shows the opened BankAccounts page.

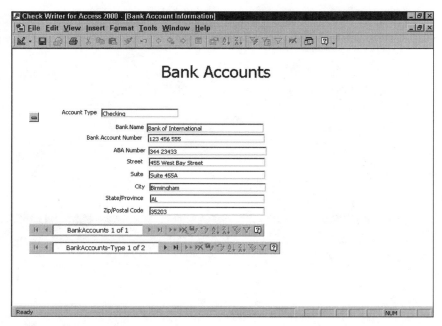

Figure 30-14
The BankAccounts page now opens in expanded mode

Done!

Remember that data access pages are stored in an HTML document. When you make changes to the page, the changes are automatically stored in the HTML document. You can see the changes you just made to the HTML document for the BankAccounts page by opening the BankAccounts.htm file in Windows Explorer. The BankAccounts.htm file opens in Internet Explorer and will display the same layout of the page as you saw when you opened the page in Access.

REVIEW

Data access pages provide a quick and easy way to build a Web-enabled application. You can use them to provide up-to-the-minute, updateable information to users in a corporate intranet environment, or to users anywhere in the world.

Because data access pages can be displayed using Internet Explorer, they can be accessed by users who may not even have Microsoft Access.

- Saving copies of reports, forms, and datasheets in HTML format is one way to distribute static information over the Internet.
- Data access pages provide a way to distribute live data over the Internet that can also be updated.
- A data access page is stored as an HTML document.
- You can use Access or Internet Explorer to work with a data access page.
- Designing a data access page is very similar to designing a form or report.

QUIZ YOURSELF

1. Where is the "code" for a data access page stored? (See "Understanding Data Access Pages.")
2. What are the two tools that you can use to view a data access page? (See "Understanding Data Access Pages.")
3. Name the three components required to work with data access pages for users without Microsoft Access. (See "Understanding Data Access Pages.")
4. What is the term for the + and – buttons that display next to each group level? (See "Working With Data Access Pages.")
5. Name the property that you set to make a group level automatically display as expanded when the page opens. (See "Modifying a data access page.")

PART

VI

Sunday Afternoon

1. True or False: An *Access Add-in* is a component that's not part of the basic Microsoft Access product.
2. List at least five examples of Add-ins provided with Access.
3. An Access Add-in uses which file extension?
   a. .MDB
   b. .MDE
   c. .MDA
   d. .ADE
   e. All of the above
4. What is the branch in the registry reserved for wizards?
5. List at least two reasons you may lose the table links in a database.
6. True or false: You use ADODB to work with Access table definitions.
7. Which of the following is used to create a new catalog object?
   a. Dim cat as ADO.catalog
   b. Dim cat as New ADO.catalog
   c. Dim cat as New ADOX.catalog
   d. Dim cat as ADOX.catalog
   e. Dim cat as New ADODB.catalog
8. What line of code would you use to set a newly created catalog object to the current database connection?

9. List four security methods that protect the program code.

10. True or false: The security objects are contained within the ADOX object model.

11. Which of the following is (or are) true of encryption in Access?

    a. Encryption is done using the JRO compact database method.

    b. Decryption requires a password.

    c. Encryption does not protect the database from being read by a utility program.

    d. Encryption uses the ADOX object model.

    e. None of the above.

12. List methods other than Access security for protecting an application from unauthorized users.

13. Two or more network workstations can share a centrally located data source in which architecture?

14. True or false: Access is a good example of a true client/server environment.

15. Which one of the following is not an MSDE object?

    a. Table

    b. Stored Procedure

    c. View

    d. Query

16. Which of the following environments is best suited for developing an application using MSDE?

    a. Ten or more simultaneous users with high volumes of updates.

    b. The business environment has a SQL Server 7.0 database and you are an off-site application developer.

    c. Five or fewer simultaneous users with modest volumes of updates.

    d. The business environment consists of outdated workstations with lower memory and minimal hard disk space.

17. A _____ is a special type of Web page that you can use to display and update data in an Access database or a SQL Server database.

18. True or false: Page objects are stored in HTML files.

19. Which of the following is/are required to view a data access page?

    a. Internet Explorer 5.0 or later

    b. A license for Microsoft Office 2000 or later

    c. Access to the database that the data access page is linked to.

    d. Microsoft Access 2000.

20. True or false: A change made to a data access page is automatically reflected in its HTML document.

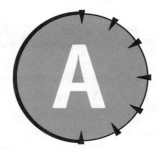
Answers to Part Reviews

Following are the answers to the Reviews at the end of each part of the book.

Friday Evening Review Answers

1. Database management systems include the ability to build tables and relationships and the ability to store data.

2. The Visual Basic editor window is a separate window in Access 2000. This is a change from Access 97.

3. The two types of procedures are *subprocedures* and *functions*. The difference is that a function returns a value to the calling procedure and a function does not.

4. Visual Basic for Applications (VBA) is the language used within Microsoft Access modules. Jet is the standard database engine used to hold the data tables in Microsoft Access and Visual Basic. The Microsoft Database Engine (MSDE) is a scaled-down version of SQL Server and used as an alternate engine.

5. False.

6. d.

7. Auto List Members

8. b.

9. general design, detail design, programming and documentation, testing, and debugging.

10. Compiling checks your program for syntax errors and resolves some of your references. It converts your program to a form your computer can understand. It allows your programs to run much faster. You should also compact your database after you compile your program.

11. The Immediate, Locals, and Watches windows.

12. A breakpoint stops a program when a specific line of code is reached. A watchpoint is set by the user and stops a program when a specific variable of control reaches a preset value.

13. property sheet

14. False.

15. a.

16. c.

17. Dim.

18. Access will run a VBA program much faster if `Option Explicit` is used once at the top of each module and all your variables are declared.

19. Public or Global define a variable to your entire program and Private limits the scoping to one procedure.

20. a, d. Text is nonsensical and is named String. Number is not a Visual Basic numeric data type. Integer, Currency, Long, Single and Double are valid.

Saturday Morning Review Answers

1. *Logical constructs* are a certain class of VBA statements that control the way a program runs. Generally, programs run one statement after another in the order in which they appear. Logical constructs are used to make the program run in the order that makes sense for the business purpose.

2. Logical constructs include conditional processing (`If-Then-Else`, `Select Case`), and Looping (`Do While`, `For Next`).

3. *Nesting* occurs when you put an `If-Then-Else` statement within another `If-Then-Else` statement. This allows you to write complex Boolean expressions.

4. The `Do Until` clause code always runs at least once and runs until the condition is met to terminate the loop. The `Do While` clause runs as long as the condition is true.

5. True.

6. Function

7. d.

8. c.

9. DateSerial

10. b.

11. True.

12. a.

13. c.

14. False

15. recordset

16. a.

17. False.

18. Pessimistic locking

19. a.

20. c.

Saturday Afternoon Review Answers

1. True.

2. False.

3. False.

4. False.

5. e.

6. False. You need to handle functions that are automatic with Access bound forms including record locking and the functions that connect the form to the data source.

7. The functions you need to include on an unbound form include: connecting to the record source, selecting/finding a record or records from a record source, loading up the controls on the form with data, retrieving the record(s), editing a record, saving a record, adding a new record, deleting a record, moving among multiple records like going to the first record, last record, next record, and previous record, and undoing changes made to the record before it is saved.

8. You would not want to use unbound forms because a lot of code is required to duplicate the functionality of a bound form. It is also difficult to provide continuous forms or a datasheet view, which a bound form can easily do.

9. A single checkbox can only have one of three states: True, False, or Null. In a situation where you need more values for the user to select, it is best to use an option group. With an option group you can have more than just three values.

10. False. Only one value can be selected in a combo box. A list box would allow you to select multiple items from the listing. This is because of the nature of the two controls. A combo box only display one item whereas a list box can be set up to display multiple rows of records or items.

11. b, e, f, and g. Review the "Basic Elements of Combo and List Boxes" section of Session 13.

12. d. Remember that to properly use the Not In List event, you need to set the Limit to List property to No. When you set this up, any entries you enter that are not in the list will initiate the code in the Not In List event. The reason for setting the Limit to List to No is that if you select Yes, any entries that are not a part of the list will trigger an error message, forcing you to select an item in the list.

13. Forms, Datasheet and Continuous.

14. False. A subform can be unlinked from the main form.

15. A continuous form allows you to format all rows and columns and use any control for each column, whereas a datasheet gives you little control over the display grid.

16. Link Child Fields and Link Master Fields.

17. You would use a tabbed control for any number of reasons. Aesthetically, you may want to standardize the Windows "look and feel." Logically, you want to segregate your data or controls by group or functionality. In addition, the physical constraints of the limited desktop area may require that you use a tabbed control in order to save space.

18. c. The On Change event is fired each time the tab selection is changed. This event can be very useful because it lets you process code in a single event for any changes in the tabs. You can add code that runs with each tab's On Change event to check for the current tab page and then to display controls or run code accordingly.

19. False. You can set the Visible property of each tab individually in addition to the entire tabbed control itself. This lets you control which pages are visible and when.

20. None, Tabbed, and Buttons. Please review "Tabbed Control Styles" in Session 15.

Saturday Evening Review Answers

1. The five parameters of the MsgBox function are the prompt text, buttons, title, helpfile, and context.

2. True. The buttons parameter also determines the icon to be displayed as well as the default button and the modality of the message box.

3. The application modal state requires the user to respond to the message box before continuing within the current application, which is suspended until the message box is cleared. The system modal state suspends *all* applications until the user responds to the message box.

4. c.

5. Access provides a few different means for importing and exporting data. In addition, you can import and export to several standard formats. The formats are listed in Chapter 17 in detail. The following is an abbreviated list.
   a. Excel (all versions)
   b. dBase (III, III+, IV, 5, and 7)
   c. Lotus (versions upto version 4)
   d. Text files (delimited and fixed width)

6. The four basic steps in doing an import are:
   a. Organizing the data.
   b. Formatting the data.
   c. Mapping the data.
   d. Appending the records.

You will first need to gather and organize the data to be imported. You then must format the data in a manner that Access can recognize and that works with your data structure. Next you will perform the most important step, mapping the data. This is the process of matching up the data being imported with the data structure you are working with. You will need to consider such issues as which tables, fields, data type, size, and so on will be matched to which corresponding parts of your data structure. These are all important aspects of the mapping process. Incorrectly matching up the field size could result in the loss of data. Likewise, matching the wrong key field from one table to another could result in corrupting the data so that it is no longer valid.

7. An import/export specification is a file that gives Access a set of rules for importing or exporting data from/to a text file. Once you've created an import/export specification, you can use it over and over, on both delimited and fixed-width text files. The specification is stored in the database and is an Access system object. You can access this feature when you initiate an import. To create a specification file you can use either of the Import or Export Text Wizards. The wizard creates a listing of information that would be critical to the import or export process such as the format of the file, field mappings, field properties, etc.Refer to "Import/Export Processes" in Chapter 17.

8. There are three main methods available for transferring data. Which method you choose depends on where the data is and whether you are exporting or importing.

   a. TransferDatabase Method

   b. TransferSpreadSheet Method

   c. TransferText Method

   Refer to the section "Methods for importing and exporting" in Session 17.

9. Memory is actually more important than the processor speed. Increasing your memory from 64MB to 128MB can easily double or triple the speed of your application, while changing the processor by 100 MHz and keeping the memory the same will make little difference.

10. Modifying a form, report, control, or module containing code. (If you don't save the modified object, your application is preserved in its previous state.)

   Adding a new form, report, control, or module. (This includes adding new code behind an existing form.)

   Deleting or renaming a form, report, control, or module.

11. Decompile.

12. You cannot view, modify, or create forms, reports, or modules in Design view.

    You cannot add, delete, or change references to object libraries or databases.

    You cannot change your database's VBA project name using the Options dialog box.

    You cannot import or export forms, reports, or modules. Note, however, that tables, queries, and macros can be imported from or exported to non-MDE databases.

13. False.

14. True.

15. True.

16. True.

17. Topic

18. True

19. d.

20. a.

Sunday Morning Review Answers

1. False.

2. Modal

3. d.

4. RowSource.

5. A Search Dialog would have several basic elements. The easiest way to derive the answer is to look at what information is required in order to do a search. In order to do a search, you must obtain the "what" — that is, the value to be searched for — from the user. You also need to determine the "where" — that is, the location(s) in which to search for the value. Therefore, you need a control to obtain the value to search for and one to select where to search. There are other elements which may be useful — for instance, adding criteria or Boolean operators — but at a minimum, the "what" and "where" are required..

A Print Dialog would have the following basic features: a control for the user to select the report to print; the number of copies; and the type of output (Preview or Print). In addition, you may want to add additional controls that give greater control of the printing options to your user — for instance, additional titles and filter options. Review the form yBank Print Dialog for an example of a basic print dialog; the form "yCheck Print Dialog" is more advanced.

6. b. The syntax and arguments for the OpenReport command are as follows:

Report Name: The actual name of the report object.

View: The type of view, either Print to the printer or Print Preview.

Filter Name: The name of a query that can be used to filter the records in the report.

Where Condition: The WHERE clause of a SQL statement that can be used to restrict the records in the report.

7. You can place code in the following events for the report:

- On Open
- On Close
- On Activate
- On Deactivate
- On No Data
- On Page
- On Error

In addition, you can also place code that is associated with a particular section or group. These events include:

- On Format
- On Print
- On Retreat

8. Concatenation allows you to build a string that can include static text as well as references to fields. This technique the one of the most flexible and powerful Access provides. It is often necessary to combine several fields into a single string. For example, if you have a FirstName and LastName field and you wanted the control to display the two as a single string with LastName first, you would type the following syntax.

[LastName] & ", " & [FirstName]

9. The SysCmd function.

10. False. The Background Compile option will compile any uncompiled code when Access's processes are not busy.

11. b.

12. Use the command line argument /x *macro*, use the macro named AutoExec, and set the Display Form/Page entry on the Startup dialog box.

13. To make sure the data links between a front-end and back-end database are correct, to install the required references, library, Active-X control, or help file, and to create desktop shortcuts and menu items.

14. False. The Package and Deployment Wizard is installed as a VBA add-in.

15. c. You can customize the Package and Deployment Wizard using Visual Basic 6.0 by modifying the Setup1.vbp program.

16. You must check the registry entries within the Setup program to deal with multiple versions of Access.

17. You should make each page of the wizard step toward completing the process; order the steps to make sense; keep buttons, fonts, and controls consistent between pages; keep pages uncluttered; and use defaults as much as possible to simplify user input.

18. The entire wizard is contained within one Access object, a form; it provides properties and methods that will simplify coding; the tabs on the Tab control can be visible or invisible depending on your needs; there needs to be only one set of navigation buttons.

19. False. You also need a Finish button.

20. a. The Back button is always disabled on the *first* page.

Sunday Afternoon Review Answers

1. True.

2. Examples of Add-ins provided with Access include control wizards, form wizards, chart wizards, field builders, object libraries, the switchboard manager, the link table manager, the documenter, the performance analyzer, and many, many more.

3. e. all of the above

4. HKEY_LOCAL_MACHINE\SOFTWARE\Microsoft\Office\9.0\Access\Wizards.

5. You may lose the table links if the data source you are linked to is not available because: the external data source has moved; the server where the external data source is located is down; the network is down; the user does not have the permissions necessary to access the external data source; or share names have changed.

6. False. You use ADOX to work with Access table definitions.

7. c.

8. `cat.ActiveConnection = CurrentProject.Connection`

9. Security methods that protect the code are share level, user level, encryption, and MDE.

10. True.

11. a.

12. Other methods of protecting an application from unauthorized users include operating system security, hiding the database window, disabling the bypass key, and disabling special keys.

13. Client/server.

14. False.

15. d.

16. b.

17. Data access page

18. True.

19. d.

20. True.

What's On the CD-ROM

Your CD contains all of the example files created or referred to in this book. There are six main directories on the CD. Some are divided into subdirectories. Most of the directories or subdirectories contain installation files with a .EXE file extension. You can simply display the directories and files using Windows Explorer and then double-click any .EXE file to launch the install program for the file you want to copy to your hard drive. Each installation file will ask you where you want to put the file and set up a Start menu shortcut for you.

The six main folders include

- Weekend Crash Course in Access Programming — Contains the sample database used throughout the book

- Acrobat Reader from Abobe — The free reader for viewing Acrobat .PDF files

- Demos — Demos of Database Creations, Inc. products for Microsoft Access

- Free Access Software — Real working software (not demos) from Database Creations

- Product Catalog — Catalogs and brochures of products developed by Database Creations, Inc.

- WinZip70 — A free utility to compress data up to 90%. Great for sending files via e-mail

Installing the Files on Your Computer

Each directory on the CD contains a standard setup file that can be selected and run to start the install. While you may be used to seeing the file name SETUP.EXE on your CDs, this generally works well when there is one installation file. We have separated all of the files by directory so you can install only the files you want and given them more readable names. Each directory (with the exception of the *Product Catalogs* directory) contains these .EXE files

You can run them from the CD by double-clicking them, or copy them to your hard drive and then double-click them. Remember that the CD is read only and you cannot install any of the files on the CD. Each of the installations will ask you for a directory name. Choose a directory on your hard drive or media (Zip or SyQuest drives) that can be written to.

If you find any of the files are read only, display the file in Windows Explorer and then right-click the file name. Select properties and uncheck the read only property. This will make the file read-write. You should not have to do this under normal conditions.

All the example .MDB files are Microsoft Access 2000 files. They only work in Microsoft Access 2000 and do not work in Microsoft Access 97, 95, 2.0, 1.1, or 1.0.

Installing and Using the Access 2000 Example Files

When you double click on the file named Crash Course Examples.exe in the directory Crash Course Examples, you will be prompted to install the example files. To open a file, go to the folder you installed the example files to and double-click the file you want to open. If you get an error message opening an Access database, you either have multiple versions of Microsoft Access on your computer and Access 2000 is not the default or you never told Windows 95/98/NT to associate.MDB files with the program msaccess.exe (Microsoft Access). Follow the instruction in the next section of this appendix to associate all .MDB files with Microsoft Access 2000.

Associating an .MDB file with Microsoft Access

To change which program starts when you open a file, perform the following operations:

1. In My Computer or Windows Explorer, click the View menu, and then click Options.

2. Click the File Types tab.

3. In the list of file types, click the one you want to change (Microsoft Access Databases).

4. The settings for that file type are shown in the File Type Details box.

5. Click Edit.

6. In the Actions box, click Open.

7. Click Edit, and then specify the program (msaccess.exe) you want to use to open files that have this extension. Make sure you choose the Access 2000 msaccess.exe if you have other versions of Microsoft Access on your computer.

A Guide to the Expanded Files on the CD

Once you install each file on the CD you may wonder how to use it. Most of the installations will create a Start menu icon for you while others simply require you to start Microsoft Access 2000 and load the software. The instructions below discuss each directory's files and what to expect when you use them. The best way to learn is to experiment so don't be afraid to simply install the file on your hard disk and open it.

Crash Course examples

These include all of the files used for the examples in this book. There are two main example files: CheckWriter2000.MDB and CheckWriter2000Data.MDB, which are used throughout the book. Several other files are included and are referred to in individual chapters.

Product catalogs

For readers who want to increase their productivity we have included the latest catalog from Database Creations, Inc. the world's largest Microsoft Access and Office mail-order company. The catalog includes the full 2000 product catalog, providing detailed information on some of our most popular products. You can view it from the CD using the included Adobe Acrobat viewer. Cary Prague, one of the authors of the Access 2000 Bible, owns this company. Mention this book and receive an additional 10% off the prices of any software product in the catalog. You can also view product updates and more information as well as new products at the Database Creations Web site, `www.databasecreations.com`, or call us to receive new printed catalogs and product descriptions at (860) 644-5891. You may also send an e-mail to `info@databasecreations.com` for information. The files are in the directory below:

Crash Course Examples\Product Catalog\2000 Database Creations Catalog.pdf

Acrobat Reader from Abobe

This free reader from Adobe lets you view and print files stored in Abobe Acrobat .PDF file formats. If you haven't discovered Adobe Acrobat, this is a great opportunity to become a fan. Adobe Acrobat is both a product and a technology. This technology allows someone using virtually any product to create an output file simply by printing it and then allowing anyone else to view the output file without any special software except Adobe Acrobat.

In the future, rather than receive a big catalog in the mail, you might be emailed a .PDF file of the catalog. In fact, in the Product Catalogs directory of the CD, you will find several catalogs with .PDF file extensions. These are also known as Acrobat formats. To view these .PDF files, you must first install the Adobe Acrobat reader. This is a free piece of software available to anyone and is found on your CD in the *Acrobat Reader from Adobe* directory. Double-click the installation file and follow the instructions. This file contains just the reader. To create your own .PDF files, you must purchase the full Acrobat program from Adobe.

To run the installation for Adobe Acrobat, run the file reader.exe found on the CD in the directory:

Crash Course Examples\Acrobat Reader from Adobe

Demos

To take advantage of the demos listed below, go to the desired directory and double-click the .EXE file. The instructions will take you through the installation process. Some of the installations will also create product descriptions in Word 2000 format on your hard drives. Check the CD directories when you are through loading the demos. The vendors and products include:

- **Database Creations** — Yes! I Can Run My Business, POSitively Business, EZ Access Tools Suite, Application Builder, Access Project Security Manager, Inventory Manager with Barcoding
- **PenSoft** — PenSoft Payroll

Yes! I Can Run My Business

Yes! I Can Run My Business is the most popular accounting software available for Microsoft Access users today. The product if fully customizable and includes all source code. It includes all typical accounting functions including sales, customers, A/R, purchases, suppliers, A/P, inventory, banking, general ledger, and fixed assets, and features multi-company accounting for any size business. Priced under $1,000 for a multi-user LAN version, it is one of the best values for small businesses. For developers, a version is available with royalty free distribution rights for around $2,500. The full product includes over 1,500 pages of professionally written documentation. Yes! I Can Run My Business received 4 1/2 stars from *CPA Software News* for best mid-range accounting software. It also won the Microsoft Access Advisor reader's choice award for best accounting system. View more information on this product at www.databasecreations.com.

You can install the Yes! I Can Run My Business demo by running:

Crash Course Examples\Demos\Yes! I Can Accounting\yes4dem2k.exe

POSitively Business Demo

POSitively Business is an add-on system for Yes! I Can Run My Business. It adds point-of-sale functionality and includes all source code. This product includes a mouseless point of sale interface, security, administrative and setup options, cashiers, cash counter, sales analyzer, barcoding and much more. The software works with standard point-of-sale hardware including cash drawers, light poles, hand-held scanners, receipt printers, and credit-card-scanning keyboards. Pricing is $595 for one register and discounts are available for multiple registers. You can also purchase a point-of-sale hardware bundle that includes a cash drawer, receipt printer, credit-card-scanning keyboard, laser scanner, light pole, and barcode font. Call for latest pricing. Developer versions of POSitively Business with royalty-free distribution rights are also available. We also have a reseller program for resellers and VAR's. Call us or visit www.positivelybusiness.com to learn more.

EZ Access Tools Suite

The EZ Access Tools Suite is specifically designed for Access 97 and Access 2000 developers to help them create great Access applications. The suite consists of eight separate products. Each can be easily integrated into your application to provide new functions in a fraction of the time it would take you to create them yourself. These products will save you hundreds of hours of development time. Think of them as a library of over 100 pre-designed, pre-programmed interfaces you can use with your applications royalty-free!

Read each of the embedded reviewer's guides in the demo for a complete overview of each product. You can purchase the entire EZ Access Tools Suite for only $395. View additional information on this product at www.databasecreations.com.

The eight EZ Access Tools in the Suite are:

- EZ Report Manager
- EZ Search Manager
- EZ Support Manager
- EZ Extensions
- EZ Security Manager
- EZ File Manager
- EZ Application Manager
- EZ Controls

You can install the EZ Access Tools Suite demo by running:
Crash Course Examples\Demos\EZ Access Tools Suite\EZ Access Tools Suite Demo.exe

Application Builder

The Application Builder provides a way for Access developers to create an application shell when building custom applications for Access 97 or Access 2000. There are two ways to use the Application Builder: either start with our application shell and add your objects (tables, queries, reports, forms, modules, etc.), or use our Application Generator Wizard to choose, configure and automatically add the components to your Access application. The Wizard guides you through the process of selecting over 40 different features and lets you add your own custom text and graphics. Then add your tables, queries, forms, and reports to the application switchboard you have selected. We even include a second wizard to help you build flexible menu systems for your application.

With the Application Builder you receive:

- Application Builder including 40 components from the EZ Access Tools Suite
- Application Generator Wizard
- Menu Editor Wizard

- On-line help
- Free Check Writer application with source code
- Five additional Switchboards not found in the Suite
- Source code

Purchase the Application Builder for only $495 or for $595, purchase both the Application Builder and EZ Access Tools Suite.

You can install the Application Builder demo by running:

Crash Course Examples\Demos\Application Builder\Application Builder.exe

Access Project Security Manager

If you use Access 2000 Projects with the new MSDE or SQL Server 7, there is no security provided for forms or reports. You only have the limited data security provided by MSDE and SQL Server 7 and no user security. With the Access Project Security Manager, you can easily add your own security. This circumvents your having to create separate application front ends for each group of users.

Purchase the Access Project Security Manager for $299 for a single developer/ single application. Multiple developer/applications and site licenses are also available. Visit www.databasecreations.com for more information and pricing.

You can install the Access Project Security Manager demo by running:

Crash Course Examples\Access Project Security Manager\APSM Demo.exe

Inventory Manager with barcode modules

The Inventory Manager is an open-source-code, fully-customizable stand-alone inventory management program for Microsoft Access 97 or 2000. This product allows you to enter inventory items, suppliers, and warehouses, and includes a simple chart of accounts and general ledger. Use the Inventory Manager as a stand-alone application or integrated with existing purchasing or sales applications you may have developed. The demo also includes a demo version of the optional barcode modules which allow you to print barcodes and adjust inventory quantities in stock or transfer goods between warehouses.

Purchase the Inventory Manager for $595 for a multi-user version or for $995 with the barcode modules. A royalty free developer version is also available. Please visit www.databasecreations.com for more information and current pricing.

You can install the Inventory Manager with Barcode Modules demo by running:

Crash Course Examples\Inventory Manager with Barcoding\invdemo2k.exe

PenSoft Payroll

PenSoft Payroll from PenSoft Corp. is a stand-alone payroll package for small to medium-sized businesses. It interfaces with Yes! I Can Run My Business to provide complete employee, hour, tax, deduction, and benefit processing. The software contains all tax tables for the United States and territories and Canada. The program also supports both English and French. For more information and pricing, please visit www.databasecreations.com.

You can install the PenSoft Payroll trial version by running:

Crash Course Examples\PenSoft Payroll\paydemo.exe

Free access software

The subdirectories under the Free Access Software contain completely usable, unlocked and unprotected versions of some award-winning products. To install each of the products, go to the subdirectory and double click on the .EXE file. This will install the .MDB file to your hard drive and also install complete documentation that you can view and print using Word 2000. The files with the word *sampler* in them are abbreviated versions of the commercially available products. The entire user guide has been provided for these products in Word format. These include:

Business Forms Library Sampler

The Access Business Forms Library Sampler is a sample of the Business Forms Library, a collection of 35 forms and reports. These contain some really innovative techniques that have never been seen anywhere else. The entire library contains tables, forms, reports, and macros for each of the forms and reports. You can integrate them into your own applications, thereby saving yourself hundreds of hours of work. Microsoft liked these forms so much they distributed this sampler in the Microsoft Access Welcome Kit with Microsoft Access 2.0. These have been updated for Access 2000 are and come with a complete user guide.

Cool Combo Box Techniques

This is a demonstration database of 25 of the coolest combo and list box techniques. Full documentation is included in the CD directory. This is from a highly acclaimed paper given by Cary Prague at the Microsoft Access conferences.

EZ File Manager Sampler

The EZ File Manager is one of eight products in the new EZ Access Suite. The complete File Utilities tool which helps you compile, compact, repair, and backup attached data databases is included along with the entire documentation set from the EZ Access File Manager to give you a complete overview of the product. Install the sampler and then copy the form and module to your own application to add file management capabilities to your application.

EZ Search Manager Sampler

The EZ Search Manager is one of eight products in the new EZ Access Suite. The complete SmartSearch tool is included along with the entire documentation set from the EZ Access Search Manager to give you a complete overview of the product. Install the sampler and then copy the forms to your own application to add an incredibly flexible search interface to your application.

Picture Builder Button Sampler

They can be used on Access 2000 toolbars or in Access 2000 buttons used for switchboards. To use these button faces simply copy the files onto your hard disk or use the bitmaps as is.

The files named ACTxx.BMP are 32x32 pixel .BMPs perfect for Access command buttons while the files named ACTxx.B24 are 24x23 pixel .BMPs perfect for Access 2000 toolbars and any Office Compatible application.

WinZip70

This directory contains WinZip70, a freeware program for compressing data files up to 90%. Great for making large Access files fit on a floppy disk or great for sending as e-mail attachments.

Reporting Problems With the Crash Course Book

If you think you have found an example that doesn't work or you have a suggestion, please let us know by e-mail or by visiting our Web site and using the contact information. We get back to our readers who ask questions about the book. While we will answer questions about the material in the Access book by e-mail we are unable to take phone calls from readers other than in the normal course of our consulting and mail order business.

All of the products in this book are available from:
Database Creations, Inc.
475 Buckland Rd.
S. Windsor, CT 06074 USA
(860) 644-5891 (US and internationally)
(860) 648-0710 (24-hour fax)
Web: www.databasecreations.com
Company e-mail: info@databasecreations.com

Index

G

Continued